Praise for *Milton*

'The 400th anniversary of Milton's birth falls this year, and Anna Beer's biography is the opening fanfare of the celebrations . . . Conscious of Milton's intimidating stature, Beer sets out to make him more approachable . . . [Her] account of his public activities is vigorous, well researched and primed with piquant detail' John Carey, *Sunday Times*

'A persuasive reading of the power and complexity of *Paradise Lost*' Peter Ackroyd, *The Times*

'Beer strikes a perfect balance . . . [She] has done a wonderful job in disentangling this largely suppressed story from its literary and social context . . . This is model literary biography, a mixture of close reading, good sense and psychological insight . . . What you get is a living, breathing, complex man, living in exciting but troubled times' Brian Morton, *Sunday Herald*

'Scrupulously researched but splendidly readable . . . Beer has all the clarity and empathy required to show us why his roles in these deadly tangles of law and doctrine, art and authority, mattered then – and matter now. Expert but accessible' Boyd Tonkin, *Independent*

'This year marks the 400th anniversary of Milton's birth – start the celebration here. In Beer's often moving study, England's great poet emerges as a man for whom political engagement was an essential part of being human' *London Review of Books*

'A truly splendid book . . . neither debunking nor idolatrous, but judicious and intelligent . . . While placing Milton firmly in his own time, this is very much a Milton for our own' Robert Nye, *Tablet*

'A portrait of a bustling and turbulent age . . . This is a valuable and authorative book, scrupulously researched and edited' *Independent on Sunday*

MILTON

POET, PAMPHLETEER, AND PATRIOT

Anna Beer

BLOOMSBURY

LONDON · BERLIN · NEW YORK

First published in Great Britain 2008

This paperback edition published 2008

Copyright © Anna Beer 2008

Map by John Gilkes

The right of Anna Beer to be identified as the author of
this work has been asserted by her in accordance with
the Copyright, Designs and Patents Act 1988

Bloomsbury Publishing Plc
36 Soho Square
London W1D 3QY

www.bloomsbury.com

Bloomsbury Publishing, London, New York and Berlin

A CIP catalogue record for this book is available from the British Library

ISBN 978 0 7475 9628 8

10 9 8 7 6 5 4 3 2 1

Typeset by Hewer Text UK Ltd, Edinburgh
Printed in Great Britain by Clays Ltd, St Ives plc

The paper this book is printed on is certified by the © Forest Stewardship Council 1996 A.C.
(FSC). It is ancient-forest friendly. The printer holds FSC chain of custody SGS-COC-2061

FSC
Mixed Sources
Product group from well-managed
forests and other controlled sources
Cert no. SGS-COC-2061
www.fsc.org
© 1996 Forest Stewardship Council

For my mother, Margaret Beer,
and in memory of my father,
John Beer, 1922–1989,
and my grandmother,
Anna Beer, 1901–1942

CONTENTS

Acknowledgements   ix

List of Illustrations   xi

Conventions   xiii

Preface   xv

Maps   xviii

PART ONE: THE MAKING OF JOHN MILTON

1   The City, 1608   3

2   Cambridge, 1625   21

3   Misrule, 1628   37

4   Masque, 1634   54

5   Elegy, 1637   78

6   Italy, 1638   91

7   Damon, 1640   106

PART TWO: JOHN MILTON, ENGLISHMAN

8   The Church, 1641   121

9   Divorce, 1642   141

10   Censorship, 1644   158

11   Poems, 1645   180

12   Revolution, 1649   202

13   Government, 1651   224

14 Defence, 1654   244

15 Crisis, 1659   271

PART THREE: POET AND PROPHET

16 Defeat, 1660   291

17 Epic, 1667   312

18 Revelation, 1667   338

19 Resurgence, 1671   365

20 The City, 1674   388

Notes   403

Select Bibliography   441

Index   443

Acknowledgements

My thanks go to my colleagues at Kellogg College and the Department for Continuing Education at the University of Oxford for their fellowship and scholarly advice, especially Adrienne Rosen, Malcolm Airs and Victoria Murphy; to David Cunnington and Manuele Gragnolati for sharing their expertise in Latin and Italian, and to Benjamin Crabstick for his exemplary work on the endnotes; to the librarians of Oxford University, who have made the task of research a pleasure; to all those students, past and present, with whom I have talked about Milton; and, above all, to those teachers who inspired me to think about Milton, most notably Elizabeth Foster, David Norbrook and Cedric Brown. My agent, Victoria Hobbs, gave early encouragement and astute guidance throughout: that this book exists at all is due to her. Thanks also to Kathleen Anderson in New York. All my friends and family know, I hope, how important their support has been to me over what has been a long period of research and writing, but special thanks go to Karen Elliott and Paul Schwartfeger for reading early drafts. Becca and Elise have tolerated having a busy writer for a mum: I am delighted to acknowledge both their many kindnesses and their healthy detachment from all things Miltonic. Roger Harvey has been the perfect companion throughout, providing cups of tea and glasses of wine at all the right moments, and much more besides.

To write a biography such as this is, of course, to stand on the shoulders of giants, and I am deeply indebted to the painstaking work of generations of Milton scholars. I simply could not have written this book without drawing heavily upon the work of biographers such as William Riley Parker, Gordon Campbell and Barbara Lewalski, not to mention the great editors of Milton, Alastair Fowler and John Carey. I am even more indebted, however, to those scholars who found time to read parts of the book and generously offered their suggestions for improvements: my thanks go to John Hale, James Grantham Turner, Joad Raymond and Sharon Achinstein. Emily Sweet in London, and Peter Ginna and Katie Henderson in New York, have all provided much-valued editorial input, complemented by the patient copy-editing of Andrea Belloli. It is Bill Swainson of Bloomsbury, however, who has worked tirelessly and constructively from first to last. His hard work has made the book a better one. I, of course, take full responsibility for any errors that remain.

List of Illustrations

Colour Plates

Milton as a ten-year-old, portrait probably by Cornelius Janssen. (© *2007 Photo Pierpont Morgan Library, New York / Art Resource / Scala, Florence*)

Part of *View of the River Thames* by Jan Visscher, 1616. (*Photo: akg-images / British Library*)

Milton aged twenty-one, artist unknown (the 'Onslow portrait'). (*National Portrait Gallery, London*)

View of Florence from *Civitates Orbis Terrarum* by Georg Braun, circa 1572. (*Private Collection / The Stapleton Collection / The Bridgeman Art Library*)

The pulling down of the Cheapside Cross by iconoclasts, May 1643. (*Private Collection / The Stapleton Collection / The Bridgeman Art Library*)

A banner from the English Civil War. (© *All Rights Reserved. The British Library Board*)

Charles I, by Van Dyck. (© *National Portrait Gallery, London*)

The execution of Charles I at Whitehall, 30 January 1649. (*Private Collection / The Bridgeman Art Library*)

Oliver Cromwell, by Robert Walker. (© *National Portrait Gallery, London*)

Parliament during the Commonwealth, 1650. (*British Museum, London, UK / The Bridgeman Art Library*)

The return of King Charles II, as illustrated in a prayer book, circa 1660. (*Lambeth Palace Library, London, UK / The Bridgeman Art Library*)

Sir Henry Vane, by R. Fortem. (*Mary Evans Picture Library*)

Milton's house at Chalfont St Giles. (*Reproduced by permission of Milton's Cottage Trust*)

Plague scenes: London, 1665–6. (© *Museum of London*)

The Great Fire of London, 1666. (*Museum of London, UK / The Bridgeman Art Library*)

1670 engraving of Milton by William Faithorne. (*National Portrait Gallery, London*)

Images in the Text

London in the sixteenth century, section of the 'Agas Map'. (*Reproduced by permission of the Guildhall Library, City of London*)

Floor plan of the house at Bread Street. (*Reproduced by permission of the Provost and Fellows of Eton College*)

Sheet music from the *Maske* at Ludlow. (© *All Rights Reserved. The British Library Board*)

A page from the manuscript at Trinity College, Cambridge, showing Milton's working copy of his early poems. (*Reproduced courtesy of the Master and Fellows of Trinity College, Cambridge*)

Frontispiece of *The Doctrine and Discipline of Divorce*. (© *All Rights Reserved. The British Library Board*)

Frontispiece of *Areopagitica*. (© *All Rights Reserved. The British Library Board*)

Frontispiece of *The Poems of Mr John Milton*. (© *All Rights Reserved. The British Library Board*)

Frontispiece of *The Tenure of Kings and Magistrates*. (© *All Rights Reserved. The British Library Board*)

Frontispiece of *Eikonoklastes*. (© *All Rights Reserved. The British Library Board*)

Frontispiece of *Joannis Miltoni Angli Pro Populo Anglicano Defensio Secunda*. (© *All Rights Reserved. The British Library Board*)

Frontispiece of the ten-book edition of *Paradise Lost*. (© *All Rights Reserved. The British Library Board*)

Frontispiece of *Paradise Regained*, incorporating *Samson Agonistes*. (© *All Rights Reserved. The British Library Board*)

Conventions

For the ease of the reader, spelling and punctuation have been modernised throughout, with two exceptions. Titles are given in their original spellings, and the verb ending -eth, as in 'God giveth grace to the lowly', has been retained. Contractions have been expanded in the prose quotations but left in the poetry, to enable the reader to appreciate Milton's scansion. Much is lost, however, by modernisation. For a taste of the original spelling and punctuation visit http://www.dartmouth.edu/~milton/reading room/.

The majority of translations of the Latin and Italian poetry are taken from John Milton, *The Complete Shorter Poems*, ed. John Carey, second edn, Longman, London, 1997. The majority of translations of the Latin prose works are taken from *Complete Prose Works of John Milton*, ed. Don M. Wolfe, 8 vols, Yale University Press, New Haven, CT, 1953–82. Where other translations are used, the source is provided in the endnote. When first mentioned, the Latin title of a work by Milton will always be given, but subsequently the English translation of the title will be used.

Preface

John Milton is one of the world's greatest poets and writers. Born into the London of Shakespeare and dying in the London of Pepys, he became a dominant influence in English literature for more than two hundred years. Yet for all his achievements, the myth of the puritanical ascetic who hated women and took it on himself to justify his God has displaced the complex, erudite man who wrote those influential works and earned his place in the canon.

At the quatercentenary of his birth, it is time for a re-assessment of John Milton's life, work and times. The young John, who was brought up on the politically charged, sexually explicit works of the Latin and Greek writers, used that education to engage in the lively, at times vulgar, debates of his time, whether at Cambridge University or in London. The slightly older Milton, hovering on the fringes of the royal court, sought patronage, produced aristocratic amusements, and kept one eye on the lavish entertainments being staged at Whitehall by King Charles I, another eye on his own more radical political and religious agenda.

To see the young John Milton most clearly, one must go to his Latin writings. In this language, he could explore areas of life that were impossible to approach, impossible even to describe in his mother tongue. To read Milton's early Latin is to explore an emotional hinterland that would inform his later writing as much as the turbulent public events of his era. Above all, Latin was the medium of possibly the most significant personal relationship in Milton's life, that with Charles Diodati. Their friendship provoked some of John's most joyful writing and culminated in a superb, crisis-driven exploration of poetry and sexuality.

Much like English today, Latin served as the language of intellectual debate and international diplomacy in Milton's time. To appreciate his mastery of it, and its role in his writing, is to understand that Milton operated on an international stage. That stage was both a violent one – this was the era of the Thirty Years War, fragile religious settlements, and Oliver Cromwell's ruthless foreign policy – and an immensely stimulating one. Milton's extended travels in Italy were packed with glorious and enlightening experiences (he was neither the first nor the last Englishman to dream of a life in Tuscany), and indeed his most eloquent prose works, including his defence of the new English republic, were written in Latin and intended for a European readership.

For all this international dimension to his work and his life, Milton was born, brought up and constantly drawn back to one small part of the City of London. Despite all his social, political and literary ambitions, despite those enraptured travels in Italy, Milton never moved far from Bread Street, in the shadow of St Paul's Cathedral, and the house where he had grown up over his father's business. But London offered a vibrant, if often dangerous, forum for Milton the writer. It was the seat of government, the eye of the religious storm, a melting pot of nationalities, and, above all, the primary producer and consumer of the new media: cheap print. Milton wrote some of his finest works from the City when it was gripped by war and regime change, and in his old age he survived persecution and poverty to produce his masterpiece, *Paradise Lost*, in part because of his familiarity with the City's underground print and political networks.

For Milton was no mere observer of the crises besetting his city, his country, his continent. Eloquent theorist though he was, Milton never remained merely in the realm of abstraction. Not only did he live and work in a culture in which reading was *for* action, not *in place of* action, but he, unlike most other writers, was involved, day-by-day, in matters of state. Whether government servant or political prisoner, advocate of religious freedom or critic of monarchy, Milton learnt, because he had to learn, how to deal with censorship and intolerance, how to make his voice heard in the clamorous debates of his time. He was immersed in, and exploited, the rapidly changing, edgy, disreputable public print culture that was growing up around him, just as Shakespeare had been immersed in, and exploited, the new theatre world of Elizabethan London. Hard-hitting and groundbreaking prose works such as his *Doctrine of Discipline and Divorce* made Milton notorious in his own time, whilst his *Areopagitica* remains one of the most eloquent defences of a free press ever written. And Milton's late, great achievements become even more remarkable in this context. *Paradise Lost*, for example, was written from a position of great practical disadvantage, but continued Milton's passionate debate with his nation and his God, a debate which produced a striking body of work that has done much to define the values of the English political nation, and which had no small influence on the Founding Fathers in America.

To write the life of John Milton is thus to survey a century of unprecedented religious, political, social and cultural struggles, and to consider a writer enmeshed in, and fascinated by, those conflicts. Milton's genius lies in the extraordinary power and beauty with which he wrote from within this turmoil, and indeed wrote out of his own personal struggles – which include his blindness, endured in an unforgiving, pre-industrial society. Throughout his life, he used his astounding learning to articulate and explore with passion and eloquence the great questions that troubled him and his contemporaries: What constitutes human liberty and how can it best be supported? What is the nature of good government and how can it be sustained? How can we understand the divine – and each other? How can we find the strength to bear suffering and death? In reading Milton, therefore, we not only journey to a troubled and exhilarating past, but are challenged, as Milton challenged his readers in his own century, to consider those questions, and to provide some answers of our own.

Anna Beer
Oxford
1 August 2007

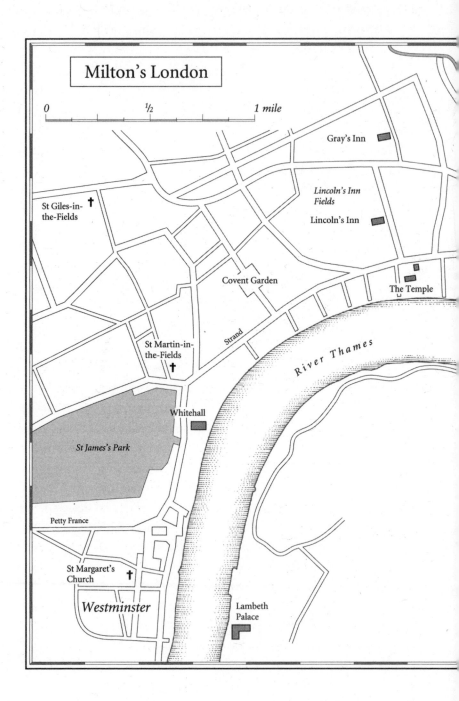

Milton's London

0 ½ 1 mile

Gray's Inn

St Giles-in-the-Fields

Lincoln's Inn Fields

Lincoln's Inn

Covent Garden

The Temple

St Martin-in-the-Fields

Strand

River Thames

Whitehall

St James's Park

Petty France

St Margaret's Church

Lambeth Palace

Westminster

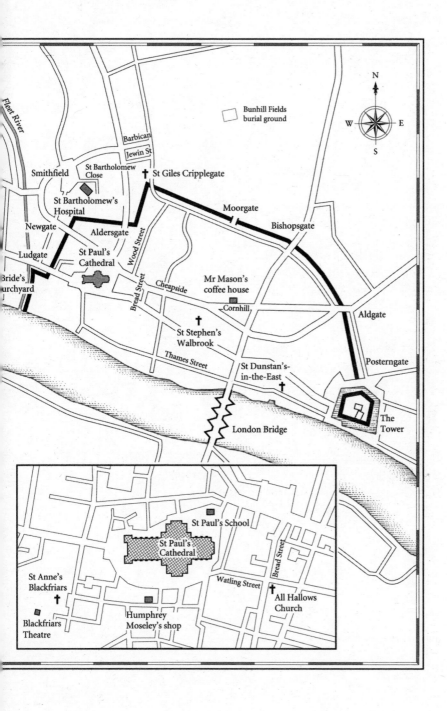

Fleet River

N
W   E
S

Bunhill Fields
burial ground

Barbican
Jewin St
St Bartholomew
Close
Smithfield
St Bartholomew's
Hospital
Newgate
Aldersgate
Ludgate
St Paul's
Cathedral
Bride's
urchyard

† St Giles Cripplegate

Moorgate

Bishopsgate

Wood Street

Bread Street
Cheapside

Mr Mason's
coffee house

Cornhill

Aldgate

† St Stephen's
Walbrook

Thames Street

St Dunstan's-
in-the-East †

Posterngate

London Bridge

The
Tower

St Paul's School

St Paul's
Cathedral

Bread Street

St Anne's
Blackfriars
†

Watling Street

All Hallows
Church †

Blackfriars
Theatre

Humphrey
Moseley's shop

The City of London in the sixteenth century.

Part One

THE MAKING OF JOHN MILTON

ONE

THE CITY

1608

O N 20 DECEMBER 1608, in the heart of the City of London, a
baby boy was baptised in All Hallows Church, on the corner
of the ancient Roman thoroughfare of Watling Street and narrow
Bread Street. The baby had been brought to the church from his
house, The Spreadeagle, a few doors up Bread Street, where he had
been born eleven days earlier. The baptism ceremony was familiar
to all those present, who were reminded, forcefully, of their sinfulness – the product of Eve's sin in the Garden of Eden – but also of
the hope of redemption and everlasting life through the incarnation
and resurrection of Jesus Christ. The baptism ceremony was the
first step towards this potential transformation, opening the door of
the kingdom of heaven to the child. Just as important, the ceremony
marked the baby boy's incorporation into a dynamic urban community in which his family played a vital part. This incorporation
was expressed not only in the church service, with the baby's
midwife, father and gossips (godparents) clustered round the font,
with the women and children of the neighbourhood in their own
special pews, but also by the gossiping afterwards, paid for by the
baby's father. This party, perhaps with banquets of sweetmeats and
other junkets, perhaps a special cake presented to the father, might
spill over into the inns of Bread Street – The George, The Star and
The Three Cups – later in the day. The baby himself would return
to his mother in Spreadeagle Court, where she remained in what
was seen as health-giving seclusion for the first weeks of her child's
life.

The baby's parents, John and Sara, had been married for about eight years, and John was already in his mid-forties, Sara in her mid-thirties. Seven years earlier, a short-lived child had been buried in the same church, on 12 May 1601. The records do not even mention whether the baby was a boy or girl. Nor do they reveal exactly when, in the intervening years, John and Sara became parents again, this time to a baby girl, Anne, who did live. Now, in the winter of 1608, John and Sara had an infant son. At the baptism ceremony, he was named John Milton. The choice of name was a recognition of his father, but John was also the most popular name in England for generations before and after 1608. There were scriptural and non-scriptural saints of that name, not to mention the Gospel of John in the New Testament, but, above all, John was seen as a thoroughly traditional English name.[1]

Sara, more so than her husband, was of the City, born and bred in the urban environment, the daughter of Paul Jeffreys, an apprentice, then a freeman, of the Company of Merchant Taylors. Paul died when Sara was about ten, but Ellen, her mother, maintained control of the family estate and stayed close to her daughter, later coming to live with her in the Milton family house in Bread Street.[2]

The brief and predictable phrases of praise that surround Sara Jeffreys Milton ('a Woman of Incomparable Virtue and Goodness', 'a woman exemplary for her Liberality to the Poor' or her son's later description of her, as his 'honourable begetter') give little sense of the living woman.[3] Sara's life, like most women's, was dominated by the business of bearing and raising children. In the years that followed baby John's birth, and as she approached and passed the age of forty, Sara continued to endure the rigours of pregnancy and labour. She gave birth to a little girl, Sara, in mid-July 1612. The baby died within a month. Another baby, Tabitha, born soon after her brother John's fifth birthday, survived longer. Her parents may have had high hopes when she passed her first birthday, since the risk of loss diminished sharply after the first year of life. Yet Tabitha was buried on 3 August 1615: she was only eighteen months old.

Families in the early seventeenth century had their own ways of coming to terms with the ever-present reality of infant mortality.

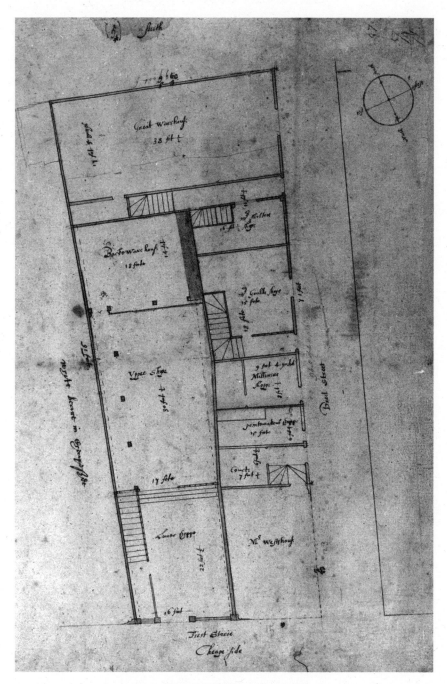

Floor plan of the house at Bread Street.

Perhaps most important for the mother was that she was celebrated not just in terms of the 'successful' delivery of a baby but for bearing the child, bringing it to birth. The ceremony of 'churching', whereby the mother was returned to her society and church, may have lost its pre-Reformation function as a rite of purification, but it remained a significant moment of public thanksgiving for the mother's survival.

Bearing and raising children may have been the dominant experience of Sara Milton's life, but it is also possible to catch glimpses of her involvement in her husband's business interests. John Milton was doing well in the City but, in contrast to Sara, had not been born and bred there. He had grown up in a village a few miles to the west of Oxford, and his move to London had not merely represented a rejection of country life but a rejection of his family's religious values. The Milton family in Oxfordshire had remained Catholic, despite the change to a Protestant state religion begun by Henry VIII and confirmed by his daughter, Elizabeth I, and her successor, the current monarch James I.

Although the Miltons in Oxfordshire would simulate conformity to the Protestant Church of England from time to time, their efforts were short-lived, and their continued loyalty to the Catholic Church proved both costly and dangerous.[4] In this part of Oxfordshire, they were not alone, however: in surrounding villages there were a number of prominent recusant families, known to offer safe houses to fugitive Jesuit priests who would pose as servants, hunters, tutors and doctors, and able to offer support to fellow, less wealthy, Catholic sympathisers.[5]

John Milton of Oxfordshire turned his back on this life when he was about twenty-three by coming to London, but his reasons may well have been economic as much as religious. He was certainly not alone in his move to the City, as inflationary and demographic pressures made the period one of great social mobility. The booming metropolis was dependent on young immigrants to keep the City open for business, in part because of the appallingly high mortality rates.[6] London was good to John. In his mid-thirties he was admitted to the Company of Scriveners (having served his apprenticeship), and shortly after he married Sara Jeffreys, thus cementing his ties with the mercantile City.

The baptism of baby John did not disrupt unduly the working life of his father: Mr Milton still found time to sign some business documents on the same day.[7]

To be a scrivener involved fulfilling a variety of roles: acting as a notary, representing clients in court, conveying land for individuals, moneylending, and operating as an estate agent and investment broker. That Mr Milton was a successful scrivener is illustrated by his leasing of the substantial house in Bread Street. The surviving floor plan shows that the house had two cellars and four further floors above the ground floor, which was the 'shop'. Above was 'Mr Milton's Hall', a large, L-shaped room with a 'little buttery' (a place to store provisions, and to get something to eat) leading off it towards a 'parlour'. This spacious room was panelled with wood and had a large window looking over Bread Street. A kitchen and a counting house completed the suite of rooms on the first floor, while above were a number of chambers for family members. Garrets at the top of the house provided tiny rooms for household servants and business apprentices.

Many years later Mr Milton's son, John, would place his family carefully within a particular social stratum: 'Who I am, then, and whence I come, I shall now disclose. I was born in London, of an honourable family. My father was a man of supreme integrity, my mother a woman of purest reputation, celebrated throughout the neighbourhood for her acts of charity.'[8] What is missing is the sense, suggested by the surviving records, that the Miltons were a busy, engaged couple, with strong connections with the merchant community (the will of a prominent Merchant Taylor left £3 to 'John Milton, and his wife to buy them Rings') and with the cultural community of the City (John Milton became a trustee of the first indoor theatre in London, the Blackfriars Playhouse, situated on the north, City, bank of the river, across from the scenes of depravity and licence surrounding the South Bank open theatres). In addition to his business talents, John Milton was a talented composer. His song 'Fair Oriana in the Morn' was published to acclaim as early as 1601, while in 1614 he contributed to a musical collection, *The Tears, or Lamentations of a Sorrowful Soul*, his work appearing alongside that of the leading names of the music business in his time such as Thomas Morley and William Byrd.[9] More importantly for the Miltons' financial security, John played the property market well.

For all the wealth that the house in Bread Street represented, and for all his father's contributions to the cultural world of his time, young John Milton grew up over the shop. In doing so, he experienced a profoundly urban childhood, rooted in the mercantile and business networks of the City. The streets around his house were dominated by St Paul's Cathedral, just a few hundred yards away. This imposing building, and the spaces around it, were far more than simply a place for worship. St Paul's both inside and out was the location for sharing news and for finding work, a convenient spot to 'gull' (con) innocent visitors, the best place to see the latest fashions. There were twenty-eight barbers living within 300 yards of its western door, fulfilling a wide range of functions, from surgeons to newsagents. By the west door, in Ave Maria Lane, were the brothels, and soliciting apparently even went on in St Paul's itself. Ironically, the very courts – 'the bawdy courts' that kept a watchful eye on sexual practices and marital relationships, as well as regulating sabbath-keeping and church attendance, tithes and wills – were held in the cathedral. 'Going to Paul's' was part of the London vernacular: all of life could be found there.

Bread Street also lay at the heart of what would become the greatest trading centre in the world over the next century, the seedbed of the new economic system: capitalism. One in five of the male population of the City (in the year of John Milton's birth still, in theory, the walled City of London) were members of the mercantile class. There was still a clear gap between the City and Westminster, the seat of government, a few miles west along the Thames. Even when these areas had merged completely, trade and finance stayed rooted in the City, where they remain to this day.[10]

Even in John's childhood, however, London was spreading far beyond its walls. The rich moved west, first to the Strand between the City and Westminster, then further still, while the manufacturing industries gradually also moved outside the walls. The City was already the country's leading manufacturing centre, its streets filled with the sights, sounds and smells of London's major industries: building, clothing, and leather- and metal-working.

The baptism ceremony on 20 December 1608 was not only designed to join the young John Milton to this vibrant urban community but to join him to his Church. It was the first step towards the possibility of salvation. There was, however, intense debate as to how the ceremony could best achieve or symbolise this vital step. The arguments about baptism represented merely the tip of an iceberg of religious controversy, partially hidden or suppressed in 1608 but lurking, ready to tear John Milton's country apart. Religion, of course, was not merely a private part of an individual's life but was utterly bound up with the political and social infrastructure of England. The country's rulers knew this and acted accordingly.

In the year of John's baptism, 1608, the English had experienced less than three generations as a Protestant nation. Only in 1534 did King Henry VIII engineer a formal break with the Church in Rome and, in doing so, establish the Church of England with himself as its head: Defender of the Faith. Over the following years the reformers set about their task of removing so-called superstition and idolatry. Images, relics and shrines which led the people to false worship were seized and destroyed, whether a crucifix that could speak or a statue of St Something, prayed to for relief by women in labour. Elizabeth I, dead five years earlier, had done much to establish religious conformity and political stability. The Act of Uniformity, passed back at the beginning of her reign in 1559, had insisted that only one text, the *Book of Common Prayer*, could be used in churches, and James I persisted in his own efforts to achieve religious compliance and consensus.

Yet despite this drive for orthodoxy, baptism – the only sacrament to be retained apart from Holy Communion in the Church of England – remained a problematic ceremony for many. The theological issue at stake was a critical one. Was the ceremony a *means* to regeneration and salvation, or simply a *sign* of it, nevertheless crucial for the joining of the individual to the body of the Church? Surrounding this central question was a series of smaller but no less vital divisions of opinion, and the furnishings and rituals connected with the baptismal ceremony became the battleground for the controversy. In churches throughout England, the baptismal font was first cherished and then neglected, removed and relocated, as, over the course of many generations, ministers and congregations engaged in what has been aptly described as an un-finished argument about religious culture and ritual.[11]

No matter that the King and his bishops sought to establish official procedure. The Church canons of 1604, for example, insisted that the sign of the cross be made on the baby's forehead, but many families, and indeed ministers, still refused to engage in this practice, which they saw as an empty gesture, redolent of the Catholicism the English nation had come to demonise. Families and ministers at the other end of the religious spectrum not only wanted the sign of the cross to be made in order fully to complete the baptismal ceremony but wanted oils to be sprinkled on the baby's head.[12] On the ground, the Church of England, and the King, the Defender of the Faith, simply did not have the resources to enforce conformity at all times, with the result that both religious diversity and religious tension characterised the Eng-land into which John Milton was born.

The earliest biographers of John Milton and his family tend to simplify this complex picture. Mr Milton's break from his own 'bigoted' father, his industry, his genteel talents (which could not be concealed despite his commercial interests) and his good wife combine to suggest a character who was exemplary of the Church of England's values and of the triumph of the Protestant work ethic. His success, in the words of probably the most reliable of the early biographers, had only positive implications for his children. Having trained as a scrivener, John Milton then 'became free of that profession; and was so prosperous in it, and the Consortship of a prudent virtuous Wife, as to be able to breed up in a liberal manner, and provide a competency for two Sons, and a Daugh-ter'.[13] (The second surviving son, Christopher, was born almost seven years after John, in November 1615.)

To some extent the statement is true. John and Sara had great ambitions for their son and the spread eagle, the sign over the shop, eventually became their son's family arms. In 1608, however, the

Miltons' gentility was precarious. So was the life of their new son. The perils of City life for young children were legion, from drowning, in ponds, ditches and the river, to road traffic. Infectious disease remained, however, the main threat. Only one in two babies survived to the age of five, and only just over a third of children survived to celebrate their fifteenth birthdays.

Despite, or because of, these perils, the Miltons focused all their energies on the education of their oldest son. This was not uncommon. But the sheer scale of young John's educational programme, its intensity and range, can seem almost chilling, the more so because of the boy's apparently eager application to the task. That John was an avid and able student is obvious. All his early biographers, and he himself, insist on just how hard-working he was in his childhood. Much, much later, when an old man himself, John's younger brother Christopher remembered his brother's studious habits: 'When he went to School, when he was very young, he studied very hard and sat up very late, commonly till 12 or one a clock at night, & his father ordered the maid to sit up for him, and in those years composed many Copies of Verses: which might well become a riper age.'[14] John, again long after the event, wrote that from the age of twelve, he rarely retired to bed from his studies until midnight.[15] In 1618, John and Sara had their son, who would be ten in December, painted as the young gentleman that they hoped would be produced by these studies.[16]

John's all-important studies would have begun, conventionally, at home, when he was about five years old. A child usually began learning letters by rote, orally from the 'hornbook' (a hand-held piece of horn with the alphabet inscribed on it) when he or she was five or six. Next the child learned to read whole words and was considered literate when he or she could read basic religious works, the primer and the catechism. Of course, it was possible to memorise these familiar texts and therefore appear functionally literate. For the vast majority of children who had schooling, whether at home or not, this was the endpoint of their education.

Learning to write was a different matter, a much more exclusive skill, and one often denied to girls, even in élite families. Anne, John's sister, was taught to write, but her future mother-in-law, despite being from a fairly wealthy family, could not.[17] John did not only learn to read and write in his own language but also began lessons in Latin. His tutor at home was a Scot, Thomas Young. Young was a Presbyterian, the form of Protestantism most influenced by the teachings of John Calvin in Geneva, and one which thrived in Scotland, with men such as John Knox doing much to form a Presbyterian Church there. As with most Protestants, Presbyterians emphasised (and continue to emphasise) the importance and authority of the Scriptures, and the possibility of salvation through faith and God's grace rather than through good works. Where the Presbyterians differed most clearly from the Church of England was in their rejection of episcopacy, the rule of the Church by bishops. Instead, the Presbyterian Church was controlled by elders, who would teach and rule the congregations. Congregations could choose their ministers.

When John was eleven, Thomas Young left England to become pastor to the English Company of Merchants in Hamburg. John, some years later, would write to him anxiously, fully aware that Young had chosen to place himself in Hamburg at the heart of the religious and military conflicts that became known as the Thirty Years War (1618–48). This European superpower struggle for territory and the control of religion burst into life in Bohemia in 1618, and in the following years, continental Europe saw relentless fighting. By 1626, northern Germany, where Young was serving, was under the complete control of the Catholic Habsburg Empire. John's tutor's life therefore demonstrated the connection between religious thinking and religious activism, as well as introducing the boy to attitudes and beliefs, such as suspicion of the established Church and support of international Protestantism, that would prove to be highly resonant in years to come. Just as significant, an educational relationship turned into a friendship. Young thought highly of his very young pupil and stayed in touch with him, later exchanging Latin and Greek verses and presenting a Hebrew Bible to John as a gift.[18]

At about the time that Young travelled to Hamburg, John Milton started formal schooling, outside the home. He had only to walk a few hundred yards to his school. There he would have had his lessons, with teachers and ushers to keep the boys under control, and senior pupils and servants doing necessary chores such as preparing the ink, stoking the fire, sweeping the room and emptying soil buckets. This was, however, no ordinary local educational establishment. St Paul's School was a renowned institution of Humanist learning that offered the rare delights of intensive Greek and, even more surprising, contemporary English literature. For the precocious John, it was probably ideal. He could add Greek to his studies (including the New Testament in its original language) and was introduced to a wide range of Classical authors, from Ovid to Cicero, from Homer to Euripides. It is probable that John started learning Hebrew in his final year at St Paul's.

It is easy to feel overawed by the amount of material that the young John Milton absorbed as a child and to pass over his vast reading with the simple statement that he was a prodigy. A more accurate assessment is that he was merely working, admittedly extremely hard and with great success, within the conventional educational models of his time. Pedagogical techniques were specifically designed to help the young boy master the vast amounts of information he was expected to absorb.

Organising one's material was crucial to success, and the commonplace book was crucial to that organisation. These items, akin to a scrapbook or notebook, were a familiar feature of life in the seventeenth century for those who were literate and had the money to buy paper. Those that have survived show individuals collecting letters, pithy quotations, scraps of poetry, 'receipts' for medicines and foods, notes for accounts, prayers – indeed any piece of information that could be useful to the owner in future. For a pupil of St Paul's, however, the compilation of commonplace books had a serious educational purpose. A boy might have an Aristotelian commonplace book in which he would set up headings according to antithesis, the favoured method of the Greek logician: pithy quotations from his favourite authors on justice and injustice, say, or joy and sorrow. He might also create a Ciceronian commonplace book, in which he would keep lists of vivid examples, culled from his reading of Classical and

Christian authors, ready to be used to persuade one's listeners of one's arguments and thus working within the rhetorical tradition championed by Cicero. Then again, he might acquire an interactive workbook such as the ever-popular *Pandectae Locorum Communium* of John Foxe, a comprehensive collection of memorable commonplaces, with space to add one's own small pieces of contemporary wisdom and to provide comments on those of the ancients.

The most important skill to develop was, however, that of memory. There were plenty of handbooks giving advice on the best ways to memorise phenomenal amounts of information. Most systems involved connecting words with images.[19] Another highly popular system was the Aristotelian place system, in which the image of a set of places, such as a street of houses and shops, is first memorised as a background. The first huge effort to be made was to picture this street over and over again, making sure that the order was absolutely right. Then, to remember a list of points, the pupil would map them on to the street of houses and shops, thus not merely memorising the things themselves but their order. Once the system was up and running, the information could be retrieved in either order, up or down the street as it were. Astonishingly, some scholars claimed to be able to retain a hundred thousand pieces of information using this method.

This emphasis on feats of memory was not as stultifying as it might sound, and the skill would be crucial to John in later life, as was fitting in a system designed to store up information for spiritual and practical use in the future. A young Princess Elizabeth, writing before she became Queen and during a period of terrifying imprisonment, wrote of the pleasure and consolation to be provided by memory. In her case, she called up the Scriptures in exemplary fashion:

> I walk many time into the pleasant fields of the holy scriptures, where I pluck up the goodly green herbs of sentences by pruning; eat them by reading, chew them by using and lay them up at length in the high seat of memory by gathering them together; that so having tasted thy sweetness I may the less perceive the bitterness of this miserable life.[20]

Princess Elizabeth was, however, that rare thing, a girl who had been educated in languages other than her own. For boys from the upper classes, Latin was a given and was the medium through which pupils learned all their other subjects, from mathematics to philosophy. Boys learned their languages through the process of double translation. So, they would first translate Latin into English, then the English back into Latin. (John, as has been seen, also learned Greek and Hebrew, as well as Italian and French, even in his early teens.) As the Milton scholar John Hale points out, in John's case, 're-translation might become multilingual, taking a passage round a ring of the languages he was learning as a teenager.'[21]

John, in academic terms, was utterly at home in this multilingual intellectual élite. Crucially for the Milton family's aspirations, education and learning had become linked with establishing gentility. John, the son of a scrivener, was well on the way to joining a powerful social coterie. Although Latin materials were slowly making their way into the vernacular, direct access to Classical authors remained a benchmark of refinement, a passport to certain parts of society and knowledge.

Direct access to the Classical authors also had some interesting implications for the young male scholar. Take the experience of tackling one particular, but representative, Classical author, Horace. The pupils

> gathered their ideas of Horace and of Horation odes from a variety of sources. They would have read the Latin text of Horace's poetry in editions which surrounded it with glosses, notes, parallel passages, and perhaps a prose paraphrase; they would have practised translating and imitating Horace's poetry at school; they would have read English translations and imitations of Horace by writers such as Jonson.

Horace, like most Latin authors, wrote about private and domestic experiences; about love and desire, both homosexual and heterosexual; about friendship and having fun; and about the passage of time. Alongside these concerns, his 'poetry also spoke of the great public events which were shaping Rome under Augustus, though often addressing such matters at a tangent, cautious about how a private citizen might speak to power or understand history, and jealous of the poet's precarious independence'.[22]

To engage with Latin every day at school thus involved not only exposure to all these subjects but a vital and constant shifting between the past and the present, savouring the differences and the connections. London was and was not Horace's Rome. On one level, the pupil could travel to a world apart, utterly different from any current experience. On another level, London *was* Rome made new, and a Classical Latin writer could be as contemporary as the latest pamphlet telling of the latest horrific battle in middle Europe, or the execution of the last of the Elizabethan heroes, Sir Walter Ralegh, in New Palace Yard, Westminster in 1618. Translation brought the ancient world – brought Athens, Troy and Rome – to London.

This was only fitting within an incipient national culture that saw its origins in the Classical world. Britain took its name, so the legend went, from Aeneas' great-grandson, Brutus, who landed at Totnes in Devon in 1100 BC. London's old name was, allegedly, Troynovant ('New Troy'). It was a short step to imagine, as many did, the transplantation of all that was great in Classical culture to the glorious nation that was England: 'It was a happy revolution of the heavens,' wrote the Humanist Gabriel Harvey, 'when Tiberis flowed into the Thames; Athens removed to London; pure Italy, and fine Greece, planted themselves in rich England.'[23] Translation itself, known as 'englishing', was thus all part of a nationalistic project underpinned to some extent with a similar ideology to that which accompanied the emergence of new nation-states in the mid-nineteenth century.[24]

What did John make of this remarkable education? When he looked back on his childhood, he conjured an image of an almost physical desire for literature of all kinds. He wrote of his childhood 'appetite' for learning and described how he 'tasted' the 'sweetness of philosophy', how he was 'allured to read' the 'smooth Elegiac poets' (a euphemistic reference to erotic Latin poetry), as well as Dante and Petrarch.[25] This is a portrait of the artist as a very young man with a sensual attraction to words, a child who achieved a kind of coming of age through literature.

What John also made clear, in later life, was that he may have read *with* desire, he may have read books *about* desire, but he remained uncorrupted by the experience. Instead, reading of these matters merely made him love chastity even more. The adult John Milton insisted that he was a child apart, one uncontaminated by his desires, one who could use his reading to transcend them. This tension between, on the one hand, appetite and desire, and, on the other, abstinence and self-control would prove both destructive and creative throughout John's life. It was perhaps never quite resolved.

The tension was not peculiar to John, however, although it was particularly extreme for him. The later Milton's emphasis on his youthful love of chastity is, in part, an implicit response to the pronouncements of commentator after commentator who warned that, for a boy, there was 'no more dangerous age than youth' because of his 'raging concupiscence'.[26] Any sign of rebellion in a child was something to worry about, whether lack of deference to age or failure of self-control. It was self-control that distinguished the civil man from the beast, the savage or, in practice within society, the non-gentleman. A book called *The Schoole of Good Manners* by William Fiston, first published in 1595, warned parents what would happen if they did not control the more repellent aspects of their young children's behaviour:

> There are some Children so slovenly, that they wet and perfume the lower part of their Shirts and Clothes with Urine, some others that bespot, and all to daub their Breasts and Sleeves filthily with dropping of drink and Pottage. Nay, which is most loathsome, with snivelling of their nose, and drivelling of their Mouth: but in any wise beware thou of this beastliness.[27]

Having conquered beastliness, however, another far more serious problem emerged: quite literally, the problem of hotheadedness. Medical theory of the time argued that the heat of the body became more overpowering at puberty. In the absence of the drier and colder qualities associated with maturity, 'striplings' of fourteen or fifteen years old, though nimble and active, were also 'wanton, unmodest, malepert, saucy, proud, without wit, and much given to toying and playing'. Their blood was at fault. It was boiling up within them, and 'seetheth in their Veins, even as new Wine, Ale or Beer spurgeth and worketh in the Tun'. The heat could lead to serious instability in the body, which could easily overpower the brain and hinder the youth's capacity for rational action.[28]

There appears to be little evidence of the 'wilful and slippery' in the adolescent John Milton, despite his engagement with Latin poetry, whether Ovid's explicit analysis of the arts of seduction (*Ars Amatoria*), which culminate in instructions to the female lover on how to fake an orgasm, or Catullus' description of an intense attachment to his male friend Licinius:

> *Hesterno, Licini, die otiosi*
> *Multum lusimus in meis tabellis*
> *[. . .]*
> *Atque illinc abii tuo lepore*
> *Incensus, Licini, facetiisque,*
> *Ut nec me miserum cibus iuuaret*
> *Nec somnus tegeret quiete ocellos,*
> *Sed toto indomitus furore lecto*
> *Uersarer, cupiens uidere lucem,*
> *Ut tecum loquerer simulque ut essem.*

> At leisure, Licinius, yesterday
> We'd much fun with my writing-tablets
> [. . .]
> Yes, and I left there fired by
> Your charm, Licinius, and wit,
> So food gave poor me no pleasure
> Nor could I rest my eyes in sleep
> But wildly excited turned and tossed
> Over the bed, longing for daylight
> That I might be with you and talk.[29]

John remained untouched, unsullied, by passages such as these. Yet he was, it seems, capable of the most intense emotional attachments. While at school, he became close friends with Charles Diodati, who came from a distinguished Protestant Italian family that had sought refuge in England. His father, Theodore, had been physician to Princess Elizabeth, the only daughter of King James. Charles's uncle, Giovanni, was an eminent Calvinist theologian, Hebraist and promoter of international Protestant collaboration, as well as the translator of the Bible into Italian in 1603. Charles himself, although a year younger than John, progressed through school and university more quickly than his friend. The Diodati family, and Charles himself, represented many of the things to which the young John Milton aspired: an international Protestant identity, high status within society, as well as talent and success.[30]

Another friend, Alexander Gill, was the son of the head teacher at St Paul's, a young man about ten years older than John. Alexander was to influence John through his adolescent years and beyond, again in the direction of an international Protestantism, already part of John's experience due to his involvement with the Presbyterian Thomas Young. Alexander Gill would be regularly in trouble with the authorities for his aggressive espousal of militant Protestant views.

There are some hints of the influence of these views in the only two English poems by John that survive from these years. The poems are translations of Psalms, probably from Latin versions of the Hebrew originals, since it is highly unlikely that John had mastered Hebrew at this age. One of, if not actually, his first preserved poems in English, is the Exodus Psalm 114, 'When Israel went out of Egypt, and the house of Jacob from the barbarous people':

> Why fled the ocean? And why skipped the mountains?
> Why turned Jordan toward his crystal fountains?
> Shake earth, and at the presence be aghast
> Of him that ever was, and ay shall last,
> That glassy floods from rugged rocks can crush,
> And make soft rills from fiery flint-stones gush.
>
> (ll. 13–18)

This very Psalm had been sung in thanksgiving at St Paul's when James I's son and heir Prince Charles had returned from Spain without his intended bride, the Spanish Infanta. The Psalm was useful to the Protestant nationalist cause, sighing relief at this close escape from a Catholic marriage alliance. John did not need to be a radical to be opposed to the marriage of a Protestant prince to a Catholic princess from the country with which England had been at war through many years of living memory. Nevertheless, his teenage Protestant nationalism shines through his choice of text.

While John progressed through school, making friends, translating Psalms, learning Greek, his only sister fulfilled her rather different social destiny by marrying. Her new husband was a government official called Edward Phillips, and the ceremony took place on 22 November 1623 at St Stephen's, Walbrook. Afterwards, the newly-weds set up home in a house in the Strand, moving west and upmarket. The marriage settlement visibly demonstrated the wealth of the Miltons, and the family's determination that Anne would remain financially secure even if her husband died. Anne's dowry of £800 was more typical of the upper gentry than a Bread Street scrivener; if widowed, she would receive substantial property (a jointure) which was secured to her interest and her future children. That the Milton family insisted upon a jointure for their daughter was a further sign that they were very much a family of property themselves. John, still only fourteen at the time, and his mother, Sara, witnessed the settlement made up a few days after the actual marriage. Clearly, the Milton family encompassed not just John Milton the scrivener but his capable wife and his almost adult son.[31]

Sara and John's responsibility towards their daughter was now complete, for, on her marriage, Anne had entered a new family. Their plan for their son John was rather different.

TWO

CAMBRIDGE

1625

T HE PRIVATE TUTORS and St Paul's all led to one place: the University of Cambridge. John was admitted to Christ's College at the age of sixteen early in 1625 and matriculated into the University on 9 April. Despite the narrowness and conservatism of the curriculum, which stood in sharp contrast to the cutting-edge approach to study at St Paul's, Cambridge was a stimulating place to live and work in the mid-1620s.

The city and the University represented a microcosm of the simmering religious, political and philosophical conflicts of the time. Most notably, within and between the colleges, competing religious factions sought to establish their vision of the Church of England. Protestants who wanted simpler religious practices and more preaching zeal lined up in opposition to those who supported ritual and tradition. One of the tutors at Milton's college, Joseph Mede, epitomised the former group. Mede was a firebrand preacher eager to apply his religious beliefs to current events, always willing to argue just how close the Second Coming of Christ was, just how active God was in the world.

There was little chance for a student at Cambridge to live the life of the recluse. Indeed there was an active blending of the worlds of University, church and town. Dons met to dispute in pubs (most famously in the sixteenth century, when Protestant reformers met in the White Horse), and shops were built right up against the church of Great St Mary's, so that the west windows were 'half-blinded up' by a cobbler's and bookbinder's.

Alongside the intellectual disputes, Cambridge (and indeed Oxford) were renowned for a different kind of conflict, the rivalry between 'town and gown', between city and University. This conflict had been exacerbated by the rapid growth of Cambridge, whose population had trebled between 1560 and 1620. At the same time, the quality of housing deteriorated, and acute poverty and overcrowding ensued. Arriving in 1625, John saw a city of building work, with colleges, old and new, expanding where they could, while the poor were crowded into older houses subdivided into tenements, 'their rudeness and straitness being only fit to harbour the poorest sort', as one contemporary put it.[1] Although the city authorities did their best, disease was rife, with a major outbreak of plague in 1625 and then again six years later. Overall, disorder and unrest were common, part of a culture of routine violent exchange, where men on both sides were quickly mobilised when group pride or boundaries of status or territory were threatened. Yet, the most serious incidents of group violence were not between 'town and gown' but internal to the University, students attacking fellow-students.[2]

Cambridge – edgy, overcrowded, full of young men ready to use fists, cudgels and swords to settle their differences – offered something special and quite different to John Milton. The University offered him a stage on which to perform – in Latin. University life was dominated by Latin, an indication not of conservatism but of the importance of the language to society at home and abroad. When John went up in 1625, Latin already dominated large areas of his life. Across Europe and into the Americas, Latin enabled international exchange, both intellectual and diplomatic. In England at large it provided the agreed language of memorial and conferred intellectual credibility on many a public occasion. Even at the end of the seventeenth century, thousands would come to hear Latin disputations in the Sheldonian Theatre in Oxford, where official University ceremonies such as student graduations are still conducted in Latin to this day, and for similar reasons. Any human endeavour with an international dimension, and some without, were conducted in Latin. So argues John Hale, the scholar who has done most to bring Milton's Latin to life, concluding that the language informed 'history, philosophy, logic, international law, science, medicine, all the most vigorous disciplines of early-modern intellectual culture'.[3] Above all, however, the experience of Latin at Cambridge was rooted in performance. The University curriculum itself may have been tedious and traditionalist in the extreme, but its mode of delivery, both in terms of the language used and the emphasis on debate, offered a superb introduction to an international world of religious, political and intellectual exchange.

At school, John had learned to read verses aloud, to recite themes, to link his learning of Latin with his mastery of rhetoric. At Cambridge this oral, performance-based education continued, if anything becoming even more central. The University's 'exercises' were debates and disputations conducted in Latin. Participants had to engage in cross-examinations and thesis defences in Latin, in public and impromptu. In a move that would become typical, John used these very exercises to criticise both the system and his fellow-students. He attacks those who only seek to provoke animosity, those who are reliant on phrases from new-fangled authors, those who insist he engage in boring tasks. Yet, equally characteristically, alongside these attacks are some grand aims. Eloquent speech and noble action, argues John the proud Englishman, are the two things that 'most enrich and adorn our country', and so he sets out a plan of study that will enable such speech and action. Young men will consider the ancient heroes, 'the customs of mankind', 'the nature of all living creatures', 'the secret virtues of stones and herbs', and gaze upon the clouds, the snow, 'the source of dew in the morning'. Above all, the mind will 'know itself'. It is all very splendid, if slightly redolent of the kinds of clichés Shakespeare's Polonius had doled out to his son a generation earlier.[4]

In these academic exercises, as throughout his schooling, John would have been judged by the quality of his Latin expression. And the fact is that John Milton was superb at Latin. His talent opened up new worlds of knowledge, and offered a connection with a wide and diverse community. European Protestants, divided by their vernacular languages, could communicate about their cause in Latin (even as they rejected it as the language of religious observance).

Mastery of the language also enabled John to write poetry. His early poems were invariably occasional – that is, composed for particular occasions; they were often Ovidian – that is, heavily influenced by the Roman erotic poet Ovid; and they were, at times, millenarian – that is, conscious of the imminence of the Apocalypse. John's Cambridge poetry, at least at first, offers a strange and heady mixture of opportunism, urbane classicism and fervent religious zeal. His *Elegia Tertia: In Obitum Praesulis Wintoniensis* (Elegy III, On the Death of the Bishop of Winchester) takes one of Ovid's erotic dream-visions of his mistress and transforms it into an ecstatic dream-vision of the recently deceased bishop, Lancelot Andrews:[5]

> *Ipse racemiferis dum densas vitibus umbras*
> *Et pellucentes miror ubique locos,*
> *Ecce mihi subito praesul Wintonius astat,*
> *Sydereum nitido fulsit in ore iubar;*
> *Vestis ad auratos defluxit candida talos,*
> *Infula divinum cinxerat alba caput.*
>
> (ll. 51–6)

As I gaze all around me in wonder at the shining spaces and the thick shadows under the clustering vines, suddenly the Bishop of Winchester appears, close by me. A star-like radiance shone from his bright face, a white robe flowed down to his golden feet and his god-like head was encircled by a white band.

John's religious zeal was of a conventional kind, an expression of a common fear that English Protestantism was dangerously threatened by a resurgent Catholic Church. In June 1625 Protestant forces had been defeated by Spanish forces at Breda in the Netherlands, another sign that reformed religion was in perilous danger. John was still in contact, through letters (in prose and in verse), with Thomas Young, ministering to his Protestant congregation in Hamburg, and, in his *Elegia Quarta ad Thomam Iunium* (Elegy IV to Thomas Young), imagines his verse letter making haste across the ocean to the beleaguered Young, who is surrounded by battles, blood 'soaking into ground sown with human flesh'. John promises Young that he will 'be kept safe beneath God's gleaming shield'. Should this be read as a hawkish expression of solidarity between radical Protestants or a dove-like hope that Young will survive the horrific violence? What is certain is that the poem vividly invokes the conflicts raging beyond the English Channel. Moreover, this concern is present even in *Elegy III*, which mourns not only the Bishop of Winchester but also the Protestant soldiers killed at Breda.

Closer to home, the threat to English Protestantism was epitomised for the many by the Gunpowder Plot of 1605. Guy Fawkes's failed attempt to blow up the Houses of Parliament at Westminster had a similar impact on the national consciousness as the attack on the World Trade Center has had on the modern United States. The anniversary of the Plot was celebrated with passion each year. John's poems on the subject, again in Latin, link the traitor Fawkes explicitly and predictably with the threat from Catholic Rome. John makes the violent and puerile suggestion that Fawkes should blow up 'filthy monks' instead of innocent English Members of Parliament.[6] In his longest poem on the Plot, and one which was possibly performed on a Cambridge college feast day, *In Quintum Novembris* (On the Fifth of November), John describes King James, the good King ruling over a happy and rich England, threatened by a fierce tyrant. With the Plot defeated, the celebrations ensue:

> *Compita laeta focis genialibus omnia fumant;*
> *Turba choros iuvenilis agit: quintoque Novembris*
> *Nulla dies toto occurrit celebratior anno.*
>
> (ll. 224–6)

There is merrymaking at every crossroads and smoke rises from the festive bonfires: the young people dance in crowds: in all the year there is no day more celebrated than the fifth of November.

Those festive bonfires were a feature of English life, and, of course, the celebration of this deliverance continues to this day in England, in a much-diluted version.

These Gunpowder poems were a public declaration of political and religious allegiance, John Milton standing up to be counted as a nationalist Protestant, vehemently opposed to Catholic threats at home and abroad. In literary terms, the longest poem in the group marked his first use (at least in terms of public occasional poetry) of the six-beat hexameter line for an entire poem. Since this was the most prestigious Latin metre, the poem signified something of a literary milestone, at least in the Latin language. These verses represent, however, only a small part of a huge undertaking. Performing in Latin constituted John's working life for more than five years, as he passed through his late teens.

It is easy to forget how young John was during his time at Cambridge: he was clearly no longer a child, but nor was he yet a man. University life was designed to change that. In intellectual terms it seems clear that he was the equal of any of his contemporaries. But élite universities have never merely been places for intellectual inquiry: they are finishing schools for the ruling classes, and in John's day, Cambridge was a place where one went to demonstrate, in highly public ways, one's masculinity, to prove oneself a man. The collegiate system represented this symbolically, making every student the 'son' of his college tutor, who was of course his 'father'. One's fellow-students, it follows, were one's 'brothers'. It was patriarchy in miniature, and highly effective.

There was, in the words of one social historian, 'considerable peer pressure to appear heterosexually active'. Bragging about sexual activities was deemed a sign of manhood, and students frequented 'suspicious houses' after curfew as a normal part of their social round, with one student boasting to a friend that 'the sweetest sport that ever he had with Bridget Edmunds was in the chair.'[7] There were, however, some brothers who did not enjoy the highly charged world, this shared culture of excess, and were thus extremely vulnerable to violent bullying. In 1622, at Trinity College, Cambridge, three men confessed that they had 'very disorderly and at unseasonable times gone to scholars' chambers violently to take them out of their lodging and to abuse them in their persons'.[8] There are hints that John

Milton, ostentatiously devoted to chastity, was one of those bullied by his peers. That there were problems for John at Cambridge, whether intellectual, political, religious or with his 'brothers', is revealed by his retreat back to London in the spring of 1627, forced out, 'rusticated', by the University authorities.[9] He was eighteen, and for the moment his University life was over.

Many biographers of John Milton, whether writing in the seventeenth or the twentieth centuries, present his Cambridge years as another step on his path towards his great poems. His time at University becomes exemplary both of his precocious genius and of his independence of mind. His 'diligent study', his vast reading, his phenomenal talent, and 'his virtuous and sober life' set him out as special in one way.[10] His disappointment with University life merely points up his uniqueness and precocity further. This interpretation is heavily reliant on Milton's own, much later, assessment. In one of his earliest prose pamphlets, he would offer an angry critique of the English system. Young men were 'sent to those places, which were intended to be the seed plots of piety and the liberal arts, but were become the nurseries of superstition, and empty speculation'.[11] This says more about John Milton than it does about Cambridge University. It conveniently obscures both the huge benefits he accrued from his time there and the personal crises (which had little to do with the intellectual debates around him) that beset him at the time. Another reason for unhappiness was suggested by John's younger brother, Christopher, who recounted many years later that Chappell, John's college tutor, whipped him.[12]

Returning to the City of London and to his family, John re-entered a challenging, yet familiar, world. Ironically, there may well have been as much if not more intellectual life around St Paul's than there had been in the whole of Cambridge. The churchyard that surrounded the cathedral was the largest open space in all the City. In one corner was Paul's Cross, for centuries a Londoner's meeting place, the open-air pulpit used for sermons and other forms of public speaking. In St Paul's itself, the dean between 1621 and 1631 was none other than John Donne, known in his lifetime more for his profound, dazzling,

inspirational sermons than his witty, metaphysical poetry. The hub of
the London book trade lay north of old St Paul's, the streets crammed
with stationers and printers. Between Friday Street and Bread Street
stood one of the best-known literary pubs in the City, haunt in the
previous generation of writers such as Shakespeare, Jonson and Donne
– The Mermaid. Moreover, despite the massive influx of poor
migrants, urban life in London was slightly more stable than in
Cambridge, in part because of the high levels of civic participation.[13]

The print shops, pubs and civic stability were only part of the
picture, however. The City of London was also a place where life was
cheap, especially for the poor. The records of one city parish note the
deaths of 'Margaret who died by the town ditch', 'Robert a vagrant
that died in the street' and 'a boy that died in a hayloft at the Red
Lion'.[14] Everyone, not only the poor, was vulnerable to plague, which
returned in 1625, killing 35,000 in London and its suburbs. Five
thousand of the victims died in just one week. It was reported that so
many people fled that in Westminster the streets were deserted and
overgrown with grass. Old women were employed, for a pittance, to
visit the houses of the dead and report back on the cause of death: the
reports of these 'searchers' remain the only historical evidence of how
people died.[15]

Within John's own family, disease and death continued to cast a
shadow, despite the Miltons' relative prosperity. The early years of the
marriage between Anne Milton and Edward Phillips echoed, uncan-
nily and painfully, the experience of Anne's mother, Sara, and father,
John. The lives of John Milton's mother and sister epitomised the
harrowing connections between mortality and sexuality, even within
the sanctity of marriage. Both couples endured the births and then the
early deaths of their children. Anne would, for example, bury her
toddler daughter, her namesake Anne, while six months pregnant
with another baby, Elizabeth, who herself would die shortly after her
third birthday. During the spring and summer of 1626, while in
London, John may well have spent time with a little nephew, *his*
namesake John, at a time when the toddler was learning to walk,
perhaps to speak his first few words. This child John would die when

he was just four, buried on 15 March 1629. Only in August 1630, seven years into the marriage, did Anne Milton Phillips give birth to a baby boy, Edward, who would survive into adulthood.

A poem – probably from the time of plague in 1625–6, if John Milton's own dating and an internal reference to the 'slaughtering pestilence' is to be relied on – commemorates the death of a child, perhaps one of his sister's children.[16] Although twenty years later Milton would think the poem good enough to go into his collected works, 'On the Death of a fair Infant dying of a Cough' is a simplistic response to grief while at the same time standing as the brilliant poem of a highly educated and thoughtful young man, at ease with the tropes of Classical mythology and Christian consolation. The poem also demonstrates John's fascination with the poet Edmund Spenser, author of the Protestant, nationalist epic *The Faerie Queene*, written a generation earlier during the 1590s. John's admiration for the writers of his father's generation, who of course included Shakespeare, shines through much of his writing in English during this period, and was perhaps fuelled by the presence of other near-contemporary writers such as Sir Philip Sidney on the curriculum at St Paul's. At this stage of his career, it was the sensuous yet pithy language of Spenser and Shakespeare that inspired John. He relished Spenser's use of archaism ('unweeting' and 'whilom' appear in 'Fair Infant'), while, formally, John adopted a six-beat closing alexandrine line for each stanza, a technique deeply characteristic of Spenser's poetry. Between them, Shakespeare and Spenser offered him phrases such as 'thought to kiss / But killed alas' (echoing Shakespeare's *Venus and Adonis*), and visions such as the 'golden-winged host' (echoing Spenser's 'bright Cherubins' with 'golden wings' in his 'Hymn of Heavenly Beauty').

Yet for all the beauty of the language, John ended by instructing the mother of the dead child, perhaps his own sister, to 'cease to lament' what he called her 'false imagined loss':

> Then thou the mother of so sweet a child
> Her false imagined loss cease to lament,
> And wisely learn to curb thy sorrows wild;

Think what a present thou to God has sent,
And render him with patience what he lent;
This if thou do he will an offspring give,
That till the world's last end shall make thy name to live.

(ll. 71–7)

When John lost those whom he loved in future years, he would find it difficult to carry out these instructions for himself.

A number of other poems from this period consider the subject of death and employ a similar language. Whether commemorating the University beadle or the aforementioned Bishop of Winchester (the illustrious Lancelot Andrewes), John occasionally resorted to a rather stilted emotionalism, writing, scarcely credibly, that on hearing the news of Andrewes's death, 'I burst into tears.'[17] This level of interest in the dead might seem strange in a young man of seventeen or eighteen but was rooted in the practice of poetry at Cambridge, and indeed in society in general. When important figures died at the University, funeral pieces were pinned on the hearse-cloth of the bier as it lay in the University Church of Great St Mary's, and then, if the author was lucky, these were collected and circulated in manuscript. Perhaps John, aspiring poet, had this very public venue in mind. John Hale certainly thinks that Milton was making an effort, through his Latin, to get a reputation.[18]

If Cambridge came to represent, in poetry at least, a nexus of power and death, London came to represent, again in poetry, a very different aspect of John's life, and one which he claimed to prefer. John chose to write of London in the form of elegy, a particular kind of Latin poem made up of so-called 'elegiac couplets', alternating hexameter and pentameter, six- and five-beat, lines. Much used by the Roman poets Ovid and Catullus for witty, even obscene, pieces, elegy did not need, and rarely had, much connection with themes of death or memorial.[19] Before considering the delights of London, however, Cambridge needed to be dismissed, as it is in a poem addressed to John's friend Charles Diodati, which insists that John has 'no concern' with, and 'no nostalgia' for, Cambridge, no regrets about escaping from the 'threats of a rough tutor' and 'other indignities which my spirit cannot endure'. (The mention of the rough tutor does suggest that there was some truth in Christopher Milton's account of his brother's beatings.)

This poem, *Elegia Prima ad Carolum Diodatum* (Elegy I to Charles Diodati), packed with allusions to Ovid and Catullus, goes on to describe London life: 'For here I can devote my leisure hours to the mild Muses: here books, which are my life, quite carry me away. When I am tired, the pageantry of the rounded theatre attracts me, and the play's babbling speeches claim my applause.' (II. 25–8) London, symbolised by the Thames, and celebrated as the place of John's birth, is infinitely preferable to Cambridge, with its 'bare fields which offer no gentle shades'.

This celebration of London living is self-consciously modern on John's part. He allies himself with new ideas of civilisation, dismissing, implicitly, the traditional ideal of the lord or the country gentleman, and celebrating a new concept of an urban élite. In the country, hospitality was the crucial indicator of gentility. In the city, it was wit, and the recognition of 'virtue of the mind'.[20] To an aspiring middle-class young man such as John Milton, unable to access the traditional privileges of a country estate, there was much to be said for an urban culture that valued wit so highly.

John's aspirations are hinted at when he represents himself as a 'worshipper of Phoebus'. Typically, this is a heavily loaded allusion. Phoebus is Apollo, the most popular of all the Greek gods, a god who presided over many aspects of life: prophecy and punishment, music, poetry and dance, pastoral life and archery, to name but a few. Above all, however, Apollo was the patron of poets and leader of the Muses. The poem suggests that it was easier to be a worshipper of all these things, easier to live the complete, active life, in London than in Cambridge.

Above all, though, London was fun and it was sexy, as the numerous invocations of the Roman erotic poet of the city, Ovid, make clear. John not only mentions his visits to the 'rounded theatre' (*'Excipit hinc fessum sinuosi pompa theatri'*) in *Elegy I* but takes time to outline some plots from plays he has seen, including that old standby of the young girl coming of (sexual) age: '. . . often, too, there is a young girl who is surprised by a warmth of feeling she never felt before, and falls in love without knowing what love is.' In an Ovidian form, the elegy, Milton recaps an Ovidian plot (straight from Ovid's 'Salmacis and Hermaphroditus' in his *Metamorphoses*) while casting himself as an Ovid-like figure, suffering exile from Cambridge as Ovid did from Rome under Augustus.

The theme of urban eroticism continues. John says he likes the shady places (not to be found in Cambridge, of course) outside the city walls, because there 'you can often see parties of young girls walking by – stars which breathe forth seductive flames.' The climax of all this praise is the explicit connection made between the beauty of 'British girls' (as he says, '. . . be content, foreign woman, to take second place!') and that of London, 'a city built by Trojan settlers, a city whose towery head can be seen for miles'.

The poem has a twist, however. John himself, as represented in this verse letter, is *not* seduced by those beautiful women breathing out seductive fires, and by implication, he is not seduced by London. The threat of the women (and of the city?) is as ever embedded in an arcane Classical reference:

> Ast ego, dum pueri sinit indulgentia caeci,
> Moenia quam subito linquere fausta paro;
> Et vitare procul malefidae infamia Circes
> Atria, divini Molyos usus ope.
> Stat quoque iuncosas Cami remeare paludes,
> Atque iterum raucae murmur adire Scholae.
>
> (ll. 85–90)

For my part I intend to quit this pampered town as quickly as possible, while the blind boy's indulgence permits, and, with the help of divine moly, to leave far behind the infamous halls of faithless Circe. I am to return again to the Cam's reedy marshes and face the uproar of the noisy scholars again.[21]

What was the significance of John's emphasis on his own restraint, his refusal to be contaminated by the constant availability of sex in the city? In part the answer lies in his age and gender. He was still in the years of dangerous heat, and any young man's struggle towards manhood was defined by his ability to achieve 'bodily equilibrium'. Balance was the ideal, a life of 'discretion, control, and containment'.[22] This insistence on balance and control was rooted in ideas about men and women's bodies. Women and men were viewed as closely related in physiology. Sadly for women, their bodies were imperfect versions of the male, with the genitals inverted inside the woman's body. This imperfection was exacerbated by the balance of the four humours within male and female bodies. Medical theory held that a woman's humoural balance was colder and moister than a man's, and it was this that made women naturally less rational and strong.

Since it was accepted that every person had male and female attributes, it was absolutely imperative to make sure that boys grew into proper men, suppressing or expelling any female attributes in childhood. In John Milton's case there appears to have been a ruthless determination to keep any female, anywhere, at a distance, rather than merely eradicating any feminine attributes within himself. In doing so, he was only taking his society's ideas to their logical extreme. Elite education and upbringing were primarily designed to train boys and girls for their future gender roles. For boys, this meant being taken away from effeminising mothers, while school and University imposed a curriculum and regime upon boys that demanded self-control and discipline, and involved a process of physical and emotional hardening. The aim was to produce men with the qualities suited to family and social leadership. The emphasis on performance and public speaking at Cambridge was yet another aspect of the same dynamic. Throughout their education, young men would learn voice production, articulation, vocabulary, forms and formulae of verbal and epistolary deference, and general principles of conversation.[23] Writers had stressed, and continued to stress, that speech should be in a 'voice, not soft, weak, piping, womanish, but audible, strong and manlike'.[24] A good style was muscular and manly, not inclined to effeminacy and verbosity.[25]

Young men learned how to speak in order to be civilised, to contribute to society: women and children learned to be silent. Men also learned languages denied to most women, another fundamental way of patrolling the boundaries between the sexes. In this context, John's insistence on his own chastity becomes a somewhat paradoxical display of his own adult manhood.

John Milton's father was, during these years, doing what *he* could to make his son a man. On top of paying his son's fees at university (£50 a year), he made sure that young John was initiated into the Milton family business. Documents from the summer of 1627, when John was eighteen, show him signing papers with his father; purchasing a property in St Martin-in-the-Fields with his father; and lending money to a gentleman-farmer in Oxfordshire, one Richard Powell. This last initiative was familiar territory for John Milton Sr, who had built up his business in part through the lending of money. The loan to Richard Powell of £500, with a return of yearly interest of £24, was standard practice, but in this case, the scrivener made over the income from the loan to his son.

At Cambridge, immersed in a culture of Latin performance, John could prove himself in one way. In London, immersed in urban life, whether financial, cultural or intellectual, he could begin to enter adult worlds in his own right. During his late teens, therefore, Cambridge *with* London made a man of him but perhaps not quite the man that his traditional biographers have represented.

For there was another aspect of John's life at this time that has not often been fully acknowledged: his intimacy with Charles Diodati. It is to Charles that John writes, in his Latin *Elegy I*, of his joy that 'at last, dear friend, your letter has reached me,' of his happiness that the letter shows 'a heart that loves me and a head so true'. It is Charles whom he compliments for being 'a charming companion'.

Once alerted to the strength of John's feeling for Charles, it is tempting to re-interpret other writings. There are perhaps hints of the intimacy between the two men in the ways in which *Elegy I* dwells on the erotics of urban living. John may write that he prefers the shady places outside the city walls, because that is where the young girls go, but he then compares the girls' 'enticing cheeks' to the 'flush of the hyacinth' and 'the blushing red of your flower, Adonis' ('*Pellacesque genas, ad quas hyacinthina sordet / Purpura, et ipse tui floris, Adoni, rubor*' [ll.61–2]). In a poem of heterosexual voyeurism, Milton incorporates an image of beautiful, doomed male youth: Adonis, the same Adonis who rejected the goddess of love, Venus, in Shakespeare's dramatic poem, *Venus and Adonis.* The 'you' addressed is on the surface at least Adonis, but in a poem addressed overall to Charles Diodati, on one level Adonis becomes Charles. Perhaps the poem's closing rejection of heterosexual sex in the city can be read as clearing a space for an allusion to love between men.

In one sense this is no surprise. In Milton's era, it was utterly normal for a man to reject the world of women (those imperfect men) and, instead, celebrate friendships with men. To distance oneself from women, even to be repelled by sexual acts between men and women, was not an expression of what has, since the late nineteenth century, been labelled homosexuality but instead a cornerstone of conventional and all-pervasive patriarchal thinking. Marriage did not represent the primary emotional bond in a man's life, although it was in slow transition towards such a status. Instead, there were numerous emotional bonds that existed and thrived outside of marriage for men (and indeed for women). Friendships with other men were thus central to men's emotional lives, and these friendships were often expressed using a language of love.

John's verse letter to his old tutor, Thomas Young, which describes with such vivid imagination the horrors of war, also, for example, contains expressions of intense feeling. Significantly, perhaps, the verse letter draws attention to the writer's presence in London ('in the midst of town distractions') and his desire to write more freely (John wants to let out 'an Asiatic exuberance of words'). Thomas is addressed as a father ('how much as a Father I regard you'), he is imagined as a Socrates to John's Alcibiades (with connotations of an erotically charged teacher–pupil relationship such as that between the Greek philosopher and his young male pupil) and, more powerfully still, as 'Dearer to me, that man, than half my soul; / I live bereft of half myself, not whole.' (ll. 19–20) It is difficult to assess what these expressions of emotion, and in particular love, mean. One man would write that he loved his court patron, another would write that he loved his cousin, yet another would write that he loved his fellow-soldier in arms. Equally, other terms used to describe loved ones are not always transparent in their meaning. The term *brother* could indicate, for example, a blood relation, a religious affiliation, erotic affection or indeed all three.

The relationship between John and Charles most obviously fell within a special category of friendship between men, referred to in those times as 'entire' or 'perfect'. Based on 'entire constancy', truthfulness and loyalty, this relationship stood at the pinnacle of models of friendship. Expressed 'in terms of love, the commitment and intensity of such friendships was likened to marriage and often compared favourably to it'.[26] Indeed, the tension between these friendships and the marital bond was a crucial one at this time, explored by Shakespeare in plays such as *The Merchant of Venice*, when Antonio and Bassanio's 'entire friendship' is tested almost to destruction by the latter's wooing of a woman, Portia.

Elegy I, addressed to Charles Diodati and written when John was in his late teens, was only one of the earliest expressions of the special bond between the two men, a bond that continued over the coming years in different forms, and with different levels of enthusiasm. It is possible to glimpse its nature from time to time, but the friendship is shrouded in complicated ways, and often by John. It is when the relationship ends that the shroud lifts for a moment, only to be swiftly replaced by Milton himself.

THREE

MISRULE

1628

A S JOHN EXPLORED urban life in his Latin poetry, real-life
London was becoming increasingly volatile. The City of London
itself was growing more hostile to the Crown, mirroring the mood in
the country, which had expected so much from King James on his
accession in 1603 but which had become weary of the King's financial
mismanagement, critical of the perceived corruption at his court, and
distrustful of his apparent tolerance of England's traditional enemy,
Spain. Apparently minor issues assumed new importance, such as the
changes being made to St Paul's Cathedral. Just as John's education
had encouraged him to see London through the filter of Ovid's Rome,
King James I and his architects were attempting to transform the
chaotic medieval city into a capital of Classical regularity. So St Paul's
received an enormous new Classical portico, designed by Inigo Jones
and sponsored by the King himself to the tune of £10,000: the ill
feeling was caused by the demolition of the adjacent parish church of
St Gregory's. The fate of St Paul's was merely symbolic of the
entrenched economic friction between City and Crown. The King
was in severe financial difficulties, yet the City refused point blank to
'lend' him £20,000. In turn, the Crown resorted to unauthorised, non-
parliamentary forms of taxation, sometimes with the claim that the
King had a traditional right to levy 'tonnage and poundage' duties, but
also simply insisting on a forced loan from its subjects. These
measures were enforced by martial law and imprisonment without
trial. Particularly inflammatory to City interests was the move to
imprison merchants who refused to pay customs duties.

With the death of James in the spring of 1625 (just as John had gone up to Cambridge), his son Charles I became King, and there was some hope for change. Instead, the Duke of Buckingham, who had risen to power during the last decade of James's reign and dominated the court and policy-making by the time of the King's death, remained pre-eminent. The Duke also became the focus of anti-monarchical sentiment, exacerbated by his transformation of York House (one of Buckingham's three London residences) into a palace, which now had 'scenes' added to a gallery that could rival the King's own Banqueting Room at Whitehall. Buckingham had a lavish art collection, buying Rubens's own collection from him for 100,000 florins, and thus obtaining nineteen Titians, seventeen Tintorettos, three Leonardo da Vincis and thirteen paintings by Rubens himself. The French ambassador reported in 1626 on the ballets, beautiful music and theatrical displays delivered during a supper at York House. It was a court in miniature, and this ostentatious display merely served to fuel the hostility of Buckingham's enemies.

The sporadic violence characteristic of the period continued, sometimes focused on individuals (Dr John Lambe, a supporter of Buckingham, was attacked and killed in London), sometimes simply an expression of hunger and deprivation, such as the riots in Maldon in Essex occasioned by the scarcity and high price of grain. The tensions in the country at large continued to be played out in miniature in Cambridge. The run-up to the elections for the position of University Chancellor of Easter 1626 exposed the deep religious and political divisions within the University. The King's candidate was the Duke of Buckingham, who was backed by William Laud, the up-and-coming cleric, soon to be Archbishop of Canterbury and a supporter of traditional Church rituals. Buckingham's opponent was Thomas Howard, Earl of Berkshire, an aristocrat sympathetic to the more austere Calvinist cause. Buckingham won, although there were loud accusations of vote rigging. Laud, who had became the focal point for opposition to what were perceived as dangerous developments in the management of Church and State, was seen as the architect of Buckingham's triumph. The following year Laud was implicated in a new crisis in Cambridge, this time over the suspension of one of the history lecturers, Dr Isaac Dorislaus. The lecturer's fault was to link a work from the past with events in the present, to cite 'dangerous passages' which were 'so applicable to the exasperations of these villainous times'.[1] More specifically, Dorislaus was accused of commenting on the Roman author Tacitus in such a way as to seem to justify popular resistance to monarchy in certain circumstances. It hardly seems a crime to quote Tacitus, but the incident reveals vividly contemporary attitudes towards history: far from being a dry academic study, it was directly, dangerously, relevant to contemporary life.[2]

As the months went by, Buckingham became more and more a figure of hate, a focus for the anger of those who felt the monarchy was at best inept, at worst corrupt. Three events in 1627 and 1628 exemplified the fears and ambitions of those who were critical of Royal policy. When La Rochelle, a Protestant enclave in Catholic France, was threatened by an army led by Cardinal Richelieu, the Duke of Buckingham initiated a series of disastrously unsuccessful military expeditions to support the city. The aim was to capture the Ile de Ré lying just off the coast of La Rochelle, from which base the resistance to Richelieu could be co-ordinated. October 1627 saw Buckingham's force of 7,000 men routed by the French, and a follow-up expedition the next year similarly failed. La Rochelle fell to French government forces in October 1628. Closer to home, in June 1628, King Charles was forced to acknowledge and sign Parliament's statement of its own powers, the Petition of Right. In July 1628, in a move that antagonised those in the Church of England opposed to 'high church' rituals, which were seen as dangerously close to Catholicism, William Laud, a vocal supporter of precisely those rituals, was appointed Bishop of London.

A month later, Buckingham was dead, the victim of an assassin, John Felton. Many rejoiced in secret. Others such as the tutor Joseph Mede at Christ's College Cambridge took care to circulate sensational accounts of the assassination, whipping up the political tension even more. Some were foolish enough to go further. Alexander Gill, one of John's old friends from St Paul's, drinking in the cellar of Trinity College Oxford, suggested that Charles I was 'fitter to stand in a Cheapside shop, with an apron afore him and say "What lack ye?" than to govern a kingdom' and that the Duke of Buckingham 'was gone down to Hell to meet King James there'. Gill was only sorry that Felton, the killer, had 'deprived him of the honour of doing that brave act' himself.[3]

Gill was in serious trouble. He was sentenced to be degraded from the ministry; he was stripped of his University degrees; and he was fined £2,000. In a move typical of its time, when punishments were acted out upon the body in symbolic ways, he was also sentenced to have one ear cut off in the pillory at Westminster, the seat of government, and his other ear cut off in Oxford, where he had uttered his treasonous words. Then he was to remain in prison until the King chose to release him. After special pleading from his headmaster-father, Gill did not lose his ears, and his fine was lowered. Nevertheless, he remained in prison for a further two years.

Back in 1623, Gill had responded with a gory, jubilant poem to what became known as the Massacre at Blackfriars, in which ninety Catholic worshippers were killed when their secret chapel near St Paul's collapsed. Gill represented the deaths as God's revenge for the Gunpowder Plot, drawing on the convenient (if arcane) numerical connection that made 15 November in the Protestant Julian calendar 5 November in the Catholic Gregorian calendar. John Milton, who wrote similar, if not quite as bloodthirsty, poems about the Gunpowder Plot, may have been in anti-Catholic sympathy with his friend with regard to the Blackfriars tragedy, but there is no indication that he went along with Gill's more radical attacks on Buckingham and the monarch.[4]

Indeed, John never got into the kind of trouble that his friend did, and the surviving documents which connect the two men are characterised by their academic rather than their political energy. Alexander was the recipient of letters and poems which explored John's experiences at Cambridge, and perhaps substituted for some of the intellectual stimulation he felt he was lacking. These writings are arcane. One, *De Idea Platonica quemadmodum Aristoteles Intellexit* (On the Platonic Idea, as Aristotle Understood It), is an extended joke in which John adopts the voice of a rather dim follower of Aristotle's thinking, a chap who simply can't get his head around Plato. The piece is only understandable in the context of two very cerebral young men, the humour (such as it is) very much reliant on an insider joke.

Although the humour of *On the Platonic Idea* might not be accessible to all, John was able to announce to Alexander in the spring of 1628 that he had been selected to provide comic Latin verses for a University occasion. This letter offers a glimpse of John's hostility to his 'brothers' there and offers a reminder that the primary function of a Cambridge education was to produce ministers for the Church. John's complaint is that his fellow-students merely recycle other people's words and ideas. In using 'worn out pieces from various sources' there is a serious risk that the 'priestly ignorance of a former age may gradually attack our clergy'.[5] But when John came to perform the comic Latin verses, these complaints were forgotten, or at least subsumed by a different agenda.

The opportunity to speak at the University occasion came unexpectedly. A student had been sent down after a so-called practical joke that entailed cutting off the water supply to the town. This same student had been supposed to be acting as 'Father' (that is, writer and presenter) of the annual vacation festival. At the last minute, John Milton was brought in to take his place.

As performing in Latin was the cornerstone of the Cambridge experience, the prospect was a familiar one in many ways. Disputations were supposed to be fun. The value came in *doing* them, the student using logic to train the mind rather than to seek out truth. In the normal run of things, there would be a thesis to be argued, for and against. Often this thesis was extremely dull or over-familiar. Some of Milton's work for these kinds of debates survives, a speech on the (dull) question of whether day or night is better (known as 'Prolusion I'), a speech on the (marginally less dull) issue of the music of the spheres (known as 'Prolusion II'), and a speech on the (almost interesting) question as to whether knowledge or ignorance leads to happiness ('Prolusion VII'). This last speech, or declamation, contains some of 'his highest and finest oratory': it would become, by accident, Milton's 'latest and greatest *performance*'.[6]

But the performance in May 1628 was a little different. John seized the opportunity of presiding over the student festival, the opportunity to be a 'Father' to the 'brothers', and produced a speech so coarse that translators in the past have tended to leave parts of it in the original. Fortunately, a recent generation of scholars has been brave enough to tackle one of Milton's most obscene works.

The occasion was a 'salting', a traditional feast of misrule, which focused on the initiation of young men into the college. Equivalent rituals occurred in most universities and continue to this day in different forms.[7] At Christ's College, Cambridge, each new student had to give a speech under extremely trying circumstances. Although it is possible that the more extreme elements of the ritual were dying out by Milton's time, the concept of performance followed by reward or punishment remained. If the student spoke well, he received a drink, of ale or cawdle, a thin gruel enhanced by beer or wine and spices. If he was average, then a salted drink would be added to his ale or cawdle, thus the name 'salting'. If he was dull, then the full punishment was meted out. He might, for example, have to drink a liquid laced with salt, and there are records of occasions when the unhappy student would be scratched on the face with sharpened nails as he drank.

This was the literal salt. Metaphorically, the occasion was full of *'sales'*: salty, sexual wit, redolent with licensed indecorum, hinting at the 'salt itch' of sexual arousal, the salt of semen.[8] John and his contemporaries were trained up in a Classical tradition (already glimpsed in some of the Latin elegies quoted earlier) in this form of wit that combined mental brilliance with sauciness and salacity. To refer to sex in the vernacular was intolerable and 'low'. In Latin it was a different matter. Not only did Latinity give access to a vast body of literary and medical lore about sex; it also provided the sophisticated, uninhibited language to discuss it. Delightfully for John Milton, the man who claimed to love London at least in his Latin writings, *sales* was profoundly linked with *urbanitas*, urbanity. A typical Humanist book of prostitute-jokes (*De Fide Concubinarum*) advertises itself as *'Jocus et Urbanitate et Sale Plenissimus'* – that is, 'Very Full of Urbane Humour and Salty Wit'. As James Grantham Turner, one of the foremost scholars of the literature of sex in this period, concludes, '. . . *urbanitas* generated *sales,* and vice versa: urbane sophistication involved mastery of every linguistic register including salty subjects, provided they were handled with salt or wit.'[9]

John Milton's role in the Cambridge salting was as master of ceremonies. He was 'Father' for the day, elevated above his 'brothers' in this licensed folly. This of course gave even more opportunity for humour, particularly for a chaste figure like the nineteen-year-old John, particularly because he had been chosen at the last minute to fulfil the role, and perhaps even because of his appearance. John Milton was, by all accounts, a beautiful young man. One of his early biographers describes him as having auburn hair, a good complexion and an 'exceeding fair' oval face, the word *fair* carrying dominant meanings at the time of femininity and purity.[10] John's portrait, painted as he approached his twenty-first birthday in 1629 (now known as the Onslow Portrait), reveals a young face with luscious full lips, an image of his innocence and, perhaps, his femininity.[11]

So when he says, 'But I ask, how does it happen that I have so quickly become a Father?', John draws attention, playfully, both to his recent elevation to master of ceremonies and to his own sexual exploits, or lack of them: how come he is 'suddenly altered from female into male', he asks (making the joke in Greek). Having raised the issue, the speech becomes, remarkably, a public performance that challenges explicitly those who had bullied, denigrated and dismissed John over the preceding years. As he puts it, 'For some have recently called me "Lady". But why do I seem unmanly to them?' He wonders whether it is because 'I never had strength to go in for drinking competitions, or because my hand has not grown calloused holding a plough-handle, or because I was not an ox-herd by the age of seven and so did not lie on my back in the midday sun; or lastly perhaps because I have not proved my manhood in the way these debauchees do'.[12] Instead, John proves his manhood verbally, with a relentless series of sexual and linguistic puns, his topics ranging from sexual exhaustion to the University decrees, from the anus to grammar:

Ego profecto si quem nimis parce diducto rictu ridentem conspexero, dicam eum scabros et cariosos dentes rubigine obductos aut indecoro ordine prominentes abscondere, aut inter prandendum hodie sic opplevisse abdomen ut non audeat ilia ulterius distendere ad risum, ne praecinenti ori succinat, et aenigmata quaedam nolens effutiat sua non Sphinx sed Sphincter anus, quae medicis interpretanda non Oedipo relinquo; nolim enim hilar vocis sono obstrepat in hoc coetu posticus gemitus: solvant ista medici qui alvum solvunt.

As for me, if I catch sight of anyone laughing only half-heartedly, I shall say it's because he is trying to hide his teeth, which are rotten and scabby and covered with disgusting gunk, or sticking out in all directions; or else he is afraid to stretch his belly any further in laughing because he has stuffed it so full at the feast already that he might give us a duet from two orifices! He might express some gastric riddles to us, not from his Sphinx but from his sphincter; his Posterior Analy-ytics. Such riddles I leave for the medical people to interpret, not Oedipus: I don't want any groaning posteriors to obstruct the sound of merry voices here. Let the medics give the enigma an enema.[13]

But he also attempts to prove his class, reclaiming the nickname 'Domina' (Lady) and using it to distance himself from the ox-herd with his calloused hands, insisting, in the way he uses language, on his own *urbanitas,* a sophistication that sets him apart from the *suburbanus,* the *rusticus,* the *vulgus.*

The performance in Cambridge was not a one-off descent into the salacious. In the Latin poetry of these years, in particular the elegies, the *sales* and *urbanites* continue unabated. *Elegy Septima* (Elegy VII) explores the predicament of a young man falling in love for the first time, while *Elegia Quinta In Adventum Veris* (Elegy V on the Approach of Spring) is an erotic study of the season:

Exuit invisam Tellus rediviva senectam,
Et cupit amplexus Phoebe subire tuos;

Et cupit, et digna est, quid enim formosius illa,
Pandit ut omniferos luxuriosa sinus,
Atque Arabum spirat messes, et ab ore venusto
Mitia cum Paphiis fundit amoma rosis.

(ll. 55–60)

The reviving Earth casts off her detested old age and yearns, Phoebus, for your embraces. She yearns for them, and she deserves them too, for what is more beautiful than she as she voluptuously bares her breasts, mother of all things, and breathes out Arabian spice-harvests and pours Paphian roses and mild perfume from her lovely lips.

Throughout, the mythological allusions are markedly sensual, the word games self-consciously Ovidian in style: *'fugit, et fugiens pervelit ipsa capi'* (she flies, yet as she flies, she would fain have herself be caught). Homoerotic references, for example in *Elegy IV* to Ganymede, Jupiter's cup-bearer, enliven and complicate hetero-erotic stories of innocent young men 'aflame' with desire. As John Hale notes, John Milton relied on Latin all his life, and 'it was through his Latin that he got up to some strange tricks.'[14]

He played some of the same tricks in Italian. John's Italian sonnets from this period consider, in utterly conventional ways and clearly following that master poet of the Italian Renaissance, Petrarch, the danger of falling in love with a woman: 'only grace from above' can save the speaker from desire being 'rooted in his heart for ever' ('Sonnet II').[15] Many poets at this time express, at best, ambivalence about, at worst, disgust at, men's desire for women, but John Milton does something a little different with the familiar predicament of the love-lorn male. When the speaker in 'Sonnet IV' is trapped by the 'snare' of love, he writes not to his beloved but to Charles Diodati, expressing naive astonishment at the turn of events:

Diodati, e te 'l diro con maraviglia,
Quel ritroso io ch'amor spreggiar solea

E de suoi lacci spesso mi ridea
Gia caddi, ov'uom dabben talor s'impiglia.

(ll. 1–4)

Diodati, (and) I'll tell you this with some amazement: I, the coy creature who used to scorn love, I who made a habit of laughing at his snares, having now fallen into his trap, which sometimes does catch a good man.[16]

John's adopted voice here is that of an innocent man awakened, surprised and perhaps even endangered by his sexual desires for a woman. Those desires are described euphemistically in the next sonnet as 'a hot cloud of steam (something I have never felt before)' pressing upon him, or the suggestive

Parte rinchiusa, e turbida si cela,
Scossomi il petto . . .

(ll. 9–10)

A turbulent part, enclosed and hidden in my breast, makes it throb.

The characterisation continues into the final sonnet, where he describes himself as '*Giovane piano, e semplicetto amante*' (a young, unassuming and artless lover). This innocent pose is counterpointed by the statement of ambition with which the poem ends. The speaker remains profoundly ambitious for 'distinction of mind and real worth', profoundly desirous for the Muses.

This sonnet not only reveals John's fascination with the topic of desire, particularly when writing to Charles Diodati, but also demonstrates the intimacy and exclusivity provided by the Italian language, something he himself draws attention to in two other poems from the series. John writes that he is like a young shepherdess watering an exotic little plant, a plant that is trying to grow far from its home, its natural climate. John (the shepherdess) instead of a watering-can has his 'nimble tongue': the plant he raises up is a foreign language, Italian, described as a new flower. By doing this, he transforms the Thames into the Arno, the river that flows through Florence. He delights in all this because he can now write 'without my worthy fellow countrymen understanding me at all'. The third element is perhaps the ground bass to the melody of these erotically charged linguistic games. In the poetry addressed to Charles, John can articulate and share his ambition to be a poet. Milton's attachment to Diodati relied, in part, on the possibility of writing *about* his writing, the opportunity it provided to experiment with different literary forms to communicate that ambition.

It would be naive to read any or all of these poems as auto-biographical confession. Milton himself reminds his audience of the distance between his true self and his literary productions. As he says just before the start of the salty 'Prolusion VI', 'If anything loose or licentious is said, you are to suppose it is not my mind and nature but the rules governing the time and the spirit of the place prompting it. So then: what the comic actors entreat when they end their performance, I demand as mine begins – APPLAUD, and LAUGH!'[17]

Yet this is not the whole story. Latin permitted John to explore areas of life that were impossible to approach, impossible even to describe in his mother tongue. Almost untranslatable Latin terms such as *amicitia* (complete friendship) and *urbanarum sodalitum* (urban companionship) are crucial to Milton's art: the former is a term reserved for Charles, as in the following letter, the latter one that encompasses him but can include other men:[18]

Non enim in Epistolarum ac Salutationum momentis veram verti ami-citiam volo, quae omnia ficta esse possunt; sed altis animi radicibus niti utrinque & sustinere se; coeptamque sinceris, & sanctis rationibus, etiamsi mutua cessarent officia, per omnem tamen vitam suspicione & culpa vacare: ad quam fovendam non tam scripto sit opus, quam viva invicem virtutem recordatione.

> For I do not wish true friendship to be weighed by letters and
> salutations, which may all be false but on either hand to rest and
> sustain itself upon the deep roots of the soul, and, begun with
> sincere and blameless motives, even though mutual courtesies cease,
> to be free for life from suspicion and blame. For fostering such a
> friendship there is need not so much for writing as for a living
> remembrance of virtue on both sides.[19]

Friendships with men have their *officia* (offices), a densely charged
term full of social significance: there is no English equivalent,
although it is translated as 'courtesies' in the passage above.[20] In
Milton's time, there was no English word for love between men. A
contemporary could write, in vague terms, of his appreciation of 'his
very entire and special friend' who is 'most loving unto and most
familiar to him'. The Bible offered two entirely negative sets of
terminology to refer to same-sex love and activities: 'effeminate'
and 'abusers of themselves with mankind'.[21] Latin therefore provided
both a lexicon for same-sex love and a veil for it. The relationship
between Charles and John, whether textual or real or both, the one
aspect feeding off the other, remains tantalisingly elusive.[22]

It is no coincidence that John Milton and Charles Diodati wrote to
each other, about each other, in any language but English. Writing in
Latin and Italian (John) and Greek (Charles), both men relied on a
multitude of insider jokes and puns, Classical references and innuen-
dos, many of which even the most erudite scholar might miss. The
language is highly self-conscious and artificial: every expression of the
relationship can seem part of a new literary pose, with Charles as
Muse and Ovid as inspiration.

In *Elegia Sixta ad Carolum Diodatum, ruri commorantem* (Elegy VI to
Charles Diodati, Staying in the Country), for example, John has
received a letter and poems from Charles.[23] The elegy ends with
John describing his own poetic activity: he refers to the writing of 'On
the Morning of Christ's Nativity,' one of his finest early English
poems:

At tu si quid agam, scitabere (si modo saltem
Esse putas tanti noscere siquid agam)
Paciferum canimus caelesti semine regem . . .
(ll. 79–81)

But if you want to know what I am doing (if, that is, you think it worth while to know whether I am doing anything at all) I am writing a poem about the king who was born of heavenly seed, and who brought peace to men . . .

The teasing tone had appeared earlier in the elegy:

But why does your muse lure mine out into the open, and not allow her to seek the obscurity which she desires? Perhaps you want my poem to tell you how warmly I return your love, and how I cherish you. You could scarcely learn that from this poem, believe me, because my love cannot be shut up in tight-fitting metres, and being sound refuses to limp along in elegiac couplets. (ll. 3–8)

These lines play a kind of literary hide-and-seek, expressing love in the same breath as an expression of the impossibility of expressing love, exploring wittily (the joke about limping refers to the elegiac metre used by John, with lines varying between five and six feet, or beats, in length) both the potential and the limitations of poetry. When John writes that a song cannot actually express his 'unbound love', he is merely offering a hint of a kind of communication that would be more direct, more free, unshackled by literary constraints. Yet it is possible that it was precisely the literary 'shackles', the Latin, the Classical allusions, the shared knowledge, that allowed Milton to write of emotion at all.

Two letters from Charles, both in Greek, both to John, do not seem particularly shackled by inhibition. Diodati may not have been a great poet, but he wrote charming letters, playful, knowing and affectionate, even flirtatious.

The present state of the weather seems to be quite jealous of the arrangements we made when lately we parted, for it has been stormy and unsettled for two whole days now. But nevertheless, so much do I desire your company that in my longing I dream of, and all but prophesy, fair weather and calm, and everything golden for tomorrow, so that we may enjoy our fill of philosophical and learned conversation.[24]

In the same letter, Charles looks forward to the next time the two men will meet: 'For tomorrow all will be lovely, and the air and the sun and the river and the trees and the birds and the earth and men will keep holiday and will laugh together with us, and will dance with us.'

The ostentatious pastoralism of these letters ('The days are long, the landscape most beautiful with budding flowers and teeming leaves, and upon every shoot is a nightingale or goldfinch or other songbird, and it takes delight in its warblings') is all part of the language of love between the two men. Although this is highly stylised writing, the energy and delight of the language involves no sacrifice of intimacy and tenderness.[25] The pastoral form is not empty here: instead it offers a kind of personal immediacy. Charles is suggesting that they live the dream, live the pastoral idyll. It may be significant that pastoral is often, in its Classical originals, a homoerotic mode of writing.[26]

None of this proves that John and Charles had a sexual relationship. All it demonstrates is that both men lived a cultural paradox. There is, predictably, little material evidence of same-sex relations in a seventeenth-century England in which sodomy was punishable by death. At the same time, male/male intimacy was necessarily ubiquitous in a society in which it was normal for men to share beds and operate in exclusively male environments. Add to this the shared experience of the Latin and Greek literature that influenced and informed men's education, a literature that had been generated in a historical era that privileged sex between men, and particularly sex between men and boys, over sex between men and women. What is most surprising is John's response to this paradox. In a society that demonised the act of sodomy, and in which, at the same time, it was perfectly possible to conduct an intimate relationship with another man without drawing any attention to one's activities, John Milton actively sought to elevate the emotional and erotic intensity of his writings connected with Charles Diodati.

It may be that the two men were bound, at least in John's mind, by the ties of 'perfect friendship'. Yet even this de-sexualised model of the friendship was not particularly normal. Most men in the period were, it seems, comfortable with passing friends with whom they could demonstrate a very obvious kind of youthful masculinity, indulging in various activities, most, if not all, fairly mild attempts to challenge authority. The transience of such friendships was precisely the point, because the young men were not committed to any long-term involvement or duties, those untranslatable *officia* noted above.[27] The opposite seems to have been true of Charles and John. Indeed, in one of Charles's letters to John (in Greek), he explicitly invokes this kind of friendship. Charles is waxing eloquent on pastoral delights, but he has one complaint. He has no one special with whom to share the delights: 'If to all this were added a fitting and well-educated companion, with a good memory of things, cut out from the herd, I would be happier than the King of Persia.'[28] On one level, this is a familiar elevation of rational human love over the bestial coupling of animals. But, in an irony that does not seem to have been lost on Charles Diodati, male/male love can be seen as particularly elevated, precisely because it is *not* mirrored in the animal kingdom. Love between men can provide unique intellectual and spiritual fulfilment precisely because it is not brutish and animalistic. Again, the paradoxes here are rooted in the assimilation of pagan philosophy and Greek homosexuality into a Christianity that rejects the body.

Another way of understanding the bond between John and Charles is to consider its roots in various cultures from which women were systematically excluded. In Cambridge, for example, they were banned from college chambers apart from exceptional circumstances such as in time of sickness. How successful these measures were is debatable, as the number of paternity suits brought against college members by townswomen testifies, but the aim was clear: to sustain an all-male society.[29]

It is ironic that, just as Charles and John sought to write women out of their lives and letters, Milton's biographers have generally succeeded, consciously and unconsciously, in writing Charles out of John's.[30] In doing so, they were only following their subject's lead. He could, and did, write of his 'unbound love' for Charles, but this future great proponent of freedom still felt it necessary to control the expression of that love, devoting his literary energies instead to celebrations of chastity and sexual propriety.

Later Milton would represent the dominant language of the relationship, Latin, as something to be displayed for its formal brilliance, a token of his precocity as a poet, rather than for its content, and certainly not for any autobiographical revelation.[31] Indeed, Milton was so keen to emphasise his youth when he wrote these poems that he dated many of them earlier than the evidence suggests they were written. For some, this shows his desire to compensate for his own sense of his late development, but it might also be an attempt to ensure that the poems, and the material they contain, are clearly placed as the work of a very young man, far removed from the mature adult that John Milton was to become.

He still had a long way to go. Later, in 1642, he would write that those who 'hope to write well hereafter in laudable things' must themselves be 'a true Poem, that is, a composition, and pattern of the best and honourablest things'.[32] This explicit connection between what one writes and how one lives goes beyond a simple link between the goodness of the man and the quality of his writing. A man is a 'true Poem': if that is the case, what kind of Poem was John Milton as he came to the end of his Cambridge studies? Perhaps sex and death are 'the best and honourablest things', perhaps to love Charles Diodati was 'laudable', but it is doubtful that John Milton saw his life that way. Instead, by the end of 1631, and his twenty-third birthday, he had never felt so old. He had achieved little, and his youth was gone. A sonnet from this period painfully recognises the individual's powerlessness in the face of passing time, and the more personal irony that although John appeared physically to be near 'manhood', 'inward ripeness' was slow to come:

> How soon hath time, the subtle thief of youth,
> Stol'n on his wing my three and twentieth year!
> My hasting days fly on with full career,
> But my late spring no bud or blossom sheweth.
> Perhaps my semblance might deceive the truth,
> That I to manhood am arrived so near,
> And inward ripeness doth much less appear,
> That some more timely-happy spirits endueth.
> Yet be it less or more, or soon or slow,
> It shall be still in strictest measure even
> To that same lot, however mean or high,
> Toward which time leads me, and the will of heaven;
> All is, if I have grace to use it so,
> As ever in my great taskmaster's eye.

FOUR

MASQUE

1634

MEANWHILE, LIFE WAS changing for John's contemporaries and his family. Charles Diodati headed for Geneva in 1631 to study theology. John's younger brother, Christopher, was admitted to the Inner Temple, embarking on his conventional and, generally speaking, highly successful career in the law. Edward Phillips, John's other brother (a status gained in his marriage to Anne, John's sister) was seriously ill. John witnessed his will in mid-August 1631, and less than two weeks later Edward was buried 'in the church at night'. He left John's sister widowed and responsible for two little boys, Edward and John, aged just one and two years old.

Anne, Edward's 'loving wife' and executor, as his will phrased it, would remarry fairly quickly, despite or because of the fact that she had been well provided for in her widowhood, through the jointure established at her marriage. On the last day of the following Christmas feasting season, she married Thomas Agar at the church of St Dunstan in the East. Anne gained a new husband, and John a new brother.[1] Agar came from a family of property and gentility, and the marriage represented an advance in social position for Anne and the Miltons.[2] Since for women the only way to change one's class was to 'marry up', Anne was in effect doing her bit for the family's aspirations. The new Agar household consisted of Thomas and Anne, with Anne's two young sons by her first marriage and Thomas's daughter by his, a little girl called Anne.[3] Thomas Agar not only replaced Edward Phillips as husband to Anne Milton; he also took over Phillips's job in the government, becoming Deputy Clerk to the Crown.

Shortly after his sister's second marriage, John Milton officially left Cambridge. Earlier, in March 1629, he had gained his BA, but, having taken his first degree, he still faced a further three years of study before he could receive the award he was aiming for, his MA. During the Lent Term of 1632, he formally supplicated for his MA degree, and, a few months later, on 3 July, he took his subscription – that is, he formally subscribed to the articles of religion of the Church of England and the University. With this expression of religious conformity, he could at last complete his University studies. He did so triumphantly, graduating *cum laude.*

What to do next seemed to be the question. He could have continued his studies at Cambridge, for there was no doubt about his intellectual abilities or his capacity for hard work. Yet John was not asked to contribute to any of the official University anthologies in his closing years at Cambridge. It is possible that his exclusion may have been caused by his unwillingness to praise Royalty, but it is equally possible that his face simply didn't fit. Instead of further University study, John decided to go home to his parents.

Home, however, was changing. The previous year, in 1631, the Milton family had moved out of the City to Hammersmith, a country village about 7 miles west of St Paul's. Five years later, John and Sara Milton would move again, even further away from Bread Street. Records show that, by April 1637, they were living in the village of Horton, south-west of London.[4] Their grown-up son moved with them, his parents presumably content to support an unproductive twenty-something while he worked out what to do with his life, John Milton Sr's income from those invariably lucrative professions, the law and money-lending, ensuring that he could provide private incomes for all his children come what may.

Again, Milton himself would offer, many years later, his account of this period, one which has been taken up and perpetuated by many biographers:

At my father's country place, whither he had retired to spend his declining years, I devoted myself entirely to the study of Greek and

Latin writers, completely at leisure, not, however without sometimes exchanging the country for the city, either to purchase books
or to become acquainted with some new discovery in mathematics or
music, in which I then took the keenest pleasure.[5]

It is a lovely picture of pastoral seclusion, five or six years of study at
his elderly father's expense, five or six years of 'complete leisure', the
ultimate indicator of his privileged social status. Early biographers
added further patina to the glossy picture, building on Milton's
description of his father as 'paterno rure', retired to the country:
John Milton Sr 'having got an Estate to his content' therefore 'left off
all business' and 'was retired from the Cares and Fatigues of the
world', settled in his 'country retirement'.[6]

The historical and what there is of a psychological record do not
quite confirm this view of the 1630s for John Milton and his family. A
strange document survives from this period. It is usually dated to
1631, the year in which John was coming towards the end of his
University education, and in which his family were moving to Hammersmith. John writes to an unknown friend. The letter was not
published during his lifetime, and yet two drafts exist in his own
handwriting. What the letter expressed was obviously important to
its author: John describes himself in psychological crisis. His life
appears like 'night'; he believes it is 'as yet obscure and unserviceable
to mankind'.[7] The letter is relentless on the subject, and highly
defensive about his choice of a continued life of study. It ends with
an offering of his poetry, prefaced by a painful expression of self-doubt:
'I am something suspicious of myself, and do take notice of a certain
belatedness in me. I am the bolder to send you some of my night-ward
thoughts some while since (because they come in not altogether
unfitly) made up in a Petrarchan stanza.' The poem he is referring
to is the sonnet that begins, 'How soon hath time, the subtle thief of
youth', which is placed after the letters in the surviving manuscript.[8]

This sense of lack of achievement is edited out of John's later
retrospective, as are, on a more material level, the Milton family's
years in Hammersmith. Hammersmith, a tiny village on the north

bank of the Thames, could be reached from London in a couple of hours of walking or a similar length of time by river. It was not exactly a rural idyll. The village, being an appropriate distance from the City, was one of the sites for the 'outhouses' or 'lazarhouses' of the London hospitals, such as St Bartholemew's and Christ's Hospital, for sufferers of leprosy. What is more, Milton scholar Gordon Campbell's meticulous research has shown that John Milton Sr did not suddenly retire from business on his removal to Hammersmith but gradually wound down his interests over a number of years.[9] Only in May 1636 did he petition to be allowed to resign from being assistant to the Scrivener's Company, the reason being his 'removal to inhabit in the country'.

The village of Hammersmith was growing fast, as is revealed by the building of a so-called Laudian Chapel of Ease, of which John Milton Sr became churchwarden. These chapels were a response to population changes in the parishes surrounding London, in this case the parish of Fulham, and were seen as the brainchild of Archbishop Laud. The residents of Hammersmith had to walk over a mile south to Fulham to attend their parish church, and 'the length and foulness of the way', which was 'in winter most toilsome sometime over ploughed land', meant that some abandoned going to church and, worse, spent their time in 'profane alehouses and ungodly exercises'.[10] The answer to the problem was a 'chapel of ease' to supplement the work of the main parish church and ensure church-going conformity.

John's father's involvement with the Chapel of Ease suggests that the Miltons were not an aggressively Protestant household and were comfortable within the mainstream of Laudian Church of England practice. Certainly, John's poetry from these years gives little hint of opposition to the established Church.[11] In the poem he wrote in London over the Christmas period of 1629, 'On the Morning of Christ's Nativity', about which he had written to Charles, there may perhaps be a gentle glance at the Book of Revelation in the very year in which vernacular commentaries on this most inflammatory of biblical texts had been suppressed, but it is only a gentle glance:

> The babe lies yet in smiling infancy,
> That on the bitter cross
> Must redeem our loss;
> So both himself and us to glorify:
> Yet first to those ychained in sleep,
> The wakeful trump of doom must thunder through the deep.
>
> (ll. 151–6)

Here John makes explicit the connection between the birth of Christ and the Apocalypse (or 'doom') foretold in the Book of Revelation, but his poem lacks the intense fervour of those radicals who believed that Judgement Day was terrifyingly imminent. Instead, John contemplates God's birth on Earth. The baby Jesus

> here with us to be,
> Forsook the courts of everlasting day,
> And chose with us a darksome house of mortal clay.
>
> (ll. 12–14)

As in much of John's early poetry in English, the language of 'On the Morning of Christ's Nativity' echoes that of an earlier generation of Protestant poets such as Edmund Spenser and Sir Philip Sidney, both offering a cultural and religious tradition in their commitment to poetry *and* to Protestantism at a time when many reformers refused to acknowledge any serious purpose to the arts. Typically, however, John negotiates with and develops his sources rather than simply borrowing from them.

Milton's poem, for example, takes up Spenser's reference (in his *Shepherd's Calendar*) to Christ as the 'great Pan'. 'On the Morning of Christ's Nativity' has a passage in which the shepherds believe that 'the mighty Pan / Was kindly come to live with them below.' This invocation of a figure who is both Christ and Pan sits alongside what constitute the most dramatic moments in the poem, the flight of the pagan gods, and the silencing of the oracles.

> The oracles are dumb,
> No voice or hideous hum
> Runs through the arched roof in words deceiving.
> Apollo from his shrine
> Can no more divine,
> With hollow shriek the steep of Delphos leaving.
> No nightly trance, or breathed spell,
> Inspires the pale-eyed priest from the prophetic cell.
>
> (ll. 173–80)

Peor and Baalim, Ashtaroth and Moloch, Isis and Osiris are all fled, powerless in the face of the 'dreaded infant's hand'.

Here John is ostensibly rejecting the Classical, pagan traditions that had informed so much of his education and reading. Christ's birth leaves no room for these false gods. And yet, though these gods no 'longer dare abide', Pan, at least, remains imaginatively in the poem since, if only in the minds of the 'silly' (here meaning unsophisticated) shepherds, Christ *is* Pan. Thus the excluded pagan gods remain within the poem, with a question mark over their complete obliteration from Milton's poetic imagination. Over the years, this kind of interplay between the Christian and the pagan would remain one of the creative tensions in Milton's poetry.

Two poems from this period, *L'Allegro* and *Il Penseroso*, explore, and indeed enact, a related and equally creative, although narrower, debate between the life of 'mirth' and the life of 'melancholy'. *L'Allegro* (the word is defined by John Florio in his dictionary of 1598 as 'joyful, merry, jocund, sportful, pleasant, frolic') endorses a life of sensuality. Long, breathless sentences carry the reader into a world of 'sunshine holiday', of

> Jest and youthful jollity,
> Quips and cranks, and wanton wiles,
> Nods, and becks, and wreathed smiles
>
> (ll. 26–8)

and offer an invitation to 'Come, and trip it as you go / On the light fantastic toe.' (ll. 33–5) The speaker desires to live with Mirth and Liberty: 'To live with her, and live with thee, / In unreproved pleasures free . . .' (ll. 39–40) This world of 'unreproved pleasures free' is a pastoral one in which

> the ploughman near at hand,
> Whistles o'er the furrowed land,
> And the milkmaid singeth blithe,
> And the mower whets his scythe,
> And every shepherd tells his tale
> Under the hawthorn in the dale.
>
> (ll. 63–8)

The shepherd-poet is, as so often in Milton's early poetry, the embodiment of an ideal: appearing in this poem are Corydon and Thyrsis, names drawn from Virgil's *Seventh Eclogue* and Theocritus' *Idylls*. Yet *L'Allegro* is not merely a pastoral vision, redolent of these Latin writers, overlaid with Shakespearean and Spenserian imagery and cadences. It also celebrates the pleasures of urban life, in particular the world of the theatre ('the well-trod stage' where 'Shakespeare fancy's child' can be seen) and music, 'such as the melting soul may pierce'.

In sharp contrast, *Il Penseroso* ('pensive') shuns society, whether in the country or the town. Melancholy is called upon, 'devout and pure, / Sober, steadfast, and demure', also Contemplation and Silence. If the speaker wanders anywhere, it will be 'in trim gardens' where he will 'walk unseen / On the dry smooth-shaven green'. The fantasy of retreat from the world runs deep in this poem:

> There in close covert by some brook,
> Where no profaner eye may look,
> Hide me from day's garish eye,
> While the bee with honied thigh,
> That at her flowery work doth sing,

And the waters murmuring
With such consort as they keep,
Entice the dewy-feathered Sleep;
And let some strange mysterious dream,
Wave at his wings in airy stream,
Of lively portraiture displayed
Softly on my eyelids laid.

(ll. 139–50)

Rich and sensuous, its imagery rooted in the natural world, the poetic inspiration the poem describes occurs only when the poet is alone, and in profoundly mysterious ways. The reward for this lifestyle is, however, as intense as, possibly more intense than, that offered in the more earthy *L'Allegro*. Music in *Il Penseroso* will 'Dissolve me into ecstasies, / And bring all heaven before mine eyes.'

L'Allegro and *Il Penseroso* eloquently compete for primacy, the debate between the poems teasingly unresolved. The tensions within 'On the Morning of Christ's Nativity' between pagan and Christian views are, in contrast, resolved or at least laid aside at the end of the poem, when the reader is offered a vision redolent of many a Baroque painting. In the stable at Bethlehem, the Christ child is also King, and the angels in their armour ('bright-harnessed') attend the Lord of Heaven.

But see the virgin blest,
Hath laid her babe to rest.
Time is our tedious song should here have ending:
Heaven's youngest teemed star,
Hath fixed her polished car,
Her sleeping Lord with handmaid lamp attending:
And all about the courtly stable,
Bright-harnessed angels sit in order serviceable.

(ll. 237–44)

The religious concerns of 'On the Morning of Christ's Nativity' appear to support John's own assertion that in his early twenties he was considering the 'labours of the church' as a career, the labours desired by his 'parents and friends' (a momentary recognition of the influence of his mother).[12] The ambition was a natural one. His father, having renounced his Catholic, recusant family in Oxfordshire, was thus a first-generation convert, eager for his son to become part of the new establishment. Indeed, it is just possible that John's relative seclusion in these years was all part of a plan to prepare himself for the Church, and a politically astute plan at that. There were increasing controls over the licensing of ministers as the conflicts within the Church of England, between the Laudians and the supporters of a more severe form of Protestantism, increased year by year. Out in Hammersmith, John was less likely to be involved with the kind of problems besetting his friends, such as Alexander Gill.

There was nothing to stop John Milton uniting the vocations of poet and clergyman. Two shining examples of this combination dominate English poetry of the period. John Donne, very much a part of Milton's world as dean of St Paul's from 1621 to 1631, was a highly successful clergyman as well as a prolific and well-connected poet. George Herbert, of the powerful Sidney/Herbert dynasty, which included several major poets in its ranks, became one of the best-loved poets of the seventeenth century and beyond. He was vicar, then rector, of the parish of Bemerton in Wiltshire.

Then as now, the decision to take holy orders was a weighty one, all the more weighty for those who saw the church as severely lacking in committed, educated ministers. The writer William Whately, in *The New Birth* (1618), exhorted prospective ministers to 'study day and night, and by continual pains, putting forth thyself to all laboriousness . . . Consider what a weighty duty, what a great honour it is to be God's instrument for the regenerating of others'.[13] Yet John decided not to take on this weighty duty and great honour. His father may not have been surprised when his son rejected, after brief consideration, a career in the law, but he may well have been confused when John abandoned any pretence of preparing to take orders. There is no hard evidence as to when exactly this happened, perhaps immediately after he left Cambridge, perhaps as late as 1640. Whenever the final decision was made, in practical terms John's reluctance to take orders meant that when his parents moved to Horton in 1635, their twenty-six-year-old son and his books came too.

Even in Horton, John was no recluse. In fact, all the evidence suggests a thoroughly social writer.[14] He needed a steady supply of books to continue his studies, and this meant regular trips back to London, and to the area around St Paul's. He could have done the journey to the City in two hours of good riding, or five of steady walking, with a break by the river at Brentford. Both his younger brother, Christopher, and his sister, Anne, were in London. Christopher was continuing his legal studies at the Temple, while Anne and her new husband were settled there, although it is uncertain where their house was situated. If there was need of a carriage to London, just by Horton was the village of Colnbrook, a busy staging post on one of the great roads that linked London and the West of England.[15]

Having acquired a new book, John would adopt an intensely scholarly approach to his reading. His edition of one of his favourite writers, the Greek playwright Euripides, acquired in 1634 and now in the Bodleian Library in Oxford, is annotated to within an inch of its life. John's comments show that he read Greek with complete ease, enjoying the sound of the language in his own mind (evident in his notes on scansion), and enjoying the dramatic effects (evident in his notes on staging and performance).[16] The level of annotation in the Euripides is surpassed only by that in a volume of Pindar, inscribed, in John's hand, with the date of purchase and the price: *Novemb' 15 1629 pret – 9s – 0.* Again, the approach is erudite in the extreme. John made notes on hundreds of the pages and then added side notes so that he could find certain passages more easily. Tellingly, he also made corrections and comments in a number of places, and even added many new references to the index, all written into the book in extremely neat handwriting.

Brilliant scholar that Milton was, this fascination with Euripides and Pindar, and countless other writers, represented no mere sterile academic pursuit. Everything in his culture, from the Humanist educational tradition at St Paul's to the all-pervasive Protestant emphasis on Bible study, encouraged him to read *for* action, not *in place of* action. John's problem was that he did not yet know what the action should be. A few years later, he would press his reading, of Euripides in particular, into action at a time of acute danger. In 1634, when he bought the book, things were much less clear. A similar dynamic can be glimpsed in John's commonplace book, started at this time in his life. In this notebook (one of a series, the others now lost), he tried to organise a dense array of references he had culled from his extensive reading. His notes are resolutely intellectual and political, in contrast to other commonplace books of the time, but it is the index that is perhaps the most striking element. Here are all these notes, all these comments, and John is trying to bring them all together somehow, linking people and ideas in different ways, attempting to make connections, reading for action, for particular projects. There are clear themes to his note-taking, but the desire for an elusive coherence seeps from the notebook's pages.

John Milton's first extended literary achievement in English dates from 1634, when he was commissioned to write the words for an important civic entertainment. The new work would be performed on 29 September, Michaelmas Night, at Ludlow Castle on the border between England and Wales.[17] *A Maske Presented at Ludlow Castle 1634* (to give the piece its full name) was designed to celebrate the installation of Thomas Egerton as the Lord President of Wales and leader of the Council of the Marches. Ludlow Castle, his new seat, was the administrative centre for the law and order of Wales and the Marches, or border areas. The castle operated like a court, providing the setting for entertainments of various kinds: the accounts show regular payments to players and musicians, with 30s for a performance by the Queen's Players or 66s 8d for musicians over the Christmas festivities. Ludlow had been the residence of Henry Sidney, father to the poet Philip, who had died tragically young on the battlefield in the Netherlands, fighting for the Protestant cause. Henry Sidney had been an impressive statesman and soldier in his own right during Elizabeth I's reign, particularly in Ireland, and Ludlow Castle was therefore deeply associated with the international Protestant cause. In the early autumn of 1634, the plan was that, after a period of travelling around his new constituency, Egerton, the incoming Lord President, would return to the castle for a lavish celebration.[18]

John Milton's task was to provide words fitting for the occasion. Superficially, at least, his involvement seems to represent a first major step towards using his 'studious labours' to prop up the somewhat tarnished image of the aristocracy in England, and to secure for himself the patronage of a member of that aristocracy. Most probably, he had been brought into the project by Henry Lawes, an established musician, actor, producer and director of masques, as well as the music teacher of one of the Lord President's children. How Lawes came to know of Milton's poetic talents remains unclear (although John Milton Sr, a composer himself, had business dealings with the Egerton family, who employed Lawes as a music teacher), but this step in John's career suggests that his work was at least visible within a London literary and musical network.[19] Lawes was a good connection to have. As a member of the King's Musick, he was involved in most if not all of the court masques in London of the 1630s. These were important events in the annual round of court life during the reign of Charles I, and it was as a place to perform them that Inigo Jones's Banqueting House had originally been designed.[20] At the court in Westminster, King Charles or his wife Queen Henrietta Maria presided over these dramatic events, with each performance promoting an exalted conception of the divine right of kings. Masques usually marked State occasions, such as marriages or visits of foreign royalty: at Ludlow, the presiding figure would be the Lord President.

Milton's *Maske* was most likely performed in the Great Hall of Ludlow Castle, usually the setting for the prerogative court of the Council of Wales but, when the musicians and players came to town, an ideal venue for performances. The resources at the castle would not have been as lavish as those that Lawes was used to in London. Lawes himself would have had to provide much of the accompanying lute music, while the instrumental music was probably provided by the waits of Ludlow or some other band specially imported, thumping out the country dance music they were used to performing. As for the actors, continuing the tradition of the Whitehall court masques, some would be professional players, but the prominent parts would be played by members of the aristocracy. At Ludlow, it is striking that the Lord President's three children Alice (aged fifteen), Thomas (eleven), and John (nine) were each given substantial roles, no mean feat if one glances at the number and complexity of the lines Milton wrote for them.

It may have helped that Alice, Thomas and John Egerton were familiar with the masque form, so alien to us now. The brothers had acted, earlier in the year, in a masque called *Coelum Britannicum*. Alice, aged eleven, and two of her elder sisters had danced in the court masque *Tempe Restor'd*, by Aurelian Townshend, in 1631, a production that typifies the genre as a whole. The plot was basic. The evil enchantress Circe 'by her allurements enamoured a young Gentleman on her person, who a while lived with her in all sensual delights until upon some jealousy conceived, she gave him to drink of an enchanted cup, and touching him with her golden wand transformed him into a Lion.'[21] When the young gentleman comes to his senses, he flees to His Majesty, King Charles (present at the performance), 'whose sight frees him from all fear'. Circe then notices the young gentleman's escape, and seeks some dubious kinds of consolation with various animals and nymphs, who 'make her sport'. This reprehensible 'sport' is interrupted, thankfully for the moral tone of the evening, by Harmony, Beauty, Virtue, Love and Cupid, who are played on to the stage with beautiful music, the music of the spheres. Order is restored: Circe gives up her magic wand to the goddess Minerva, and Tempe (the peaceful haunt of Apollo and the Muses) is restored.

It is not much of a plot, but it did not need to be, because what the court wanted, and what the court got, was a spectacle. The dramatic experience was dominated by the operation of elaborate scenery, by songs, by dances and, above all, by the participation of Royalty in the fiction. Everything was designed to amaze. As such, the visual spectacle was far more important than the words: as one critic has sternly pointed out, 'no poetic invention could prosper in a theatre where everything was tense with excitement about who or what was going to appear or disappear or change into something else.'[22]

Sheet music from the Maske *at* Ludlow.

The most famous 'inventor' of masques was the architect Inigo
Jones, who engineered, quite literally, *Tempe Restor'd*, as the title page
makes clear: 'The subject and Allegory of the Masque, with the
descriptions, and Apparatus of the Scenes were invented by Inigo
Jones, Surveyor of his Majesty's work.' This emphasis on Jones as
'inventor' did not endear him and his like to those playwrights more
concerned with the words than the spectacle. Indeed, Ben Jonson,
never renowned for his placidity, ended up engaged in a vicious
theatre-land spat with Jones, his one-time collaborator. The two
men had worked together on a masque in 1631 (*Love's Triumph
through Callipolis*). When it was published, Jonson put his name above
Jones's. The latter complained furiously, and with some justice: there
really are very few words in the masque. Jonson in turn turned his
scorn on the masque genre itself, using bitter irony in his poem 'An
Expostulation with Inigo Jones':

> O Shows! Shows! Mighty Shows!
> The Eloquence of Masques! What need of prose
> Or Verse, or Sense t'express the Immortal you?
> You are the Spectacles of State![23]
>
> (ll. 29–33)

Jonson was right. Masques *were* 'Spectacles of State'. They were a
deeply conservative form of drama, designed to deny the need for
change. So, in the masque outlined above, the audience were told,
if they had missed the point amid all the singing, dancing and
scene-changing, the precise meaning of the performance, and just
how it confirmed the divine right of the King to rule: 'Circe here
signifies desire in general,' which leads 'some to virtue and some
to vice'. Virtue, meanwhile, is signified by 'the King's Majesty,
who therein transcends as far common men, as they are above
Beasts'.

Crucial to the aim of the traditional masque to glorify the court or a
particular member of the aristocracy was the involvement of the
nobility in the performance, most notably in the form of dance.

Performances ended with a breakdown of the barrier between the
stage and the audience, all designed to confirm the power and
authority of the presiding figure, whether King, Queen, Duchess
or, indeed, Lord President of Wales and Lord of the Marches.[24]

So when, in Milton's *Maske*, an Attendant Spirit flew on to the stage
in the Great Hall at Ludlow, the audience thought they knew what was
coming. The Spirit explains that he has come to Earth, precisely to
Wales and the Marches, in order to serve the Earl of Bridgewater,

> A noble peer of mickle trust, and power
> Has in his charge, with tempered awe to guide
> An old, and haughty nation proud in arms:
> Where his fair offspring nursed in princely lore,
> Are coming to attend their father's state
> And new-entrusted sceptre.[25]
>
> (ll. 31–6)

Typically, fact and fiction are blurred, the children already hovering
between their masque identities and their real social identities.

The drama truly starts when the Attendant Spirit warns of a
terrible threat to the children, one Comus. He is the son of Circe
and Bacchus, the god of wine, the latter as prone as the former to
mutate innocent bystanders, in his case into dolphins. It is no surprise
that Comus, 'much like his father, but his mother more', has his own
unpleasant practices: he has a magic potion that turns the 'visages' of
his victims into beasts. Those afflicted do not even realise that they are
bestial; instead they 'roll with pleasure in a sensual sty'.

In a marvellous dramatic moment (between lines 92 and 93),
'Comus enters with a charming rod in one hand, his glass in the
other, with him a rout of monsters, headed like sundry sorts of wild
beasts, but otherwise like men and women, their apparel glistening,
they come in making a riotous and unruly noise, with torches in their
hands.' The colour, noise and light, together with the grotesque
animal heads, presumably caused gasps of astonishment in the audience: this is what they had come to see. They might have been

differently astonished by what happened next. Speech after speech after speech followed, many fifty, sixty, seventy lines in length. Comus' first speech, for example, takes fifty lines to demonstrate his glib moral relativism: ''Tis only daylight that makes sin.'

Although dances, songs and spectacle punctuate the proceedings, it is speech that dominates Milton's *Maske*. Comus' eloquent attempts to seduce the Lady (who is lost, frightened, troubled by a 'thousand fantasies') are countered by her articulate assertions of her own Conscience, Faith and Hope, and, above all, Chastity. She is also something of a political commentator. When Comus disguises himself as a lowly shepherd, she follows him, justifying her trust with the pointed comment that 'honest-offered courtesy' is sooner found in 'lowly sheds with smoky rafters' than in the tapestried halls and courts of princes. Is there a suggestion of irony in these words being spoken in one such tapestried hall?

At the heart of the *Maske* is Comus' threat to the Lady's chastity: lest the audience forget, her virgin status is referred to relentlessly by her brothers. The boys want, quite naturally, to fight Comus, but the older and wiser Attendant Spirit gently reminds them that 'here thy sword can do thee little stead,' since Comus has the power 'with his bare wand' to 'unthread thy joints / And crumble all thy sinews'. Instead, the Spirit conveniently remembers a 'certain shepherd lad' who 'loved me well', who knew of a flower called 'haemony' that could act against all enchantments. The Spirit, even more conveniently, has the flower with him, and now it will be of use.

The second major spectacle of the evening is revealed to the audience: a stately palace, Comus' court, 'set out with all manner of deliciousness: soft music, tables spread with all dainties'. The verbal battle between the Lady (now imprisoned in a chair) and Comus continues. Both have some good lines, but the Lady probably has the best: 'Fool do not boast, / Thou canst not touch the freedom of my mind,' she snaps at her would-be seducer. She even takes the opportunity to counter Comus' hedonistic arguments with a remarkable critique of a society dominated by excess, displacing his rhetoric of sexuality with her own language of economics and politics:

If every just man that now pines with want
Had but a moderate and beseeming share
Of that which lewdly-pampered Luxury
Now heaps upon some few with vast excess

(ll. 767–70)

then the world would be a better place. To Comus this is 'mere moral babble': as he offers her a sip of the drink that will lead to delight 'beyond the bliss of dreams', the brothers rush in, breaking Comus' glass on the ground and seeing off his bestial followers. Comus, however, escapes, leaving the Lady chained by evil magic to her seat, yet another plot twist in a production that has already offered a rare level of complexity to its audience.

It takes a virgin to free a virgin, and Sabrina, the goddess of the Severn, the river of Ludlow, is called on to intercede. (In the interests of his drama, Milton changes his source and his geography in the interests of a hapy ending: Sabrina, in the myth he is working from, is actually killed in the river, and the river of Ludlow is the Teme. There will be no deaths in the Severn tonight.) The resolution of the *Maske* is achieved in both spectacle and song, as a singing Sabrina sprinkles water on the Lady's breast and frees her from Comus' spell.

It falls to the Attendant Spirit to close out the evening's celebrations by linking the children of the *Maske* back to the real world of Ludlow Castle. He is urgent in his desire to leave the fictional world of Comus' wood:

Come Lady while heaven lends us grace,
Let us fly this cursed place,
Lest the sorcerer us entice
With some other new device.

(ll. 937–40)

At their 'father's residence' there are many friends waiting 'to gratulate his wished presence': the *Maske* steps back into the present moment, the celebration of the installation of Egerton. The Attendant Spirit pictures the festivities, the dancing, the jigs, and imagines that 'our sudden coming' will 'double all their mirth and cheer'. So, the scene changes for the last time, revealing Ludlow Town and the President's Castle, breaking down the porous barrier between stage and audience. In come Country Dancers followed by the Attendant Spirit and the children. A song dismisses the dancers until the 'next sunshine holiday', and another presents the children to their parents:

> Noble Lord, and Lady bright,
> I have brought ye new delight,
> Here behold so goodly grown
> Three fair branches of your own,
> Heaven hath timely tried their youth,
> Their faith, their patience, and their truth,
> And sent them here through hard assays
> With a crown of deathless praise,
> To triumph in victorious dance
> O'er sensual folly, and intemperance.
>
> (ll. 965–74)

In the reconciliation with their parents, the Lady and the Two Brothers finally leave the dangerous world of Comus (undefeated still, and out there with his wand) and become Alice, John and Thomas once again. The Attendant Spirit returns to the deliciously sensuous spirit world, probably rising up whence he had come some hours earlier: 'Up in the broad fields of the sky: / There I suck the liquid air.' He enjoys the endless summers; he sees true lovers in eternal happiness. The *Maske* ends by suggesting to his audience that they too can reach this breathtaking place:

> Mortals that would follow me,
> Love Virtue, she alone is free,
> She can teach ye how to climb
> Higher than the sphery chime;
> Or if Virtue feeble were,
> Heaven itself would stoop to her.
>
> (ll. 1017–22)

It is a superbly optimistic, inspiring ending to the evening, with a moral edge to it that adds depth to the experience. The young protagonists have been tested, and have gained in stature and in wisdom in the process. The audience is encouraged to 'love virtue', whose rewards are presented in the most sensual and enticing ways, and, if sometimes frail and feeble, there is comfort in the knowledge that 'heaven itself' will reach down and offer help.

Milton's *Maske* gives some indication of his place within what has become known as the Caroline literary culture of the 1630s, designated 'Caroline' (from Carolos, the Latin for Charles) in recognition of the social and aesthetic influences of the reigning monarch and his Court. Indeed, that Milton was even engaged with theatre suggests a clear gap between him and some groups of Protestants, epitomised by the Presbyterian William Prynne, the author of one of the most savage attacks on the theatre known in English history, entitled *Histrio-mastix, the player's scourge, or, actor's tragaedie* (1633), which in its 1,100 pages of vitriol takes a moment to be shocked that 'Shakespeare's plays are printed in the best Crown paper, far better than most bibles.'[26] Later, other like-minded commentators would condemn the corrupt form of the masque and its proponents, the nobility and gentry. Lucy Hutchinson (the highly educated wife to one of Oliver Cromwell's most senior officers), looking back at this period, would thunder that the 'generality of the gentry of the land soon learnt the court fashion, and every great house in the country became a sty of uncleanness. To keep the people in the deplorable security till vengeance overtook them, they were entertained with masques, stage plays, and various sorts of ruder sports.' These masques, stage plays and rude sports led, inevitably in Hutchinson's mind, to 'Murder, incest, adultery, drunkenness, swearing, fornication, and all sorts of ribaldry . . .'[27]

But was Milton therefore firmly set within this dominant 'court fashion' which so incurred the wrath of the Prynnes and the Hutchinsons? Caroline writers tended to celebrate aristocratic codes of love and honour in erotic, witty language. John Suckling epitomises the breed, a cynical rake by all accounts, and a man who would lead a battalion of men in 1639 not so much in battle, as in fashion, paying £12,000 to make sure his soldiers looked the part. No cynical rake, Milton did produce a masque that is nevertheless full of echoes of the court masques of recent years such as *Tempe Restor'd,* Carew's *Coelum Britannicum* or Jonson's *Pleasure Reconcil'd to Virtue.*[28]

Yet Milton's *Maske,* although clearly working within the traditions of the Caroline court masque, does some very strange things with the genre. This could simply be the result of its author's competition with his fellow-poets, Milton's attempt to surpass the efforts in the masque form of Townshend, Carew and Jonson, despite the limitations of the setting in Ludlow Castle. Questions remain, however. Is John Milton imitating these celebrated exponents of the genre? Or is he parodying them? Milton does not quite play the Caroline game, interrogating the very aristocratic codes he portrays. In writing his *Maske,* he might be placed in the *company* of his fellow Caroline poets and inventors of masques, but what remains tantalisingly uncertain is his underlying attitude towards his contemporaries' poetics, politics and, indeed, religion.

That Milton's *Maske* is resistant 'to simple resolution', at least by modern critics, is perhaps the strongest indicator of its strangeness.[29] To be effective, it should have been simple and should have resolved into clear celebration of the Lord President, his family, and their happy rule over Wales and the Marches. Some of the complexities were created by Milton's plotting and his unwillingness to supply crucial details. What on earth *is* 'haemony', for example?[30] Other complexities are rooted in the disputational skills he learned during his Cambridge years. Milton would always give both sides of the argument. He had after all been trained up to do so. In his *Maske,* Comus' arguments can sound more convincing than the Lady's and invariably sound more convincing than those of the boys. There are links here with John's *L'Allegro* and *Il Penseroso.* Much to the exasperation of readers, it has proved impossible (although many have tried) to decide which poem represents the views of the flesh-and-blood John Milton.

What *is* clear, and what remains the most remarkable aspect of the work, is the *Maske's* intense, explicit exploration of chastity. The work as a whole celebrates virginity and demonstrates sexuality to be terrifying. For some critics, its focus can be stated even more baldly: '*Comus* is about rape.'[31] The argument can be taken even further: It is not only the Lady who is at threat from Comus and his wand; the young boys are endangered too.

This is not such an outlandish interpretation. One Latin commentary informed readers that Comus had a 'sexuality [composed of] both Mercury and Venus: the rest of the adornment was such as would *effeminate* a man . . .'[32] Not only does Comus look like a woman, but his followers were traditionally cross-dressers, suggesting that no individual was safe from his desires. As ever, Milton uses allusions to hint at what he cannot spell out explicitly. The greatest threat from Comus, for example, is that he will 'unthread thy joints / And crumble all thy sinews'. The allusion is to Dante, an author who had been part of English literary tradition from the time of Chaucer and an author loved by John, who read his works assiduously. Milton is echoing Dante's description of the punishment of the 'sodomite' in Canto XV of the *Inferno* (ll. 110–14). Other commentators link Comus to Belial, the devil of the Old Testament. Belial, like Comus, is sexually androgynous and connected to sodomy, as a quick glance at the violent story in Judges 19 demonstrates.[33]

The clearest threat, however, is to the Lady. It may or may not have been coincidence that Thomas Egerton, the Lord President, had personally interceded in a legal case prior to the *Maske*. A young girl of fourteen called Margery Evans had been raped. In a travesty of justice, the rapist remained free and Margery was put in prison. Egerton conducted an inquiry into Evans's case and eventually helped to have her freed. It is therefore just possible that this case, one in which the Lord President's decency, uprightness and civic role had been demonstrated, lurks behind the emphases of the *Maske*.

There was, however, another topical context for the *Maske*, one which was far more notorious than the false imprisonment of a girl of fourteen in Ludlow. The Lord President's wife had a sister, who was married to Mervin Touchet, 2nd Earl of Castlehaven. The earl's title offered him no protection when his sexual practices emerged. Touchet forced one male servant to rape Lady Touchet and his stepdaughter, married another servant to his own daughter, and throughout conducted openly sodomitic relationships with his servants. One Henry Skipwith was such a favourite that Touchet sought to leave his inheritance to him, bypassing his own son. The court that condemned Touchet hardly needed to hear that he was also a papist. Condemned in general of 'unchastity', and specifically of sodomy, he was sentenced to death, in 1631, a penalty re-instituted under Elizabeth I and which remained law until the nineteenth century.

Could this notorious and terrible case from just three years earlier have influenced the choice of subject at Ludlow? Did the Bridgewater family's need for, and John's desire for, the ideal of the chaste life set the tone for the work? By featuring parents and children in a performance that celebrated chastity, temperance and the charms of 'divine philosophy', not to mention the virtues of familial loyalty, the *Maske* demonstrated to all the purity of the Lord President and his family. On the other hand, to draw attention in such an explicit way to the issue of chastity (and, implicitly, to the topic of sodomy) may have been a gross error on the part of the young Milton, unwittingly opening old family wounds in the interest of his own personal agenda.

That agenda was, of course, chastity. In a move that would become increasingly characteristic, Milton linked the religious and moral issue explicitly to considerations of economics and government. Moreover, while it is clear that the audience was being encouraged to condemn Comus (in other words, the sexual politics of the piece are straightforward), it is not so clear that the audience were simply allowed to celebrate the aristocracy. Not only does the Lady stringently criticise an economics of excess in which the rich get richer and the poor poorer, but the very image of Comus (again linked with Belial) perverts the moral will of the declining aristocracy. Politically speaking, the work is distinctly short on flattery.[34] The hero of the hour is Sabrina, a supernatural being, rather than the real-life person being honoured (usually the monarch, here the Lord President). If all these elements are considered together, the *Maske* starts looking like a veiled criticism of the aristocracy rather than of simple conservatism.

The most daring and problematic element in the *Maske* is, however, the dominance of Comus (to the extent that the work is usually known, incorrectly, as *Comus*). His kind of character would normally appear in an anti-masque, offering a brief glimpse of exotic evil or grotesqueness. Invariably the characters in the anti-masque would be 'Indians', 'savages' or 'lunatics', all grist for the entertainment mill. In Milton's hands, Comus is the protagonist, and he remains undefeated, complicating the inspirational ending in interesting ways. Milton seems to be reminding his audience that the evil Comus represents, whether of unchastity, corrupt courtliness or excess, or indeed all three, is ongoing. Even though there may be a few notes of criticism and warning in his representation *of* the aristocracy *to* the aristocracy, these notes are muted and respectful. It is not these notes of criticism, however, that make the *Maske* so problematic. Instead, it is the fact that it bursts at the seams, crammed with too much literary and moral intensity for its small frame. It is unsurprising that a flurry of further aristocratic commissions did not follow.[35] The complexity and intensity of the *Maske*, if not its relentless defence of chastity and its ambivalence about courtly excess, meant that, if John was looking seriously for patronage and for a place on the fringes of the aristocracy, he had failed in his intention.

FIVE

ELEGY

1637

THE *MASKE* OF 1634 was only one expression of a remarkable obsession with chastity and virginity dominating John's life at this time. His outlook is exemplified by the strange fantasy of marriage without sex at the end of the *Maske*, a passage probably added after the performance, when Cupid and Psyche produce Youth (immortality) through an immaculate birth.

It is tempting perhaps to see John's own shame and fear, his desire to contain his own desires, his horror of the whole business of sex. Yet, he was only expressing in his own way a prevalent view in his society, where the sexual act with a woman was often viewed with disgust. This view was fuelled by the Church's anxiety about sex, even within marriage, an anxiety authorised by the Bible, which insisted that the reward for virginity was salvation: 'These are they which were not defiled with women; for they are virgins. These are they which follow the Lamb withersoever he goeth' (Revelation 14:4). Writers from Shakespeare to Andrew Marvell propagated a similar view. Shakespeare's famous sonnet, which begins 'Th'expence of Spirit in a waste of shame / Is lust in action . . .', explores with what has been called 'clinical precision and pathological disgust' the contemporary physiology of sexual desire. In the phrase 'waste of shame', Shakespeare was punning not only on the word *waste* ('to squander' *and* 'the waist', 'the erotic zones') but also on the word *shame*, the English word for *pudendum* (Latin for 'genitals'). Lust in action is a terrible thing: 'All this the world well knows yet none knows / To shun the heaven that leads men to this hell.' A man might desire a sexual encounter, but in the act of orgasm he expended his vital spirit. Each sexual emission, it was believed, shortened a man's life: in Shakespeare's sonnet this becomes a metaphorical representation of the larger loss of selfhood that occurs when a man succumbs to unregulated desire.[1] John Milton would later write that this precious seminal fluid is 'the best substance of his body, and of his soul too as some think', far too precious to be spilled for no good reason.[2]

John's insistence on chastity, his attempt to dispense with male/ female sexual relations, may be representative of his culture, but it was also an aspect of his continuing friendship with Charles Diodati. Through John's early twenties, Charles was represented as the dominant figure in the friendship, determining its pace and progress: whether that dominance was expressed sexually, socially or emotionally (or any combination of the above), or was simply part of a broader literary convention, is harder to tell.

Certainly, when the relationship surfaces in the historical records again, in November 1637, the twenty-eight-year-old John seems to be teasing both his friend and himself about precisely this imbalance. Typically, he builds his involvement with Charles into the very syntax of his Latin: '*Illud vero queror, te* . . .' can be translated as 'But what I really complain of is that you . . .', but the emphasis is all on the '*te*', 'you'. John's complaint is that Charles has not written to him: 'Now at length I plainly see that you are trying to outdo me once in obstinate silence. If so, congratulations; have your little glory; see, I write first.'[3] He complains that Charles has sent letters to his bookseller and to his brother, both in London, and that he could therefore have written to John 'conveniently enough, on account of their nearness'. John admits that he himself has twice sought out Charles in London. Once, he had been on his way to see Charles's brother earlier in the autumn and tried to find him, with no joy. The second attempt to make contact was even more charged: John had heard that Charles might be in London and had rushed off to find him but ''twas the vision of a shadow! for nowhere did you appear.'

A letter such as this demonstrates once again that Diodati was more to Milton than merely a 'boyhood friend', more even than an *amicus*, a 'perfect friend'. Touchingly, John could joke with Charles in a way that he was unable to with others, asking him to remove his strict prohibition that he 'be sick without your kind permission'.[4] It's not that funny, but it *is* affectionate since Charles has teasingly said that John can't even get ill without his permission.[5] Desire and playfulness, alongside the staginess, seep through the writings associated with Charles.

So too does John's fascination with his own writing. The teasing erotic intensity of his correspondence with Charles becomes a further aspect of his exploration of his own ambition to be a writer. In the heightened world of their correspondence, books become male friends, loved ones that connect John and Charles. John asks to borrow a book on early Italian history from Charles. The potential book borrowing becomes an opportunity to anticipate their meeting up: 'On my word I shall see either that he [the book] is well cared for until your arrival, or, if you prefer, that he is returned to you shortly.'[6] Many of John's puns play on the connections between sex and writing: as any schoolchild knows, one can get a lot of mileage in the English language out of a word like *intercourse*.[7] John writes to Charles that he cannot delay his writing 'until I reach [*pervadum*, 'penetrate'] where I am being driven, and complete, as it were, some great period of my studies', the sexual imagery of penetration lying beneath the literary surface. Milton was not alone in his sexualisation of writing: many of his contemporaries and predecessors made much of the spending of ink and sperm, the expense of spirit, poetry as ejaculation. So when he jokes that he is slow and lazy to write (literally, in Latin, that he is 'cowardly in the use of his pen'), he is in familiar territory for poets of this period, happy to link pens with penises in endless bad, and some good, puns. These are in-jokes, shared between highly educated young men, and redolent with ironies, as when John uses a colloquial word like *garrire* ('chat') to describe his erudite communications with Charles.[8]

For all the jokes and irony, the presence of desire, whether acted upon or not, would, of course, have made the friendship profoundly awkward. Even if straightforward fear for one's life did not suppress homosexual acts, then the mind-forged manacles of Church teaching would ensure that every minute of every day a man would know that his desire was sinful. John himself, in his commonplace book, began listing sins: after Avarice and Gluttony comes Lust, and the first note

on the subject is 'Lust for boys or men' (noted in Greek, of course).[9]
John Milton had problems. He was still living with his parents. He still
did not have a profession. He was (it could be argued) still reading far
too many books. And he appears to have been in love with a man.

John did at least discuss his career options with Charles. In the letter
of November 1637, he writes that he is considering a legal career, or at
least taking a room in the Inns of Court.[10] The four Inns of Court (the
Middle Temple, the Inner Temple, Lincoln's Inn, Gray's Inn) were in
effect a set of colleges for the study of the law, with each Inn, as with each
Oxbridge college, having its own dining hall, library and chapel. If John
had taken this path, the demands on his time would not have been too
onerous. In Milton's time the education delivered to young lawyers was
hardly rigorous and could drag on for years. The qualifications, and the
time they took to gain, were not as important as the exclusive world one
joined. Only gentlemen could enter the Inns, and their lives were
regulated in both major and minor ways: they had to attend chapel,
shave at least once in three weeks, wear their gowns even outside the
Inns and, once inside, take off their swords and bucklers, boots and
spurs, great hose, great ruffs, silks and furs. Entertainment was an
important aspect of life in the Inns: Shakespeare's *Twelfth Night* and *The
Comedy of Errors* played in the great halls in the intervals between the
'dancing and revelry with gentlewomen'. For others, the legal training
was crucial to the development of their political beliefs and aspirations,
with distinguished parliamentarians and historians, such as John
Hampden and John Selden, completing their education at the Inns.
They were places where many a young gentleman aspired to be. More
than 1,700 students were admitted to the Inner Temple alone between
1600 and 1643. In yet another instance of his reluctance to follow a
conventional path, John Milton would not, however, be one of those
young gentleman, though his brother, Christopher, would be.

John did at least know what he wanted, and he knew how difficult it
was to achieve. To Charles, he wrote, 'What am I pondering, you ask?
God help me, immortality.'[11] Desiring immortality, he insists on the
importance of his programme of learning. For a man so apparently
unclear about his future path, this is an important claim, demonstrat-

ing both his commitment to his studies and his increasing sense of urgency in pursuing them. Yet there was still no sight of the 'end' he was making for. These concerns resound through a long Latin poem from this time, written by John to his father: *Ad Patrem* (To My Father).[12] John gives his father the gift of a poem, knowing full well that this is a poor repayment of all the gifts he has been given by his father: '. . . this page shows you what I do possess'. As the modern critic Frank Kermode wrote, if John represented 'his father's chief investment', then there was not much evidence of payback yet.[13] *To My Father* tackles head on John's father's apparent hostility to his son's vocation of poetry, asking him not to 'despise divine poetry, the poet's creation', asking Mr Milton (daringly) to drop the pretence that he hates 'the Muses', reminding him of his own great talent as a musician 'able to fit a thousand notes to apt rhythms', insisting that he has given birth to a 'kindred spirit'. Most important, John argues that he *will* be great – one day. He ends with the hope that 'this eulogy and my father's name' will survive 'as an example for a far-off age'. The poem makes almost painful reading, revealing a vulnerable son seeking to bridge a gap with his father and unable quite to do so.

The publication of the *Maske* in 1637 at first sight seems to have been part of this renewed quest for poetic immortality. Masques were notoriously ephemeral works, the text existing often only in performance. Milton's *Maske*, as we have seen, made far greater claims for the poetry than most works in the genre, but if its publication was designed to increase its author's fame, the aim was thwarted by its appearing anonymously.[14] It was Henry Lawes who published it, and with a familiar excuse in a culture where authors still had to justify any move away from coterie manuscript circulation to the less élite world of print. Using the (again highly conventional) metaphor of the work as the child of the author, Lawes writes that although the Maske is 'not openly acknowledged by' its author, it is nevertheless 'a legitimate offspring, so lovely, and so much desired, that the often copying of it hath tired my pen to give my several friends satisfaction'.[15] Lawes's letter thus presents the *Maske* as a successful and popular work within its original aristocratic coterie.

A cryptic Latin epigram offers some clues to the author's attitude towards the appearance of his 'offspring'. Translated it reads: 'Alas, alas, what misery I have brought upon myself! The Southern Wind ruined my flowers.' The words quoted are from Virgil's *Eclogue II*: the shepherd Corydon is pining for the handsome youth Alexis and lamenting the consequences of his intemperate desire for him. This Latin tag may just be a conventional formula to show that Milton was reluctant to publish, a nod towards the stigma of print at this time. It may express his anxiety about presenting a work that 'defies expectations, generic and cultural'.[16] Or, controversially, John's use of the Virgil quotation may tease the reader with a glimpse of a literary tradition that works against the apparently innocent agenda of the masque, an agenda that John (or some other person) had just underscored by adding further vindications of chastity to the published edition. For to invoke Virgil's *Eclogue II* was to invoke homosexual love poetry. To take on the voice of Corydon was to take on the voice of a homosexual lover. Yet, as ever, the real John Milton is hidden away behind teasing Classical allusions, inviting interpretations from the banal to the sensational, leaving the reader forever guessing.

The game continues in the great poem from these years, *Lycidas*. One of the most surprising, and puzzling, features of this superb elegy for a Cambridge man, Edward King, is the abrupt revelation at its end that the speaking voice, the 'I' of the poem, is not John Milton himself but an 'uncouth swain'.

> Thus sang the uncouth swain to the oaks and rills,
> While the still morn went out with sandals grey,
> He touched the tender stops of various quills,
> With eager thought warbling his Doric lay:
> And now the sun had stretched out all the hills,
> And now was dropped into the western bay;
> At last he rose, and twitched his mantle blue:
> Tomorrow to fresh woods, and pastures new.
>
> (ll. 186–93)

The authorial voice, and the reader's expectations of the poem, are both disrupted, John playing a game of 'now you see me, now you don't'. The disruption is the more disconcerting because it is couched in such wistfully beautiful phrases. While recent theories of literature have challenged the notion that any author speaks directly to the reader, insisting that even the first-person voice is precisely that, a voice representing but not embodying subjective authority, it is true to say that John did not have the dubious advantage of studying post-Structuralist critical theory. Instead, he simply demands that the reader *not* read the poem as a direct confessional moment, even when it is written in the first person. It is as if Milton is warning his readers *not* to plunder his poems for his life, warning his readers that there is no transparent relationship between the poem and the man.

This move towards detachment, in different form, can be seen in the pairing of *L'Allegro* and *Il Penseroso*. Readers are drawn to choose which one is the 'real' Milton, but there is no way of deciding. They are poems, not autobiographical statements. This relates to his culture's understanding of poetry as occasional, responsive to a particular historical moment or event, commemorative of a person – poetry with a purpose beyond individual self-expression. A poem stood as a performance, a display of learning, that placed its author within a long and Classically driven élite tradition. Seventeenth-century readers would have found alien the concept of a poem as an open-ended or confessional moment, or even the distillation of personal experience.

At first sight, *Lycidas* seems to return John to the University world he had left some years before. Invited to contribute to a collection of poems to mark Edward King's death, he wrote a piece which, like so many of his early poems, was both an elegy and rooted in the world of performance for the University, as *Lycidas* makes clear in its references to Cambridge (personified as Camus) and to the speaker's and the dead man's time as students 'together'. The name Lycidas (a character who appears in both Theocritus' *Idyll VII* and Virgil's *Eclogue VII*) clearly suggests that Milton was placing his work within the Latin pastoral tradition so familiar to his fellow Cambridge scholars. Indeed the most recent translator of Theocritus begins his introduction to the *Idylls* with a quotation from *Lycidas*, pointing out that Milton's source 'is to be traced to the *Boukolika* ("ox-herding poems") of Theocritus of Syracuse who bequeathed to the Western tradition the lament for the death of a pastoral poet (Idyll I), the peculiar pathos of death by drowning (Idylls I and 13), and the very name Lycidas (Idyll 7)'.[17]

Yet, despite all these nods towards familiar traditions, and for all its distancing techniques, *Lycidas* engages directly with John's most passionate plea in his letters to Charles of 1637: 'What am I pondering, you ask? So help me God, immortality.' In confronting the sudden and early death of Edward King, John again contemplated his own mortality, his past life and his future one. He grappled with the ways in which immortality could be achieved through the creation of poetry and, even more significantly for him, through an assurance of Christian salvation. *Lycidas* expresses explicitly the fears underlying John's poem to his father – that to write poetry is to follow a 'thankless muse' – but then adds a further, even more profound fear. If 'fame is the spur' that pushes the writer on, it is a precarious process since the 'blind Fury' (fate) will come with 'th'abhorred shears' and slit 'the thin-spun life'. And yet, in the face of these fears, a vision of true Fame is offered:

> Fame is no plant that grows on mortal soil,
> Nor in the glistering foil
> Set off to the world, nor in broad rumour lies,
> But lives and spreads aloft by those pure eyes,
> And perfect witness of all-judging Jove;
> As he pronounces lastly on each deed,
> Of so much fame in heaven expect thy meed.
>
>   (ll. 78–84)

Perhaps scorning delights and living laborious days will be worthwhile, but neither the struggle nor the reward should be measured in earthly terms.

It is not the consideration of fame, however, that makes *Lycidas* the remarkable work it is. Other qualities take it and its author beyond the concerns of the Cambridge years. For, quite apart from the strange ending with its inspirational closing line, 'Tomorrow to fresh woods, and pastures new', *Lycidas* is no ordinary Cambridge elegy. It is markedly different in style and content from those offered by the other contributors, as Milton avoided the clever metaphysical complexities of his contemporaries (who were still imitating witty John Donne from the previous generation). Instead, he forged a passionate, lyrical, pastoral style all of his own. Just as he had done more than ten years earlier in his elegy for an infant, perhaps his sister's child, he offers a Christian consolation, a vision of the dead man in heaven. It is beautifully done, but the real power of the elegy is that this consolation is so difficult to achieve.

As the poem begins, the passionate repetitions of the lost one's name emphasise that the speaker is trapped in a moment of grief:

> For Lycidas is dead, dead ere his prime.
> Young Lycidas, and hath not left his peer:
> Who would not sing for Lycidas?
>
> (ll. 8–10)

Only by moving through the stages of grief, presented in ritualised ways, can consolation be found. *Lycidas* explores the process whereby 'frail thoughts' struggle with 'false surmise', and the grieving clutch at answers that are no answers, feel anger and despair. Only by moving through these states is it possible to reach a point when a vision of Lycidas in heaven can be meaningful, the point at which the tears are wiped 'for ever' from the dead man's eyes, and from the eyes of his mourners. In 'the blest kingdoms meek of joy and love' and 'through the dear might of him that walked the waves',

> There entertain him all the saints above,
> In solemn troops, and sweet societies
> That sing, and singing in their glory move,
> And wipe the tears for ever from his eyes.
> Now Lycidas, the shepherds weep no more . . .
>
> (ll. 178–82)

In *Lycidas*, the pastoral mode, which up to this point in John's work had been predominantly mined for its playful homoeroticism, takes on a new seriousness. Virgil's *Eclogues*, the ultimate model for would-be pastoral poets, were not just concerned with quaint tales of sexually adventurous shepherds and their sheep. Or, rather, the shepherds and sheep provided a way of approaching far more weighty matters. As the Elizabethan writer George Puttenham put it, 'under the veil of homely persons' pastoral can look 'at greater matters and such as perchance had not been safe to have been disclosed in any other sort'.[18] John Milton seized his chance in *Lycidas* to tackle some great matters, using the veil of pastoral to shroud a passionate critique of contemporary religious life. For in the midst of the lament for Edward King, a startling voice, that of St Peter, interrupts the poem, denouncing the churchmen of the time. They are the 'blind mouths' who have betrayed their flock. The flock now 'rot inwardly, and foul contagion spread'. The passage speaks of John's desperate conviction that the Church of England, under the leadership of Archbishop Laud, had lost its way, its increasing authoritarianism together with its excess ritual and cere-mony making ground at the expense of preaching. Milton uses the images of pastoral, of pipe-playing shepherds, of flocks of sheep, to reveal a clergy who do not care and a people who are starving for religious direction:

> And when they list, their lean and flashy songs
> Grate on their scrannel pipes of wretched straw,
> The hungry sheep look up, and are not fed,
> But swoll'n with wind, and the rank mist they draw,
> Rot inwardly, and foul contagion spread.
>
> (ll. 123–7)

It is a powerful expression of the fear that the people of England were rotting 'inwardly', the psyche and soul of the nation, as much as the body, in perilous danger. In two mysterious and apocalyptic lines, *Lycidas* moves into prophetic mode: there will be a violent end to this corruption: 'But that two-handed engine at the door, / Stands ready to smite once, and smite no more.' (ll. 131–2) The very vagueness of the image (no one is quite sure what the 'two-handed engine' is) suggests that, whether in London or in Horton, there was little relief from the sense that there was something rotten in the state of England. The dark pastoral of *Lycidas* was not only an exploration of John's own sense of the precariousness of life and art but one of the first clear expressions of his engagement with the political and religious crisis in his country.

'Dark pastoral' could be one way of describing John's continued life at Horton. Accounts of these years tend to be distorted by an enduring romantic vision of English country-village life. Barbara Lewalski, for example, describes Horton as a 'peaceful village close to Windsor, nestled among the trees and brooks and meadows of Berkshire.'[19] What is more, the coincidence of John's rural existence with what became known as King Charles I's Personal Rule (the years between 1629 and 1640, when the King ruled without Parliament) has encouraged, implicitly, the characterisation of these years in John's life as ones of personal retreat. In fact, in Horton as elsewhere, rural life had its crises and conflicts. The countryside around the village was flat and wet, encouraging the presence of paper mills, powered by the River Colne and its tributaries, alongside the water meadows and wheat and bean fields. These paper mills generated the most obvious tension in the area, since the small English papermaking industry was both in crisis and deeply unpopular throughout this period. Most paper supplies were imported from France, where the linen scraps necessary for paper production were readily available. In England, clothing was traditionally and predominantly made of wool (cotton would only be imported during the seventeenth century), so there was no indigenous tradition of collecting 'rags' to make paper. The few rag-gatherers there were suffered from persecution, accused of begging and spreading disease. Matters came to a head during the plague epidemic of 1636–7, when legislation to stop the rag-gatherers was passed: the Privy Council ordered the Justices of Middlesex to search the twenty or more rag-shops on the outskirts of the city and burn their contents. About a week later an order was issued for the closing-down of paper

mills. The paper would not be much missed: it was common knowledge that paper produced in the English mills was of extremely poor
quality, that one could not actually write on it.[20] It is no surprise,
therefore, that the mills of Horton were viewed with great suspicion.
It was not just the unpleasant smell generated by the fermenting rags
used to make the paper; there were social problems as well. The
gentry of the county complained that 'the paper-makers have brought
many poor and indigent persons into their parishes, whom they ought
to maintain; that their workmen have double wages in comparison
with other labourers and may well save; that the paper-makers
brought the plague into the country places where they work by
means of their rags, as into Horton where sixteen or seventeen people
died.'[21]

In 1637 the death toll in Horton did indeed double. One victim was
John's mother, who died on 3 April and was buried three days later in
Horton church. She was in her mid-sixties. There is no way of
knowing how John felt about her death, except for one short mention
of her in his later account of these years: 'I became desirous, my
mother having died, of seeing foreign parts, especially Italy.'[22]

This was indeed the new plan. John's thoughts turned away from
his own country. As the deaths continued through a summer of plague,
he remained unready, yet, to engage in any practical way in the battle
for the souls of the suffering English people. Instead he raised money
for his projected trip to Italy, loaning out £150 on 1 February 1638 at
8-per-cent interest (ensuring an addition to his regular income), and
selling land in St Martin-in-the-Fields in April to raise capital.
Instructions for Forreine Travell, published in 1642, suggested that a
gentleman would need more than £300 a year to pay for his travels,
not forgetting the £50 a year for an accompanying manservant.

Aside from the money, John needed high-level support simply to
leave the country. A key figure in the process was Sir Henry Wotton,
previously ambassador to Venice, an impressive linguist and a long-
time friend to the poet John Donne. Wotton was a writer himself,
producing a slim volume in 1624 – *Elements of Architecture collected from
the best authors & examples*, in which he shared his appreciation of Italy

and its buildings – and the author of accomplished poetry, often in praise of the Crown. John's literary endeavours conveniently brought the two men into contact. Wotton by this time was old and sick but remained in his post as Provost of Eton College. He had been given a copy of the *Maske* to read at his home only a few miles away from Horton, the work bound into a book of poems, as was often the practice of printers and stationers. Wotton liked it, calling it a 'dainty piece of entertainment', a 'delicacy' and, in subsequent correspondence with Milton, thanked him for revealing his authorship, 'intimating unto me (how modestly soever) the true Artificer'.[23] Within an élite coterie, John was happy to put his name to his work. Similarly, although only John's initials were attached to *Lycidas* when it appeared in the University collection, the readers of this coterie collection would have recognised his style; other, less exclusive, readers did not need to know he was the author. Although there had been no requests for more masques from the pen of John Milton (unless, being ephemeral, they have been lost), the writing, the performance and, most importantly, the circulation first in manuscript and then in print of the *Maske* had proved a passport into a rarefied social world. It was an important factor in Wotton's support for the Italian journey, while Henry Lawes, the court musician who had brought Milton into the Ludlow performance, would send John his letter and passport giving him permission to leave the country. The web of contacts established over the preceding years was starting to yield results. With his travel documents and advice from the old Italian hand Wotton, John was ready to set off on his journey to continental, Catholic Europe. It is quite possible that, up to this point, he had been no further away from London than Oxfordshire or Cambridge.

SIX

ITALY

1638

I N MAY 1638, John sailed for France. His father's money (the trip would be expensive, perhaps £300 a year), the influence of Henry Lawes in the matter of a passport, and a letter of introduction to intellectuals in Paris from Henry Wotton got him to France. His success in Italy, his next destination, was to be of his own making.

In Paris, John met with the eminent intellectual Hugo Grotius, an eloquent commentator on the tragedy of religious conflict and the author of a seminal work in international law, *De Jure Belli ac Pacis* (On the Law of War and Peace). In 1618 a conflict in Bohemia, involving King James I's daughter, Princess Elizabeth, had precipitated what would later be known as the Thirty Years War. Grotius looked on in horror, writing in the prologue to *On the Law of War and Peace,* 'I saw in the whole Christian world a license of fighting at which even barbarous nations might blush. Wars were begun on trifling pretexts or none at all, and carried on without any reference of law, Divine or human.' The country to which Milton was travelling was a case in point. Italy was something of a battleground for France and Spain, the two European superpowers of the time. English troops may have been only rarely engaged in the conflicts, but within the English court there were those who supported France and those who supported Spain. Every move on the continent was carefully monitored. Through the early decades of the seventeenth century, the Catholic Spanish Habsburg dynasty was struggling to deal with the threat posed by Protestant interests within their empire: for example, in 1621 Dutch rebels attempted to overthrow Spanish power in the Netherlands. To make matters worse, in 1635, only three years prior to Milton's sortie into continental Europe, France, in the ascendant since 1598 when her own internal wars of religion came to an end, became actively involved in the conflicts, the aim being to destroy the Habsburgs completely. To that end, Catholic France found itself supporting Protestant powers against the Spanish.

If only human beings listened to their consciences, given by God as a sovereign guide, then they would reject those ideas by which 'the mind is stupefied into brutal hardness,' argued Grotius. This European intellectual caught up in the maelstrom of war and religious difference achieved much, both intellectually and practically, but failed in the end, at least in his own estimation, to accomplish anything through his attempts to understand the world. His final words were, allegedly, of disillusion: 'By understanding many things, I have accomplished nothing.' When John Milton met him, however, in 1638, disillusion and death were still some years away. In Paris, John encountered an intelligent and free-thinking figure with a clear international role to play. It may well have been an inspirational meeting.

John did not, however, stay long in Paris.[1] Henry Wotton had advised him not to miss the city but then to head south to Marseilles 'and thence by sea to Genoa, whence the passage unto Tuscany is as Diurnal as a Gravesend Barge'.[2] This route would avoid the necessity of crossing the Alps; the reference to the regularity of the Gravesend Barge suggested that it was a popular and efficient route into Italy. Wotton had also given John the benefits of his memories of his time in Italy, including an account of his stay with the steward of a family who had been strangled. This is a typical anecdote of Italian life, redolent of the pamphlets available to English readers which depicted a country that was dangerous, exciting and, of course, Catholic. One pamphlet offered a 'true and terrible narration of a horrible earthquake which happened in the province of Calabria (in the kingdom of Naples, under the dominion of the King of Spain) in Italy' involving 'the death of some 50000 persons, of all degrees, sex, and age. The like never heard of in precedent times', while a news pamphlet of 1635 recounted the wonderful conversion of the Marquis of Vico from 'popery' – no matter that the news had first appeared nearly fifty years earlier. George Sandys's relation of his travels in remote parts of Italy was a best-seller, republished in 1637, while *The history of the Inquisition: composed by the Reverend Father Paul Servita, who was also the compiler of the Councell of Trent. A pious, learned, and curious worke, necessary for councellors, casuists, and politicians. Translated out of the Italian copy by Robert Gentilis* would provide the English reader with everything he ever wanted to know about the Inquisition, and could be bought at Humphrey Moseley's shop in 'Paul's Church-yard, at the sign of the Prince's Arms'.

The terrors of Italy may have been a literary construct, but John was travelling through a Europe still in the grips of war. Italy, controlled by Spain, had become embroiled in complicated ways in the ongoing conflict. The Pope, Urban VIII (from the Barberini family), was, in very broad terms, supportive of the French, while Cardinal Borgia was pro-Spanish. Predictably, the two men disagreed over the conflict in Germany, and soon there was an open rift between the Borgias and the Barberinis. The feud culminated in 1634, when Pope Urban asserted his authority, and that of the Barberini family, and banished Cardinal Borgia from Rome.

This act marked the end of Spanish dominance in Rome, at least for the time being. Yet the Pope's power remained precarious. John Milton missed, by a year, an attempted coup d'état directed at the papacy. Pope Urban VIII had fallen ill late in July 1637, prompting the leader of Spanish-controlled Naples to move 6,000 of his infantrymen and 1,000 cavalry to the borders of the Papal State. The Spanish were openly hoping for the Pope's death. The Pope, in turn, and his family did the only sensible thing: stripped the papal apartments and locked themselves in the Castel Sant' Angelo. Urban survived this scare but then created another crisis himself. He decided that he wanted to take over the Duchy of Castro, an independent enclave just north of Rome. Understandably, the family who owned it (indeed had been given the land by a previous Pope, Paul III) were unhappy with the idea. Yet another small but vicious conflict ensued.

Undeterred, John Milton travelled south through France, then sailed from Nice (after about two weeks of travelling overland) to

Genoa, then on to Leghorn and Pisa. Although most of Italy remained in the control of Spain, there were variations in practice in different regions. Genoa was technically independent but strongly loyal to Spain. Leghorn, or Livorno, was a free port and thoroughly cosmopolitan, a blend of Jews, Turks and Protestants as well as Catholics.

John, perhaps to his surprise, arrived in a country in which the situation on the ground was surprisingly stable, if rigidly stratified. The native dynasties (the houses of Savoy, Gonzaga, Medici, Este, Farnese) had been ruling in 1600 and were still ruling in 1700. Similarly, the republics of Genoa, Venice and Lucca remained intact. More important still, for a young man from England, Italy was not merely the battleground of Europe but the home of what nineteenth-century scholars would call the Renaissance, and far more advanced in social and cultural life than faraway England. City life in particular was remarkably well established, civic facilities such as hospitals gaining the admiration of visitors from across Europe. The celebrated Ospedale degli Innocenti had been founded in Florence back in the fifteenth century. Even Martin Luther, no friend to the papacy, had been impressed by the hospitals in Rome, and an English traveller of the 1590s had written, with awe, that '400 or 500 paupers' were being fed by his local Italian city hospital.[3] Even closer to Milton's time, the inveterate (and highly entertaining) traveller Thomas Coryate noted that in Milan's Ca' Granda 'an hundred and twelve chambers and four thousand poor people are relieved.' Hospitals fulfilled many roles within society, from providing wet-nurses for abandoned babies to teaching the poorest children their letters: put simply, Italian cities offered welfare to their citizens on a scale unknown back in London.

The first city that John spent any great time in was Florence. When he looked back, over fifteen years later, he recalled the pleasures of Tuscan city life.

In that city, which I have always admired above all others because of the elegance, not just of its tongue, but also of its wit, I lingered for about two months. There I at once became the friend of many gentlemen eminent in rank and learning, whose private academies

I frequented – a Florentine institution which deserves great praise not only for promoting humane studies but also for encouraging friendly intercourse. Time will never destroy my recollection – ever welcome and delightful – of you, Jacopo Gaddi, Carlo Dati, Frescobaldi, Coltellini, Buonmatthei, Chimentelli, Francini and many others.[4]

These men were members of the intellectual élite of Italy, and some of them were delightfully young. Carlo Dati was only nineteen when John, approaching his thirtieth birthday, visited, and the two men remained friends for many years. Literary exchanges cemented the friendships. Milton would write to Buonmatthei enthusing about his work, while another writer, Malatesti, would dedicate a volume of sonnets to Milton. These sonnets, *La Tina: Equivoci Rusticali* (The Vat: Rude Puns), were erotic or obscene, depending on one's viewpoint, with echoes of the values of *sales* and *urbanitas* so crucial to the success of John's most exuberant Latin performance at Cambridge.

These 'private academies' which John enjoyed were unique to Italian city life, looking for their inspiration, in theory at least, to Plato's Academy and, more recently, to the neo-Platonic Academies presided over by towering Renaissance figures such as the wealthy Florentine banker, politician and patron Cosimo de' Medici and the intellectual Marsilio Ficino. It was all certainly more exciting than University life at Cambridge.[5] The academies had self-consciously urbane names, such as the Apatasti (the Passion-less or the Apathetics) or the Svogliati (literally, the Will-less) in Florence. Protected by cryptic pseudonyms, the members could discuss subjects unbroachable in other social contexts.

For John Milton, the proceedings were heaven on earth. There would be literary readings, then critiques and defences of the readings; there would be translations from Greek and Latin, analysis of literary texts, ancient and modern, and debates on linguistic matters. John had been born for this environment. On 6 September 1638 he read one of his poems (it is not known which one, but it was in Latin hexameters) to the Svogliati Academy and was feted for it. John had become something of a star – after all, it is only in an English idiom that one can be too clever by half. In Italy, John was too clever and they loved him for it.

But there was more to the experience than being appreciated as a poet. The whimsical pseudonyms existed alongside a pseudo-republican government for each society, which served to conceal the huge rifts in society. In the world of the academies, a poet would be named 'Il Fisso' (the Solid One) and a prince would be 'Il Solitario' (the Solitary One), and both would be judged on their poetry alone. It appeared to be a meritocracy, valuing an ideal of manhood based on one's abilities as 'a conversational being' who could use reason and intellect and 'come to know the truth and understand the good'.[6] At last, John had found a milieu in which he could flourish. In this, at least, he was rare among English travellers, the Italian private academies not often featuring on the travellers' itinerary.

There were, of course, dangers involved for Milton in his travels. Some were endemic to seventeenth-century life. He was lucky to miss the famine of 1628–9 and the plague epidemic in northern Italy, which claimed up to 40 per cent of the population. Censorship might have been inefficient at times, but there were still notorious cases of persecution by the Inquisition. In Florence, John met the scientist Galileo's illegitimate son, Vincenzo, at the Academy, and he would write, later (in *Areopagitica*), that he met Galileo himself in the course of his travels (although there is no other indication that the two men met).[7] The discoverer of the telescope was now seventy-five years old and almost totally blind but remained under house arrest, as he had been for the previous five years.

But when John arrived in Rome in the autumn of 1638, all was calm. Pope Urban VIII's policy of using the support of the French to counter Spanish control of Italy but at the same time to offer support to the Spanish/Austrian Habsburgs in their mission to crush Protestantism within their own empire appeared to be working. John arrived for one of the most spectacular events of the decade. On Sunday, 21 November there were huge celebrations when the French King, Louis XIII, produced an heir, the future Sun King, Louis XIV. With Pope Urban VIII supporting the French cause, Rome threw an extravagant party,

vividly confirming the crucial alliance between France and the Barberini family. A cavalcade of horses and carriages rode from the Ponte
Sisto down the Via Giulia, past the Palazzo Farnese, decorated for the
occasion, through the arch across the Via Giulia laden with torches,
the windows of the great buildings lit with white candles. At the
Piazza Navona, another great Roman family, the Orsini, did their bit,
decorating their sumptuous palace and placing a large banner with the
French monarch's coat of arms over the balcony. Everywhere there
were torches and candles, and fireworks shooting into the night. The
greatest display took place at the Palazzo Barberini, where 300
torches illuminated the coats of arms, and Classical inscriptions
informed the world that Louis XIII was the new Hercules, the killer
of the monster Spain. Wine flowed from the foundations 'celebrating
not just the birth of the new French prince but the birth of the new
French power in Rome'.[8]

John was staying in a city dominated by the Barberinis. Their family
symbol, bees, appeared on all the public buildings and on the family's
carriages. A fresco in the Palazzo Barberini glorifies Pope Urban's
reign, overwhelming the viewer with grand illusions, the images
surrounded by countless garland-bearers, shells, masks and dolphins,
all in simulated stucco. Using what has been described as an 'intense
and impetuous visual language', architects and artists such as the
papal favourite Gian Lorenzo Bernini were remodelling St Peter's to
express the splendour and power of the Counter-Reformatory Catholic Church. During Milton's visit, the architect Borromini's church
San Carlo alle Quattro Fontane – 'an extraordinary design with
nothing copied or borrowed from any architect but founded on the
antique and on the best architectural authors' – was being built.[9] The
aim of both art and architecture was the endless stimulation of the eye.

It is all the stranger, therefore, that Milton never commented on
any visual aspect of his time in Italy. His English contemporary Lord
Arundel created a special room to house his two hundred books of
drawings by Leonardo, Michelangelo, Raphael and others, while the
diarist John Evelyn, twelve years John's junior and travelling six years
later, is eloquent on the subject. It is clear that Evelyn consulted

guidebooks, and when he wrote up his travels, he used them to fill in any gaps in his notes: indeed, a number of his reactions come straight from the guides he was using. Evelyn was fascinated by the art he saw and employed a nineteen-year-old artist, Carlo Maratti, whom he called 'my painter', to make copies of the paintings and antique sculptures he liked. Evelyn's trip was all about art appreciation, and the Italian religious system did not seem to trouble him unduly. He would, for example, attend Mass, and he watched religious processions with interest.[10]

In contrast, apart from one mention of the 'antiquity and venerable repute' of Rome,[11] it was the world of Italian books and letters that provoked a response in Milton. He was made welcome by Cardinal Barberini and met Lucas Holstein, a Vatican librarian. Again John was delighted by what he found, 'men endowed with both learning and wit'.[12] (John Evelyn, like Milton, was well treated by Cardinal Barberini, who loaned him his Correggio painting *Madonna and Child with Saints Catherine and Sebastian* so that Evelyn's painter-servant could copy it.) Later, in December in Naples, where he would have turned thirty, John met Giovanni Batista, Marquis of Manso, 'a man of high rank and influence', the biographer of the great Italian poet Tasso, and the founder of the Accademia degli Oziosi (Academy of the Idle), which met at his villa. John was introduced to Manso by 'a certain Eremite Friar, with whom I had made the journey from Rome', another example, if one were needed, that he felt quite comfortable dealing with Catholics and moving in Catholic circles. He may not have attended Mass, but on 20 October 1638 he signed his name into the Pilgrim Book of the English College, the home of the Jesuits in Rome: 'Mr Milton with his servant'.

The connection with Manso was an important one for Milton as he moved into Spanish Italy. Naples was seen as bandit territory, with the Spanish authorities turning a blind eye to the gangs eager to make trouble for the Papal State further north.[13] Under the protection of Manso, John was presented to the Spanish vice-regal court in Naples, at the brand new Palazzo Reale, and saw the sights, which included the impressive fortifications and *arsenale*, as well as the startlingly new grid-plan arrangements of streets around the palace, still known as the Spanish Quarter. (Herculaneum and Pompeii were only discovered in 1738 and 1748, respectively, so were not on Milton's tour.)

Manso inspired John's longest Latin poem from this period, probably written in January 1639. It is not one of his most fascinating works, but it is as ever a well-connected text, crammed with allusions to other works, some of which might even have made sense to Manso himself. There seems little doubt that John would have expected the poem, *Mansus*, to reach a wider audience. It had several aims in mind: 'to repay a kindness, to immortalize a patron, to claim a similar immortality for poets, to continue a conversation, to answer a backhanded compliment, to bridge as well as to acknowledge the gap between poet and recipient'. Above all, however, it was yet another poem about poetry.[14] This is hardly surprising, given John's relentless preoccupation with the world of letters and his place within it. What is perhaps new is the emphasis, couched defensively but nevertheless there, on John's status as an *English* poet. He encourages Manso *not* to be 'scornful of a Muse from a far-off land' who 'has recently been rash enough to venture a flight through the cities of Italy'. The defence of John Milton, with his Muse from a far-off land, develops into a defence of English poetry in its entirety and the claim that John wants to bring King Arthur back to life in his poetry. (Hints of this nationalist poetic appeared back in 1628 in the English poem that ended John's Latin salting at Cambridge. The poem, which begins 'Hail native language . . .', celebrates the potential of English.)

When Milton looked back at his time with Manso, he remembered the following moment: 'When I was leaving he gravely apologized because even though he had especially wished to show me many more attentions, he could not do so in that city, since I was unwilling to be circumspect in regard to religion.'[15] John makes much of his refusal to worship with his Catholic hosts, and the theme is developed when he tells a story of real danger. He was aiming to return to Rome from Naples. On the point of leaving,

I was warned by merchants that they had learned through letters of plots laid against me by the English Jesuits, should I return to Rome, because of the freedom with which I had spoken about religion. For I had determined within myself that in those parts I would not indeed begin a conversation about religion, but if questioned about my faith would hide nothing, whatever the consequences. And so, I nonetheless returned to Rome. What I was, if any man inquired, I concealed from no one. For almost two more months, in the very stronghold of the Pope, if anyone attacked the orthodox religion, I openly, as before, defended it. Thus, by the will of God, I returned again in safety to Florence, revisiting friends who were as anxious to see me as if it were my native land to which I had returned.[16]

This may have been what happened, but it is telling that this vision of John Milton, the plain-speaking Protestant hero defending the 'orthodox religion', protected from evil Jesuits by the will of God, emerged in 1654, over fifteen years after the Italian journeys, and as part of a defence both of the English people and of Milton himself entitled *Joannis Miltoni Angli Pro Populo Anglicano Defensio Secunda* (John Milton Englishman Second Defence of The English People). There were indeed dangers in Italy in the late 1630s, but at the time of Milton's visit the papal dominions at least were relatively welcoming to the English, with Cardinal Barberini even assuming the title 'Protector of the English Nation' and known for his courtesy to English visitors. Moreover, the merchants John mentions had been requested to give assistance to him on his journey by the English ambassador in Paris, Viscount Scudamore, and their support would have eased his passage considerably.

It seems that at no time did John's religion stop him meeting the people he wanted to meet and seizing the opportunities for pleasures along the way. Take the events of 17 February 1639, when he was back in Rome. He went to the opera at the Palazzo Barberini, where there was an audience of 3,500, including the future Cardinal Mazarin.[17] To John's delight, Cardinal Barberini 'singled me out in so great a throng', and, ever ambitious, he assiduously followed this moment of notice up by visiting the next day.[18] He was, by all accounts, received kindly and courteously. Elsewhere in Rome, John heard Leonora Baroni sing. Baroni was a celebrity there, the subject of much gossip: Was she the mistress of Cardinals Mazarin and Rospigliosi? She was certainly something unfamiliar to John Milton: a female professional performer. As with Manso in Naples, so with Baroni in Rome. John turned to poetry, writing a series of epigrams in honour of the singer. To another Roman figure, the poet Salzilli, he wrote yet more poetry, describing himself, in Latin, as 'Young Milton, London born-and-bred' and 'Milton, who recently left his nest and his own little bit of sky . . .'[19]

In Italy, John Milton did at last fly the nest. Everything points to the most glorious of experiences, a journey that affirmed him in his ambitions to be a poet, affirmed him in his own sense of Englishness and Protestantism, while never the less allowing him to relish and engage with everything that sophisticated, intellectual, Catholic Italy could offer. The ways in which his Italian friends and acquaintances responded to him epitomises the success of the journey. Among numerous tributes, the poet Malatesti dedicated his erotic sonnet sequence *La Tina* to 'the great English poet John Milton of London', while Salzilli paid tribute to 'John Milton, Englishman who deserves to be crowned with the triple laurel wreath of poetry, Greek certainly, Latin and Tuscan'.[20] Italy had a reputation – not only was it a Catholic land and the leading force in the aggressive Counter-Reformation, but it was also a land of republics and city-states, the land of Machiavelli and his *Realpolitik*. But for John, well aware of the country's dangerous repute ('a refuge or asylum for criminals'), Italy had proved to be the promised land, 'the lodging-place of *humanitas* and of all the arts of civilization'.[21]

And yet he cut his travels short, deciding during the winter of 1638/9 not to continue to Sicily and Greece but to return to England. The reason he gave later was that he heard 'sad tidings of civil war from England' which summoned him home, for 'I thought it base that I should travel abroad at my ease for the cultivation of my mind, while been true, but the dates do not quite work, since the first minor conflict of the civil wars, the First Bishops' War, only broke out in March 1639, and in January John was already on his way north again, leaving Naples for Rome. Moreover, he hardly rushed home. In March 1639 he was again in Florence, reading his poetry, again, at the Svogliati Academy (and, as he said later, 'gladly lingering there for as many months as before'), writing to the friends he had made in Rome, including Holstein, the Vatican librarian.[23] In April he travelled west to Lucca, then to Bologna and Ferrara, before staying a month in the Republic of Venice. While there, he arranged for his books (including a couple of chests of music books, with works by Marenzio, Gesualdo and Monteverdi among others, yet another reminder of the pleasure that John gained from the music of Italy, if not its art) to be parcelled up and sent back to England, before making his own arrangements to travel home. Nevertheless, he had a month to enjoy the delights of the city. All around him building work was going on, most notably the erection of the remarkable church of Sta Maria della Salute, which dominates the entrance to the Grand Canal and celebrated the city's survival of the plague of 1631.

Plague may have threatened Venice, as all cities, but in other respects the place was (and remains) unique. The Republic kept as far as possible out of the wars of the seventeenth century: the city's life was trade.[24] In terms of intellectual life, Venice was the most liberal city that John visited. The Accademia degli Incogniti was the most daring of the academies, its members including the proto-feminist thinker Arcangela Tarabotti, its meetings the uninhibited gathering of Italian libertines.[25] Throughout the Veneto, the Palladian villas of the Venetian aristocracy brought the pastoral visions of the Classical poets to life in stone, wood and pasture. If John had visited an estate such as the Villa Barbaro, the triumphant collaboration between Palladio and the painter Veronese, he would have seen perhaps the most beautiful secular building in Europe. Built for the Cornaro family, who had made their money in trade in Venice but now wanted the stability and prestige of a country estate, Palladio's design meshed practicality with an idealised recreation of Classical villa life. Veronese, in his wall paintings, added the wit: while real windows looked out on to the external agricultural landscape, painted windows framed by columns offered views of illusory landscapes redolent of Arcadia. The play between reality and illusion continued throughout, with the eye drawn to objects (is that weapon in the corner real or painted?) or a small girl peering round a half-open door – another example of Veronese's talent for playful deception. The Villa Barbaro played delightfully with the social and historical in-jokes of a super-confident élite, providing the perfect setting for a lifestyle of wit and leisure.[26]

From Venice, relieved of his books, John could make the journey across the Alps to Geneva, through the Veneto via Verona and Milan. It was May 1639, a good time of year to make the arduous overland journey. Geneva, the heartland of Calvinism, was a world away from the Italian cities in which John had spent the previous twelve months or so. There, he met up with Charles Diodati's uncle, the eminent theologian Giovanni Diodati, a liberal by the standards of that Calvinist stronghold and an important figure in international Pro-testant circles.[27] John had earlier visited the Diodati family home in Lucca, a significant diversion on his northward journey towards Venice. The family meant a lot to him. And then he continued his journey home, arriving back in England probably in midsummer 1639.

Only a couple of years after his return to England, John wrote proudly of his acceptance and indeed success in the

private academies of Italy, whither I was favour'd to resort, perceiv-ing that some trifles which I had in memory, compos'd at under twenty or thereabout (for the manner is that every one must give some proof of his wit and reading there) met with some acceptance above what was looked for, and other things which I had shifted in scarcity of books and conveniences to patch up amongst them, were received with written Encomiums, which the Italian is not forward to bestow on men of this side the Alps.[28]

His account of his remarkable achievements in the literary and intellectual world of Italy is then overlaid by a highly conventional representation of Italy as a land of danger. When Milton looked back he represented a more hostile Italy than the one he met in actuality, perhaps invoking, consciously or unconsciously, an earlier era, much more antagonistic to Protestantism, one in which English travellers had to be very wary of revealing their religion. Back in 1620, one travel adviser wrote that loyal Protestants could avert danger in Rome by avoiding churches during services and simply never talking about their religious beliefs. To be English was to court danger. Indeed, the traveller Moryson claimed to have met a man who said he was German, but when Moryson spoke to him in German he could not reply. The story changed: he was actually from the French-speaking part of Germany, but, unfortunately, he had no French when pressed. Moryson tried him in Italian: only then was the gentleman exposed as an Englishman abroad. The Englishman fled the conversation, assuming that Moryson, rather than a fellow-countryman desiring a chat, was a ruthless spy seeking out English Protestant aliens.[29]

There is an element of audience-pleasing here: what English Protestant would not be titillated by the thought of the terrible dangers of travelling in a Catholic world? What English Protestant reader would not be delighted by John's plain-speaking refusal to renounce his beliefs? But these statements are also important assertions of his Protestant identity. He might enjoy the pleasures of Italian culture, the charms of the academies, the discussions with learned friends, but he could walk away from it all firm in his religion.

This view of himself is encapsulated in words he wrote at the time of his journey. When in Geneva, he stayed with an Italian Protestant family, the Cardogni. He wrote in their visitors' book: '*Caelum non animu[m] muto du[m] trans mare curro.*' The Latin tag is loosely based on a quotation from Horace ('*coelum, non animum, mutant, qui trans mare currunt*': 'those who cross the sea change their sky but not their mind'). John, however, personalised the statement, making it sound almost defiant: 'When I cross the sea, I change my sky but not my mind.' He also, however, wrote a couple of lines of English verse: '. . . if virtue feeble were / Heaven it self would stoop to her.' These lines are, of course, from the closing speeches of his own *Maske* and suggest some fragility, a consciousness of the possibility of sin, a recognition that virtue may sometimes be feeble, and that at these times, God's mercy must reach down to us.

This strange mixture of confident intransigence and suggestive vulnerability hints at the conflicts within John but does not even begin to indicate the emotional crisis he was facing at this time. For, at some point in the second half of his Italian journey, perhaps as early as Naples, perhaps in Venice, he received devastating news.[30] Charles Diodati was dead. He had been buried in London, at St Anne's Blackfriars, on 27 August 1638. It is impossible to know if the receipt of this news, months after the event, was one of the reasons, perhaps *the* reason, that John cut short his planned journey to Sicily and Greece. Perhaps the itinerary of his return journey, taking in Lucca, the Diodati family home and Geneva, the home of Charles's uncle, became, consciously or unconsciously, something of a journey of commemoration. The records do not even reveal what killed Diodati, although his sister had succumbed to the plague only two months before his death. What is certain is that in Geneva, John would have been in mourning for his friend.

Only when he returned to England, however, did John, *could* John, properly absorb the impact of Charles's death and explore its relation to his own experiences in Italy. Predictably he turned to poetry to mourn. Less predictably, he wrote his longest, most intense Latin poem, a passionate lament for the loss of the man he loved.

SEVEN

DAMON

1640

T HE POEM, *Epitaphium Damonis* (Elegy for Damon), was John Milton's final work of poetry in Latin. The form he chose, pastoral elegy, was an entirely appropriate one in which to mourn Diodati, given the two men's history. Latin, as it had done for many years, provided both the vehicle for the expression of feelings inexpressible in English and a screen for those feelings. Even in a dry English prose translation, the poem expresses a raw desolation:

> But we men are a hard race: a race harassed by cruel fates. Our minds are unfriendly, our hearts discordant. It is hard for a man to find one kindred spirit among thousands of his fellows, and if at last, softened by our prayers, fate grants one, there comes the unexpected day, the unlooked for hour, which snatches him away, leaving an eternal emptiness. 'Go home unfed, lambs, your shepherd has no time for you now.' (ll. 106–12)

The challenge was to celebrate this 'one kindred spirit', this 'rare love', and the pastoral elegy provided the ideal framework.[1] Pastoral suggested intimacy and shared experience (John had used it in this way in *Lycidas*), invoked the shared worlds of St Paul's and the universities, of the Ovidian elegies, the Latin and Greek letters. As the 'Argument' to the poem makes clear, Thyrsis (John) is mourning Damon (Charles) because they are 'of the same neighbourhood, had cultivated the same interests and been the closest possible friends from childhood'. Most important, however, the pastoral mode provides a framework for the expression of love between men.

John draws on a range of Latin allusions to inform the emotional core of the poem, allowing that love to emerge in subtle ways. He invokes, for example, Heracles' pursuit of a boy, desperate with desire for him, or mentions the 'lovely Amyntas', alluding to the sensuous world of Theocritus' *Idyll VII* in which

> Eucritus and I and pretty Amyntas turned aside
> To the farm of Phrasidamus, where we sank down
> With pleasure on deep-piled couches of sweet rushes,
> And vine leaves freshly stripped from the bush.
> Above us was the constant quiet movement of elm
> And poplar, and from the cave of the Nymphs nearby
> The sacred water ran with a bubbling sound as it fell.[2]

Elegy for Damon is built around a refrain that occurs seventeen times in the poem: '*Iti domum impasti, domino iam non vacat, agni*' (Go home, unfed, lambs, your shepherd has no time for you now). The line is a distorted mirror of the final line of Virgil's last eclogue, which runs, 'Go home, my full-fed goats, the evening star comes, go home.' Where Virgil's lines suggest the completion of a natural process, the fulfilment of the shepherd's duty, the variation here suggests failure and despair. Thyrsis, the shepherd-speaker, cannot now act as a shepherd. Yet John Milton, the poet, can perhaps begin to ease the burden of pain with these words, as if, in rejecting the pastoral, he is also pushing away the pain of grief.

This love elegy offers a number of consolations, at least for the dead man. Damon/Diodati is reassured that his fame will live for long years to come: he 'kept the faith of his fathers, observed justice, cultivated the arts of Pallas, and had a poet for his friend'. The rather bathetic final clause may be a moment of self-mockery, a moment when John allows for the fact that he might not have been that important to Charles's life, or indeed his reputation. It could also be read as a confident claim, a celebration of perfect friendship (although he does not use the term *amicus* here). Charles's virtues will be remembered *because* he had a poet for his friend.

That friendship is described as an enduring one, surviving through difficult times, relishing of the good times. The praise of Charles is fulsome, and painful to read, so linked is it with the representation of his loss. 'To whom shall I open my heart?' and 'who will bring back again for me the charms of your talk, who will bring back your laughter, your flashes of Attic wit and your cultured jokes?' These lines lie at the heart of the poem, as James Grantham Turner, fully appreciating the subtleties of the Latin original, explains:

> What Thyrsis misses most about Damon, even more than the soft pears and firm nuts roasting by the fire, are 'blanditias tuas,' 'risus,' 'Cecropiosque sales . . . cultosque lepores'; your blandishments, your smile, your Athenian salty wit, and your cultivated charms. In these lines heavy with longing Milton blends the language of *sal et lepos* with the language of erotic love. Diodati was the unique *lepidus sodalis* or charming companion promised to him, and Milton never uses *lepos* or *lepidus* (in poetry) except in close association with his Tuscan friend. It is Diodati, in Elegy 6, who is encouraged to write sensuous Dionysan poetry, produced by festivity, wine, music, dancing girls, cheerful fires – that is, *lepidos focus* – and the heat of sexual desire rushing through his bones (lines 9–48).[3]

As Turner's analysis makes clear, Charles was fun. He was also a 'kindred spirit'. With his loss, there came 'an eternal emptiness'. There was also guilt. Now the trip to Italy started to look like self-indulgence. If John had been in England, he could 'at least have held your dying hand and gently closed your lids in peaceful death, and said "Goodbye!" '. And yet, Thyrsis/John is comforted by his recollections of Italy, focused here (to provide a connection with Diodati, whose family came from Lucca) on Tuscany: 'O how grand I felt, lying by the cool, murmuring Arno, in the shade of a poplar grove . . .' He was so happy that he imagined Charles with him, imagined what he longed for in the future occurring in the present: 'Hallo there! What are you up to? If there's nothing else you have to do let's go and lie down a bit in the chequered shade beside the streams of Colne or among the acres of Cassivellaunus.'

This striking passage recalls John's Italian fantasy of Charles, surely a fantasy laden with erotic overtones, and places it firmly in England, by the banks of the Colne (the river at Horton) and the Thames ('Cassivellaunus' is an arcane reference to the Thames region). Indeed, the poem begins by bringing the Latin pastoral form right into the heart of London, asking the muses of Sicily to come to the 'Thames-side towns'. There is no sense that Latin pastoral elegy is being kept safely at a temporal, Classical or geographical distance. It, and the kinds of desires it is designed to express, are brought home.

And yet, the penultimate passages of *Elegy for Damon* bid farewell to Latin pastoral poetry. John Milton will in future write British epics, or, if he does write pastoral, he will 'rasp out a British tune'. This is not just a self-conscious statement of poetic intent but a putting aside of the most important aspect of Latin pastoral poetry for John to this date: its ability to provide a language in which, among many other things, he can celebrate love for men.

In one further twist, however, the poem ends with a vision of Charles in heaven. This is the reward for Charles's 'youth without stain', a youth without 'the delight of the marriage bed', a reward full of 'virginal honours'. But this is an unfamiliar heaven and a seriously strange expression of 'virginal honours': 'Your radiant head circled with a gleaming crown, the joyful, shady branches of leafy palm in your hands, you will take part for ever in the immortal marriage-rite, where singing is heard and the lyre rages in the midst of the ecstatic dances, and where the festal orgies rave in Bacchic frenzy under the thyrsus of Zion.' (ll. 215–19) Whether it is the references to Bacchic dance (a frenzied simulation of sexual intercourse in which the gods enter the dancers) or to the thyrsus (a staff twined with ivy and vine carried by Bacchus' followers, and representing the phallus), which are both linked with Zion (the heavenly city of God) and the 'immortal marriage-rite' (the marriage of the Lamb in the Book of Revelations), or simply the heightened vocabulary of raging and raving, orgies and frenzies, this is a potent (in every sense) vision of a heaven both pagan and Christian, and in which Charles Diodati is having the time of his life.

These lines could be reduced to a crude litmus test of John's sexuality (or a crude comment upon Charles's). They have been used to demonstrate John's homosexuality, or his attempt to come to terms with his friend's homosexuality by assimilating it into Greek and Christian models of love. They have been used to show John asserting his own chastity, if not heterosexuality. Most often, the lines are taken to be yet another expression of Milton's poetic manifesto, a discussion of the proper use of poetry, a reading that carefully ignores the sexual imagery. In this reading, Milton, having turned his back on the pastoral genre, has one last look at a model of the poet that he will also reject: the Bacchic one. In doing so, he takes on the mantle of the vatic poet instead.[4]

It is, however, far more revealing to read *Elegy for Damon* as a crisis-driven exploration of poetry *and* sexuality. At times, John's expressions of his special purpose in life, his claims to unique status, can seem self-regarding, even arrogant. This poem suggests instead that his relationship with Charles epitomised his 'radical state of loneliness' in the world, his 'raw sense of otherness'.[5] Over the preceding years, John had represented himself as a man of chastity and austerity, sipping his water while Charles quaffed his wine. But alongside this severe self-presentation, another John Milton appeared, most visible in his communications with Diodati, a man comfortable with *sales* and *urbanitas*, a man at ease with Ovid as much as the Holy Scriptures. Throughout Milton's poetry, pagan and Christian discourses vie for supremacy: the Christian vision appears to triumph most notably in 'On the Morning of Christ's Nativity', when the pagan gods are silenced, yet the dialectic between the two remains a creative force, particularly in the Latin poetry. The tragic realisation in *Elegy for Damon* is that these two kinds of life, these two kinds of poetry, cannot coexist. Perhaps, as Turner argues, 'this possibility died with Diodati.'[6]

Yet, returning to that vision of Charles in his Bacchic heaven, whatever its significance, the belief that he is 'among the gods' does at least provide a consolation. It is the only thing in the poem that does: 'Nothing is here for tears. I shall weep no more.' (l. 202) Charles's death did indeed mark a turning point. Astonishingly, John would never again refer to his dead friend. There is not so much as a mention of his name in any of his later writings. This part of his life was over.

If *Elegy for Damon* was a farewell to Latin poetry, as well as a farewell to Charles, if the Italian journey had confirmed John Milton in his determination to become a British poet, it remained unclear which of the many routes ahead he wanted to take. Between the end of 1639 and early 1641, he made notes of nearly a hundred titles of works he *could* write. For some he even sketched out plans.

Meanwhile, other changes were taking place. When John had departed for Italy he had left at Horton a Milton family that appeared to be thriving. His brother Christopher had just married (or was on the point of marrying) Thomasina Webber, the daughter of a tailor from the City: not a great match in terms of social class, but at least Christopher was getting married and his new wife came from the world of Bread Street. Christopher and Thomasina came to live in Horton, where their first child (possibly first children) were born. John's older sister appeared happily settled with her new husband, Thomas Agar. Anne probably stayed in Horton during the period of mourning for her mother, arriving with her husband, their new baby, also called Anne and born in 1636, and her two sons from her previous marriage, John and Edward.

During or soon after John's return from Italy, this stability would be shattered. Anne died, leaving a young daughter to be cared for by Thomas Agar, and two orphan sons. This personal, familial loss was made more critical by the increasing instability in the country at large. The years immediately after John's return from Italy were characterised by the Milton family's attempts to navigate these crises, attempting to safeguard the wealth and status that John Milton Sr, and indeed his wife, had worked so hard to accrue.

In practical terms, this meant a number of house moves for all concerned. John may have spent a short time at Horton on his return from Italy but soon rented a room in a house in St Bride's Churchyard back in the City. He stayed there for about a year before moving to a 'pretty garden house' in Aldersgate Street, probably in the early months of 1641, certainly before 29 April of that year.[7] It was a return to familiar territory. Aldersgate, surmounted with a statue of King James, was one of the four oldest entrances to the City of London, the street of the same name running south towards Cheapside, and thus towards St Paul's and John's birthplace. Living in Aldersgate, he was poised between two very different urban environments. Outside the walls, the workshop of the capital was full of the sights and smells of its industries. Inside, controlled by the City oligarchy of the Lord Mayor, sheriffs and aldermen, the streets reflected the more ordered world of merchants and professional men, John Milton among them.[8]

The pretty garden house was also large, designed to accommodate John himself, his books (of course) and his pupils, a new development in his life. John would become a professional tutor in due course, but in 1641, his first pupils were his own nephews, Edward and John Phillips. Everything the boys achieved suggests that their uncle gave them a fine if demanding education. John Phillips, for example, would go on to translate works from Latin, Greek, French, Spanish and Italian – and possibly Dutch.

Their uncle was, however, far more than a tutor to Anne's boys. John Phillips, aged about eight years old, was the first nephew to come and board with his uncle: he was put completely under John's 'charge and care'. Edward, his older brother, joined the household shortly after. At about this time, John also took on a servant, Jane Yates. Nothing more is known about her, but she would have been busy. (There is no more mention of the male servant who accompanied John to Italy.) Although the precise dates of these various moves are impossible to pin down, the primary reasons for the boys coming to live with their Uncle John were the illness and death of their mother.

At first sight it seems strange that Thomas Agar, their stepfather, did not keep the boys in his household. He was a successful govern-ment official and could well afford to pay for the kind of care they needed. That John took responsibility for his nephews suggests the values of his society as well as his own sense of familial duty. The bonds between nephews and maternal uncles could be strong and enduring, the uncle at times crucial in the safeguarding of a child's financial interests after his or her mother's death.[9] In more general terms, high mortality rates, particularly in urban families, necessitated this kind of movement between households. More than a quarter of all gentry householders had kinsfolk who came from outside their immediate nuclear family living with them. (The percentages decreased the lower down the economic and social scale people were. A labourer's family could not afford to fund this extended concept of family.) To be able to take on responsibilities for relatives in one's own household was thus both a practice and a sign of gentrification, fitting for such an upwardly mobile family as the Miltons.

As is always the case, however, individual families' arrangements depended on the personalities involved, with wide variations within groups as to how close individuals might be.[10] John's willingness to take on the responsibility of raising his sister's children, and his success in doing so, can be contrasted with Thomas Agar's presumed unwillingness to continue in his role as stepfather. Agar never formally adopted Edward and John, his priority presumably being the care of his one surviving daughter, Anne.[11] John's action, above all, underlines the salient characteristic of effective family life in England at this time: fluidity.[12]

The Milton family's ability to cope with crisis was going to be tested over the coming years, as the country descended into civil war, the 'sad tidings' of which had, John claimed, called him home from Italy in 1639. The problems had begun in Scotland when the Scottish Presbyterians, known as Covenanters, moved to challenge the power of King Charles I and his Church. The relationship between Charles and the Scots had not been a happy one with the King aggressively seeking to achieve religious conformity between his three disparate kingdoms. The moment of confrontation was precipitated by his attempt to introduce a new prayer book to Scotland. If the King's Laudian reforms were unpopular in England, they were anathema in Scotland, where the Protestant Reformation had taken hold most strongly.

The King should, however, have been able to deal with any military challenge from within his borders. Charles's army was stronger than that of the Scots, in particular his cavalry, and overall, he was better equipped and better funded for a long campaign. As John Milton continued his long journey overland back to England during 1639, it seemed that the Scottish crisis was going to be resolved quickly, if not by force itself then by a show of force. King Charles, writes the historian Richard Cust, 'believed that simply appearing in the field would be enough to secure him victory, since the Covenanters would never actually have the nerve to fight'.[13] Charles and his army marched north, sending 3,000 infantry and 1,000 cavalry ahead to assess the Scots' strength. As the English approached the town of Kelso, Alexander Leslie, the veteran Scottish commander, decided to use a tactic familiar on the continent during the Thirty Years War. His infantry went into a shallow formation, but showed extra sets of colours, giving the impression that the Scots' army outnumbered that of the King several times over. The English withdrew. By the time John returned to England, his fears for his country had been confirmed, and in the autumn of 1639, further hostilities between the English and Scots seemed inevitable. Both sides made nods towards peacemaking, but in reality both were exploring what help they could receive from foreign governments to fight their war. Charles I hoped for £10,000 from the Spanish, the Scots looked to Louis XIII of France for help. After the humiliation of Kelso, Charles and his First Minister, Wentworth, aimed to raise a massive army of 35,000 men, including 8,000 from Ireland. The possibility of support from Spain would help, but the King needed much more, a further £1,000,000 for his war fund, at one estimate.

How to raise the money? The King had received as many loans as he could hope for from the City of London, and the aldermen of the City refused point blank to bankroll another campaign. The King had moreover raised as much money as he could from deeply unpopular customs and excise revenues. There was no more to be hoped for there. Even the Spanish money disappeared when the Spaniards were distracted by problems in their own backyard, a revolt in Catalonia.

The King's advisers saw the truth of the matter: 'If you think to make a war with your own purse you deceive yourself. The only way to prosper is to go back and call a parliament, and so shall you have money enough and do your business handsomely'.[14] King Charles replied that there were 'fools' in the last Parliament, back in 1628. He was reminded that there were wise men too. With no other option, he reluctantly summoned a Parliament, a desperate step for a monarch who had seen fit to dismiss the one of 1628 and rule without its troublesome interference for the previous twelve years.

Whether full of fools or wise men, the Parliament that convened on 13 April 1640 knew it had a rare moment of power, an opportunity to challenge the legitimacy of the King's personal rule. Predictably, instead of voting large sums of money for the war, the members insisted on considering their own grievances. Moreover, many members simply did not accept the argument that the war was necessary. Behind the scenes, the King and his supporters made the case for fighting the Scots, reminded MPs of their oaths of loyalty to the Crown, and made promises about reforms. Parliament was not listening, and Charles used his Royal prerogative to suspend proceedings. This spring 1640 session at Westminster became known as the Short Parliament. Its failure merely confirmed the King's opinion of parliamentary government. He had tried to enlist Parliament's support, and Parliament had failed him. Charles now went to war regardless.

As if this political and military crisis were not enough, at the same time the simmering problems in the Church were coming to a boil. Archbishop Laud, who was, ironically, attempting to distance himself from the Scottish issue, chose this moment to publish new canons (church laws) requiring conformity. All clergymen now had to take what was called 'the etcetera oath' concerning the organisation of the Church; they had to swear allegiance to 'the government of this Church by Archbishops, Bishops, Deans and Archdeacons, etc. as it now stands established and by right ought to stand.' To some, it seemed likely that the English Church was very close to adding 'Pope' at the beginning of this list.

This proved to be the last straw for many ministers and congregations, not to mention Parliament, which declared the canons illegal in December, whether out of a concern for the implications for religious freedom (such as it was at the time) or the desire to find a scapegoat in a time of acute tension. In May 1640, there were riots in the City of London on account of the 'etcetera' clause, and a huge mob of London apprentices attacked Lambeth Palace, Archbishop Laud's residence.

Milton and his nephews, in their house in Aldersgate, were therefore living in the middle of a city in which the national crisis was being played out politically and socially. It cannot have been comfortable. Christopher Milton, on a visit to London, was, it seems, attacked. He was visiting from Horton, where he, Thomasina and their children were still living with the widowed John Milton through the year 1640.

Elsewhere, other families were being hit hard by events. The Powell family in Oxfordshire, for example, who had been repeatedly borrowing from the Miltons, father and son, over the previous decade and more, were struggling. Despite receiving the lease of some lands from the King himself in Shotover Woods, between Oxford and their home in the nearby village of Forest Hill, they still could not remain solvent. In June 1640, the Powells were forced into mortgaging their land to raise money. It was John Milton, his father's son, who was the mortgagee. The months went by; again the Milton family regrouped. Christopher moved with his family to Reading, and his father came to join them.

Meanwhile, King Charles needed some good news. There was none. On 28 August 1640, in a battle at Newcastle (part of what became known as the Second Bishops' War) the King's forces were routed by the Scots. The Scots were gaining confidence, and heading south. The defeat at Newcastle

left Charles in a much weakened position, both militarily and politically. He still had a force of around 16,000 men at York, but it was costing £40,000 a month to keep together and at the start of September there was only £1037 in the Exchequer. The presence of a Scots army on English soil was also threatening to transform English politics. For the first time since the fifteenth century there was an alternative to the crown as a source of power around which critics of the regime could rally. The army's presence was also a stark reminder of the king's failure in battle, which was still the ultimate test for a monarch.[15]

On the ground, the Scottish victory in the Bishops' Wars created immense volatility and uncertainty. A rebellion had taken place against the monarch and had succeeded. This remarkable event shattered the taboo against such armed resistance, one of the most significant constraints operating in favour of the political status quo. The very fact of success destroyed the belief, assiduously cultivated by the Tudors, that rebellion always failed. What was more, the Scots had rebelled in the name of religion and conscience, and had apparently met with divine approval for their actions. All this served to reinstate armed resistance as a legitimate response to a tyrannical ruler, thus opening up a whole range of political possibilities, not just for the English but (perhaps even more inflammatory) for the Irish under English rule.

A month after the defeat at Newcastle, Parliament began to flex its muscles in earnest against the King, or at least against his ministers. It moved to impeach his chief minister Wentworth (accused of conspiring to use Irish armies to subdue both the Scots and the English), and proceedings began in the spring of the following year. By now, the charge against Wentworth was that he supported arbitrary government. Wentworth had indeed used a ruthless dictatorship, a policy known as 'thorough', in Ireland with vicious effectiveness. There were those who feared that his experiences there were merely a pilot scheme for the 'thorough' government of England.

Wentworth, however, offered a superb defence, and the impeachment procedures foundered. Parliament therefore changed tack and produced a bill of attainder, which in effect accused the chief minister of treason. There were unprecedented crowds around Parliament, the multitude baying for Wentworth's blood. It was said the great parliamentarian John Pym used his contacts with radical groups in the City to organise marches of apprentices and others to Westminster, all with the aim of ensuring Wentworth's successful prosecution.[16] Others thought these public demonstrations were spontaneous expressions of deep-seated political and religious divisions within the country. What was clear was that men such as Pym were happy to create fears of a Popish Plot, a Catholic threat to Protestant England. King Charles, seeking support from Catholic Spain, married to his Catholic Queen Henrietta Maria and loyal to his High Church archbishop, did nothing to stop these fears, and did something to inflame them.

The crowds got their wish, primarily because a plot (known as the Army Plot) came to light. The plan had been to bring the King's northern army down to London, seize the Tower of London, release Wentworth and dissolve Parliament. It was a not a particularly brilliant idea, and its discovery sealed Wentworth's fate. King Charles, who had sought to protect his loyal minister, agonised over the decision but in the end admitted the truth: 'I am forced to give way.'[17] Wentworth was executed on 12 May 1641. Two days earlier, Parliament had passed a bill saying that it could not be dissolved except by itself. Parliament had achieved a victory as crucial and as bloody as that of the Scots.

In the midst of these unprecedented events, a slim volume was privately published in London. John Milton had arranged for the printing of his elegy for Charles Diodati. It was his first separately printed poem. He sent copies to friends in Italy, and possibly to friends in England. A rare copy survives in the British Library.[18] The quarto has only four leaves and is undated, and there is no name of author, printer or bookseller. On the last page, in the bottom corner, is the word *Londini*. John Milton was writing of his grief from London, a city torn by conflict, the city he loved, and the centre of government for a country in crisis. Just months after the publication of *Elegy for Damon*, in the first part of 1641, as Wentworth's impeachment and then attainder dragged on, John turned to writing prose in English. The decision, he wrote later, was based on his consciousness that his country needed him. Since he had always had 'greater strength of mind than of body', and any 'stout trooper might outdo' him in the 'toils of war', he chose to serve his country in a different way, seeking to excel in the labours of the mind.[19] His country did need him, and he would indeed excel.

Part Two

JOHN MILTON, ENGLISHMAN

EIGHT

THE CHURCH

1641

JOHN MILTON'S ASSERTION that his pen would be effective was, never the less, a bold one. His family background (some wealth, aspirations to gentility) and his talents suggested various familiar career paths for a man who wished to have a voice in social and political life, most obviously a place in the Church or the law. John, as has been seen, had seriously considered the priesthood, a path taken successfully by men who sought political influence such as John Donne in the previous generation, or indeed Archbishop Laud in the current one. He had toyed with the idea of a legal career, the profession chosen by his brother, Christopher: this would be the profession of many of the most influential parliamentarians in the period. Neither priest nor lawyer, however, John Milton almost single-handedly created the identity of the writer as political activist, of writing as a political vocation.

He was helped by being in the right place at the right time: London in 1640. There were new politics (Parliament was in action again), new conditions for writing (censorship had been relaxed) and new uses for that writing.[1] In July 1641 Parliament formally abolished the Court of the Star Chamber, for years the State's most effective means of censorship. As Milton himself put it later: '. . . as soon as freedom of speech (at the very least became possible), all mouths were opened.' His aims were magnificent. Now 'thoroughly aroused', he saw that men were 'following the true path to liberty' and making the 'most direct progress towards the liberation of all human life from slavery'.[2] He would play his part in the struggle. He put aside his literary ambitions, whether in the Latin, Greek, Italian or English languages. In 1640 he was still planning a major new literary work, his thoughts turning to tragic drama after his time in Italy. He sketched out four drafts for a drama, each focusing on the events recounted in the Book of Genesis, when Adam and Eve are expelled from Eden, having eaten the fruit of the Tree of Knowledge. The notes survive in the Trinity Manuscript (owned by Trinity College Cambridge) and demonstrate that John was much preoccupied with finding the right shape for his ideas. The third draft outlines briefly, for example, a five-act drama. In Act Three, Lucifer contrives Adam's ruin, and a Chorus 'fears for Adam and relates Lucifer's rebellion and fall'. Act Four jumps to a scene that occurs after Adam's 'ruin':

Act 4

Adam   }
          }   fallen
Eve   }
Conscience cites them to God's examination
Chorus bewails and tells the good Adam hath lost

The fourth draft sets out in prose a similar narrative, with a little more detail ('Eve having by this time been seduced by the serpent appears confusedly covered in leaves'), and ends with the comment, 'Compare this with the former draft.'[3]

There were no further versions, no attempts to compare draft with draft. Instead, this kind of creative work was laid aside, and John Milton transformed himself into a writer of polemical prose. Often vicious, often funny, his voice would be insistent and powerful in defence of the ideas he believed in.

The print culture he was now engaged with was characterised by rapid turnover, as satirised in a pamphlet of 1641 in which Suck-bottle the hawker (street-seller of pamphlets) is looking for a 'new book being out today', while the poet who sold a book the night before already has another to sell, but 'nobody will buy it because it is not

A page from the manuscript at Trinity College, Cambridge, showing
Milton's working copy of his early poems.

licenceable.' Authors, book-sellers, printers, 'mercuries' and 'hawkers' were all thoroughly dependent on each other: '. . . when fortune late hath frowned / All five are fallen, all five do kiss the ground' went one jingle. *Mercury* became a common word for a newspaper, from the 'mercuries', or messengers, who brought news in person, but the term's other meanings ('go-between', 'nimble-fingered thief') suggest vividly the edgy atmosphere surrounding news and other cheap print in this rapidly changing society.

Suddenly, print was all that mattered. Old manuscripts from the 1620s were picked up, dusted down and published. Milton, of course, was familiar with the world of the London book trade, the area around St Paul's. It was home territory: from his house in Aldersgate, Paul's Churchyard was a short walk away.[4] He had always been a buyer of books, amassing a much-loved collection, referring to books as friends, taking meticulous notes. Through his adult life, he went to his favoured book-sellers and bought books either already bound or in loose leaf ready for his own personal binding, each detail of purchase and presentation (usually carefully noted) indicating the relationship between book and reader.

In 1640, however, John Milton was still predominantly a consumer of print rather than a maker of it. His reputation as a poet, such as it was at this time, was not based on published works. *Lycidas* had been printed in the rather obscure University collection *Justa Edouardo King Naufrago*, Henry Lawes had put out a discreet edition of the *Maske* from Ludlow, but otherwise there was little of Milton's work in print.

Nor was there much of his writing circulating in manuscript, which seems stranger in a culture in which scribal publication – the copying and circulation of manuscripts – was an important indicator of a writer's status. The Trinity Manuscript (which contains those drafts of a biblical drama) also has versions of *Lycidas* and the *Maske*, as well as many of the short poems that John had written in his twenties and thirties. Perhaps the Trinity Manuscript, along with others, was used to prepare copies of his work for those who wanted to read it. There is plenty of evidence that poems were sent to friends or potential supporters in manuscript, but these did not then appear in verse miscellanies, whether scribal or printed. In this John was in good company. George Herbert, one of the greatest religious poets of the century, does not appear in manuscript verse miscellanies, and his masterpiece *The Temple* was only published after his death in 1633. Yet, for John Milton, what limited circulation of his work there was did not lead to any kind of wider literary celebrity.[5]

There was no guarantee that the move into print would provide any celebrity either, let alone the immortality that John sought from his writing. His chosen format was the pamphlet: quick to write, cheap to print, cheap to buy, a form constantly in dialogue with itself, as pamphleteer responded to pamphleteer. But, step by step, he became more and more actively engaged in this rapidly changing world of print and politics.

The crisis in the country was growing, as the King's absolute power (and that of his Church) was challenged from both within and without the political and religious establishment. Milton's first cause, in the early 1640s, was the best way to reform the corrupt Church. The problems were painfully obvious. The clergy were ill-educated, some held more than one living, and many did not live in their parishes. The élite of the Church were viewed as personally corrupt, and their cathedrals 'dens of loitering lubbers'. Tithes, the tax upon parishioners, ended up in the pockets of the already rich, whether clergy or laymen. More sinister, the Church, backed by the power of the State (bishops held a greater number of secular government positions than at any time in the previous century) enforced uniformity of belief and practice among the people of England. Where before, it was claimed, many shades of Protestant opinion had been, more or less, accommodated within the Church of England, through the 1630s a narrow orthodoxy had been increasingly insisted upon, linked to complete allegiance to the Crown. The Thirty Years War, with its vicious series of battles between Protestants and Catholics, only encouraged the authorities to police the State religion in England more brutally, to 'protect' the nation from the perceived Catholic threat. The wars in Europe also encouraged caution in those who, in seeking reform, were anxious to avoid the conflagrations occurring on the continent.

The city in which John Milton lived and wrote was becoming more and more politically alive. The new climate was epitomised by a remarkable petition which demanded that episcopacy, the rule of the bishops within the Church of England, 'with all its dependencies, roots and branches, be abolished'. This so-called Root and Branch Petition attacked the policies of Archbishop Laud, who was represented as encouraging Catholic-style idolatry, and, in a vital linking of religious and social concerns, the petition connected the government of bishops with other grievances, even the decline of 'neighbourliness'. The petition's rhetoric exemplifies the tone of the new debate, aggressively hostile to the ministers of the established Church, and exposing

> the great increase of idle, lewd and dissolute, ignorant and erro-
> neous men in the ministry, which swarm like locusts of Egypt over
> the whole kingdom; and will they but wear a canonical coat, a
> surplice, a hood, bow at the name of Jesus, and be zealous of
> superstitious ceremonies, they may live as they list, confront whom
> they please, preach and vent what errors they will, and neglect
> preaching at their pleasures without control.[6]

In January, one Bishop Joseph Hall had offered a tract to the new Parliament defending episcopacy. Two months later, a group strongly opposed to Hall's arguments responded. They called themselves Smectymnuus, a strange, wonderful and almost unpronounceable name created from the members' initials. One of the group, Thomas Young, had known John Milton for more than twenty years, so when Milton entered the debate himself, he dedicated his first contribution to the man who had once been his tutor and was now his friend.[7]

Milton's pamphlet *Of Reformation Touching Church Discipline in England: And the Causes that hitherto have hindred it. Two Bookes written to a Freind* was published in May 1641.[8] Its full title (actually quite short compared to many other pamphlets) suggests that it would consider, rationally, the history and causes of the current problems in the Church. Its author was writing in civil terms to a friend, after all.

Once into the body of the text, however, the atmosphere gets more heated. Milton expresses deep anxiety that the Reformed Church is going 'to backslide one way into the Jewish beggary, of old cast rudiments, and stumble forward another way into the new-vomited Paganism of sensual idolatry'.[9] Since England was, according to Milton, the *first* Reformed country, it was particularly important for England to keep the flame of Reform alive. God is, of course, on the side of those who oppose episcopacy. God, in fact, actually vomits over the bishops.

> And it is still Episcopacy that before all our eyes worsen and slugs the most learned and seeming religious of our Ministers, who no sooner are advanced to it, but like a seething pot set to cool, sensibly exhale and reek out the greatest part of that zeal, and those gifts which were formerly in them, settling in a skinny congealment of ease and sloth at the top: and if they keep their learning by some potent sway of nature, 'tis a rare chance; but their devotion most commonly comes to that queasy temper of luke-warmness, that gives a vomit to God himself.[10]

In a move that would become crucial to Milton's political identity, he was as much concerned with the failure of the English people to *see* the problem, the failure of people to *voice* the problem, as he was with the problem itself. He was appalled that the English nation remained silent about the peril of the Church, personified as female as was usual: '. . . we blanch and varnish her deformities', the pamphlet thunders. 'Our understanding' has 'a film of ignorance over it', our sight is bleared 'with gazing on false glisterings'. What was needed, and immediately, was the purge of a 'sovereign eyesalve'. That eyesalve was Holy Scripture. Only in a complete reliance on the words of the Bible would truth be found, would English eyes be opened. *Of Reformation* ends with a vicious invective against those who want to maintain episcopacy: the bishops, these 'vassals of perdition', are imagined in hell, where they will be treated with 'a raving and bestial tyranny' such as is normally handed out to 'slaves and negroes . . .'[11]

In the early years of this remarkable decade there were many, many pamphlets arguing similar cases, in similar (and, to modern eyes, offensive) terms. Milton's central argument, that episcopacy was a corruption of the practices of the early Church, would have been familiar to many of his readers. So would his argument that those who defended episcopacy were relying on tradition rather than Scripture. So would his argument that the corruptions of the bishops were a threat to monarchy itself: since the power of the monarchy depended on 'justice and heroic virtue', it was diminished when it was chained to the 'gaudy rottenness' of episcopacy. Milton was merely one new voice in a clamour of new print voices, but he himself had come a long way from 1626, when he had been able to write (admittedly formulaic) elegies celebrating the virtues of dead bishops, to be circulated in manuscript among a Cambridge coterie readership.

There were dangers involved in this nascent print culture, both psychological and physical. Later Milton would write of his fear that a volume of his own poetry would be 'scraped by the dirty calloused hand of an illiterate dealer'.[12] Illiterate dealers were perhaps a minor problem in a political and religious regime that still persecuted and mutilated authors, and that seized and burned their books. As recently as June 1637, the authors Prynne, Bastwick and Burton had suffered horrific physical punishments at the instigation of Archbishop Laud. Their crime had been 'to write against a bishop or two'. For this, the men had, variously, ears cut off, cheeks sliced away, and faces branded.[13] As with the Internet in this century, people expressed real fears about the sheer number of new works appearing. Others condemned the whole notion of publication, particularly for money. Publication was imagined as 'epidemical contagion', and 'Pamphlet-mongers' were castigated for writing for 'a little mercenary gain, and profit', as 'poetical Needy-brains, who for a sordid gain, or desire to have the style of a witty railer, will thus empoison your pen'. The proliferation of new pamphlets was also resented by more (allegedly) serious writers, who complained that 'such a book as that of thirty or forty sheets of paper is not like to sell in this age were the matter never so good, but if it had been a lying and scandalous pamphlet of a sheet of paper . . . to hold up Anarchy' then the printers would print it, knowing it would sell, be 'vendable ware'.[14]

Some even worried, in more practical terms, that the paper stocks of the nation would be exhausted, while many more feared that the new Babel of voices would lead only to chaos and social breakdown. This last group had a point. Much of what was being printed was unauthorised and unlicensed. For decades, the Company of Stationers had controlled all aspects of the printing trades, including apprentice-ships, the succession of printing houses, the control of copyright and the prevention of piracy. Controlling the Company of Stationers was the Court of the Star Chamber, whose ordinances of 1637 had increased the penalties for printing unlicensed books, tightened up the restrictions on who could grant licences, and ordered that no English books were to be printed abroad or foreign books sold without permission of the Church. The Star Chamber had teeth: it was this body which had meted out the vicious punishments on Prynne, Bastwick and Burton. Now, in 1641, Parliament abolished the Star Chamber, in one stroke removing the vast majority of the licensing controls. The floodgates opened.

John Milton's tract against the bishops was representative of this phenomenon. It was neither registered nor licensed for publication, and its author remained anonymous. It was a pirate edition, standing outside the system, the names of the printers not even mentioned. Only the bookseller is identified, one Thomas Underhill, who had himself only set up business that year, his shop being 'At the sign of the Bible, near the Compter in Great Wood Street'. Although up to a thousand copies might have been printed (between 500 and 1,000 was the standard number for a new pamphlet), Milton's first prose work was in its very nature ephemeral: news one week, scrap paper the next.

Milton, however, did not see his own work in this way. In an act profoundly indicative of his own evaluation of authorship, he presented a copy of his first tract to the Bodleian Library. Nine of the corrections noted in the published errata are made in the text, almost definitely in his own hand. The existence of this corrected presentation copy demonstrates that Milton did not see his pamphlet as narrowly topical and thus ephemeral, that he did not see his pamphlet, however cheap it had been to print and to buy, as a mere scrap in the ever-growing pile of papers.

This double vision – the desire to be actively engaged as a writer in the heat of the historical moment, and the desire to transcend that historical moment and achieve immortality – is deeply characteristic of John Milton. The vision informs his writing throughout his life, producing works enmeshed in the events and causes of his own time and his own nation, yet attempting to speak to future generations, and to the widest possible audience. This double vision is related to another, equally paradoxical aspect of his identity as a writer. As the scholar Stephen Dobranski has shown, Milton was utterly reliant on all the other members of this changing print world, 'amanuenses, acquaintances, printers, distributors, and retailers'. Yet the image he projected, and the image that generations of readers have wanted to see, is that of the completely independent writer and thinker, standing above the messy business transactions of the publishing world. As Dobranski points out, the reality was that an awful lot of people were needed to create precisely this image of the independent author.[15]

Of Reformation may have been an ephemeral work, but it appeared to do its job. In June 1641 the 'Root and Branch' Bill to abolish episcopacy was passed by Parliament. In the following months, Milton took on Bishop Joseph Hall again. Hall had had the temerity to attack the Smectymnuans. Milton took each and every one of his arguments and systematically dismantled them all.[16] His new pamphlet was full of righteous anger, obscene references and crass puns. It reads like a dramatic speech as Milton engages with each of Hall's arguments in turn, in dialogue form, with Hall's *Remonstrance* quoted verbatim and Milton, the Answerer, punching back:

Remon: What a death it is to think of the sport and advantage these watchful enemies, these opposite spectators will be sure to make of our sin and shame?

Answ: This is but to fling and struggle under the inevitable net of God, that now begins to environ you round.

Remon: No one clergy in the whole Christian world yields so
        many eminent scholars, learned preachers, grave, holy
        and accomplished divines as this Church of England doth
        at this day.
Answer: Ha, ha, ha.
Remon: And long, and ever may it thus flourish.
Answer: O pestilent imprecation! Flourish as it does at this day in
        the Prelates?[17]

These works were developing within a culture accustomed to the
immediacy of the spoken word and the intimacy of handwritten
documents, and Milton, along with many of his contemporary
authors, had received an education rooted in performance skills and
debate. All these elements are visible in his early tracts.[18]

In August, Bishop Hall was sent to prison by Parliament,
another victory for John Milton, pamphleteer. It is no surprise
that his confidence soared at this time. He was gaining much from
his new engagement in print journalism. It was not a matter of
money. This was probably unimportant, since John was protected,
by his father's relative wealth and a regular income from property,
money-lending and investment, from the need to write for sordid
gain like other pamphlet-mongers.[19] So it was not money but a new
kind of power that Milton gained from his engagement with print
polemic.

His confidence manifested itself in very material ways. In contrast
with the pamphlets of most writers of his time, Milton's had strangely
empty margins. Most writers surrounded their main text with
numerous annotations and cross-references in order to demonstrate
their orthodoxy and their familiarity with established authorities on
the subject. Milton himself wrote, a few years later, of his own
practice, arguing that he gave his readers 'the good health of a sound
answer' rather 'than the gout and dropsy of a big margent, littered and
overlaid with crude and huddled quotations'.[20] What he was doing
with his strangely bare page was showing his authority in the *body* of
the text, without any need for nervous footnoting. His vast reading

was fully absorbed, revealing not so much his independence of mind (though it does that) as his remarkable, coherent authority.

However, just a few months after these confidence-building triumphs, Milton and those campaigning for the abolishment of episcopacy faced a setback. On 29 December 1641, in a reversal of previous policy, the bishops were allowed to return to their places in the House of Lords. They promptly ruled that no law that had been passed would stand. Milton was incensed at this backsliding and took up his pen again, writing *The Reason of Church-government Urg'd against Prelaty* over the Christmas period of 1641–2. As before, his wrath was directed at the bishops, but he also focused with intensity on the threat posed to manliness by any falling back to popish religion and politics.

> In *Reason of Church Government* Milton's most frequent charge against prelacy is that, reform it however you choose, it will inevitably lead the country back to popish slavery; his second most frequent (and related) allegation is that prelacy un-mans men. As an ecclesiastical system it promotes servility among otherwise manly Christians; it makes merchandise of men's souls and bodies; and prompts abjection and self-loathing among Christian men for whom a proper sense of self-esteem is not only healthy but soteriologically necessary.[21]

It is clear that Milton saw himself as a manly Christian. A decade or so later, he would reminisce happily about his own potency at this time: 'I brought succour to the ministers, who were, as it was said, scarcely able to withstand the eloquence of this bishop, and from that time onward, if the bishops made any response, I took a hand.'[22] He explained, clearly, his motivation and role in these years:

> Some complained of the personal defects of the bishops, others of the defectiveness of the episcopal rank itself . . . Now thoroughly aroused to these concerns, I perceived that men were following the true path to liberty and that from these beginnings, these first

steps, they were making the most direct progress towards the liberation of all human life from slavery – provided that the discipline arising from religion should overflow into the morals and institutions of the state . . . I decided, although at that time occupied with certain other matters, to devote to this conflict all my talents and all my active powers.[23]

Milton's sense of his own strength was rooted in a common analogy between the public speaker/writer and the soldier. In times of crisis and division, the orator was as good as a soldier, better indeed, since an orator could 'kill' his opponents several times over, and a well-aimed publication could do more damage than any artillery.[24] Milton, the confident print warrior, had chosen his battle, and he seemed to be winning.

Milton had found his public voice, an important part of the prescribed development of a young man. The ability to speak out set men apart from women and children, who, rather than finding a voice, were instructed, indeed coerced, to remain silent. So a young man would work on his voice production, articulation, vocabulary, forms and formulae of verbal and epistolary deference, and general principles of conversation.[25] John's education and life experience, from the disputations at Cambridge to the Italian academies, were at last coming to fruition. It was perhaps this confidence in his own abilities, in the progress he had made, that led him at thirty-three to take the next step in his life.

In the summer of 1642, John Milton married. The step is only surprising given his previous history, whether his intense relationship with Charles Diodati or his passionate advocacy of chastity. In material terms, he had everything a man needed to get married: a place to live, preferably of one's own; furnishings for house and body; prospects of an assured income in the years ahead, from land, investments, profession or trade; and ready cash for the initial costs and the ensuing babies. When a social historian comments that 'marriage defined women's status, their economic lives, and their social contacts,' and that 'for women, the moment of marital choice could be the moment of deciding an identity,' the statement can be seen to have been as true for a man, particularly a man such as John.[26] In taking a wife, he finally achieved a (rather delayed but nevertheless prestigious) identity in society.

Whether his new bride, Mary, was equally ready for marriage is another question. Putting aside for a moment the question of emotional attachment, there were some awkward social and financial issues to be resolved before the marriage could be deemed a success. Mary was the daughter of one of Milton's business associates, Richard Powell of Forest Hill. John had loaned money to Richard Powell on a regular basis for many years. In view of the fact that in England, traditionally, the couple and their parents accumulated and contributed all the assets to the new marriage, Mary Powell would have been expected to bring a marriage portion, whether an annual income or a lump sum, to complement the considerable assets that her husband provided.[27] John's new bride, so the marriage settlement said, was going to bring with her the substantial sum of £1,000.[28] The Powells, already in debt to the Miltons and with eleven children, did not in reality have the money. Moreover, since, on the whole, parents were not prepared to cripple themselves financially to pay marriage portions to daughters, Mary's parents were unlikely to descend even further into debt in order to raise the money. It is possible, however, that the Milton family had hopes that they would.[29]

Financial matters aside (and these were a vital aspect of early modern marriage), the most significant social concern was Mary's age. She was seventeen. Although in physiological terms, she might have been at an ideal age for motherhood, she was still an adolescent in the terminology of the time, in which youth for women lasted from about twelve to twenty-one. Marriage for a teenage girl was viewed as a particular challenge. The new wife would, by definition, have to leave her family home and set up a new household. Women would separate from their families of origin, would manage a separate economy, and would largely bring up and socialise their children using their own skills and resources. It was therefore essential to be self-sufficient and competent.[30] No wonder one commentator warned that 'to marry children together is the way to make whoremongers and whores.' The language here is clearly exaggerated for effect, but in general, couples did indeed marry in their mid- to late twenties, having gained the skills, resources and experience necessary to do so.

The financial and geographical position of the Powell family, and Mary's and John's ages, are the aspects of the marriage that are documented. Almost everything else is shrouded in mystery. There is no record of the ceremony, so the precise date and place remain unknown. Whether the story told by an early biographer that the poet went off to Oxfordshire on a little trip and surprised everyone by coming back with a young wife is accurate is impossible to verify.[31]

In the absence of facts, speculation abounds. Biographers suggest what a seventeen-year-old girl would have seen in a man double her age: 'One imagines it was Milton's wit, his good looks, and his musical ability that attracted her,' combined with Mary's desire to escape her 'mother's chatter', suggests A. N. Wilson. John's apparently sudden decision to marry, after many years advocating chastity, is explained by Wilson in sentimental terms: 'Instantly in love, Milton's deeply passionate nature hastened on to marry this pretty young teenager whom he hardly knew.'[32] (It is assumed that Mary is 'pretty': there is no portrait, however, and therefore, again, no evidence either way.) The author of the standard twentieth-century biography of Milton, William Riley Parker, offers a related portrait of John in his London life: 'At thirty-three, he was still a bachelor, high-minded, fastidious, and lonely.' Having 'mastered his masculinity' (sic) through his years of study, John at last knew what true love was.[33]

Perhaps; but it seems more likely that financial and broad social concerns ensured the achievement of the marriage in the first place, as was fitting in a society in which marriage was still seen in contractual and familial rather than romantic or individual terms. John and Mary's wedding, just before harvest time, linked even more securely two families already connected by financial interests. Mutual attraction, goodwill, indeed love, if they were present in the couple, were optional extras.

Following the marriage, Mary was required to set up home in Aldersgate, leaving her large household in Oxfordshire. London was still in ferment. A year earlier there may have been a sense that the military, political and religious crises would blow over, and normal monarchical business be resumed. Feeling confident in the summer of 1641, King Charles, having brokered a peace with the Scots, had received a lavish welcome back to his capital from the City aldermen. Over the coming months, he took the opportunity to launch stinging attacks on the 'irreverence of those many schismatics and separatists, wherewith of late this kingdom and this city [London] abounds . . .'[34] Milton may have insisted in *Of Reformation* that it was the corrupt system of episcopacy that was doing damage to the monarchy, but famously, Charles I, like his father, saw his own power as linked inextricably with that of his State Church: no bishop, no King. In taking on the bishops, men like Milton were in effect challenging the power of the monarch. Charles was asking for help from the City to suppress such irreverent 'schismatics and separatists'.

He did not get the assistance he sought, because of events far away from London. The Irish Rebellion began in October 1641 and destroyed the precarious stability. Propaganda in England, such as Sir John Temple's *The Irish Rebellion* published five years later, presented the Rebellion as a horrifying massacre of English settlers in Ireland. The number dead was put at 40,000, though the figure was probably closer to 4,000. The number killed was not really the point: it was the image of Catholic violence against Protestants that inflamed people brought up on a diet of anti-popery.

For years there had been growing fears about the prevalence of 'popish' practices at court and the rise of ritual in the churches of Laudian England, and regular scare stories concerning invasions from Catholic powers. The simple word *popery*, invoking the fear of foreign subjection, of anarchy and chaos, could be used to justify many causes. News of the rebellion in Ireland came at a moment when rumours of an Irish invasion were once again spreading through the country. Fearful fantasy appeared to be becoming reality.

In this climate, King Charles's demand for assistance in dealing with 'schismatics and separatists' commanded much less authority than the spectre of a Catholic-inspired invasion. When Charles, distrusted by his own Parliament, tried to raise an army to fight the Irish rebels, it prevented him doing any such thing, fearful that he would use the army for other purposes. By the closing months of 1641, Parliament was actively taking steps to control the army, instituting its own recruitment drives and musters. For generations, the Lord Lieutenants and Deputy Lieutenants in the counties had been responsible for supervising the only regular armed force in the country, known as the militia, which, in theory, consisted of every able-bodied man between the ages of sixteen and sixty. These men were expected to keep weapons (and horses as well if they were wealthy) and to bring them to annual musters organised by the Lord Lieutenants and Deputies. Although the general efficiency of the militia was known to be very poor, it was nevertheless crucial in the build-up to any conflict for each side to seize control of this potential source of men and weapons.

The King would be equally thwarted by the City of London. In the City elections of December, the ruling oligarchy was defeated, to be replaced by a faction with close ties to the parliamentary leadership. The elections were characterised by mass demonstrations in support of the policies of John Pym, the most eloquent of the parliamentarians. Further rallies ensured that bishops were not able to attend the House of Lords. In a related move, in September 1641, the work of the radical Reformation began in physical earnest: the iconoclasts commenced business. Altar rails, crucifixes and images were ripped from parish churches throughout London and beyond.

As Parliament moved to secure control of the army, they offered a 'Grand Remonstrance' of their grievances, ostensibly to the King, actually to the people. As one political moderate wrote, 'When I first heard of a Remonstrance, I presently imagined that like faithful councillors we should hold up a glass unto His Majesty . . . I did not dream that we should remonstrate downwards, tell stories to the people and talk of the King as of a third person.'[35] It was a new political era.

On 3 January 1642, King Charles attempted to move against his parliamentary opponents, targeting the group led by Pym. The plan was that five key MPs should be arrested in Parliament. The attempt ended in abject failure, with any trust that remained in the King gone.

Parliament appointed an experienced and successful soldier, Philip
Skippon, as Sergeant Major-General of the City Trained Bands. On
his very first day in the job, 11 January, Skippon and the Trained
Bands, or militias, welcomed back to Westminster the five Members of
Parliament whom King Charles had attempted to eject. Charles, now
seriously alarmed, had already retreated down the Thames to Hampton Court Palace with his Queen.

Parliament's aims were simple. They wished to remove evil councillors, control the military, and eject the bishops from the House of
Lords. There was popular support for their aims, and not just in
London. On 11 January, the people of Buckinghamshire (or 4,000 to
5,000 of them) presented a petition supporting the reforms, followed
by representatives from Warwickshire and other counties. These huge
marches were impressive and threatening, with London becoming
more politically explosive with each passing month.

John Milton's engagement with the conflicts of his time was
therefore representative of a much larger religious and political
mobilisation. Print was the lifeblood of this increasingly politicised
public, and new forms emerged to record and incite the conflicts. The
newsbook was one such, evolving from the purely commercial 'corantos', single broadsheets that conveyed news and had been in
circulation since 1620. Corantos were seen as unreliable and dangerous by the political establishment, used to controlling all news. The
courtier John Chamberlain wrote in 1622 that corantos contained
material that 'the common people know not how to understand,' yet
still appeared 'every week (at least)' with 'all manner of news, and as
strange stuff as any we have from Amsterdam'.[36] Now, in the 1640s,
news became a political tool, printed in a new form, the newsbook: a
regular, rather than sporadic, publication, with a consistent number of
pages, and an unchanging, short title.[37] This new medium was
exploited to full effect by Parliament, with newsbooks actively sponsored by the Pym circle that so threatened King Charles. If anything,
newsbooks and their writers were even less respectable than pamphlets and pamphleteers, with journalists caricatured as men who would
pick up the excrement that other books let fall.[38] The typical news-

book writer was caricatured as sexually immoral and religiously suspect: he would even go shopping on a Sunday. But the new medium did not need to be highly respected. It was politically effective, and that is what counted. The political landscape had changed forever with the conscious use of cheap print by those who sought to oppose first the bishops and then the King's policies, if not the King himself.

Of course, the avalanche of cheap print did not consist entirely of politically and religiously motivated works. A quick glance at some of the titles published at this time suggests that readers were as interested in strange disasters and self-help as they were in the crisis in episcopacy. Alongside sermons (*The power of love: a sermon*, London, 1643) and political/military tracts (*The city of London's resolution . . . concerning their loyalty to the King and their love . . . to the parliament. Together with a command from the House of peers concerning the stopping of ammunition in the northern road*, London, 1642), there also appeared sensationalist accounts of violent death (*Strange and horrible news which happened betwixt St John's Street and Islington . . . being a terrible murther committed by one of Sir Sander Duncome's beares*, London, 1642) and advice for the single man (*The godly man's choice: or A direction how single godly persons, who intend marriage, may make a choice of a fit and meet yoak-fellow*, by Caleb Grantham, 1644). Writers, printers and book-sellers competed with each other, both for their share of the new market and for the hearts and minds of their readers. John Milton, for one, learned a few tricks: one way to deprive your political or religious opponent of sales would be to quote his entire tract in order to present disagreements with it. No need, therefore, for the reader to bother buying the original.[39]

Print proliferated because almost every opinion generated a response, which in turn necessitated a counter-response from the maligned author. When the Smectymnuans, for example, attacked Bishop Hall, he replied, condemning their views, to which their response was a 219-page answer. The speed of these exchanges was often remarkable. Milton's own first pamphlet on Church reform received a reply within days of its publication. Vicious abuse of one's opponents characterised much of the debate. When in May 1642, around the time of his marital expedition to Oxfordshire, Milton wrote *An Apology against a Pamphlet* (in itself a response to a response), he claimed to be furious at the way he had been personally attacked. Immersed as he was in this world of cheap print, he cannot have been genuinely surprised. Colourful, personal and at times obscene invective was the order of the day, the religious and political pamphlets picking up the techniques of the earlier forms of popular writing, whether ballads or jestbooks, almanacs or tales.

In June 1643, however, Parliament sought to stem the tide by reintroducing licensing in its Printing Ordinance. It was an act of defiance, therefore, when John's next print campaign opened, in the summer of the year following his marriage, with the publication of an unlicensed, unregistered pamphlet that appeared without an author's name, without a preface and carrying merely the initials of its printers. Only the crucial information as to where readers could buy the pamphlet, Goldsmiths Alley, was included. Buyers there were: the first print run in August 1643 of at least 1,200 copies sold out. A second edition, double in size, appeared just six months after the first, in February of the following year. This time Milton put his initials to the front page and gave his full name in the preface, but there was still no mention of a book-seller or printer. For this second edition, he explicitly announced that his work had been published in defiance of the Printing Ordinance, claiming also that he had honestly attempted to get it licensed and failed to do so.

The new pamphlet was ostensibly addressed to two audiences, Parliament and the Westminster Assembly of Divines. The latter was the Presbyterian council that had taken over the running of the State Church after episcopacy had been abolished. The Assembly was busy at this time considering just how the Church could and should be reformed, and one of their principal concerns was the extent to which canon law would operate within the Reformed (Presbyterian) Church of England. Milton was offering his perspective on the issue. So far, so conventional, with the author merely continuing with his concern for Reformation of the Church. There was nothing conventional, however, about the content of the pamphlet, Milton's notorious *Doctrine and Discipline of Divorce*.

NINE

DIVORCE

1642

D IVORCE WAS A TABOO SUBJECT.[1] Not content with merely raising it, Milton, remarkably, used his pamphlet to advocate a relaxation of the law. This was to fly in the face of centuries of tradition and, what is more, to do so at a time when fears of social collapse were running high. Daniel Rogers, for example, writing about marriage in 1642, was dismayed to see (or imagine) couples 'of all sorts . . . abandoning each other by law or lawless divorce', a phenomenon he claimed to see occurring at all levels of society.[2] The blame was placed squarely on the wives' shoulders. Women were refusing to work at marriage since 'if so be they cannot agree upon everything, then straight nothing but separation.' The reality was that formal separation, let alone divorce, was almost impossible for the vast majority of women and men, but reality could not compete with mythic fear. The vision of women abandoning their husbands was a potent symbol of a society that could not 'agree upon everything'. As often happens, when all else is crumbling, traditional family values are policed all the more rigorously.

Milton was taking on some of the fundamental beliefs of his Church in his new work. One of the reasons that divorce was not permitted, except in truly exceptional circumstances, was that Jesus Christ denounced the practice. In the Old Testament Book of Deuteronomy (24:1–2), a husband is instructed that he can 'send' his wife 'out of his house' if she has 'some uncleanness'. Christ, however, states explicitly in Matthew 5:31–2 that if a husband should 'put away' his wife, then he will be committing adultery and encouraging the wife to do so too. The only exception would be if the woman had committed 'fornication'.

Milton, in order to justify divorce on any ground other than a woman's infidelity, had to challenge Christ's revision of Deuteronomy. So he returned to Hebraic law and argued that the original phrases in Deuteronomy do indeed express God's intentions because they link so well with God's vision of marriage in Genesis 2:18, a vision that is not focused on the sexual act. So, in *The Doctrine and Discipline of Divorce*, he argues that God 'in the first ordaining of marriage taught us to what end he did it, in words expressly implying the apt and cheerful conversation of man with woman, to comfort and refresh him against the evil of solitary life, not mentioning the purpose of generation till afterwards'.[3] The issue of sexual relations and therefore adultery is immediately relegated in importance, clearing a space for Milton to claim that the permitted cause of divorce in Deuteronomy has been mistranslated as 'some un-cleanness'. Instead

> in the Hebrew it sounds *nakedness of ought, or any real nakedness:* which by all the learned interpreters is referred to the mind, as well as to the body. And what greater nakedness or unfitness of mind than that which hinders ever the solace and peaceful couple, and what hinders that more than the unfitness and defectiveness of an unconjugal mind.[4]

At one stroke, Milton expands the idea of 'uncleanness' to include 'unfitness of mind'. He then returns to Genesis and clinches his argument by appealing to God's avowed purpose in joining woman to man:

> And what his chief end was of creating woman to be joined with man, his own instituting words declare, and are infallible to inform us what is marriage, and what is no marriage; unless we can think them set there to no purpose: *It is not good,* saith he, *that man should be alone; I will make him a help meet for him.* From which words so plain, less cannot be concluded, nor is by any learned interpreter, than that

THE
DOCTRINE
AND DISCIPLINE
OF
DIVORCE:
RESTOR'D TO THE GOOD
OF BOTH SEXES,

From the bondage of Canon Law,
and other mistakes, to Christian freedom,
guided by the Rule of Charity.

Wherein also many places of Scripture, have
recover'd their long-lost meaning.

Seasonable to be now thought on in the
Reformation intended.

MATTH. 13. 52.

*Every Scribe instructed to the Kingdome of Heav'n, is like the Maister
of a house which bringeth out of his treasurie things old and new.*

LONDON,

Printed by *T. P.* and *M. S.* In Goldsmiths
Alley. 1 6 4 3.

in God's intention a meet and happy conversation is the chiefest and noblest end of marriage; for we find here no expression so necessarily implying carnal knowledge, as this prevention of loneliness to the mind and spirit of man.[5]

Having established that God intended 'meet and happy conversation' to be the foundation of a good marriage (rather than sexual fidelity), it only remained to prove that Jesus did not intend to contradict God in the Gospels. Milton argued that Christ was at the time reprimanding the Pharisees for their attitude towards the law and therefore used exaggeration to make his point.

In making this argument, Milton had to attack 'this great and sad oppression' of the 'strictness of a literal interpreting'. These literal interpretations of Scripture, he claimed, overburdened, indeed overwhelmed, many Christians. This was an important step in Milton's thinking, as the scholar Barbara Lewalski points out. Previously in his tracts against episcopacy he made the basic assumption, following a core Protestant belief, that there was a single sense of Scripture easily understood by the elect, by those who had been selected by divine will for salvation. By the time of his divorce tract, according to Lewalski, his 'primary interpretative touchstone [was] the essential spirit of the gospel, charity'.[6] Milton was asking his readers to think about Christ's intention rather than his precise words, a step that opened up the act of interpretation in profound ways.

In *The Doctrine and Discipline of Divorce*, therefore, Milton distanced himself from 'obstinate literality', from what could be called a fundamentalist religious position, at least with regard to the Bible. In defending divorce, he had to challenge the pronouncements of the two most important figures in conventional Protestant thinking, Christ and St Paul. In doing so, he moved towards a more monist, or anti-Trinitarian, belief, perhaps even towards a more Hebraic understanding of God, one which placed the pronouncements of Moses (the word of God) above those of Paul (who was just Paul).[7]

The extent to which Milton was willing to modify his previous understanding of scriptural truth is an indication of the strength of his feelings about the necessity of divorce. He did not, however, need to modify one of his other most dearly held beliefs, that of the superiority of chastity over sexual activity, in order to back up his arguments. Since it was generally believed that if divorce was made easier, there would be an increase in sexual immorality, he worked hard to emphasise that he was not, in any way, advocating a relaxation in strict sexual propriety. Instead, he was arguing that sexual infidelity should not be the *only* reason for a marriage to be deemed to have failed. For Milton, compatibility was the key. Without compatibility, sex was, in any case, a mechanical and deeply unpleasant act: husband and wife 'grind in the mill of an undelighted and servile copulation', 'two carcasses chain'd unnaturally together'.

The venom with which John Milton denigrated the sexual act perhaps says more about the author than his argument. Sex between men and women was the 'promiscuous draining of a carnal rage', the 'quintessence of excrescence', a 'carnal performance'. Sexual relations were seen as an utterly repellent transaction between men and women. The man's semen was paid out to the woman, extorted from his body. Semen was the 'best substance of his body, and of his soul too', and the poor man did not even get 'recompense'. There is certainly no celebration of loving sex, of an act that might be delighted and non-servile. When he returned to the theme of divorce in a later tract, *Colasterion,* Milton did defend the 'amiable and attractive society of conjugal love, besides the deed of procreation, which of it self soon cloys, and is despis'd, unless it bee cherished and re-incited with a pleasing conversation'.[8] He was arguing that in and of itself, the sexual act is soon despised, and that it needs 'pleasing conversation' to make the 'deed of procreation' bearable.

It is perhaps no surprise that Milton's ideal model of married life involved the woman becoming as similar to the man as possible. His vision of companionate marriage was of a kind of manly friendship, possibly modelled on that described by Socrates in Plato's *Symposium,* at heart 'a same-sex model of ideal companionship'.[9] It is a kind of back-handed compliment that these works suggest that women might be capable of imitating these ideal manly friendships, but Milton did, by implication, help to create a modern understanding of companionate marriage.

Although his particular emphasis was unique, Milton was not alone in his concern to celebrate friendship within marriage. Popular works exhorted husbands and wives to 'be as two sweet friends', while reminding husbands that they 'must not enjoin your wife' to do things 'unmeet in themselves, or against her mind'.[10] Ballads such as 'Hold your hands, honest Men' encouraged husbands to withhold violence, while songs like 'Keep a Good Tongue in your Head' reminded women to keep quiet whatever happened. For men might be exhorted to moderate their violence towards their wives, but the reality for many women was that if they were married to a man who abused them, there was little that could be done to prevent it. The experience of the three wives of one Rowland Muckleston of Myddle, a 'man of bold and daring spirit' (or, put more bluntly, a violent man), illustrates this graphically. His first wife was 'a quiet, low-spirited woman' who accepted his total domination and died young. His second wife was of a 'masculine spirit, and would not suffer him to intermeddle with her concerns within doors'. This predictably led to severe and violent quarrels: the husband lost an eye, but eventually the wife lost her life. Muckleston's third wife was a widow, a woman who had therefore experienced some degree of independence. This marriage ended in stalemate and eventual separation, with the widow going to live with her grown-up children. The prevalence of these kinds of small, domestic tragedies had encouraged Protestant thinkers in continental Europe to advocate divorce for women as protection against abusive husbands. Milton may have argued, radically for his time, that both men and women should be free to marry again after divorce. Never the less he remained unconcerned about the plight of women trapped in abusive marriages.

For, fundamental to his arguments is Milton's basic belief that men are superior to women. After all, he asks, '. . . who can be ignorant that woman was created for man, and not man for woman,' complacently echoing the misogyny of St Paul, who reminded his early Christian readers that only men are made in the image of God. Having had to demolish many central biblical arguments to make his case for divorce, Milton was on much more conventional ground when it came to man's natural, God-given, power over woman. The title page of *The Doctrine and Discipline of Divorce* may state that if the doctrine was restored, it would be 'to the good of both sexes', but the emphasis throughout, from Adam in his 'unkindly solitariness' to the present day, is on the man's predicament.

Casual misogyny was the bedrock of Milton's society. A lively tradition of humorous ballads on the subject of wife-beating was one side of the coin. Take, for example, the tale of the drunkard who beat his scolding wife and broke her arm. When asked why he had paid the bone-setter double the fee requested, he joked that he would break her other arm next time and so was paying in advance. The other side of the coin was the celebration of that immensely rare item, a virtuous woman. As the pamphlet *A Strange Wonder or a Wonder in a Woman* (1642) reminded its readers, it was possible to find a good woman, but among 'many thousands . . . you shall scarce find one that is not guilty of one abominable crime or another'. Put bluntly, as social historian Bernard Capp does, a 'sketch of the gender order in early modern England will suggest a regime deeply misogynistic, the product of male contempt, fear, and self-interest packaged as principle'; the primary aim of all writing on marriage was 'to secure male authority, not to compromise it'.

Despite his apparent liberal intent, this is precisely what Milton sought to do in *The Doctrine of Discipline and Divorce*: to secure male authority. He argued that

> the freedom and eminence of man's creation gives him to be a Law in this matter to himself, being the head of the other sex which was made for him: whom therefore though he ought not to injure, yet neither should he be forced to retain in society to his own overthrow, nor to hear any judge therein above himself.[11]

To make it easier for men to divorce their wives would make men masters of themselves again. This in turn was all part of the great project of reform, as he reminds one of his audiences, Parliament, in the preface to the pamphlet:

> Ye have now, doubtless by the savour and appointment of God, ye have now in your hands a great and populous Nation to Reform; from what corruption, what blindness in Religion ye know well; in what a degenerate and fallen spirit from the apprehension of native liberty, and true manliness I am sure ye find: with what unbounded licence rushing to whoredoms and adulteries needs not long enquiry . . .[12]

In a later pamphlet on the same theme, *Tetrachordon*, he claims that 'nothing now adays is more degenerately forgotten, than the true dignity of Man, almost in every respect, but especially in this prime institution of Matrimony, wherein his native pre-eminence ought most to shine.'[13]

Underlying this insistence on 'true manliness' and men's 'native pre-eminence' is a radical political argument. The political dimension to Milton's arguments about divorce would have been apparent to his first readers, brought up to understand the ideological and practical interconnectedness of family and State. The political was the personal in the seventeenth century, and imagined in those terms. So, the King was the Father of his people. The husband was the head of the household, which in turn was a microcosm of the State. Milton, building on the Protestant understanding of marriage as a covenant between two people rather than a sacrament, argued that if one of those who made the covenant was deeply unhappy or lonely, then the purpose of the marriage had not been achieved. Milton took a conventional model (the idea of tyranny, for example, was used to provide a check on husbands, with most writers balancing their assertion of men's authority with a denunciation of domestic tyranny) and ran with it in radical political directions.

For husband and wife, read Parliament and King, also in covenant with each other rather than joined in sacramental mystery: Milton linked the two worlds metaphorically, arguing that 'no effect of tyranny can sit more heavy on the Common-wealth, then this household unhappiness on the family.' It may have been no coincidence that Milton also took the opportunity to criticise marriages in which the husband and wife were not of the same religious persuasion: Put most crudely, Catholic wives doomed good Protestant marriages to failure, a point made again, if more subtly, in *Tetrachordon*, in which a marriage 'where the religion is contrary' is seen as deeply problematic.[14] The hint is that the reader only had to look at his King to see an example.

First and foremost, however, Milton was arguing that those who were unhappily married were useless to society. They were 'unserviceable and spiritless to the Common-wealth' or, as he put it in *Tetrachordon*, 'unactive to all public service, dead to the Common-wealth'. The crucial point was that a man had to be useful to society, and a man trapped in an unhappy marriage could not be useful. Considered in this context, Milton's myopia about the position of women is understandable, if not laudable. Why should he have argued that women should have the same right to divorce as men when there was no possibility of a woman being useful to the Common-wealth? His claims for male superiority over women, his suggestion that men's powers were being eroded and needed reclaiming, reveal Milton's gender politics as rooted in the political franchise of his time.

If Milton was merely reasserting the patriarchal values of his own society, trying to shore up threatened male powers, then why did these tracts on divorce provoke such a strong response in his contemporaries? His pamphlets were denounced in sermons, vigorous attempts were made to suppress them, and the list of their author's enemies (at least in print) grew rapidly, from the Bishop of Exeter to leading Presbyterian parliamentarians.

John Milton was hated because, to many of his early readers, he appeared to be arguing for complete sexual freedom, for a world in which 'the bonds of matrimony are let loose to inordinate lust.'[15] And this in a country riven by civil war, in which prostitutes travelled openly with the armies, in which men went to the wars never to be seen again. (Charles I, ever the idealist, put out a proclamation in July 1643 aimed at dissuading his soldiers from using prostitutes. It seems the proclamation was ignored.)

The divorce tracts were therefore viewed as merely engineering yet further immorality, and their author was consigned to the lunatic fringe by his enemies. Now John Milton was simply another representative of the religious sects who were beginning to emerge in the early 1640s. These multifarious sects were joined only in their insistence upon the primacy of the inner spirit of every individual and their hostility to the State Church. Suddenly, Milton was an extremist. *The Doctrine and Discipline of Divorce* conferred notoriety on him, previously merely one voice among many on the more conventional subject of episcopal reform.

What is remarkable is that, despite the overwhelmingly hostile response to *The Doctrine and Discipline of Divorce*, Milton kept to his theme, repeating and developing his arguments in successive tracts over the following years. There were four editions of *The Doctrine* in total, with two appearing in 1645, and the proliferation of editions suggests that this pamphlet at least was selling, and selling in thousands, not hundreds. In the summer of 1644, Milton would offer a new translation of the work of Martin Bucer, a German Protestant reformer active in the religious conflicts of the first half of the sixteenth century, who had found a home in England at the court of the Protestant King Edward VI.[16] The Bucer translation, put with some extracts from the great Humanist scholar Erasmus, were designed to bolster Milton's own arguments concerning divorce. He was seeking to show Parliament and a wider readership that he was 'no forger of new and loose opinions'. Finally, almost two years into the campaign, in March 1645, and facing ever more hostile responses, he published *Tetrachordon* and *Colasterion* together, blending measured and rational argument with aggressive abuse of his newfound enemies.

These enemies included Herbert Palmer, who denounced *The Doctrine and Discipline of Divorce* in a sermon to Parliament, and William Prynne, who attacked Milton for advocating 'divorce at pleasure'.[17] Milton was, however, utterly determined to speak out, despite his layman status and despite the State's attempts to control printing. Taking on the voice and authority of the Old Testament prophet Josiah, who did that which was right in the eyes of the Lord at a time when the Law was suffering, Milton insisted that he did not need to be a man of the Church to take on his topic: 'I want [i.e. lack] neither pall nor mitre, I stay neither for ordination nor induction'. 'In the firm faith of a knowing Christian' truth will be spoken.

Milton may have been speaking truth to those in power, but he was also speaking from bitter personal experience. For, in August 1642, Mary Powell Milton left her husband John after only a few weeks of marriage and went home to her family in Oxfordshire. This single event is possibly one of the most misrepresented and misunderstood moments in John Milton's life. In the absence of any concrete, historical evidence, every generation has been quick to fill in their own version of John and Mary's short-lived marriage. Perhaps the most pervasive image is that of a man hated by women (a month was enough for Mary, poor girl). More subtle, but equally speculative, is the vision of an innocent, intellectual John Milton, out of his depth with women. Milton himself is entirely silent concerning his relationship with his wife, unless the divorce tracts are to be read as starkly autobiographical texts. The earliest biographers, including John's own nephew, are notoriously vague on the subject, but all at least agree that Mary did indeed return to her family soon after the marriage. The most neutral account has her simply wishing to go home because her friends expressed a desire to see her, the plan being that she would spend the rest of the summer in Oxfordshire before rejoining her new husband in the City.

That Mary left London and returned to Oxfordshire is clear. Why she did so is not. Among the broader social issues that might have hindered the success of the marriage was Mary's youth. Suddenly at seventeen, she was expected to take over the management of a large house in the city, with all the necessary accompanying domestic tasks taking place in an urban environment, rather than the self-sufficient rural estate in which she had grown up.[18] The City of London presented an alien environment even if she had spent time in the city of Oxford, a few miles from her home. London, more particularly Aldersgate, suited her husband, but Mary Powell Milton may well have been, in practical terms, out of her depth, emotionally isolated and physically disorientated.

Her youth aside, any incomer to London was likely to feel overwhelmed by the new experience of urban living. Whereas outside the city walls, there might be fifteen houses per acre, inside the density might be as high as ninety-five. With the recent surge in population, open spaces had been increasingly built over and large buildings subdivided into thin-walled tenements, exacerbating the sense of overcrowding. Mary's new world was a complicated network of streets, alleys and courts, a confusing mass of shops backed by kitchens and yards. In this environment, most people had relatively short personal histories, and one's neighbours might be unknown quantities. Newcomers, previously used to small, stable, rural communities, had to adapt to a life in which they were sharing the public spaces of the street with people whose families and histories were unknown to them. At the same time they lived in unusually close quarters with these strangers. Predictably, there were very public discussions of neighbours' lives, in particular the issue of sexual honour, as these rapidly changing communities tried to place newcomers.[19] The City thus offered a challenging combination of anonymity and closeness. Add to this the unprecedented instability in the City at this time of acute civil unrest, and it could be argued that many a new bride would have been unsettled.

However difficult these early weeks in Aldersgate were for the new Mrs Milton, it was nevertheless an extreme and highly public step to return to her family so soon. Worse still, she showed no readiness to return to her husband and London. This is the more remarkable because, while in many societies a woman is entitled to family support from her kin group after a divorce or separation, in seventeenth-century England the position was very different. Once joined in marriage, and therefore to another family, there was, in theory, no kin group to return to. A woman's brothers, parents or more distant kin had no responsibility to shelter and maintain her, or her children if there were any. Once married, a woman was under the absolute *couverture* and power of her husband.[20] If, in extreme circumstances, a woman was pushed to abandon the marriage altogether, there was no guarantee that her relatives would take her in, since by offering shelter, they could be prosecuted for detaining a woman from her lawful husband. For this reason as much as any other, a woman's family usually encouraged her to return to her husband, whatever dangers lay ahead. If the matter went to court, the response was similar.[21] Her status ensured that she stood outside the law, with her husband retaining all rights over her property and income, and the woman unable to conduct a legal action by herself or have a claim on access to her children.[22] Despite all this, Mary headed home to Oxfordshire, and her family took her back.

Whatever the reasons for Mary's departure, events in the country as a whole would ensure that this particular pair of newlyweds would have little chance of patching up their differences. The nation was preparing for war. A military conflict had been likely since June, when the war of words between the King and Parliament had become yet more intense, fuelled by unprecedented public debate. King Charles had responded to Parliament's demands by offering them a terrifying vision of popular revolution: the common people would be encouraged

> to set up for themselves, call parity and independence liberty, devour that estate which had devoured the rest, destroy all rights and properties, all distinctions of family and merit, and by this means this splendid and excellently distinguished form of government end in a dark, unequal chaos of confusion, and the long line of our many noble ancestors in a Jack Cade or Wat Tyler.[23]

Parliament remained undaunted, and, in a radical step, its Ordinance of March 1642 (unsigned by the King) argued that, in the interest of His Majesty's safety, and in the face of a threat from 'Papists', the Lord Lieutenants of the counties were authorised to assemble and call together all those who were 'meet and fit for wars, and them to train and exercise and put in readiness'. King Charles responded two months later with a Royal proclamation condemning the Ordinance and promising retribution on all those who obeyed Parliament's illegal command.[24] In London, a battle for the control of the assembled armed bands raged through the winter and spring of 1642. Parliament, and its nominated military leader Philip Skippon, won out, increasing the number of men at their service to 8,000 and organising the first general muster of the reformed Trained Bands in Finsbury Fields, an event that represented a carefully orchestrated display of parliamentary firepower. It involved a celebration attended by thousands of Londoners, with members of both Houses of Parliament entertained lavishly at the City's expense.[25] By June, Parliament was seeking out 'defaulters', those who did not support its cause. In these conditions, small details of daily life suddenly became significant – the length of one's hair, for example, short hair becoming a notable symbol of parliamentary allegiance. A pamphlet of 1644, *A Gag for Long Haired Rattleheads who revile all civil Roundheads*, traced a connection between long hair and 'pride, lust, wantonness, effeminacy' through a bizarre series of ancient and modern examples.[26] London was no longer a safe place for those who supported the King, or even those who had their doubts about Parliament's military ambitions.

Then, on 13 August 1642, King Charles I issued a Royal proclamation calling for the University of Oxford to place the city in which it was located, only a handful of miles from Mary Powell Milton's family home, in a state of defence. All this was only preparation. On 22 August the King raised his standard at Nottingham, formally declaring hostilities. Civil war had begun.

Although there had been skirmishes all over the country during the preceding months as bands of men tried to get hold of ammunition stores, most famously in Hull and Manchester, and individuals had to decide their allegiance, there remained a deep-seated reluctance underlying all these actions, with few expressing open enthusiasm for war. Crucially, 'the language of politics for so long had been couched in terms of king *and* parliament, that it took an enormous mental adjustment to come to grips with the concept of a parliament in arms against a king.'[27] The death of 5,000 men at the battle of Edgehill on 23 October 1642 meant that no one could ignore the reality: the country was at war with itself. King Charles had been attempting to march on London, to regain his capital. The parliamentary forces intercepted the King's army, more by luck than by judgement, at an escarpment, Edgehill, between Kineton and Banbury. It was a vicious day of fighting, Englishman against Englishman, acts of bravery and military prowess occurring alongside errors and confusion. At the end of the day, the two armies retired. In the morning, neither side wanted to continue. Both sides, predictably, claimed victory. The Earl of Essex and his army retreated to Warwick Castle. The road to London was undefended. The King moved inexorably towards his capital, claiming the towns of Banbury, Oxford (where he set up his court) and, a few days later, Reading. London would be next.

These were the terrible conditions under which, it seems, John Milton asked his wife to return to London. The city was gripped with fear at the prospect of the return of its King. Shops closed, prayer meetings were called, barricades went up, and the rumour mill went into overtime, with tales of atrocities committed by Charles's forces circulating through the streets. Then London mobilised. On 13 November, the London Trained Bands, led by Skippon, mustered at Turnham Green, a village west of London.

That they could do so gave an indication of the fusion of parliamentary, City and military groupings in the preceding months.[28] Armed with their staffs, pikes, muskets and swords, the Trained Bands waited for their King at Turnham Green. By mid-November, there were 24,000 London soldiers stationed there. As had happened earlier, in the First Bishops' War, Charles's military judgement failed him. He could have retaken his capital. He could have at least *tried* to retake his capital. Instead, he retreated, leading his forces back to Hounslow, then Reading, and at last to his court in Oxford. Turnham Green was the battle that never was, demonstrating once again the reluctance of both sides to engage, for while Charles was unwilling to take on the Trained Bands, they in turn allowed him to return to Oxford.

It is not surprising, therefore, that Mary Powell Milton remained in her family home through this winter of violence and upheaval. One of the earliest biographies of Milton, by John Aubrey, recognises the reality of these wartime conditions. Aubrey dismisses any idea that

Mary was unfaithful to her husband but feels sympathy for John: '. . . what man (especially contemplative) would like to have a young wife environed & stormed by the sons of Mars and those of the enemy party.'[29] Violence against women was and remains a hidden tragedy of war, and Aubrey saw Mary as a potential victim, unprotected by her bookish husband.

Commentators on both sides of the political divide recounted appalling events: war 'enforceth the Mother to behold the Ravishment of her own Daughter'. In Somerset it was reported that Royalist soldiers arrived in a village and demanded the services of a woman. In fear, the villagers handed over a particular woman who was 'given to them all'. In the morning, the woman was ostracised by the village.[30] Even if the stories were exaggerated for propaganda purposes, the climate of fear they generated was very real. It was no time for Mary to travel to London.

Another early biographer spells out the impact of the Civil War upon the marriage. It faltered because the Powell family were 'generally addicted to the Cavalier party' – that is, were supporters of the King.[31] This makes a lot of sense in an era when a marriage was never merely between two individuals, but it raises an important and problematic question. Why did neither the Miltons nor the Powells see this coming?

One answer might be that in 1642 it was quite possible to be anti-episcopal (as John Milton certainly was) without seeking to challenge in any explicit way the power of the King. Precisely how and when Milton's politics became more radical vexes scholars even now. It seems plausible that the Powell family, and possibly Milton himself, had no idea just how extreme his politics would become in the following years. Moreover, no one knew, although some feared, in the summer of 1642 that the stand-off between Parliament and the King would escalate into outright civil war.[32]

A strange little poem from 1642 seems to offer a glimpse of Milton's response to wartime conditions without offering any explicit indication of his political allegiances. It is a sonnet, in English, addressed to 'Captain or colonel, or knight in arms', and subtitled 'When the assault was intended to the City'. It is a plea from Milton to whichever member of the military might come to get him, whether captain, colonel or knight. The poem's message is apparently simple: the captain or colonel can take the poet's house but should save the poet, because the 'defenceless' poet has the power to confer fame:

> him within protect from harms,
> He can requite thee, for he knows the charms
> That call fame on such gentle acts as these,
> And he can spread thy name o'er lands and seas.
>
> (ll. 4–7)

Somebody, not Milton, added a note to the manuscript copy to say that the sonnet was pinned 'on his door'. Whether or not the poem was indeed pinned to the door of the house in Aldersgate, there is a highly self-conscious literary game going on in this little verse, which invokes Milton's literary hero, Euripides, in the final lines:

> Lift not thy spear against the muses' bower,
> The great Emathian conqueror bid spare
> The house of Pindarus, when temple and tower
> Went to the ground: and the repeated air
> Of sad Electra's poet had the power
> To save the Athenian walls from ruin bare.
>
> (ll. 9–14)

This refers to a story, told by the Roman historian Plutarch, that a man was heard singing the first chorus from Euripides' *Electra* when Athens was being attacked. All hearers melted with compassion and refused to destroy a city that had produced such great men.

In Milton's sonnet, therefore, London is Athens, and its author is both the singer *of* Euripides and Euripides himself. The hope is that the poet will not only survive 'the assault' himself but save his city. 'Running through the whole allusion is the delighted emulation of Euripides, alike as poet and as citizen and human being,' writes the critic John Hale. Delighted emulation is certainly present but so is fear, masked but not entirely concealed as urbane Classical wit.[33]

TEN

CENSORSHIP

1644

E ARLY IN THE NEW YEAR, it was announced that no travel would
be permitted between London and Oxford. By this stage, however, it was evident that a further divide existed between Mary and
John. The Powell family were committed to the cause of the King,
Mary's brother Richard already working as an intelligence agent for
the Royalist forces. The situation in Oxford was as fraught as it was in
London, the University city filling with refugees, including those who
opposed Parliament. Meanwhile, by the spring of 1643, the city of
Reading had become the new war zone, and John's brother Christopher and his young family were there. Christopher, unlike his brother,
openly supported the King, his name on the muster roll of October
1642 showing him committed to furnishing arms and supplies to the
Royalist armies.

Reading fell to parliamentary forces on 27 April 1643 after several
months of siege during which Christopher's wife, Thomasina, moved
with their children to London, to her mother's house. Thomasina was
pregnant, and her son John, Milton's newest nephew, would be born
there in June. After the fall of the city, Christopher was forced to leave
Reading (where it appears that his property was seized by parliamentary forces) and travelled west, via Wells, to Exeter.[1]

At some point in the midst of all this upheaval, John Milton Sr also
made the journey to London. Christopher's household in Reading was
just too dangerous; his son John's house in Aldersgate would be safer.
There life continued as normal in many respects, despite (or because
of) the continued absence of Mary. When the poet looked back at this

period in his life, he referred only to his desire to find a 'place to become established, could I but find one anywhere in such upset and tumultuous times', presumably a reference to civil war rather than his marital problems.[2] In the meantime, while waiting for the unlikely reform of canon law that was needed for a divorce, life still needed to be lived, and one of the early biographers writes that 'our author, now as it were a single man again, made it his chief diversion, now and then in an Evening to visit the Lady Margaret Lee [Ley]', a woman of 'great wit and ingenuity'.[3] Lady Margaret was the wife of a parliamentary captain called Hobson, and the couple were Milton's neighbours in Aldersgate Street.

This faint hint that neighbours John and Margaret diverted each other while *his* wife Mary remained in Oxford and *her* husband was risking his life for the defence of the city has troubled more recent biographers, who have rushed to reassure readers that although the relationship led to something 'beyond social friendship', it 'almost certainly' did not lead 'given Milton's strict principles, to an affair'.[4] Given John's personal history up to this point, at least with regard to women, the reassurance seems unnecessary. Moreover, although Milton did write a poem for 'honoured Margaret' at about this time (it would be published in 1645), his sonnet shows little interest in Margaret in and of herself, and is instead utterly concerned with her status as the daughter of a politician, James Ley, whose death was, hints the sonnet, hastened by King Charles's actions, which were 'fatal to liberty' and to Ley.

It seems unlikely that, in the continued absence of Mary, John Milton turned to another woman. Instead, he committed himself more and more to his teaching. In Aldersgate, he gained a new student, Cyriack Skinner, in addition to his two nephews, whom he continued to teach and to raise. This role was obviously important to Milton, and after completing his writings on Church Reform, and in the midst of the wars (both the pamphlet wars raging over his divorce tracts, and the military battles around the country) he found time to write a short but compelling tract outlining his vision of education. This was a thoroughly respectable work compared to the divorce pamphlets. Published on 11 July 1644, the piece was even formally registered for publication.

Of Education engages with the European Protestant debate about education, particularly the ideas of Samuel Hartlib (to whom the tract is addressed). Broadly speaking, Milton advocates a child-centred theory of education, arguing that boys, being young, have 'empty wits' and should not be forced to write what they cannot understand. Such work is 'wrung from poor striplings, like blood out of the nose, or the plucking of untimely fruit'. But, as with divorce, Milton proves less liberal than many continental Protestant thinkers who advocated pleasurable education for all, boys and girls, able and 'dull'. In contrast, he wants to produce 'steadfast pillars of the State', in contrast to the current crop of 'poor shaken uncertain reeds, of such a tottering conscience', and is therefore only concerned with boys and men. Milton's devotion to the idea of the useful (and by definition male) public citizen blinds him to some other possibilities in his own argument.

Underpinning Milton's arguments is the optimistic religious conviction that although all men are sinful, ruined by 'our first parents' Adam and Eve, it is possible through education to 'know God aright, and out of that knowledge to love him, to imitate him, to be like him, as we may the nearest, by possessing our souls of true virtue, which, being united to the heavenly grace of faith, makes up the highest perfection'. These arguments are related to the wartime conditions in which *Of Education* was produced, with dark comments on a nation perishing for lack of education, and hopeful visions of education leading to 'honest living with much more peace'. The curriculum envisaged is wide-ranging, from agriculture to weapons training, from the study of harbours and ports to wrestling.[5] With its emphasis on fresh air and nature, Milton's tract offers his country a bold and idealistic vision of a complete education of mind and body. Young men, when they are 'unsweating', should learn music, while the study of poetry, 'simple, sensuous, and passionate' poetry, can show a young man 'what religious, what glorious and magnificent use might be made of poetry, both in divine and human things'. Music and poetry together can make manners and dispositions 'smooth', 'make them gentle from rustic harshness and distempered passions'. As ever, the ideal is gentility through urbanity, something John Milton believed his own education had, eventually, achieved.

Of Education is a real joy to read, very different in tone and purpose from the divorce tracts written during the same period. When making a consistent and positive case for something he was truly committed to – the importance to the nation of an all-round education for boys and young men – Milton could relax into accessible, vigorous and coherent prose.

> I call therefore a complete and generous education that which fits a man to perform justly, skilfully and magnanimously all the offices both private and public of peace and war. And how all this may be done between twelve, and one and twenty, less time than is now bestowed in pure trifling in grammar and sophistry, is to be thus ordered. First, to find out a spacious house and ground about it . . .[6]

When grappling with the much more painful and complicated issue of liberalising divorce law, Milton could not sustain the same sense of sincerity and focus, although throughout these years and well into 1645 (and his divorce tract *Tetrachordon*) he continued to urge his arguments for the 'necessity of ordaining more wholesomely and more humanly in the casualties of Divorce, than our Laws have yet established', demanding, at times passionately, occasionally hysterically, a remedy for the 'most urgent and excessive grievance happening in domestic life'.

Did Milton really believe that the law on divorce might be changed according to the ideas expressed in his tracts? *Of Education* is certainly a confident work, suggesting that its author's belief in his own abilities was still strong. After all, Milton had argued that the bishops had to go, and they had gone. The one purpose of the Assembly of Divines ordered by Parliament in 1643 was to decide what should replace it, and, in September 1646, episcopacy would be formally abolished. Writing *could* change the world. But there was no sign that the divorce laws would go the way of episcopacy.[7] If, and it seems unlikely, John was waiting for a reform that would enable him and Mary to start new lives separately, he was being overly optimistic.

Under the current law, and as the months and years went by and his wife remained in Oxfordshire, John, and indeed Mary, faced some difficult decisions. John could have initiated divorce proceedings, which, if successful, would have allowed him to remarry, but he would have had to prove in court that the marriage was not valid, either because it had never been consummated (due to his own impotence or Mary's frigidity), or because Mary had previously been engaged to another man. Even if either of these had been true, and there is no evidence either way, it is unlikely that he would have wanted the marriage to end in such a public and humiliating manner.

There remained the option, open to either John or Mary, to apply for a judicial separation through the spiritual courts (divorce *a mensa et thoro*, 'from bed and board'), the very courts that John was seeking to replace with civil proceedings. As a man, he would have had the stronger case. Mary had deserted him, and that was sufficient grounds. Neither party would, however, have had the right to remarry. This may have been particularly critical for the still teenaged Mary, who furthermore would have received no guarantee of financial provision after a judicial separation, whoever initiated it. Any action would have incurred intense public scrutiny of both parties' private lives.

In the end, no formal action was taken by either Mary or John to end the marriage, and, to complicate matters further, action was taken to link the two families, if not John and Mary, more closely. On 12 June 1644, Richard Powell, her father, defaulted on his interest payment of £12, owed to his son-in-law. John's response was to begin attempts to repossess the Powell family property. Despite the fact that John may have been bitter about Mary's treatment of him, and despite the fact that the Powells appeared by this stage to be his political and religious opponents, this step may not have been quite as predatory and vindictive as it looks at first sight. It is possible that, at a time of intense instability, the Milton and Powell families were, rather than fighting each other, closing ranks. The Powells were in trouble. They were dangerously close to the battlegrounds of the Midlands, they were Royalist, and they were penniless. Milton was reasonably secure both in practical terms in London (where there had been no military engagements) and financially, with his successful tutoring complementing his investments, loans and property management. It made sense for him to take over the Powell property. As their son-in-law, if not son-in-reality, it kept the Forest Hill estate in the extended family during a time of national crisis.

For the summer of 1644 saw some of the most vicious fighting of the English Civil War. Now the English Parliament had allied itself with the Scottish Presbyterian Covenanters, the two groups brought together by the threat of King Charles's linking up with the Irish. On 25 September 1643, Parliament and the Scots signed the Solemn League and Covenant against the perceived Royalist/Catholic challenge to English parliamentary government and Protestantism. The English offered the Scots a commitment to religious reform 'according to the word of God and the example of the best reformed Churches'. The Scots agreed to use their army to fight against King Charles. If this had ever been an English civil war, it was no longer: Britain was a battleground, with Scottish, Irish and English troops now all in conflict with each other. Battles were played out in the north-east and north-west of England, the scale of violence escalated, and the usual accompaniments of war became horribly familiar: reprisals, rape, executions, massacres.

Each side had early victories in the renewed hostilities. The great parliamentarian general Lord Fairfax defeated the Irish Royalists at the Battle of Nantwich on 24 January 1644, while on 29 June 1644 the Royalists won a battle at Cropredy Bridge. Only a few days later, parliamentary armies defeated the King's forces, led by Prince Rupert, at the Battle of Marston Moor, thus ending the Royalist threat from the north-east. This victory was evidence of the successful reforms – financial, administrative, military – that had taken place within the parliamentary forces, and the successful collaboration of armies from Scotland, Yorkshire and the eastern counties of England. The latter – the Eastern Association – was the most successful of the regional military associations set up by Parliament. It was led by the Earl of Manchester and the man who would come to dominate the military and political history of the nation over the coming years: Oliver Cromwell.[8]

In contrast, the Royalist campaign was in crisis. Queen Henrietta Maria fled to France on 14 July, and stayed there.[9] York surrendered to Parliament, and further leading Royalists headed into exile. Yet the King still had loyal support in the south-west, where his leaders were assembling an army, and Oxford remained a Royalist stronghold in the Midlands. Once again the tide turned. On 1 September 1644, Charles's new Scottish commander, the Marquess of Montrose, defeated the Scottish Covenanters at Tibbermore, in alliance with the Earl of Antrim, who brought a Scots army over from Ireland. A day later, the parliamentary commander, the Earl of Essex, led an assault on Royalist forces in Cornwall, stretching his supply lines to breaking point. His army was decimated at Lostwithiel. Essex himself fled, in disguise, by sea, and what was left of his army surrendered to the King.

It was Parliament's turn to feel desperate. Matters were not helped by growing divisions between the Scottish Covenanters and Parliament, the latter concerned that a rigid Presbyterianism would be introduced in England. Fears grew that the powerful Scots, now occupying Newcastle, would negotiate with Charles in order to ensure that Presbyterianism survived in Scotland. So, on through the autumn of 1644, the battles continued, with inconclusive results. What was emerging, however, was the continued rise in influence of the parliamentary commander Oliver Cromwell, whose radical policies threatened his more conservative colleagues. It was as if Cromwell's determination actually to *win* the war served to expose the latent ambivalence in many of the parliamentary leaders. As the Earl of Manchester said, expressing the deep-seated fears of many of his countrymen at taking arms against their King, 'If we beat the King 99 times he would be king still, and his posterity, and we subjects still; but if he beat us but once we should be hang'd, and our posterity be undone.'[10]

John Milton was living in a country paralysed and debilitated by a war that many saw as futile. Implicit in his writing at this time is a fear that the hard-won gains of the early 1640s, in particular the moves towards Church reform and the development of Parliament's powers, were being eroded with each passing month of unresolved military and political conflict. Milton had been steadily moving away from his support for the Presbyterian cause during the early 1640s, and as the Civil War dragged on, he became disillusioned with Parliament as well. The failure of the parliamentary armies in 1643 and 1644 to follow up on their occasional victories, the deal made between Parliament and the Scottish Presbyterian Covenanters in September 1643, the attacks by Presbyterians on his divorce pamphlets, and Parliament's apparent willingness to sanction such attacks all led Milton to reconsider his positive view of the men he had previously described as of 'mature wisdom, deliberate virtue, and dear affection to the public good'.[11]

Out of these experiences came a unique piece of writing, one of the most powerful and inspirational works in the English language. That work was *Areopagitica*. It had its genesis in the often bitter, sometimes crass, territory of the divorce tracts. In writing on divorce, Milton had been forced to engage with, in practical and theoretical ways, the issue of free speech. In his translation of Martin Bucer, for example, he claimed to be shocked that, in contrast to previous eras, his tract containing similar ideas to those expressed in the past 'shall in a time of reformation, a time of free speaking, free writing, not find a permission to the Press'. The polemic continues, becoming more and more impassioned, and culminates in the following plea:

> I refer me to wisest Men, whether truth be suffer'd to be truth, or liberty to be liberty now among us, and be not again in danger of new fetters and captivity after all our hopes and labours lost: and whether learning be not (which our enemies too prophetically fear'd) in the way to be trodden down again by ignorance. Whereof while time is, out of the faith owing to God and my Country, I bid this Kingdom beware; and doubt not but God who hath dignify'd this Parliament already to so many glorious degrees, will also give them (which is a singular blessing) to inform themselves rightly in the midst of an unprincipled age; and to prevent this working mystery of ignorance and ecclesiastical thraldom, which under new shapes and disguises begins afresh to grow upon us.[12]

AREOPAGITICA;

A

SPEECH

OF

Mr. JOHN MILTON

For the Liberty of Vnlicenc'd PRINTING,

To the PARLAMENT of ENGLAND.

Τὺλδ'θεϱον δ' ἐκεῖνο, εἴ τις θέλẹ πόλẹ
Χρηςὸν τι βάλδ μ' εἰς μέσον φέρειν, ἔχạν.
Καὶ]αῦθ' ὁ χϱύζων, λαμπϱὸς ἐϑ', ὁ μὴ θέλωγ,
Σιγᾷ, τί τὐτων ἐςιν ἰσαίτεϱον πόλẹ;
Euripid. Hicetid.

This is true Liberty when free born men
Having to advise the public may speak free,
Which he who can, and will, deserv's high praise,
Who neither can nor will, may hold his peace;
What can be juster in a State then this?
Euripid. Hicetid.

LONDON,
Printed in the Yeare, 1644.

In a further plea to Parliament, this time in the preface to *Tetrachordon*, Milton linked his fear of backsliding into ecclesiastical thraldom, which only needs the ignorance created by censorship to thrive once more, to a rousing appeal to the nation's manhood. Milton knew which side he was on: that of real men and free speech.

> And if men want manliness to expostulate the right of their due ransom, and to second their own occasions, they may sit hereafter and bemoan themselves to have neglected through faintness the only remedy of their sufferings, which a seasonable and well-grounded speaking might have purchas'd them. And perhaps in time to come, others will know how to esteem what is not every day put into their hands, when they have marked events, and better weighed how hurtful and unwise it is, to hide a secret and pernicious rupture under the ill counsel of a bashful silence.[13]

It is powerful rhetoric in defence both of his arguments about divorce and of his right to be heard expressing those arguments.[14]

This rhetoric did not, however, offer Milton much protection but rather inflamed his enemies further. In turn he reaffirmed his loyalty to Parliament ('that supreme and majestic Tribunal'), his complete reliance on 'Expositions of Scripture', and his utter loathing for opponents such as Herbert Palmer, an ignorant man who had clearly not even read his tracts but merely attacked them in the 'most open and invective manner, and at the most bitter opportunity that drift or set design could have invented'.[15]

The threat from Palmer was a real one. He had accused Parliament of laxity in their failure to suppress Milton's work, as part of a general assault on all calls for toleration: he thundered that 'a wicked book is abroad and uncensored, though deserving to be burnt, whose author hath been so impudent as to set his name to it and dedicate it to yourselves.'[16] In a menacing move, a Stationers' Petition was issued against Milton's divorce tracts in August. On 31 October *An Answer to a Book* specified the street where he lived (alleging that he had made a covenant with a man in Hackney to exchange his house in Aldersgate Street) and made ironic, and rather pointed, attacks on his attitudes to women: 'It is true if every man were of your breeding and capacity. . . you count now woman to due conversation accessible as to you, except she can speak Hebrew, Greek, Latin & French, and dispute against the canon law as well as you, or at least be able to hold discourse with you.'[17]

Through November and beyond the attacks on Milton the Divorcer continued unabated. In response, he turned his mind in the autumn of 1644 to the issue of freedom of speech. His belief in its necessity derived in part from his need to be heard on the subject of divorce. But even in the divorce tracts, he went beyond this personal agenda, linking free speech with the continuance of true Reformation and with the restoration of English manliness. His actions had already shown him to be opposed to Parliament's reinstatement of licensing back in 1643, since he had continued despite censorship to put his radical views in print. Now he would marshal his arguments on the subject.

On 23 November, *Areopagitica* went on sale to the public for 4d (a reasonable price for a substantial pamphlet, given that a single-sheet one might cost 1d, and two sheets 2d). It is a sustained attack on pre-publication censorship, driven by the kind of raw energy that fuelled the divorce tracts but resolutely focused and coherent in its defence of free speech. The little pamphlet carried no printer or book-seller's name, again a sign that it was a dangerous work with which to be connected. Milton's name appears defiantly on the title page, however: *A Speech of Mr John Milton.* Like other radical propagandists of the mid-1640s, Milton as author was protecting his printer and distributor while inviting prosecution himself.[18]

The title (not perhaps the most accessible that Milton could have chosen) referred to the Areopagus, a court and senate of republican Athens made up of about 300 members elected by the entire body of free Athenian citizens. This was not democracy, but it *was* conciliar, elected government, and it was definitely not monarchy. Milton was linking his own address to Parliament with the kind of public speech made to the Athenian Areopagus, a link echoed in the prefatory quote from his favoured Euripides: 'This is true liberty, when free-born men

/ Having to advise the public, may speak free . . . What can be juster in a state than this?'

It is easy to forget 'just how raw and new an enthusiasm for Athens would have been at this time', how exciting its invocation would have been in political terms.[19] Milton himself wrote that he had 'got the power within me to a passion'. He was desperate to communicate his central argument that life is never perfect, that there will always be problems in any political system, 'but when complaints are freely heard, deeply consider'd, and speedily reform'd, then is the utmost bound of civil liberty attain'd that wise men look for.'

In contrast, censorship and licensing would be the 'stop of truth'. The people of England would become stupidly docile: 'dull ease and cessation of our knowledge' would lead to 'obedient unanimity', a 'rigid external formality', 'gross conforming stupidity'. This of course was exactly what those who sought political power wanted (and still want): an unthinkingly obedient populace. For John Milton this was a nightmare scenario, rendering the nation politically frigid, 'a stanch [i.e., watertight] and solid piece of frame-work, as any January could freeze together' or, later 'a stark and dead congealment of *wood, and hay and stubble* forced and frozen together'. Milton's imagery was taken from the Bible and the domestic world around him: the fusion is powerful.

He was even more eloquent on the subject of books themselves: 'For books are not absolutely dead things, but do contain a potency of life in them to be as active as that soul was whose progeny they are: nay they do preserve as in a vial the purest efficacy and extraction of that living intellect that bred them'.[20] He conceded that because books are alive they can indeed be dangerous, but the remedy was worse than the threat: 'as good almost kill a Man as kill a good Book'. To spill the 'life of man preserved and stored up in books' was a 'kind of homicide', even 'a martyrdom'. If the whole edition of a book was destroyed, it was 'a kind of massacre' in which was killed 'the breath of reason it self . . . an immortality rather then a life'. Books became human beings, as they were in John's playful letters to Charles Diodati, but now men were pouring their 'life' into books, a triumphant re-imagining of the wasteful pouring of semen into women with no recompense explored in the divorce tracts. Now, in *Areopagitica*, Milton could forge his playfulness and his anger into a powerful vision of a world free from censorship and persecution.

The enduring legacy of Milton's arguments can mask the fact that *Areopagitica* is absolutely rooted in its time and in the physical processes of the print trade which its author knew so well. One passage, for example, moves from theory to a very down-to-earth description of the practical problems facing everyone within a print culture stifled by censorship, describing the very moment the licenser interrupts the printing process. The presses grind to a halt, the author falls into melancholy and vexation, then rushes across the city to plead with the licenser, who may well be having a long lunch and thus cannot be found. It is a small moment, but it describes both the frustration and the corruption of the system perfectly. *Areopagitica* is full of relish of the very physicality of the book trade – the 'wet sheets' of paper, the sermons 'printed and piled up at bookseller's stalls' – and believed in its value, in the particular value of cheap, accessible print: '. . . a wise man will make better use of an idle pamphlet, then a fool will do of sacred discipline'.

There is an irony in Milton's celebration of cheap print. So often he is seen as a rather precious intellectual, someone who would value a superbly bound copy of Euripides far higher than an 'idle pamphlet'. Instead, he celebrated what for historians of printing 'are the worst years in history' if production values are considered.[21] Indeed, he tackled head on his contemporaries' fears about the proliferation of printed matter, offering a pragmatic analysis of current conditions. There were so many books coming out that even if censorship were desirable, it would not be enforceable. If the authorities really did want to suppress the sectarians and the extremists, then tackling their printed output was not the way to do it. Milton recognised that it was 'unwritten traditions' that kept the radicals going, and argued that indeed 'the Christian faith, for that was once a schism, is not unknown to have spread all over Asia, ere any Gospel or Epistle was seen in writing.'

This comment is a reminder of Milton's core argument. In funda-

Milton as a ten-year-old, portrait probably
by Cornelius Janssen.

Part of *View of the River Thames* by Jan Visscher, 1616, with
St Paul's dominating the skyline.

Milton aged
twenty-one, in what
is known as the
'Onslow portrait',
artist unknown.

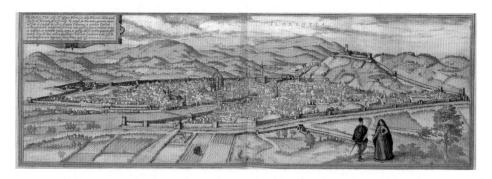

View of Florence from *Civitates Orbis Terrarum* by Georg Braun, circa 1572.

The 2 of May, 1643. y Crosse in Cheapeside was pulled
downe, a Troope of Horse & 2 Companies of foote wayted
to garde it & at y fall of y tope Crosse dromes beat tru-
pets blew & multitudes of Capes wayre throwne
in y Ayre & a greate Shoute of People with ioy,
y 2 of May the Almana ke sayeth, was y invention
of the Crosse, & 6 day at night was the Leaden
Popes burnt in the pla ce where it stood with
ringinge of Bells & a greate Acclamation &
no hurt done in all these actions.

The pulling down of the Cheapside Cross by iconoclasts, May 1643.

EXOSVS : DEO : ET : SANCTIS :

ROOTE : AND : BRANCH :

A banner from the English Civil War.

This is a day of good Tydings. 2 Kings. 7.9.

5.   55

And he brought forth the Kings son, put the Crowne upon him, and gaue him the testimony, and they made him King, and anoynted him and they clapt their hands, & said, God saue ỹ King 2K:11·12·

The return of King Charles II, as illustrated in a prayer book, circa 1660.

Sir Henry Vane.

Milton's house at Chalfont St Giles.

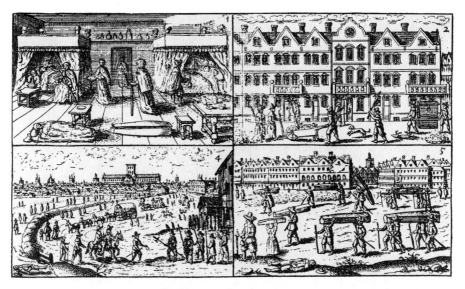

Plague scenes: London, 1665–6.

The Great Fire of London, 1666.

Gul. Faithorne ad Vivum. Delin. et sculpsit.

Joannis Miltoni Effigies Ætat: 62.
1670.

1670 engraving of Milton by William Faithorne.

mental terms, there is good and evil in the world, and human beings have to confront both.

> He that can apprehend and consider vice with all her baits and seeming pleasures, and yet abstain, and yet distinguish, and yet prefer that which is truly better, he is the true wayfaring Christian. I cannot praise a fugitive and cloistered virtue, unexercised and unbreathed, that never sallies out and sees her adversary, but slinks out of the race, where that immortal garland is to be run for, not without dust and heat. Assuredly we bring not innocence into the world, we bring impurity much rather: that which purifies us is trial, and trial is by what is contrary.[22]

This is a remarkable statement, passionately invoking an engagement with the 'dust and heat' of the world, passionately celebrating humanity's ability to survive the 'trial' of deciding for themselves the difference between evil and good.

Modern readers may respond to *Areopagitica*'s insistence on human reason, but in Milton's time it was the emphasis on the progressive religious revelation which can only be achieved through 'trial' that was most significant.[23] What had been latent in the *Maske* at Ludlow back in 1634, when the Lady's virtue of mind and body had been tested by Comus and not found wanting, was now explicitly politicised. Milton was seeking the best form of society for 'the true wayfaring Christian'.

That society could be created in England, land of the (Protestant) free. Milton had himself travelled, and foreigners had envied his luck in living in 'such a place of philosophic freedom'. In Catholic Italy, predictably, 'nothing had been there written now these many years but flattery and fustian', and the situation was worse still in the Muslim Ottoman Empire, where the authority of the Koran was maintained 'by the prohibition of Printing'. In contrast to these benighted places, *Areopagitica* ends by invoking a vision of the English nation aroused to action: 'Methinks I see in my mind a noble and puissant Nation rousing herself like a strong man after sleep, and shaking her invincible locks.'

Milton did his best in *Areopagitica* to wake the nation, but his words would find their most responsive audiences generations later. In 1644, the pattern of self-interested persecution allied to incompetence that he satirised so successfully continued unchecked. In fact, the work simply provoked new attempts from the House of Lords and the Stationers Company to control 'the frequent Printing of scandalous Books' by John Milton.[24]

Despite this kind of intervention, Milton's printer, Matthew Simmons, remained loyal to his author and continued to print his works. Within only a few weeks, a new edition of *The Doctrine and Discipline of Divorce* came from his press, followed swiftly by *Colasterion* and *Tetrachordon.* Whether this was a sign of courage in the face of persecution on the part of Milton the author, and Simmons his printer, or a sign that the bark of the Lords and the Stationers was worse than their bite, or that nobody was really very interested in pursuing the matter in the midst of a gruelling civil war, is hard to tell. What it indicates for certain is the importance of collaboration between different members of the print community, and how this collaboration engendered a particular attitude towards the pursuit of knowledge: '. . . only through such cooperation could an author like Milton have his texts produced during the seventeenth century and only through such a collaboration, as Milton repeatedly insists, could knowledge be discovered and increased.'[25]

Working with, and in support of, a collaborative print culture, John Milton wrote *Areopagitica* despite and because of the war destroying his country, despite and because of the collapse of his marriage and the overwhelmingly hostile responses to his divorce tracts. The experiences of the previous few years had changed him. He was no longer searching for transcendence but was acutely aware that the challenge was to live *in* the world: 'to sequester out of the world into Atlantick and Utopian polities, which can never be drawn into use, will not mend our condition.' Instead, the challenge was to use God-given reason 'to ordain wisely as in this world of evil, in the midst of which God hath placed us unavoidably.'[26] In this brave, sophisticated, passionate work, Milton came of age as a prose pamphleteer.

At precisely the time he was writing *Areopagitica*, however, John Milton was faced with a new challenge, a new enemy, one he could not battle in print. It was in the autumn of 1644 that he first noticed a deterioration in his eyesight. Ten years on, he would describe his experience in painful detail:

> I noticed my sight becoming weak and growing dim, and at the same time my spleen and all my viscera burdened and shaken with flatulence. And even in the morning, if I began as usual to read, I noticed that my eyes felt immediate pain deep within and turned from reading, though later refreshed after moderate bodily exercise; as often as I looked at a lamp, a sort of rainbow seemed to obscure it. Soon a mist appearing in the left part of the left eye (for that eye became clouded some years before the other) removed from my sight everything on that side.[27]

In Milton's own time, his condition was described as *gutta serena* (glaucoma in modern terminology).[28] It was incurable. No one was sure what caused the condition, although some suggested that it was connected with gout. Similarly, there were suggestions as to what might help, including the use of belladonna, but no consensus.

The onset of blindness is a terrifying experience for anyone at any time. For Milton, the values of his society laid a particular and complicated burden upon him. A comment of Leonardo da Vinci distils the attitudes of the period: '. . . he who loses sight is like one expelled from the world, when he does not see it any more, nor anything in it. And such a life is a sister to death.'[29] Not only that, blindness, as with any disability, was invariably viewed as a punishment from God.

Later in the century, one diarist, Samuel Jeake, described vividly his spiritual and practical experience of encroaching blindness. He spent nearly six hours riding to London from his home in Kent, 'where I arrived safe about 3h 30 p.m. Excessive hot weather which discomposed me. The intention of my journey was to find a medicine for my eyes.'[30] The medicine did not help, but prayer offered some respite, giving Samuel an 'assurance about the recovery of my sight. Vowed £50 to the poor on the healing of my eyesight.' His next diary entry is equally optimistic: 'In my evening prayer I believed God would heal my eyesight with joys.' Yet a few months later, he had returned to his medicines, 'both purgers and alteratives', which he continued daily for three months.[31]

Did John Milton seek out 'purgers and alteratives'; did he pray that his God would heal his eyesight? Probably both. Yet the 'trials' of these years merely seemed to fuel his commitment to his cause. Although he was called to be examined by the House of Lords in December 1644 to answer charges of unregistered and unlicensed printing, he still published the third and fourth editions of *The Doctrine and Discipline of Divorce* over the following months, precipitating yet further attacks from his enemies.[32]

Repeatedly, he envisioned authorship as battle: 'I refuse no Occasion, and avoid no Adversary, either to maintain what I have begun, or to give it up for better reason.'[33] The adversaries continued to proliferate, so he continued to write, at times merely attacking his opponents rather than making any new case. Since August 1643, he had written four works on divorce (*The Doctrine and Discipline*, first published in August 1643; *The Judgement of Martin Bucer* of July 1644, and then *Tetrachordon* and *Colasterion*, both published in March 1645); *Colasterion* still shows him able to sum up a bad marriage in two pithy words: 'ransomless captivity', as well as willing to insult his opponents: 'I mean not to dispute philosophy with this pork, who never read any.'[34] It is not surprising that, despite his relentless insistence that all he was arguing for was 'divorce upon extreme necessity' rather than 'divorce at pleasure', there was no stemming the tide of disapproval for Milton's ideas. The attacks upon him continued undiminished through 1645.

Even without a failed marriage, encroaching blindness and relentless vilification as a 'Divorcer', daily life was becoming increasingly difficult as the Civil War continued. Even before the war, poverty had been deeply rooted in the economic structure of the nation, and un- and underemployment were common. Add a run of bad harvests, such as had occurred during the 1620s, 1630s and 1640s, and conditions became appalling for many. Now war had divided communities and families throughout England and inflicted considerable economic, social and psychological damage upon the nation. In the region of 80,000 soldiers were killed or injured in the numerous battles, sieges and sackings of the war, and a much greater number of civilians suffered from the food shortages, diseases and unprecedented financial demands which the armies brought in their wake.[35]

No matter that London, encircled by newly created defences, safe from surprise attack, was a relatively stable place to live and work, certainly far safer than the Midlands or the north-west of England. In their control of cities such as Reading and Oxford, the Royalist armies were able to disrupt much of the traffic of food into London, blocking grain from the south Midlands – which would normally have come down the Thames – and livestock from further afield – usually driven from Wales and northern and western England to be fattened in the Midlands and then finished on pastures close to the capital. Food shortages in London started to bite in the summer of 1643 and motivated acts such as the complete destruction of a Royalist house near the Thames at Henley, in order to ensure the free travel of barges to London. Coal supplies to the City were disrupted by Parliament's own blockade of the north-east coast, leading to an over-reliance on dwindling wood supplies in London. By 1644, Parliament was considering the bringing in of peat from areas as far away as the Fens.

The religious, economic, political and military crises all came to a head at the beginning of 1645. In December 1644, the newly powerful Oliver Cromwell, deeply frustrated with the military command of the Earl of Manchester, had pushed the Self-Denying Ordinance through Parliament. The Ordinance allowed army leaders to retire honourably, paving the way for a complete restructuring of the army.[36] In January, Archbishop William Laud was executed for treason, giving the people what they wanted.

Laud's death was a terrifying sign of the power of the new Presbyterian Church establishment. Many were finding religious life as unsatisfactory as it had been a few years earlier, at the height of

Laudian practice. There was certainly no place in the State religion for the more radical sects and their beliefs. Any call for toleration appalled those still reeling from the apparent breakdown of religious and social consensus in the aftermath of the collapse of the episcopal system, as well as those who believed that a State Church was the only viable form of religious organisation. In the face of the rising numbers of religious groups or sects who disassociated themselves completely from the State Church, the new Presbyterian establishment closed ranks, desperate to stem the tide of sectarianism. Religious toleration would only create more chaos and heresy.

Thomas Edwards was a prolific spokesman for the new orthodoxy, the author of the *Gangraena: or a Catalogue and Discovery of many of the Errours, Heresies, Blasphemies and Pernicious Practices of the Sectaries of the time* (London, 1646). Edwards saw the sectaries as dangerously successful manipulators of print and speech. They broadcast 'all victories', 'crying them up in pulpits, news-books, conferences, calling them the saviours of kingdoms; and for this purpose they have certain men that are criers and trumpeters between the army, city and country, who trumpet forth their praises . . .'[37] (In an historical irony, Edwards's detailed accounts of the hated sectarians provides one of the most valuable sources for their practices.) Edwards insisted that the sectaries were masters of false rhetoric: simply by saying that they were successful, they had become so. What were they after? They wanted to empty the churches, stop paying tithes, get in their own preachers, 'mechanic preachers, who come from London, the armies, and other places to preach in and corrupt the people'. They were even opposed to the singing of Psalms: if they could not get the practice stopped in their church, then 'they in a contemptuous manner clap on their hats in the time of singing psalms, and having been pulled off, put them on again; yea, in prayer also many of them keep on hats.'[38]

Gangraena was designed to shock, designed to inspire fear of a complete social breakdown, and thus the need for renewed censorship. In Edwards's eyes, John Milton's advocacy of divorce-law liberalisation, together with his desire to speak out, was just another assault on the (precariously new) order of things. In the *Second Part of*

Gangraena, Edwards recounted the story of Mrs Attaway, a lace-maker, who read *The Doctrine and Discipline of Divorce* and promptly ran off with a sectarian.

Whether Mrs Attaway did run off with a Baptist is irrelevant. Edwards had a point. John Milton's divorce tracts signalled just how far he had moved away from the Presbyterians. Milton had found that although he had not liked the Laudian bishops, he liked the ensuing system of Presbyterian Church government even less. One of his most powerful poems from this time, 'On the New Forcers of Conscience', savages the new regime, in particular the joining of Church and State: the 'civil sword' should never be used to 'force our consciences that Christ set free'. The Presbyterians did not abhor the sins of those they had defeated; instead they envied them, and had now 'seized the widowed whore plurality'. Good men 'Must now be named and printed heretics / By shallow Edwards and Scotch What-d'ye-call' (the latter probably a reference to another critic of Milton's divorce pamphlets, one Robert Baillie). 'On the New Forcers of Conscience' argues that the Presbyterians had embraced the very vices – plurality, holding more than one church living, religious persecution – against which they had campaigned. The poem ends with a rousing couplet that looks forward to a time 'When they shall read this clearly in your charge / New *Presbyter* is but old *Priest* writ large'. (ll. 19–20)

Does Milton's break with Presbyterianism also mark a political turning point for him, perhaps even a move towards republicanism? Scholars remain divided, but what is certain is that during these years of civil war, he thought long and hard, under difficult conditions, about the relationship between the personal and the political, asking, in different ways and at different times, two similar questions: How can a man be most useful to his nation, and what is the best form of government for that nation?[39]

Others were asking the same questions and coming up with some very practical answers. Not only that, but they had the power to implement their vision of a new religious and political order. Oliver Cromwell, like Milton a supporter of 'liberty of conscience' and an opponent of formalism, like Milton a stern critic of corrupt monarchy, would emerge in 1645 as the undisputed leader of the parliamentary forces. It had been a rapid and somewhat mysterious rise. Born into a prominent family in rural Huntingdonshire, Cromwell's first forty years were unexceptional. Why, without money and contacts, he was elected to Parliament in 1640 remains unclear. But once he reached the battlefield in 1642, his rise was swift and seemingly inexorable.

On 3 April 1645, the Self-Denying Ordinance was passed by the House of Lords; all MPs except Cromwell were required to resign their commissions within forty days. Two months later, Cromwell became Lieutenant General of what was now called the New Model Army, and on 14 June, his victory over Royalist forces at the Battle of Naseby marked the end of King Charles's attempts to achieve a military resolution to the conflict. The King's army was defeated again on 10 July, at Langport, opening up the West Country to the parliamentarians. Bristol surrendered on 11 September, and the young Prince of Wales was sent to France. The reorganisation, the remodelling, of the parliamentary armies in 1645 was one component in this new success, allied to Parliament's superior administrative and financial organisation as instituted by John Pym. Just as important for Parliament were the twin weapons of spying and propaganda. The exposure of the King's 'secret cabinet', containing revelations of his secret dealings with the Irish and continental Catholic powers, inflicted almost as much damage to his cause as the losses in battle, yet another reminder of the importance of print and propaganda.[40]

Oliver Cromwell's military abilities were, however, exceptional. He was a natural soldier and an inspired tactician. At the Battle of Marston Moor he ensured victory with the simple addition of horses to the parliamentarian army. Equally important, he was a military meritocrat, famously claiming in September 1643 that he 'had rather have a plain russet-coated captain that knows what he fights for, and loves what he knows, than that which you call a gentleman and is nothing else'.[41] For himself, he believed, utterly, in the providential manifestation of God's will and thus continually sought 'remarkable providences'. Every success on the battlefield confirmed his belief that his cause, and the cause of his army, was just: '. . . let us look into providences; surely they mean somewhat. They hang so together; have been so constant, so clear and unclouded.'[42] This was a far cry from the vacillations of a commander such as the Earl of Manchester, unsure of the legitimacy of his position, fearful as to the consequences of both defeat and victory. Cromwell imagined himself as Moses, and the English as the Israelites. He was leading the people of England/ Israel out of the bondage of Egypt/tyranny.

Above all, in the words of the historian John Morrill, Cromwell cared about ends not means and was loyal to no one but God.[43] Religion was the most important determinant in his life, encouraging the development of a new kind of fundamentalist tyranny, and often overruling the (secular) law. His New Model Army was a force to be reckoned with, replacing bodies such as the Trained Bands of London who gradually melted away. Above all, Cromwell was successful, and, once he had taken charge, 1645 would become the year in which Parliament at last seemed to have achieved dominance over the King. Charles would now have to negotiate the disputes over Church and State government that had precipitated the war in the first place.

It was also the year in which Mary Powell Milton returned to London and her husband, John. Again, there is no conclusive evidence, only hearsay about the circumstances from the early biographers. Edward Phillips writes that there were rumours that, after years of separation, Milton was planning to marry 'one of Mr Davis' daughters, a very handsome and witty gentlewoman' but also notes that 'the then declining State of the king's Cause . . .' prompted the Powells to put pressure on the marriage to work. Another has it that Mary said, on her return, that 'her mother had been the chief promoter of her forwardness.'[44] Whatever the reasons, Mary did return to John.

By the end of 1645, as the Civil War appeared to be stuttering to a close, and a new era of negotiation between King and Parliament appeared to be beginning, John Milton was presenting a thoroughly conventional exterior to the world, at least in his personal life. He and his wife moved to a larger house in the Barbican, still in the City of London, and that autumn, Mary became pregnant.[45] Milton's next step as an author would seek to confirm his new respectability.

ELEVEN

POEMS

1645

POEMS OF MR JOHN MILTON was published on 2 January 1646. (The title page has 1645, most likely because the old calendar, whereby March marked the beginning of the new year, was being used.) The little book presented as conventional an appearance to the world as the reunited Miltons did in their new house in the Barbican. The printer of the *Poems* may have been that still uncommon but not unknown creature, a woman, Ruth Raworth, but Milton's book-seller was the eminently respectable Royalist sympathiser Humphrey Moseley, who added a preface regretting the dominance of controversial prose in the publishing world. The work was 'Printed and publish'd according to Order', precisely the Order that Milton had been attacking in *Areopagitica*. Everything about the appearance of the *Poems* suggests that he was taking a step back from his role as controversialist. The volume offered the world a retrospective of his poetry to date, with his English poems culminating in *Lycidas* and his Latin poetry culminating in *Epitaphium Damonis*. His readers may have found the collection confusing. In the *Poems of Mr John Milton* the reader finds obsequious praise for a bishop, Lancelot Andrewes, destined for heaven, in a poem written twenty years earlier. In *Of Reformation*, the tract of 1641, Milton had consigned all bishops to hell in no uncertain terms.

Why did Milton collect together his poetry, almost all of it written prior to 1640, and publish it now? Among other things, to publish what was in effect a Complete Works was to provide another assurance of literary immortality. Milton was an author who took good care of his own work in a material sense: as we have seen, he kept copies of his poems and his tracts, and he circulated his works to friends and to libraries so that even the most ephemeral of them would survive. The publication of the *Poems* was just one further element in this process. It is possible to go further, and see the collected poems as Milton's offering up of the documents illustrating his development as a writer, another indication of a poet 'obsessed with his own genius', a man 'profoundly self-regarding'.[1] Certainly, much of the poetry, including that in Latin, is presented as a virtuoso display of precocious talent, with poems classified by how young he was when he wrote them: just fifteen when he translated the Psalms, just seventeen when he mourned the Bishop of Winchester in a Latin elegy.

The *Poems* also helped to signal Milton's distance from the radical sectaries who had embraced, somewhat embarrassingly, his work on divorce, and whom he had disowned in 'Sonnet XII' ('I did but prompt the age to quit their clogs'), in which they are characterised as those 'that bawl for freedom in their senseless mood'. Milton himself, in this sonnet, praised, somewhat predictably, men who were 'wise and good'. The *Poems* of 1645 show Mr John Milton to be just that: educated, intellectual, moral and from the social élite.

Nevertheless, there are traces of the infamous prose polemicist of the previous five years, reminders of the campaigning Milton. A triumphalist note is added to the heading to *Lycidas*, the poem that had denounced the clergy of England for their corruption back in 1637. Eight years earlier Milton had foretold the 'ruin of the clergy'. Now, with the destruction of episcopal power, the execution even of Archbishop Laud, the clergy had indeed been ruined. By a poetic sleight of hand, Milton achieved prophetic power by turning his *wish* for ruin into a historical record of the events of the intervening years. Blink, however, and a reader would miss this headnote: Milton wears his political and religious beliefs lightly in the 1645 *Poems*.

It was not the religious politics of his poetry that caused Milton anxiety in 1645 but its sexual politics. Stung by accusations that he had encouraged sexual looseness in his divorce tracts, he felt it

necessary to apologise for some of his Latin poems, in a headnote to
Elegy VII of the 1645 *Poems*:

> *Haec ego mente olim laeva, studioque supino*
> *Nequitiae posui vana trophaea meae.*
> *Scilicet abreptum sic me malus impulit error,*
> *Indocilisque aetas prava magistra fuit.*
>
> (ll. 1–4)

These lines are the trifling memorials of my levity which, with a
warped mind and a base spirit, I once raised. This, in fact, is how
mischievous error seduced me and drove me on: my ignorant youth
was a vicious teacher.[2]

Milton went on to say that once he reached 'the shady Academy' with
its 'Socratic streams' (a reference to his reading of the works of Plato
and his subsequent championing of platonic love), from 'that moment
on the flames were quenched'.

This little Latin poem can be read as a remarkable admission as well
as a rebuttal. It is something akin to a modern politician admitting
that, yes, he did have same-sex relationships or take drugs while at
university, but that was then, this is now. In the context of Milton's
own life, there is something poignant about the intensity with which
he announced his distance from his 'ignorant youth'. Now, in 1645,
'My heart is frozen solid, packed around with thick ice; so that even the
boy himself [Cupid] is afraid to let the frost get at his arrows, and
Venus fears the strength of a Diomedes.' (ll. 8–10) Milton is now
Diomedes, friend of Odysseus and a great military champion of the
Greeks against the Trojans, and the enemy of the goddess of love. This
new strength comes at a price. He is now without emotion at all. It has
been argued that these lines cannot date from the time of the
publication of the *Poems* because they would 'come oddly from a
married man'.[3] Given the likely state of John's relationship with Mary
(even the Mary who had returned to live with him and bear his
children), it does not seem strange at all. Perhaps the marriage could

Melpo∫mene   Erato.

IOANNIS MILTONI ANGLI EFFIGIES ANNO ÆTATIS VIGE∫. Pri:.

Urania.   Clio

Ἀμαθεῖ γεγράφθαι χειρὶ τήνδε μὲν εἰκόνα
Φαίης τάχ' ἄν, πρὸς εἶδος αὐτοφυὲς βλέπων·
Τὸν δ' ἐκτυπωτὸν ᾗκ ἐπιγνόντες φίλοι
Γελᾶτε φαύλυ δυσμίμημα ζωγράφυ

W·M· ∫culp

The frontispiece to Poems of Mr John Milton.

only function if John's heart was indeed frozen solid. What is more, in using the familiar language of the humours of heat and cold, Milton was insisting that he had moved from a 'hot' sexually experimental youth to a 'cold' passionless, indeed sexless, adulthood. Is it fanciful to see a hint of (well-hidden) regret for what has been lost? Mischievous error may well have seduced the young John Milton, but surely the alternative, to be a violent block of ice, was hardly more appealing. Moreover, while it is clear that Milton was rejecting the poetry of 'levity', the little poem remains silent as to what kind of writing a Diomedes would produce.

Milton also added some verses in Greek to the engraved portrait of himself in the frontispiece to the *Poems*, a portrait he felt to be grossly inaccurate. The verses satirised the artist, William Marshall: '. . . my friends, laugh at this rotten picture of a rotten artist.' Was this a very public joke? Or was it yet another example of Milton using a little-known language, Greek, to play games with his friends, and to exclude those who did not have access to that language? Marshall himself would have engraved the condemnation of his skill in a language he did not understand. Milton's small act of vengeance may have been fuelled by Marshall's role as engraver for one of the works that had attacked Milton in 1645 (Daniel Featley's *Dippers Dipt*), a work that had placed Milton in the same camp as the radical sectarians. Apparently, the choice of Marshall was a desperate one in any case. Engravers were in short supply in wartime.

The Greek verse was an empty gesture, but it nevertheless remains confusing to see Milton published by Humphrey Moseley, a collaboration that placed the writer in the company of such Royalist poets as Waller, Carew, Shirley, Suckling and Cartwright. There are, however, hints that Moseley took control of the work, producing a volume that reflected his agenda rather than Milton's, which would have been standard practice at the time. Milton could not have been unaware that he was not in control of his work once it had been signed over to a printer or book-seller. Printers made hands-on decisions during the physical creation of a text, such as its spelling and punctuation; publishers were printers or, more often, book-sellers, who, having put up the capital for a book, could choose the format, determine the layout and design the title page.[4] With Moseley involved, it should have been no surprise that Milton started looking like a Royalist poet. It was not, however, a good time to make a bid for literary celebrity, let alone Royalist literary celebrity.

London was becoming a hothouse for radical ideas and radical action. The Civil War had led to the collapse of hierarchies and a new social fluidity: a symbol of the changing times was that St Paul's was converted into a cavalry barracks, with up to 800 horses of the parliamentarian army stabled in the nave. In this tense climate, it was not only Milton who opposed the new Presbyterian regime and its parliamentary supporters. Others, far more radical than he, would emerge to claim much greater rights and freedoms.

Just at the time that Milton appeared to be retreating, at least in public, from his oppositional stance, the Leveller movement came together in London.[5] Led by men like John Lilburne, the Levellers challenged Parliament's record. Parliament had not brought about a godly Reformation, the complacent religious/political élite (now Presbyterian rather than Laudian) maintained a tyrannical power, tithes were still being collected, and 'thousands of men and women [were] permitted to live in beggary and wickedness all their life long', as William Walwyn put it in 1647, collecting together a number of petitions in a single volume, *Gold tried in the fire: or the burnt petitions revived*.[6] The *Humble Petition* of September 1648 was the culmination of months of activism, as, in the closing phases of the first Civil War, radical sectarian congregations joined with radical urban politicians on the streets of London, linked by their opposition to the Presbyterian settlement and their defence of religious nonconformity. (The Solemn League and Covenant with the Scottish Presbyterians had been a carefully worded document, avoiding a commitment to any specific form of Church government in England but never the less setting the English Church on a Presbyterian path that left little room for 'independents' in religion.)[7]

But where the Leveller movement differed from all other radical movements of the time was in its explicit demand for political rights for the people, based on principles of natural equality and government by consent. The radical concept of 'one man, one vote' went against the basis of traditional parliamentary government, where only property owners were enfranchised. The King and Lords were 'negative voices' while an ideal House of Commons, representing the English people, was the 'supreme power'. It was not quite a fully fledged republican position, but it was pretty close.[8]

Despite the attempts at forcible suppression, the movement spread from London into Cromwell's New Model Army. Now Parliament had a serious problem: a politicised army. The very soldiers who had brought it into power were questioning its authority. Too late, Parliament attempted to take control, but by 1647 even some of the officers in the New Model Army were listening to the radicals. In late May, the army seized the King himself from the Scots at Holdenby House in Northamptonshire and began moving towards London. The political landscape was changed forever, now the army had a manifesto. The soldiers insisted they were no 'mere mercenary army' but created to 'the defence of our own and the people's just rights and liberties'.[9] They wanted parliaments of fixed duration, an increase in the electoral franchise and 'liberty of tender consciences'.

When the army reached London, the result was not violence but an extraordinary debate about government. Representatives of the officers and men from each regiment in the New Model Army met with the senior officers in Putney Church, by the Thames, between 28 October and 9 November. They were there to debate Leveller policies. The Putney Debates were rather like the pamphlet wars but live. The energetic, passionate arguments were scribbled down as they happened, offering a remarkable glimpse of history in the making. With startling modernity, factions within the army spoke up for the common man's rights to participate in government. As one Col. Thomas Rainsborough put it, 'for really I think that the poorest he that is in England hath a life to live as the greatest he.' Moreover, he argued, '. . . every man that is to live under a government ought first by his own consent to put himself under that government.'[10]

With arguments like these, it is no wonder that contemporaries were appalled by what they saw as a destruction of valuable hierarchy and order, coining the term *Leveller* as one of abuse. One opponent imagined the terrible political consequences of giving ordinary people the vote. If the populace listened to 'the language of the Levellers in their late petition' then monstrous tyrants and demagogues would be elected to positions of high office by a politically illiterate electorate. More bluntly, the fear was that they 'would level everything. There would be no government, no property, no family. All would be held in common'.[11] This fear reveals that the link between Church and State, strong as it was, was nowhere near as fundamental to the seventeenth-century mindset as the link between governmental and family structures. A simple injunction such as that a child should obey his or her parents was merely one manifestation of a society built upon legitimising obedience to one's God-given superiors, thus ensuring that 2 per cent of the population controlled the other 98 per cent, and that men controlled women. The Levellers' arguments threatened the status quo at almost every point, and even within the New Model Army, the majority could not accept their claims. Many of the army commanders, including Cromwell, although radical in their own ways, resisted the Levellers' arguments about the franchise, insisting that a man should not have a share in the political life of a kingdom unless he had what was called a permanent fixed interest in this kingdom – that is, property and land.

In the light of this heightened political activity it is all the more strange that John Milton was keeping very quiet. His *Of Education* was being read in European intellectual circles, and he was still being attacked for his divorce pamphlets, but the author himself was not responding. He did not even make many notes in his commonplace book between 1646 and 1648.

This may be because the sheer effort of surviving these tumultuous times engrossed all his energies. It was a world in chaos. Men would leave home to fight, women might have to leave home to escape whichever army was in town, and no one was able to keep track of the individuals involved, alive or dead. Such were the disruption, and lack of reliable records, that legislation was passed later to allow a woman to remarry if she had not heard from her husband after three years, or if her husband had been understood to be dead by 'common fame'. Shortages of food and fuel affected everyone. Throughout the country, church interiors were being broken up by one arm of the Presbyterian and parliamentary alliance, determined to remove all traces of superstition and popery. William Dowsing's diary of his efforts in East Anglia was characteristic. Seeking to destroy all 'monuments of idolatry and superstition' in parish churches, he recorded a relentless trail of violence:

> Ditton: January 3 1644 We beat down two crucifixes, and the twelve apostles, and many other superstitious pictures.
> At Little Swaffham, we brake down a great many pictures super-stitious, twenty cherubims, and the rails we brake in pieces and digged down the steps.[12]

Sunday sports were banned. The Christmas festival was abolished.[13] The Royalist rich were leaving the country on the heels of their Queen.[14]

It was indeed a world turned upside down, and the Miltons, like all other families, faced formidable challenges. The exceptionally poor harvest of 1647–8 pushed many to the brink of bankruptcy or starvation. In that year, Milton received a relatively low income from his new (ex-Powell) properties in Wheatley, only £2 13s. If he did focus on maintaining his estate through these years of uncertainty, he succeeded, and this despite his later complaints that his private income was withheld during the 'civil commotions' and that what he did have was being heavily taxed to pay for the armed struggle. But war and poor harvests were there to be overcome, and the new Oxfordshire property was there to be developed and exploited; in September 1648 Milton received rents to the value of £31 13s 6d. His social and economic prosperity was helped by his being on the winning side in the wars, even if the parliamentary forces were increasingly divided among themselves.

Within the wider Milton family, there were those who had supported the Royalist cause and were facing the fallout of military defeat. John's brother Christopher had journeyed to Exeter after the fall of his hometown of Reading. (Queen Henrietta Maria retreated to Exeter as she approached the birth of her daughter, Henrietta, since Oxford was too unsafe.) On 13 April 1646, however, Exeter had surrendered to the parliamentary army led by Gen. Fairfax, with correct wartime etiquette rigorously observed, the articles of war followed to the last letter. On 13 April, the Royalist leader mustered his men within the walls for the last time, and at midday he led his garrison out, drums beating, colours flying. The King's daughter, Princess Henrietta, was carried out of the city in a litter, accompanied by the ladies of the court. The parliamentarian soldiers standing by did not even jeer the departing soldiers. By two in the afternoon, Oliver Cromwell, leading the New Model Army, had taken possession of the city.[15]

After the fall of Exeter, Christopher seems to have travelled to London to be reunited with his family. Life went on. Thomasina, his wife, would bear him another son, Thomas, in February of the following year. In political terms, Christopher opted for security, expressing his complete allegiance to Parliament and Presbyterianism by taking the Covenant in London on 20 April 1646. Things had worked out as well as could be expected for Christopher Milton, Royalist.

The Powell family were less fortunate. Also in April 1646, King Charles's wartime capital, Oxford, was under siege by parliamentary forces. On 27 April, Charles himself left Oxford in disguise. He chose to surrender to the Scottish army in Nottinghamshire rather than to the parliamentarians. The Powell family at Forest Hill, having been in financial crisis for years, now faced destitution. They packed their bags and left their property to its fate, heading in the first instance for Oxford. In June, Richard Powell's household goods were sold off by parliamentary sequestrators for Oxfordshire to one Matthew Appletree of London for £335. A week later, Oxford fell to Parliament, and the property at Forest Hill was taken over by Robert Pye, a reward for his military service in the parliamentary cause.[16] Three days later, the parliamentary Gen. Fairfax gave a pass to Richard Powell allowing him and his family to leave Oxford.

What is surprising is the Powells' destination. The family (Anne and Richard and at least five of their children) went to John and Mary Milton's house in London. Mary was already seven or eight months pregnant. With John's nephews and his father already in the house, it must have been crowded, but in the crisis the two families came together as a matter of survival.

Family concerns loomed large over the next two years. To begin with, there was the birth of Mary's first child, an experience fraught with dangers, physical and spiritual. Deaths in childbed were at least a hundred times more prevalent than they are now. All went well, however, and on 29 July 1646, John and Mary's daughter Anne was born, named, presumably, for Mary's mother but also a commemoration of John's sister. Her proud father wrote in the family Bible, which can still be seen in the British Library, that Anne was born 'on the fast at evening about half an hour after six'. (The phrase 'on the fast' refers to a Day of Public Humiliation, as designated by Parliament, another reminder of the times. There were many of these Days, a typical example being the monthly fast appointed by the King at the request of Parliament on 8 January 1641 to mark the Irish insurrection and massacre. The fast was to be observed every last Wednesday in the month as long as the calamities of the nation should require it.)

A month later Richard Powell made his first moves to attempt to recover his property. (More precisely, his son-in-law's property, since it had been mortgaged to Milton.) The victorious parliamentary government insisted that Royalists 'compound' for their estates – that is, pay money in order to have them returned. If he paid up, then any defeated Royalist, having sworn an oath of loyalty to the new government, could get on with his life again. So, on 6 August, Richard Powell petitioned to compound, claiming to the 'honourable committee sitting at Goldsmiths Hall of Compositions' that since his estate was lying 'for the most part' in 'the King's Quarters', he could do little else than 'adhere to his Majesty's party against the forces raised by the Parliament in this unnatural war'. Powell recognised that this was 'Delinquency', the term applied by Parliament to describe the actions of those who had assisted Charles I by arms, money or personal service during the war and beyond. He pointed out, however, that his case was covered by 'those articles at the surrender of Oxford', since the Powells had 'lived there whilst it was a Garrison holden for the King against the Parliament and was there at the time of the Surrender'.[17] Put more plainly, Powell suggested, perhaps quite sincerely, that his support for the King was purely on account of his own family property lying 'in the King's Quarters', and that since his family were in Oxford at the time of the surrender of the city, they were protected by the 'articles' devised at that time. The committee agreed.

A day later, it was Christopher Milton's turn to petition precisely the same committee. He too appealed to 'Articles', in his case the articles of surrender agreed at Exeter. He lamented that of 'personal estate I have none but what hath been seized and taken from me, and converted to the use of the state'. He wished to compound 'to free it out of sequestration' and offered to pay whatever fine was necessary, as set by 'this Committee for Compositions with Delinquents'. Just to make his political loyalties absolutely clear, Christopher took the Oath of Covenant again. He was fined £200 at first, but this was reduced to £80, which he paid in two instalments, on 24 September and 24 December. The committee found Richard Powell's circumstances more complicated to deal with, partly because he was in such serious debt.[18] Once the sums were done, however, and Powell too had taken the necessary Covenant and Oath, his fine was set at £180 in early December 1646.

Mary's father had only weeks to live, perhaps one of the reasons that he formally handed over the management of his estate to his son-in-law in mid-December. On or around 1 January 1647, he died, his will having been drawn up a couple of days earlier, 'at the House of Mr John Milton Situate in Barbican'. Only two months later, John's own father died at the age of about eighty-three or -four. He was buried in St Giles Cripplegate, a church that still survives at the heart of the modern Barbican complex in the City of London.

Milton was now acting head of both the Powell and Milton families, and, in a move that showed him to be his father's son, he moved swiftly after Richard Powell's death to ensure his control of such property in Oxfordshire to which he had a right. On 16 July 1647 he obtained 'an extent' on the mortgaged estate. Four months later, he was permitted to take possession of the Powell property. Quite properly, he handed over one third of the income from the estate to Powell's widow, Anne (her 'widow's thirds'). Although his primary aim in these actions might have been to recover the debt owed to him by Powell, with a possible secondary aim of gaining his wife's long-delayed dowry, this deal was not only beneficial to John Milton. It also provided security for Anne Powell at a time when her own sons were unable to support her and, through John's marriage to Mary, kept the Forest Hill property in the extended Powell family.

Although legal wrangles over the Forest Hill property would continue for years, Milton was on more secure ground in the neighbouring village of Wheatley, where he now owned cottages and received the tithe income. He was soon into his stride as an Oxfordshire landowner, leasing both tithes and cottages to John Robinson for six years for an annual rent of £60. Overall, Milton made about £100 a year from the Oxfordshire estate and does seem to have paid his mother-in-law her 'widow's thirds' of the income. This Powell/Milton rapprochement exemplified many families' response to the upheaval of the war. Family came first for most people, meaning that in practice parliamentarians often did support their defeated Royalist kin.[19]

No records of any kind survive to provide any clues as to the Miltons' domestic arrangements.[20] Whereas many seventeenth-century husbands made explicit notes about their wives' reproductive cycles in their diaries, or jotted down household expenditures in their commonplace books, nothing of this kind appears in the five volumes of Milton's *Life Records*. Did Mary feed her own children, or did she display her genteel status by hiring a wet nurse? Even if her husband, ever keen to assert his distance from the 'vulgar', wanted this, conditions would have worked against them. Not only were engravers in short supply in wartime London: wet nurses were thin on the ground as well.

What is clear is that all was not completely well with John and Mary's daughter Anne. Edward Phillips, Milton's nephew, remembered much later that 'whether by ill Constitution, or want of Care', his cousin 'grew more and more decrepit'.[21] While it is certain, from later evidence, that Anne suffered from some 'bodily infirmity, and difficult utterance of speech', and probably did not learn to write, Phillips's suggestion that she lacked care is contentious and unsubstantiated.[22]

Aspects of seventeenth-century parenting (such as ruthless swad-
dling, or the discouragement of crawling, in case the baby became too
much like an animal) may have meant that it was quite some time
before John and Mary realised that their child would be 'lame' and
'decrepit'. Once they did, their culture would have insisted that the
parents take the responsibility, indeed the 'sign of sin' of illness or
infirmity, upon themselves. The man was responsible spiritually and
morally for the whole family: to have a lame child was thus a failing in
some way on his part. The mother, being a woman, was systemically
flawed: diseases such as jaundice, scabs and measles were attributed to
the child's nine months in the womb in contact with corruption from
the impurities in the mother's blood. There were dire warnings to
prospective parents, with medical writers cautioning husbands and
wives against too frequent copulation, which would weaken their seed
and create stunted offspring. There was no escaping from the conclusion. John and Mary were responsible for their child's disability:
Mary simply by virtue of being a woman, John, spiritually and socially,
by failing to be a good governor.

Soon, however, they would be parents again. On 25 October 1648,
John would add the information to his Bible that his wife had borne
him another daughter, this time christened Mary. She was, as with
Anne, born 'on a fast day', but this time the baby arrived at about six in
the morning.

Births, deaths, and battles for estates therefore characterised these
years for John Milton as his country struggled towards a period of
calm. By May 1647 Parliament was voting to disband the army: the
Civil War was over, it seemed. In London, a parliamentary ordinance
(that is, legislation passed through Parliament but lacking Royal
assent) permitted apprentices to take up their old jobs after the
disruption of military service. Life was returning to normal.

It is curious, in the light of all these personal developments in
Milton's life, that in April 1647, he wrote to his Italian friend Carlo
Dati of his 'almost perpetual loneliness'.[23] This correspondence enacts
the kind of friendship Milton simply could not find in England at this
time and was a vital link with a world in which he had taken great

pleasure.[24] Carlo Dati, known as 'Smaritto' (the Bewildered One) in one of the Florentine academies, wrote to Milton about language and poetry, offering for example a detailed analysis of translation and stylistic issues in Petrarch: 'It grieves me much that the disorders of the realm have disturbed your studies, and I am anxiously awaiting your poems . . . All your friends, whom I greeted affectionately in your name, send you their respectful salutations'.[25] Milton ended up sending two copies of his 1645 *Poems*, and his friend responded in a way that would have presumably delighted his correspondent, thanking him for his 'most erudite poems'. Dati in turn was delighted because he had just been made chair of Classics at the Florentine Academy.

Yet as the Milton scholar Barbara Lewalski points out, fond as John was of his friends, whether Dati in 1647 or Charles Diodati in the 1630s, 'keeping up with friends through correspondence was not one of Milton's strong points', as the numerous, often rather strained apologies for failure to write indicate.[26] This apparent weakness can be linked with the problems he appeared to have with putting pen to paper during this period of his life. For Dati, far away in Italy, it appeared, however, that it was the war that was interrupting his friend's intellectual literary endeavours, but even when it came to writing to very close friends, it seems that Milton found it all too easy to defer.

He, Mary and baby Anne moved, around September 1647 (about a year before baby Mary was born), to a smaller house in High Holborn, as far from the City as Milton would move when he lived in London. The house backed on to Lincoln's Inn Fields and permitted 'a private and quiet life': Milton himself represented the move as providing an opportunity to continue his studies, perhaps even, after several seasons dominated by births, deaths and compoundings, to allow him to start afresh. Still he was attacked in print and indeed in manuscript for being a 'divorcer', and still he hardly wrote.

Characteristically, he continued to make efforts to preserve for posterity what he had written to date. He sent eleven of his prose tracts to the Bodleian Library, with a little inscription addressed to Rous the Bodley Librarian, and a list of contents in his own hand. Later he found that the copy of his 1645 *Poems* that he had sent to the

Library had gone astray, and so he sent another to Rous, this time with a Latin ode attached. These efforts, and the Latin ode, speak volumes about Milton's longing to escape from the conditions he found himself in during the late 1640s. He was deeply nostalgic for a time when his 'boyish hand' wrote while its owner 'wandered in play' through Italy and England, and lamented 'this damnable civil war'.

There is something cloying about Milton's address to his little lost book. He imagines it 'taken and thumbed over by a block-headed bookseller with calloused grimy hands' (in contrast, of course, to Rous, who will treasure his copy). Above all, Rous will provide a home for the book 'which the insolent clamourings of the rabble will never penetrate, far away from the vulgar mob of readers'. It is a strange but powerful fantasy. Tellingly, the ode concludes with a prose passage in which Milton explains, with precision, even pedantry, exactly which metric constructions he has used: '*Ode tribus constat Strophis, totidemque Antistrophis una demum epodo clausis, quas, tametsi omnes nec versuum numero, nec certis ubique colis exacte respondeant . . .*' (ll. 88–90) (This ode consists of three strophes and the antistrophes with a concluding epode. Though the strophes and antistrophes do not exactly correspond either in the number of their lines or in the distribution of the particular metrical units . . .) Rarely does he sound so pompous. Allied to the coy sentimentality of the preceding poem, the impression is of a man who has lost his way.

The scraps of writing that do survive from this time suggest great distress at national and perhaps domestic events, and yet an inability to see ways forward. In April 1648, John Milton turned to the Hebrew Bible, offering new translations of a selection of Psalms.[27] These are songs of lament for the nation beset by civil war, and they plead with God to act on behalf of those suffering from the horrors of conflict:

> Regard the weak and fatherless
> Despatch the poor man's cause,
> And raise the man in deep distress
> By just and equal laws.
> (*Psalm LXXXII*, verse 3)

The images are ones almost of rape, certainly of violent desecration (the nation is female), with Milton transforming the landscape of Israel into a very English one of hedges and fences:

> Why has thou laid her hedges low
> And broken down her fence,
> That all may pluck her, as they go,
> *With rudest violence?*
> > (*Psalm LXXX*, verse 12)

(The italics are Milton's, indicating any addition he made to his source text, in this case Psalm 80, and yet more evidence of his academic scrupulousness.) The Psalms also voice the fears of a weak man ('I am a man, but weak alas / And for that name unfit'): Milton adds the note, just in case this is unclear, that this is a reference to 'a man without manly strength', the spectre of improper manliness lurking behind his insistence.

These are beautiful translations. Another poem from the time demonstrates that Milton had not forgotten how to write but perhaps did not know for what cause he *should* write. His sonnet addressed to the parliamentary general Lord Fairfax is a case in point. It was never printed by Milton: What was its purpose? The first eight lines celebrate Fairfax's glorious military achievements: 'Fairfax, whose name in arms through Europe rings . . .' But then Milton uses the turn of the sonnet to point out that

> O yet a nobler task awaits thy hand;
> For what can war, but endless war still breed,
> Till truth, and right from violence be freed,
> And public faith cleared from the shameful brand
> Of public fraud. In vain doth valour bleed
> While avarice, and rapine share the land.
> > (ll. 9–14)

These eloquent lines are a powerful indictment of war, and a lament for a nation ruled by violence, avarice and rape.

This sonnet was a response to the shocking renewal of the Civil War. For while John and Mary set up home in High Holborn and cared for their two little daughters and two much bigger nephews, now sixteen and seventeen, the war had erupted once again, with new ferocity. King Charles, now allied with the Scots, and those who were disaffected with Parliament, declared war on the New Model Army and those in Parliament who supported it. The second Civil War was even more vicious than the first. When in the summer Lord Fairfax led the parliamentary forces in their siege of Colchester, capturing the town on 27 August, the Royalist leaders Sir Charles Lucas and Sir George Lisle were immediately shot after trial by court martial. But by the end of August, and Cromwell's defeat of the Scots at the Battle of Preston, the fighting was over.

Charles had lost again. Parliament opened talks with the King immediately. The Treaty of Newport (on the Isle of Wight) marked the final attempt to reach a negotiated settlement and was under-mined, rather predictably, by Charles's secret instructions to his allies to ignore anything he seemed to agree to or say. John Milton's implicit question in his sonnet to Fairfax, about how 'truth' and 'right' could be freed from violence, was very much the question of the time.

John Milton, new to fatherhood, new to encroaching blindness, living with his in-laws, having lost the father who had shaped his life, and living in a city in the eye of the storm, did not have an answer. The impression is of a man withdrawing, both from the developments in his own family (the return of his wife, the birth of his children, the death of his father) and from any clear opinion about the momentous events transforming his country. His identity as a writer stood on a knife edge. Was he a sophisticated Caroline poet, like Waller or Suckling, determined to celebrate and maintain the vanished values of the pre-war period? Was he a religiously independent, socially radical, republican-minded prose pamphleteer, urging political change? Or was he an alien in his own country, a writer who could only find his real audience in the multilingual universities and academies of Italy and beyond? More speculatively, had his marriage, had fatherhood, resolved the conflicts over his sexuality of the previous decades?[28]

As had happened during the period after his return from Italy, events would force Milton's hand and provide some answers. In December, the New Model Army took steps to end the political inertia that had characterised the previous years. They moved against the King himself. On 6 December, about 100 MPs, all either opponents of the army or supporters of continued negotiation with the King, were either imprisoned or secluded. A further group of MPs chose to keep well away, either in fear or protest.[29] What was left was a 'rump' of those loyal to the army. Pride's Purge, named after one of its leaders, Col. Thomas Pride, ensured that there would be no more futile negotiations with the King. Instead, what became known as the Rump Parliament voted that Charles, 'the principal author' of the nation's calamities, would be brought to trial 'according to the fundamental power that rests in themselves'.[30] The charge against the King was that he had been the reason, author and continuer of the 'unnatural, cruel, and bloody wars, and therein guilty of High Treason and of the murders, rapines, burnings, spoils, desolations, damage, and mischief to this nation acted and committed in the said war and occasioned thereby'. It was not only the life of Charles Stuart that was at stake. Crucial to the proceedings was a conflict over two views of monarchy and government. Parliament argued that Charles was 'admitted King of England and therein trusted with a limited power to govern by and according to the laws of the land and not otherwise'. Charles accepted no such thing: 'England was never an elective kingdom but an hereditary kingdom for near these thousand years.'

In the trial that ensued, Parliament attempted both to maintain a proper dignity (the Clerk of the Court's table was 'covered with a rich Turkey carpet', the Lord President would enter the hall in great ceremony with the mace and sword of state carried before him) and to permit access to 'all persons without exception desirous to see or hear'. Each day's proceedings began with the Lord President's cere-monial entry. The King, for his part, made every effort to demonstrate his contempt for the court, whether by failing to remove his hat or show 'any other sign of respect', interrupting the court officials or, above all, refusing to answer the charge against him.

His silence did not help him. The court adjudged that for his 'treasons and crimes' the 'said Charles Stuart, as a tyrant, traitor, murderer, and public enemy to the good people of this nation, shall be put to death by the severing of his head from his body'. It would be done quickly. The sentence would be executed 'in the open street before Whitehall, upon the morrow, being the thirtieth day of this instant month of January, between the hours of ten in the morning and five in the afternoon of the same day, with full effect'. The warrant for execution was signed by the Lord President, by Oliver Cromwell and by fifty-seven other commissioners.

The Lord President, the only man in English history to sign a death warrant for his own monarch, was John Bradshaw. John Bradshaw was John Milton's lawyer. He had become powerful on account of his close links with the City militia and the politically radical elements in the London City Council, the latter having seized control from the more conservative Lord Mayor and aldermen. Bradshaw's elevation to Lord President was yet another expression of the increasing influence of City radicals, his smart apartments in New Palace Yard, and later in the dean's house at Westminster Abbey, another expression that the radicals were becoming the new establishment.[31]

Equally remarkable, however, was the transformation in John Milton. The proceedings against King Charles galvanised him into action. The prose polemicist was back. Between 15 and 29 January, as the trial unfolded, he wrote *The Tenure of Kings and Magistrates*, his defence of the people's right to 'call to account a Tyrant, or wicked King' if the 'ordinary magistrate have neglected or deny'd to do it'. Many still believed that, having waged war on King Charles, it was unthinkable to take the next steps – trial, deposition and execution – which, for Milton, were 'the necessary consequences of their own former actions'.

From the very first sentence of his tract, Milton took on these weak-minded men:

THE TENURE OF

KINGS

AND

MAGISTRATES:

PROVING,

That it is Lawfull, and hath been held so through all Ages, for any, who have the Power, to call to account a Tyrant, or wicked KING, and after due conviction, to depose, and put him to death; if the ordinary MAGISTRATE have neglected, or deny'd to doe it.

And that they, who of late, so much blame Deposing, are the Men that did it themselves.

The Author, J. M.   *K*

LONDON,

Printed by *Matthew Simmons*, at the Gilded Lyon in Aldersgate Street, 1649.

If men within themselves would be govern'd by reason, and not generally give up their understanding to a double tyranny, of Custom from without, and blind affections within, they would discern better, what it is to favour and uphold the Tyrant of a Nation. But being slaves within doors, no wonder that they strive so much to have the public State conformably govern'd to the inward vicious rule, by which they govern themselves. For indeed none can love freedom heartily but good men; the rest love not freedom, but license; which never hath more scope or more indulgence then under Tyrants.[32]

Milton thundered that men's base compliance with tyranny was now being rebranded as loyalty and obedience.

Overall, as Barbara Lewalski points out, '. . . several elements are intertwined here, somewhat disjointedly: castigation of backsliding Presbyterians, rhetorical appeals to the fragmenting revolutionary parties, defenses of tyrannicide, and development of a republican political theory derived from classical and contemporary sources, and the Bible.'[33] From these entangled elements emerged a work that is notably radical in its resistance theory: Parliament and army are doing the right thing, and are therefore both justified in, and able to achieve, their aims. Their success proves that God supports Parliament and the army. This claim alone makes the *Tenure* a revolutionary work.[34]

In the three years between the publication of the *Poems* in January 1646 and the writing of the *Tenure* in January 1649, John Milton had undergone an extraordinary change. His political and religious beliefs, his emotional passion and his intellectual rigour at last coalesced, forming around a single aim. Tyranny must be eradicated from the English State. King Charles and his monarchy had to be destroyed. Even before the court at Whitehall pronounced the death sentence on the King, Milton had come out as a revolutionary republican.

TWELVE

REVOLUTION

1649

A S THE INK DRIED on *The Tenure of Kings and Magistrates,* the event it looked for with such eagerness took place with shocking speed. King Charles I was executed on 30 January 1649. For one New Model Army soldier, '. . . that the king is executed is good news to us: only some few honest men and a few cavaliers bemoan him,' while others remained singularly unmoved: 'A little before supper we saw a diurnal with news that the King was sentenced to die this night: I paid Mr Watson his five pounds for my black mare.'[1] The soldier was wrong. Even those who would come to support the new regime were stunned by events. Bulstrode Whitelock, an MP who kept a fascinating day-by-day diary of events throughout these years, could not bring himself to make an entry on 29 January, such was his distress. The next day, Whitelock did not attend Parliament 'but stayed all day at home, troubled at the death of the King this day, & praying to God to keep his judgements from us'.[2] Fear accompanied shock as the nation struggled to absorb the execution of their King.

An eyewitness account of the execution captures the mood.

I stood amongst the crowd in the street before Whitehall gate where the scaffold was erected, and saw what was done, but was not so near as to hear any thing. The blow I saw given, and can truly say with a sad heart, at the instant whereof, I remember well, there was such a groan by the thousands then present as I never heard before and desire I may never hear again. There was according to Order one Troop immediately marching from Charing Cross to Westminster and another from Westminster to Charing Cross purposely to master the people, and to disperse and scatter them, so that I had much ado amongst the rest to escape home without hurt.[3]

The English people knew that they had witnessed a unique moment in history and wondered, fearfully, what would happen next. As soon has Charles's head had been severed from his body, a contest for hearts and minds began, epitomised by rival interpretations of the crowd's 'groan', one side hearing it as relief, the other sorrow. John Milton would play a crucial role in this battle over the coming months and years.

In the immediate aftermath of the execution, the Rump Parliament had some very practical concerns. Tellingly, the new regime decided that the mechanisms of execution should be removed as quickly as possible, as if the event had never happened. At the same time, they insisted that Charles's body should be put on display to the public 'that all men might know that he was dead'. Accordingly, in a show of respect not usually offered to those executed for treason, the body was embalmed after its head had been sewn back on.

The Rump moved more slowly when it came to enacting the constitutional reforms in the name of which it had executed the King. Through February and March, however, the necessary Acts were passed and the revolution completed. The monarchy was abolished. It was ruled that 'the office was unnecessary, burdensome, and danger-ous to the liberty, safety, and public interest of the people, and that for the most part, use hath been made of the regal power and prerogative to oppress and impoverish and enslave the subject'.[4] The House of Lords, the Privy Council and the Prerogative Courts were all abolished, and the Crown's administrative departments (such as the Exchequer and the Admiralty) replaced by a Council of State. This Council would be supported by a raft of subcommittees with executive powers.

In an appeal to history, the new regime argued that the English nation had at last recovered 'its just and ancient right, of being governed by its own representatives or national meetings in council, from time to time chosen and entrusted for that purpose by the people'. Just as Protestants had asserted that they were merely returning the Church to its original uncorrupt state, the new government was merely returning England to its ancient liberty. Finally, on 19 May 1649, the Act was passed declaring England a 'Commonwealth and Free State'.

England was now the political new world. Over the preceding centuries, various Italian city-states had flirted with republicanism (Venice had been the longest-lasting, Florence had the purest form). Milton, and those of his contemporaries who travelled, might have known the system at first hand on a small scale. They would certainly have read the theory of republicanism, whether in the words of Classical Livy or Renaissance Machiavelli. But it was one thing to read about a political system, or to travel for a month to Venice, another thing to fight a civil war, and to establish a viable republic based on clear anti-monarchical principles. This is what the Rump Parliament did, and there were few who followed their lead until the late eighteenth century.

It did not make England popular in 1649. Throughout Europe, monarchies looked warily at the example of the Commonwealth. Within and beyond the nation's borders, there were many who immediately started working for the counter-revolution. The threat to the Commonwealth was real and urgent, as recognised in the Act for the abolishing of monarchy, in which there were fearsome warnings of what would happen to anyone who tried 'by force of arms or otherwise' to aid, assist, comfort or abet 'any person or persons' who supported the 'setting up again of any pretended right of the said Charles, eldest son to the said late King, James called Duke of York, or of any other the issue and posterity of the said late King'. There is much more of the same. The Act sought to cover any eventuality, and promised 'the same pains, forfeitures, judgements, and execution as is used in case of high treason' to those who challenged the Rump's authority to govern. In other words, the Act told the English people, support any attempt to reinstate monarchy, and you die.

Despite these threats, there were many willing to support the executed King's two sons, Charles and James Stuart, who were still very much alive. Over the next two years, resistance in Ireland in particular proved vicious and prolonged. Henry Ireton, a leading military commander and Cromwell's son-in-law, lost his life at the terrible siege of Limerick, but eventually and bloodily, Cromwell's armies eradicated opposition. There remained the problem of Charles Stuart, who on 1 January 1651 had been crowned King of Scotland, and by September had led an army as far south as Worcester. But Charles's forces were routed in battle there, and the would-be King fled to France. The military threat to the new republic was being dealt with: after all, this was a revolution based on Cromwell's success on the battlefield.

There was, however, a more insidious internal threat to the new regime. Many individuals had expected more, much more, of the revolution. Many would be disappointed in their hopes for religious, social or political change. John Milton in the early months of 1649 was among them.

Most of the more radical religious groups discovered fairly quickly that there was no room for their views in the Commonwealth. At first, hopes were high. In the aftermath of Charles's execution, Fifth Monarchists like John Owen (Cromwell's chaplain) believed even more fervently that the Apocalypse was imminent. If only the rule of the saints could be established in England, then God would 'sooner or later shake all the Monarchies of the Earth'. Another group of religious extremists, the Ranters, were successfully recruiting from the London poor: 'No matter what scripture, saints or churches say, if that within thee do not condemn thee, thou shalt not be condemned,' argued the Ranter Laurence Claxton in 1650. Abiezer Coppe, prosecuted in 1651 for asserting that 'there is no sin', that 'there is no God', 'that God is in man, or in the creature only, and no where else', expressed the Ranters' antinomianism.[5] Many Ranters went further and believed that an individual attained perfection *through* sinning. The aim was to enact a sin as 'no-sin', and the result was a complete rejection of the family unit, the bedrock of seventeenth-century life: 'Give over thy stinking family duties' was the Ranter command.[6]

Other sects, perhaps understandably, distanced themselves from the Ranters while sharing their antinomianism. The Quaker George

Fox took care to argue that he was clear of sin because of the love of Jesus Christ, but that did not mean he *was* actually Jesus Christ: 'Nay, we are nothing. Christ is all.'[7] Nevertheless, Fox received a six-month imprisonment for his blasphemy, 'contrary to the late act of Parliament'.

The 'late act' that convicted Fox was Parliament's response to the religious radicals and merely fuelled disillusion with the revolution among these groups. Further Acts insisted on the observation of the Sabbath, authorised strong punishments for profane swearing or cursing, and, most shocking, instituted the death penalty for those who committed adultery, fornication or incest. Indeed, fear of the radical fringe meant that the Rump Parliament was extremely slow to overturn the statutes that compelled individuals to attend the national Church. It would wait nearly three years to introduce a limited form of religious toleration.

The more explicitly political radicals who welcomed the execution of the King and the abolishment of monarchy also had their hopes shattered in the early months of 1649. To many it seemed as if England had merely replaced a tyrannical monarchy with a tyrannical oligarchy, with government by one man replaced by government by an unaccountable élite. As the Leveller John Lilburne's pamphlet of that year had it, he had *England's New Chains Discovered*. Lilburne questioned 'what now is become of that liberty that no man's person shall be attached or imprisoned, or otherwise dis-eased of his Freehold, or free Customs, but by lawful judgements of his equals?'[8] Disillusion led to demands for military action. Lilburne's ally, Richard Overton, proposed that a joint council of officers and men from the New Model Army, who had, after all, achieved the removal of the King, should rule the country. Overton urged the soldiers and the people of England to fight for this cause.

Oliver Cromwell responded aggressively, but the funeral of one Trooper Lockyer, shot by Cromwell's men, became something of a public demonstration of support for the Army. A hundred people walked in front of the corpse, which was decorated with bunches of rosemary for remembrance, stained with blood. Lockyer's sword was laid upon his body. Soldiers on horseback followed, and then thousands of foot soldiers, wearing sea-green and black ribbons, green the colour of the Leveller movement, black a sign of respect. Behind the men came a procession of women. At Westminster, near the churchyard where Lockyer was to be buried, 'some thousands more of the better sort' joined the mourners, unwilling to march in the procession but keen to show their support. It was a remarkable and unprecedented display of political will.

There were more unprecedented political developments to come. The Levellers' democratic ideals were rooted in their Christian beliefs: all men (and, even more remarkably, all women) were equal before God.[9] And now it was the Leveller women's turn to make their case to Parliament. Thousands of women, led by Lilburne's wife, presented a special petition. They were told to go home and wash their dishes. The women replied that they had at home neither food nor dishes. The women's *Petition* is a passionate and eloquent argument for all women's common humanity with men, and a record of these particular women's sufferings during wartime and beyond. Years of 'unjust cruelties' inspired them, but the execution of Robert Lockyer and the imprisonment of the Leveller leaders – 'our friends in the Tower', as the *Petition* put it – triggered their extraordinary action in 1649. Commanded to stay at home, the women invoked their Christian duty to speak out, to bear testimony:

Nay, shall such valiant, religious men as Mr. Robert Lockyer be liable to law martial, and to be judged by his adversaries, and most inhumanly shot to death? Shall the blood of war be shed in time of peace? Doth not the word of God expressly condemn it . . . . And are we Christians, and shall we sit still and keep at home, while such men as have borne continual testimony against the injustice of all times and unrighteousness of men, be picked out and be delivered up to the slaughter . . .[10]

Parliament was not listening, *could* not listen, to such outrageous proto-feminist claims as these.

Nevertheless, a petition signed by 90,000 people, 'Remonstrance of many thousands of the free people of England', appeared in September, suggesting that the movement was thriving. In fact, the 'Remonstrance' was the Levellers' death rattle. Their political ideas were far ahead of their time. More importantly, they faced the implacable opposition of Oliver Cromwell. Looking back, a few years later, at the state of the nation in 1649, Cromwell described it as 'rent and torn in spirit and in principle from one end to another . . . family against family, husband against wife, parents against children, and nothing in the hearts and minds of men but "Overturning, over-turning, overturning . . ."'[11] His task, as he saw, was to stand firm against those who sought merely to 'Overturn', against those who pursued a 'levelling principle' that would 'tend to the reducing of all to an equality'. For Cromwell, however, standing firm invariably meant violent action. As he warned his Council, 'I tell you . . . you have no other way to deal with these men but to break them in pieces. If you do not break them, they will break you.'[12]

Cromwell's determination to crush the Army Levellers was one factor in the movement's collapse. Less violent but perhaps as effective, the Rump Parliament took care to pay the New Model soldiers, something the parliamentary leaders of 1646–7 had often failed to do. Once paid, many soldiers lost interest in their political ambitions: radicalism was perhaps not actually as deep-rooted in the Army as it first seemed.[13]

There was, however, a third grouping in the radical challenge to the new Commonwealth, a movement that reached beyond religious and political claims towards a complete revolution in the economic and social basis of English society. This movement had its beginnings in the particularly harsh economic conditions of the period from 1648 to 1650, when, in the face of grinding poverty and the threat of starvation, agrarian communities came together to farm common lands for food. The most famous of these 'Digger' communities was based at St George's Hill in Surrey, and later at Cobham Heath, also in Surrey. Its leader was Gerard Winstanley, and his tract of 1649, *The New Law of Righteousnes*, demanded the return of all public lands to the people. Winstanley told his readers that he had received a simple but revolutionary message in a trance: 'Work together, Eat bread together.' The Surrey commune was his attempt to put his vision into practice. On common land, the Diggers grew corn, parsnips, carrots and beans. It did not take long for persecution to begin. The community was attacked and its buildings burned. Winstanley merely became more urgent in his pamphleteering, offering *A Watch-word to the City of London and the Armie*, in which he argued that freedom is won not given, and urging the people to take action on their own behalf. The utopian Digger movement, so much smaller than the Leveller movement (and condemned even by them), was, however, as doomed to destruction as all the other radical movements of the time. In the face of the hostility of local landowners, harassment by soldiers and lawsuits, the commune could not survive. There was no trace of the Diggers by July 1650.

As the Digger movement demonstrated, it was the poor who suffered most in these years of failed crops and uncertain government, but no one was exempt from at least some misery. The diarist John Evelyn recalled the freak weather conditions of 1648, a 'most exceeding wet year, neither frost or snow all the winter for above six days in all, and cattle died of a murrain [infectious disease] every where'.[14] The traditional response to hunger was to see it as God's will, as the preacher Robert Wilkinson had advised corn rioters back in 1607: 'Therefore, consider and see I beseech you, whence arise conspiracies, riots, and damnable rebellions; not from want of bread, but through want of faith, yea want of bread doth come by want of faith.'[15] It remained to be seen whether the new republican Commonwealth would be any better than previous governments at delivering the poor from starvation, or whether the 'want of bread' would remain, conveniently, simply an incontrovertible sign of God's displeasure with his people.

And what of John Milton? No Ranter or Digger, no Leveller or Quaker, Milton was nevertheless a disappointed man in the spring of 1649. He expressed his disappointment with the new regime by writing an astonishing fifty thousand words in six weeks, the first four chapters of his (admittedly already researched) *History of Britain*, together with a 'Digression' considering the state of the nation. The work would not be published for more than twenty years, but this was Milton's response to the crisis of the English revolution, his *History* 'just the swift review needed for historical instruction at a critical time'.[16]

Milton recognised that the country was at a transitional stage but feared that England was sliding back to its old political ways. Members of Parliament ousted by the Rump, those who had voted in favour of further negotiations with the King back in December 1648, were being allowed to return to Westminster, having conveniently changed their minds about their earlier decision. Milton in his 'Digression' lamented that the opportunity to establish republican government was being squandered within a month of the execution of the King. He was angry and fearful: 'they who had the chief management', who were 'masters of their own choice, were not found able' to create even the hope 'of a just and well amended commonwealth to come'.[17] As ever, Milton was worried about the condition of English manhood. The heat of the violent man, happy to start civil wars, could not be sustained and would turn to weakness; the cool temperance (not to mention the Classical and Mediterranean political thinking) needed to run a country was nowhere to be found.[18]

Just one fortnight after the execution of Charles, Milton had been happy to quote Seneca in the printed preface to his *Tenure of Kings and Magistrates*:

> There can be slain
> No sacrifice to God more acceptable
> Than an unjust and wicked king.

Only a few weeks later, he was already wondering if it had all been worth it. Yet the sacrificial slaying of King Charles was to prove a turning point for Milton. Only six weeks after the execution, and four weeks after he had leapt back into print with his *Tenure*, he was invited by the new government to become Secretary for Foreign Tongues to the Council of State at a salary of £288 per annum. He accepted the position, a sign, perhaps, that his fear of political backsliding was transitory. Whether out of pragmatism or idealism, he joined forces with the new regime. If Bradshaw and Cromwell were indeed going to transform England into a beacon of republican good governance, then John Milton was going to be part of that transformation.

The Council needed someone to handle their diplomatic correspondence with foreign nations. Much of the correspondence would be in Latin, still the political lingua franca of Europe. They chose Milton. His talent for Latin was indisputable; his *Tenure* had established his political loyalty, even before Charles's head had rolled; and his connection with John Bradshaw can have done no harm.

Bradshaw had not stopped at sentencing King Charles to death. Having chaired the high court of justice set up to try Royalist military leaders, on 14 February 1649 he became one of forty-one peers, politicians, judges and soldiers chosen by MPs to sit on the new Council of State. This Council would be the principal executive organ of the Commonwealth of England and Ireland. The day after the executions of the Royalist military leaders, Bradshaw was appointed Lord President of the Council by his colleagues, making him in effect England's first elected executive head of state.

Whether Lord President Bradshaw pulled the necessary strings or not, John Milton was now the Council's Secretary for Foreign Tongues. At last he was in a position to exploit all his linguistic abilities. Back in 1644 in his tract *Of Education*, he had worried about the poor Latin pronunciation of his fellow Englishmen: 'For we Englishmen, being far northerly, do not open our mouths in the cold air wide enough to grace a southern tongue.' Now he could, quite literally, open his mouth wide in the northern air, speak and write in Latin to the honour of his country. Crucially, Milton's ability in Latin gave credibility to the new government: there were not too many highly educated intellectuals who would have served the Commonwealth in 1649. Milton was in a superb position to reply, intelligently and fluently, to the attacks that flowed from Catholic, monarchical Europe.

John Milton was where he wanted to be. His talents were now in the service of a political regime that he supported in principle, and all doubts were laid aside. Looking back at this period later, he wrote that he abandoned the pessimistic *History* in the face of his new responsibilities.[19] He may have been writing to the Council's orders, but he had a clear focus and a clear path ahead of him.

The Council quickly realised that Milton also had his uses as a propagandist. His first major assignment looked like familiar territory. He was asked to respond to a pamphlet. This was no ordinary pamphlet, however: it was *Eikon Basilike* (The King's Image), a short work allegedly written by King Charles I himself. *Eikon Basilike* turned Charles I from a villainous and inept leader who had been rightfully removed from office, and from life, into a saintly figure, sanctioned by God himself to lead his country and martyred by vicious extremists. The pamphlet built on the indisputable fact that Charles had died well. Even his opponents had to admit that the King had demonstrated courage and firmness on the scaffold, the more surprising because these qualities were not natural to him. Some years later, the poet Andrew Marvell would capture the moment in a poem ostensibly in praise of the man who replaced Charles as leader, Oliver Cromwell:

> He nothing common did or mean
> Upon that memorable scene,
> But with his keener eye
> The axe's edge did try:
>
> Nor call'd the gods, with vulgar spite,
> To vindicate his helpless right,
> But bowed his comely head
> Down, as upon a bed.[20]

To many, this composure revealed that God was with the King, something that Charles repeatedly pointed out in his comments on the scaffold.

Typical of *Eikon Basilike*'s religious tone is the chapter recounting Charles's captivity at Holmby, which enabled him 'to study the world's vanity and inconstancy'. God sees 'tis fit to deprive me of wife, children, army, friends, and freedom, that I may be wholly His, Who alone is all.' The work ends with the King's meditations on death, his prayers and the prophetic (or canny) comment that 'the glory attending my death will far surpass all I could enjoy or conceive in life.'[21]

John Milton, who had already written so passionately in support of the legitimacy of removing the tyrannical Charles in his *Tenure of Kings and Magistrates*, rose to the challenge presented by *Eikon Basilike*. His reply was published on 6 October 1649 and entitled *Eikonoklastes* (The Image Destroyer). Milton used the technique he had first deployed in the early 1640s, whereby he took the very phrases of the enemy and turned them against him.

> *That I went*, saith he of his going to the House of Commons, *attended with some Gentlemen*; Gentlemen indeed; the ragged infantry of stews and brothels; the spawn and shipwreck of taverns and dicing houses ... The House of Commons upon several examinations of this business declared it sufficiently proved that the coming of those soldiers, Papists and others with the King, was to take away some of their Members, and in case of opposition or denial, to have fallen upon the House in a hostile manner. This the King here denies; adding a fearful imprecation against his own life, *If he purposed any violence or oppression against the innocent, then*, saith he, *let the enemy persecute my soul, and tread my life to the ground and lay my honour in the dust*. What need then more disputing? He appealed to God's tribunal, and behold God hath judged, and done to him in the sight of all men according to the verdict of his own mouth.[22]

Eikonoklastes is not only a savage attack on Charles I, who whipped 'all his Kingdoms' with 'his two twisted Scorpions, both temporal and spiritual tyranny', and pursued 'his private interest' at all times, but a defence of the new political order: 'For who should better understand

ΕΙΚΟΝΟΚΛΑΣΤΗΣ

IN

Anſwer

To a Book Intitl'd

ΕΙΚΩΝ ΒΑΣΙΛΙΚΗ,

THE

Portrature of his Sacred Majesty

in his *Solitudes* and *Sufferings*.

The Author I. Milton

PROV. 28. 15, 16, 17.

15. *As a roaring Lyon, and a ranging Beare, ſo is a wicked Ruler over the poor people.*

16. *The Prince that wanteth underſtanding, is alſo a great oppreſſor; but he that hateth covetouſneſſe ſhall prolong his dayes.*

17. *A man that doth violence to the blood of any perſon, ſhall fly to the pit, let no man ſtay him.*

Saluſt. Conjurat. Catilin.

Regium imperium, quod initio, conſervandæ libertatis, atque augendæ reipub. causâ fuerat, in ſuperbiam, dominationemque ſe convertit.
Regibus boni, quàm mali, ſuſpectiores ſunt; ſemperque his aliena virtus formidoloſa eſt.
Quidlibet impunè facere, hoc ſcilicet regium eſt.

Publiſhed by Authority.

London, Printed by *Matthew Simmons*, next dore to the gilded Lyon in Alderſgate ſtreet. 1649.

their own laws, and when they are transgressed, than they who are governed by them, and whose consent first made them: and who can have more right to take knowledge of things done within a free nation, than they within themselves?'[23] Milton's reply became a rallying cry to the recently liberated nation. If they only had virtues such as piety, justice and fortitude, joined with contempt for avarice and ambition, then the people 'need not Kings to make them happy, but are the architects of their own happiness'.[24]

It was an optimistic assessment of the English people, based on Milton's belief in the necessity for shared government, an independent Church and the value of meritocracy. The benefits of a society should never again 'come to be within the gift of any single person'. Yet the pamphlet's closing sentences recognise that the image of King Charles that Milton had spent so many pages destroying still had power, if only over the 'rabble'. There was hope, if the English people could just break the spell of monarchy and 'recover'. *Eikon Basilike* might gain Charles

> after death a short, contemptible, and soon fading reward; not what he aims at, to stir the constancy and solid firmness of any wise man, or to unsettle the conscience of any knowing Christian, if he could ever aim at a thing so hopeless, and above the genius of his cleric elocution, but to catch the worthless approbation of an inconstant, irrational, and image-doting rabble. The rest whom perhaps ignorance without malice, or some error, less than fatal, hath for the time misled on this side sorcery or obduration may find the grace and good guidance to bethink themselves, and recover.[25]

John Milton's political journey may have been a long and uneven one (and remains a subject of contention among Miltonists), but he was now the voice of republican England. The Council also drew on his considerable experience of the practicalities of the book trade. Milton liaised with stationers on the Council's behalf and arranged publication of official works, as well as contributing his own writings to the political effort. So far, so good, but suddenly, John Milton, the author who had cut his political teeth with numerous unlicensed, illegal publications and defended a free press so eloquently in the (unlicensed and thus illegal) *Areopagitica*, found himself on the other side of the censorship fence. He now had to enforce the Rump Parliament's Act of 20 September 1649, which renewed some of the restrictions on the liberty of the press. This was a step backwards for the regime, which had previously taken 'the calculated risk of allowing full reporting of every stage of the trial in the newsbooks, even though this meant relaying Charles' sharp retorts against his judges'.[26] In the early months of 1649, the Rump had wanted the execution of the King to be public, not private tyrannicide. Now they were keener to control opinion.

By the end of 1649, Milton was a government insider, busier and more productive than he had been at any other stage in his life. That year has been described with some justice as his annus mirabilis. It was the year in which he wrote the *Tenure*, the first four books of the *History*, the *Observations* (a work for the Commonwealth concerning their policy in Ireland) and *Eikonoklastes*.[27] He also prepared numerous Latin letters of State for his masters. All this was achieved as his eyesight continued to decline.

By the end of the year, he and his family were actually living at the heart of government, in Whitehall Palace. On 19 November 1649, a note stipulated that 'Mr Milton shall have the lodgings that were in the hands of Sir John Hippely in Whitehall for his accommodation as being Secretary to the Council for Foreign Languages.'[28] From his house in Scotland Yard, one of the Whitehall courtyards, Mr Milton was on hand to attend the informal, unminuted Council meetings held at the palace, as well as his more formal business for the Commonwealth. Whitehall was not terribly palatial in the seventeenth century. Instead, its tiny courtyards and passageways were reminiscent of a cramped medieval town.[29] The palace had been given something of a facelift in the time of Charles I, gaining Inigo Jones's Banqueting Hall with its Rubens ceiling, but it still remained a sprawling, rambling structure of about 2,000 rooms. As ever, there is nothing to indicate whether and how family life for the Miltons changed with the move.

Mary Powell Milton, still only twenty-four years old, would presumably have packed up her clothes, her spices, her plate and her linen, and set up home, bringing her two daughters, now aged three and one, with her.[30] Servants of the State had started to bring their families to live with them at Whitehall during the reign of Charles I: Scotland Yard and the Royal Mews had been developed to house 'every mean courtier' and his family, much to the dismay of some.

As one would expect, the accommodation for civil servants such as Milton and his family remained far away from what had been the Privy lodgings. Little had changed in the layout and significance of these lodgings now that the monarchy had been abolished. The rooms at Whitehall remained organised according to a system whereby access to each new room signified a further element of trust and acceptance by the ruling power. The names of the rooms had, however, been changed, and in practical terms access had been improved. So, the Queen's Presence Chamber became the new Council Chamber, and a new route was created to it directly from the river. The various committees that administered the Commonwealth now met in rooms previously used by Royalty. Through the Civil War, Whitehall had been neglected, the gardens suffering in particular. In 1650, they were restored and re-turfed. The palace remained well furnished. The Rump Parliament may have sold off the vast majority of the goods and personal estate of the King but could not resist holding on to about £10,000 of material from Whitehall. By 1651, this figure had risen to £50,000, the goods kept for the use of Parliament. In a move typical of regime change, hundreds of pounds were voted to set up appropriate lodgings for the Council of State and to increase security for Council members.[31]

As the months went by, the pace of life at Whitehall did not slow. The Council had plenty of uses for their Latin Secretary. Milton was recruited to help with the new government newspaper *Mercurius Politicus*, launched in June 1650. The newspaper was run by Marchamont Nedham, who, only a year earlier, had been arrested for producing a Royalist newspaper, fittingly named *Mercurius Pragmaticus*. *Mercurius Politicus* was an attempt to beat the King's supporters at their own game. Newsbooks and pamphlets had emerged from Charles's central command at Oxford, and the Royalist newspaper *Mercurius Aulicus*, which had run from January 1643 to September 1645, had set a new standard of sophistication in propagandist war reporting. Under Nedham, and with a bit of help from Milton, *Mercurius Politicus* became the predominant newsbook of the 1650s with Nedham, a 'pioneer in the development of journalism', using his editorials to disseminate republican theory.[32] It was all part of the republic's attempts to control any internal challenge, epitomised by Parliament's enforcement of the Engagement of 2 January 1650, in which all men over eighteen had to swear loyalty to a Commonwealth without a King or Lords.

It was harder to inspire or coerce the loyalty of those opponents to republicanism who had fled abroad. In Holland, the exiled English Royalists, led by the son of Charles I, commissioned Claude de Saumaise, one of the great Classical scholars of the period, to write *Defensio Regia Pro Carolo I* (Defence of the Reign of Charles I). De Saumaise, or Salmasius as he was called in European Latin circles, was, like Milton, known for his remarkable facility with languages at an early age, with Hebrew, Arabic and Coptic among his linguistic armoury. Milton's new task was to take on Salmasius and his work. The battle between the two men would be one of the most celebrated, not to mention nasty and prolonged, literary and political clashes of the period.

With some cunning, *Mercurius Politicus* derided Salmasius for months before Milton's response emerged, creating an audience for the comeback of England's combatant. At last, Milton's *Pro Populo Anglicano Defensio* (The Defence of the English People) was published, on 24 February 1651. Alongside the satire of Salmasius' grasp of English (the plural of 'hundred' is not 'hundreda', Milton pointed out gleefully in a prefatory poem), there was no holding back on the personal insults. Salmasius is described as 'a talkative ass sat upon by a woman', 'a eunuch priest, your wife for a husband', an 'agent of royal roguery', a 'hireling pimp of slavery', 'a gallic cock' and 'a dung-hill Frenchman'. His wife is a 'barking bitch'.[33] Abusing his French opponent (and his wife) was the easy part. There were many other areas where Milton had to tread more carefully. Salmasius accused the Council of State of tyranny, something Milton was happy to refute, but he also accused the Council of being made up of the 'wickedest rabble', since those of noble blood had been excluded. Milton had a problem here, in that he, the son of a scrivener (hardly from the rabble but certainly not from the nobility), had to demonstrate his own natural nobility in the face of this kind of attack. This is one of the reasons that, when writing about himself in the 1650s, Milton was relentless in his assertions of his own gentility, and the nobility of the men he was serving.

Less personal to Milton himself, but equally problematic to the new republic, was Salmasius' appeal to the traditional interlinking of God, King and Father. In removing the King, the English people were rejecting both God and the family. Milton tackled this head on, bravely taking kingship out of the equation:

> But upon my word, you are still in darkness since you do not distinguish a father's right from a king's. And when you have called kings fathers of their country, you believe that you have persuaded people at once by this metaphor: that whatever I would admit about a father, I would straightway grant to be true of a king. A father and a king are very different things. A father has begotten us; but a king has not made us, but rather we the king. Nature gave a father to people, the people themselves gave themselves a king; so people do not exist because of a king, but a king exists because of the people.[34]

For all the confidence, however, Milton's own anxieties seeped into the *Defence*. His ideal political models derived from Mediterranean countries, and it appeared genuinely to trouble him whether, for example, the republicanism of Athens or the Senate of Rome *could* be transplanted to a cold northern country. More importantly, there was a suggestion that the business of the Commonwealth had not been completed: 'Our form of government is such as our circumstances and schisms permit; it is not the most desirable, but only as good as the stubborn struggles of the wicked citizens allow it to be.' The crucial issue for the English nation was how to win the peace, having won the war ('*ad ultimum sibi constare, et sua uti victoria sciebant*'), above all to know 'the purpose and reason of winning'.

The hope expressed was that popular liberty had been secured by the army. Again, however, there is a qualification of this apparent support for the people hidden away in the Latin. Milton used a Latin form of 'popular' which links the word to the *sanior*, a fit, appropriate minority. As ever, he was worried by any form of democracy. Government had to be concentrated in the hands of suitable people. Overall, Milton trod carefully, showing some political caution. Charles Stuart in exile had many supporters, and the new Commonwealth needed to rally its own supporters in Europe. Many of the states they were wooing were monarchies, and so the *Defence* demonstrates the supremacy of law rather than attacking the system of monarchy itself. One Milton scholar goes so far as to say that Milton 'argues that he is defending the rights of a particular people at a particular time to deal with a particular king, rather than the merits of republicanism'.[35] In this reading, there is no republican ideology at work in the *Defence*, just raw political pragmatism, an attempt to soften the edges of the English political experiment.

If this was the intention, then the plan misfired. While the *Defence* sold throughout Europe (being Milton's most frequently reprinted work during his lifetime, with at least ten editions published in the first year alone, including a translation from the original Latin into Dutch), it was also the most viciously attacked. It was publicly burned in cities throughout Europe, most often in the absolutist France of Louis XIV and his Cardinal Mazarin, with the fires lit in Toulouse and Paris in the year of the work's publication. However cautious the *Defence* might have been, Milton, as the scholar David Norbrook suggests, still made clear the connection between abuses of Royal power and the very nature of the monarchical office, with its inbuilt tendency to aggrandise the human will.[36] In a sign of Milton's inexorable journey away from establishment respectability, the boy who had played the Elder Brother in the *Maske* at Ludlow would grow into the man who would write into a copy of the *Defence*, '*Liber igni, Author furca, dignissimi*' (The book is most deserving of burning, the author of the gallows).[37] The *Defence*, for good or for evil, established Milton as something of a European intellectual celebrity, described by the Dutch philologist and poet Nicholas Heinsius as extremely well educated, 'born in a noble position, and brought up in luxury. He is an extremely little chap and in precarious health',[38] or celebrated for his talent by another European intellectual, Isaac Vossius, who argued that the burning of Milton's *Defence* would never extirpate his writings since 'they rather shine out with a certain wonderful increase of lustre by means of those flames.'[39]

From being one small, if notorious, drop in the ocean of polemical pamphlet writings in the 1640s, Milton's learning had earned him a voice in government, a voice that would define the new England to a sceptical Europe. It was a voice that he had sought since his return from Italy. In one of his earliest pamphlets on Church Reform, he had outlined his literary plans. An epic and a tragedy were hinted at; both would look back to a time before the Norman Conquest, when the English were free and Christianity was a purer faith, and, above all, both would be 'doctrinal and exemplary to a nation'.[40]

His value to the Council was obvious. Just after the publication of the *Defence*, there was an attempt to remove 'Mr Milton out of his lodgings in Whitehall'. The pressure was coming from the parliamentary MPs, who wanted Whitehall for themselves, demanding the 'best conveniences' and quite happy to move the civil servants out. The Council members stood up for Mr Milton, insisting that he remain in Whitehall, 'where he is in regard of the employment which he is in to the Council, which necessitates him to reside near the Council'.[41]

It is unlikely that he had ever been so busy. A fascinating correspondence between him and a visiting ambassador, Herman Mylius, reveals the day-to-day details of his life in government. Milton writes from Westminster, postponing his meeting with Mylius because he has been delayed in a parliamentary meeting. In another letter, he is concerned to get his business done by two in the afternoon, because the Council will be meeting in the evening. There is, of course, an element of diplomatic man-management here, and Milton may well have been buying time. When he does finally respond to Mylius (again claiming a hectic schedule), it happens to be on the same day that the Council approves the motion to consider Mylius' business, the Oldenburg Case.

Herman Mylius had been sent to London by Count Anthon

Gunther of Oldenburg in the summer of 1651 to secure from the English government a safeguard which would give Oldenburg merchants protection from seizure of their goods and vessels by English warships, which were at the time engaged in undeclared naval wars with both France and Portugal. The County of Oldenburg, lying between the United Netherlands and the Hanseatic city of Bremen in the north-west of Germany, had remained neutral during the Thirty Years War and was determined to stay neutral now. Mylius believed that Milton was the man who could ensure that he returned home to Oldenburg with his safeguard.

Mylius needed a bit of managing. His letters are intense creations, diplomatic correspondence at an exalted emotional level. Milton is his 'dear adornment', while Herman (quoting the Roman author Horace) is the lover deceived. Mylius signs off that he is 'yours even in death' and, in another letter, reminds Milton of 'yesterday's promise after our morning embrace'. Mylius even characterises himself as a lover: 'You must have observed how lovers sicken, who want what they crave at once. But I shall loiter in your love and so die.' Admittedly, Mylius did have a lot to thank Milton for, or at least that's how Milton wanted him to see it, hinting that it was he who had pushed the Oldenburg Case through, 'most eager in your interests and your honour'.[42]

Meanwhile, through these turbulent years of regime change, economic crisis and diplomatic business, Milton continued to manage his financial resources with exemplary skill, and continued to pay his mother-in-law her widow's thirds every autumn and spring from the Oxfordshire estate.[43] Anne Powell and John Milton were both involved in attempts to establish their rights to the land and property in Forest Hill and Wheatley, and there is much evidence of cooperation between them. The relationship between Anne Powell and her son-in-law had, however, soured by the spring of 1651, as post-war legislation gave to Milton what it took from Anne. When, in March 1651, Milton paid the final fines (two payments of £65) to free the Wheatley estate from sequestration, the Committee in question instructed him to keep all the money from the Powell property rather than hand over a percentage to his mother-in-law. Anne Powell, understandably, petitioned for redress, complaining that she lived in poverty and needed the money 'to preserve her and her children from starving'. Her youngest child was still only about eleven years old. Her testimony, which survives in the National Archives, was offered in July 1651 and gives a rare glimpse of Milton family life, at least as seen through Anne Powell's eyes. Anne claims that she cannot raise the issue with her son-in-law, whom she describes as a 'harsh and choleric man', because he will take it out on her daughter Mary.[44] It is not a pleasant image, of John the bullying husband. At the time she made the claim, John and Mary had just become parents again. On 16 March 1651, Mary Powell Milton gave birth to a baby boy named John, born at 9.30 in the evening at the family's apartment at Whitehall. By the summer, Mary was pregnant again.

Anne Powell was back in court repeatedly the following year, determined to gain reparation for her losses in the Civil War. Her argument was that Parliament had seized far more than it was entitled to by the Articles of War, including her possessions. The process of litigation was slow and stressful, and cannot have been easy for her, but the tension between her and John seems to have been resolved. Eventually, in May 1654, she did receive a rebate from the state of £192 4s 1d. Others who had supported the Royalist cause were also finding life hard. Thomas Agar, Milton's brother-in-law, lost his government post in the last years of the Civil War and did not regain it. He had retreated from London to Lincoln by 1650, and it is unclear how he survived over the following years.

John Milton, property owner in London and Oxfordshire and now father to a son, was, in contrast, doing well. The estate at Wheatley yielded only 50s in November 1648 but £10 in October 1650. In 1649, Milton installed a new tenant in the property and, over these years, took in about £280 a year in tithes. Overall, the two years following the execution of Charles I were filled with achievements for Milton. He was exceptionally productive in his writing; successful in his financial dealings; making a political name for himself in England and beyond; the father of a new baby boy; the husband of a wife pregnant with their fourth child. These were, perhaps, the best years of his life.

THIRTEEN

GOVERNMENT

1651

Y ET DAY BY DAY Milton was struggling with the illnesses and pain connected with the final destruction of his eyesight. His contemporaries knew he suffered from illness. Herman Mylius, for one, noted that he had 'headache' and 'inflammation of the eyes' in a letter written on 1 January 1652.[1] But they did not realise the whole truth, partly because Milton tried so hard, for so long, to continue to write, to continue to be independent. There were good reasons to do so. His blindness and the related illnesses could all too easily be seized upon by his enemies and used as weapons against him.

The final loss of Milton's eyesight can be tracked in his dealings with Mylius. In late October 1651, Mylius noted in his diary, in his strange mixture of Latin and German, that Milton *'hat in me praesentia die notata ad marginem selbst gesetzet'* (in my presence he set down the notes in the margin himself).[2] Milton was doing everything in his power to maintain the façade of a sighted man. Still in December, he concealed from Mylius the nature of his problem. Unspecified 'ill health' was his 'perpetual enemy' while on 31 December, he apologised for a two-week delay in writing caused by 'for the sake of my health, a necessary and sudden move to another house, which I had chanced to begin on that very day on which your letter was brought to me'.[3]

This house move took the forty-three-year-old John and his family, in the depths of winter, to a house in Petty France in Westminster, opening into St James's Park. There they remained close to the seat of government, with Mary expecting their fourth child, the baby John only nine months old, and the girls still only five and three. It is, however, possible that little John was away from his family at this time, since many small children were sent out to nurse during their early years, only returning home once weaned. Some nurses did live with families, however, and perhaps this is how things were organised in the 'pretty garden house' with its view of the park.

Over the coming year, this young family would be torn apart. By May 1652, Mary was preparing for her fourth labour. For any mother and father, the time leading up to a birth was an anxious one. Many women prepared themselves spiritually for death, knowing the appalling interconnection between maternity and mortality. Only God could know who would survive, who would thrive. One Londoner, Nehemiah Wallington, wrote, with anxiety, that 'one or two weeks before my wife fell sick, I did hear of three score women with child and in childbed that died in one week in Shoreditch parish, and scarce two of a hundred that was sick with child that escaped death.' Another diarist, Nicholas Assheton, recorded his wife's labour:

> February 16. My wife in labour of childbirth. Her delivery was with such violence as the child died within half an hour, and, but for God's wonderful mercy, more than human reason could expect, she had died; but he spared her a while longer to me, and took the child to his mercy; for which, as for one of his great mercies bestowed on me, I render all submissive, hearty thanks and praise to the only good and gracious God of Israel.[4]

In many cases, women returned to their mother's house to give birth, or the mother came to the daughter. Anne Powell was living in London, and so may well have supported her daughter, if her other family responsibilities and her financial difficulties permitted her to do so. Overall, however, it was the responsibility of the husband to ensure, for example, that the midwife would be in attendance. But which of the following fairly typical exertions on the part of one expectant father in 1645, the minister Ralph Josselin, could John manage in his blindness, and what could he not?

I had prayed with confidence of good success to her. About midnight on Monday I rose, called up some neighbours; the night was very light, Goodman Potter willing to go for the midwife, and up when I went; the horse out of the pasture, but presently found; the midwife up at Bures, expecting it had been nearer day; the weather indifferent dry; midwife came, all things even gotten ready towards day. I called in the women by daylight, almost all came; and about 11 or 12 of the clock my wife was with very sharp pains delivered November 25 of her daughter intended for a Jane; she was then twenty-five years of age herself. We had made a good pasty for this hour, and that also was kept well. Wife and child both well, praise be my good and merciful Father.[5]

Did Milton ensure that a 'good pasty' had been made in preparation for his wife's labour? Did he, as one husband did, make sure that his wife, desperate to eat sprats, felt pleased that he had arranged her desired fish supper before 'she lay down'? It is hard to imagine, but scepticism may be an unfair response to the paucity of domestic documents in the Milton archive. Some of these events, or ones similar, must have occurred in the household: John was not, and could not have been, completely detached from the ordinary stuff of life. Yet the very difficulty of imagining him organising a 'pasty' for his wife suggests a triumph both for Milton's own self-representation and its perpetuation by many of his biographers and critics: as one puts it, no one would be interested in 'the ordinary Circumstances of his Life' 'which are common to him with all other Men'.[6]

In May 1652, when Mary successfully gave birth to a daughter, John made another entry in the family Bible. Still struggling to write despite his blindness, he wrote, 'My daughter Deborah was born . . .' but could not complete the sentence. Someone else had to write that she was born at about three in the morning of 2 May. The choice of name demonstrates a particular political and religious consciousness in Milton at this time. Deborah was an uncommon name, setting this third daughter apart from her sisters Mary and Anne. (Mary and Anne were the second and third most popular names for girls through the preceding three decades behind Elizabeth: Deborah came in at twenty-eighth.) Since there were no family members called Deborah, the choice must have honoured the biblical Deborah, a radical Christian heroine for centuries and, in the Civil War and beyond, a figure of vengeance. Her song in Judges 5 was used to justify armed struggle against tyranny.[7]

The choice of name may well have been entirely Milton's, a signal of his commitment to the godly overthrow of his monarch, to the continuation of the republican revolution. Traditionally, godparents chose a baby's name, but this was now viewed as popish superstition in Reformed households. Moreover, Mary Powell Milton was too ill to consider the matter: the birth had been a difficult one for her. Indeed, the note in the family Bible recording Deborah's birth would have, when seen in its entirety, a devastating conclusion: 'My daughter Deborah was born the 2d of May, being Sunday somewhat before 3 of the clock in the morning 1652. My wife her mother died about 3 days after.'[8] As Mary lay dying, the passing bell tolled for her so that both Mary and her neighbours would know her end was near. Nine strokes of the bell were tolled for a man (popularly called the Nine Tailors), six for a woman and three for a child: these were then followed by one stroke for each year of the dying person's age. In Mary's case, there would have been only twenty-seven strokes. She had been married to John for exactly ten years and lived with him for seven, during which time she had borne him four children, including a male heir. Anne, disabled in some way, was nearly six; her sister Mary three and a half, toddler John just fourteen months old, and now there was three-day-old Deborah.

To whom did Milton turn at this time? His sister and mother were dead. His nephews had left or were leaving his house to start their own lives, and in any case young men would not be expected to help in this way. Perhaps he called on one of Mary's sisters, or her mother. To some extent, the impact of Mary's death would have been slightly mitigated by the contemporary practices in raising young children, with Deborah fed by a wet nurse (to protect her from the perceived dangers of colostrum, the 'first milk' produced by the mother immediately after birth), and fourteen-month-old John probably with his own nurse.[9] Childcare was women's work, of course, but not necessarily the mother's work. Since wealthy mothers did not expect to care for their very young children physically, it is no surprise that fathers were completely excluded (at least in theory) from the process. It was, insisted commentators, both odd and effeminate for men to handle babies. These traditions of child-rearing meant that Milton could have established, relatively easily, a network of support, created in part from his extended female family, in part from professional help, to ensure the care of his four children. Whatever system he put in place, his priority remained his work.

As father and as husband, however, he still had important responsibilities. Deborah needed to be baptised, and his wife Mary buried. When John's grandmother and mother had been buried, the bells had been rung, the burial had taken place within the church or churchyard, a sermon had been preached. But by 1652, these traditional burial rituals had been officially banned, all part of the effort to achieve full godly Reformation. Other rituals connected with death were fading out at this time, such as the wake, where people would eat, drink and be merry while sitting with the corpse. In practice some individuals still found ways to pursue the old practices, John Evelyn reporting, for example, that he managed to have one Lady Brown buried in Deptford Church in September 1652 'according to the Church Office . . . after it had not been used in that church of 7 years'.[10] It is hard to see Milton, servant to the Commonwealth, not conforming to the new orthodoxy. There is, however, no record of Mary's burial place, nor is there a record of her daughter's baptism. This lack of evidence is to some extent a result of the upheavals in the Church during the Commonwealth period and the breakdown of the system of ecclesiastical records.

Wherever and whenever Mary was buried, the ceremony was, on the face of it, one that insisted on the joyful release of death, full of references to living and rising, resurrection and life, felicity and joy.[11] The belief in an afterlife offered a very real consolation for many. Oliver Heywood, a Nonconformist minister in a small town near

Halifax in Yorkshire and an eloquent diarist, recounted the loss of his much-loved 'comfortable' wife of six years:

> In the midst of these public fears and woeful disasters God called home to himself my dear and precious wife after she had lived with me to my exceeding comfort six years and about a month; it was the heaviest personal stroke that ever I experienced, yet the Lord hath abundantly satisfied my heart and supported my spirit under it, partly upon the consideration of her happy condition, partly upon our grounded expectation of approaching judgements.[12]

Heywood was partly comforted by his belief that his wife was now in heaven, in a 'happy condition', partly by his sense that the end of the world was truly nigh, that Judgement Day was near. Did this mirror John's feelings about Mary's death? Again, there is simply nothing, anywhere, to indicate his emotional response or even his husbandly attitude to his wife. There is no evidence either that John thought Mary 'comfortable', or that he felt assured of her salvation or indeed of the imminence of Judgement Day. Yet, even if their relationship is seen in the most reductive way – an arranged marriage in 1642, a non-marriage for three years, a marriage of social convenience and respectability for seven – the fact remains that for ten years, Mary had been John's wife. She had borne him four children. She had survived the Civil War and shared in his subsequent political good fortune. She had managed his households in Aldersgate, Scotland Yard and Petty France.

Oliver Heywood, in a moment of spiritual crisis, expressed the intense sense of loss that his wife's death brought to him, and also his struggle to accept God's will: 'I want [lack] her at every turn, everywhere, and in every work. Methinks I am but half myself without her. But why should I complain? She is at rest, God's will is done.' Heywood had two young sons, and went on to describe the new domestic arrangements necessary in his widowhood: 'I keep house with one only maid and my two little sons, and I bless God we live sweetly together.' Heywood was fortunate in his maid. He, as a minister, saw her as 'my child as well as servant, one of my first and best converts to the faith, and that spiritual relation hath much endeared us; sober, solid, and of a tender conscience, though full of scruples yet fearing God above many, laborious, faithful, in who the children take great delight, a great mercy to me in this solitary condition'.[13] There are hints that John Milton was tragically less fortunate in his choice of childcare.

Only a few weeks after Mary's death, there came a new entry in the Milton family Bible: 'And my son about 6 weeks after his mother'. Little John died at only fifteen months old. Edward Phillips, John's nephew, threw out dark insinuations many years later about 'the ill usage or bad constitution of an ill-chosen nurse'.[14] Phillips's allegation was rooted in the values of his time, in which, painfully, responses to the death of children were often rooted in a simple misogyny whereby, since women were responsible for children, they were blamed when things went wrong. Phillips could not blame Mary Powell Milton, because she was dead, but he could point the finger at an unnamed nurse. But, easy as it was to blame women, that defective sex, for these personal tragedies, men also had a burden of responsibility on their shoulders. A father's sense of responsibility, however much countered by religious faith, created agonies in the bereaved. One father reported in anguished detail the dying of his very young son. He watched the seriously ill baby every night, relieved at signs that 'it revived again,' devastated at the next relapse: 'This night again my son very ill. He did not cry so much as the night before, whether the cause was want of strength I know not.' The baby's eventual death is recorded in quiet terms: 'This day my dear babe Ralph quietly fell asleep, and is at rest with the Lord.' But the diary entries that follow are less calm: '. . . these two days were such as I never knew before; the former for the death, and this for the burial of my dear son.' The father hopes against hope that 'my God shall make me see this dealing of his to be for the best.' A few days later, he is looking for a reason for his son's death and sees only his own sin. He blames himself for 'unseasonable playing at chess', for his excessive 'lusts': so 'God hath taken away a son.'[15] The beliefs of his time would encourage any bereaved father to consider his own sins. Did John Milton look at himself and wonder why God had taken away a son? Had he indeed failed his son? The household over which Milton was governor was coming to ruin. His wife and only son were dead, his eldest daughter was lame. And he himself was blind.

Despite, or perhaps because of, his personal losses, Milton continued his work through this traumatic period, giving his talents as a writer and linguist to the Commonwealth government. Whether his work offered a welcome contrast to the domestic tragedies around him or whether he was operating at breaking point is impossible to know. He certainly did not voluntarily retreat from his political work, nor was he sidelined because of his blindness. Milton remained highly visible in European circles, responding to attacks from abroad, exchanging letters with the politicians and thinkers of other nations, defending the English Commonwealth's position, and all in Latin. In August 1652, for example, he was ordered by the Council to reply to a new attack on *The Defence of the English People*, which appeared in two further editions that year. Also during 1652, Milton received visits from political and intellectual figures from Germany, and offered his support to a number of people, including the poet and playwright William Davenant, and to various projects, including the Polyglot Bible. John even took the time to add another weapon to his linguistic arsenal, this time Dutch, the language of the nation emerging as England's greatest trading rival and soon to be England's most dangerous military threat.

Through this period of intense activity the political landscape was, however, changing. The future began to look uncertain for Milton, and potentially inhospitable. This was in part because the man who had proved to be his most significant patron during the Commonwealth period, John Bradshaw, had stepped down, reluctantly, from being Chair of the Council on 26 November 1651. Although Bradshaw remained influential, it was his colleague Oliver Cromwell who was emerging as the most powerful figure in the Council. Crucially, Cromwell commanded the support of the army. He was carefully watched by his contemporaries at the time. As John Dury (the man who translated Milton's *Eikonoklastes* into French during that year) wrote to Herman Mylius, 'Things will shortly happen which have been unheard of . . . [Cromwell] alone holds the direction of political and military affairs in his hands. He is ONE equivalent to all, and, in effect, King.'[16]

Milton was worried, and with good reason. He had felt disillusioned with the pace and purpose of the revolution in government in the early months of 1649. Now this further evidence of backsliding to monarchical practices, if not monarchy, gave further cause for concern. His worries are expressed in a series of sonnets written to various political leaders. The first in the series was addressed to Lord General Cromwell himself and written in May 1652, the month of Mary Powell Milton's death. On one level, the sonnet is a direct response (as is explained in a note in the Trinity Manuscript) to a Committee meeting, evidence if it were needed that Milton, despite blindness and bereavement, was still keeping track of political events. The Committee in question, for the Propagation of the Gospel, was a divided body. There were those who advocated an established Church, with ministers paid by the State and dissenters permitted freedom of worship so long as they agreed to fifteen fundamental tenets. And there were those (including Cromwell) who argued for almost unlimited liberty of faith. This was the issue tackled by Milton in his sonnet. The poem, given here in full, goes beyond the specific issue of religious tolerance, and the specific occasion of the Committee meeting, to offer a complex assessment of Cromwell and the larger historical moment:

> Cromwell, our chief of men, who through a cloud
> Not of war only, but detractions rude,
> Guided by faith and matchless fortitude
> To peace and truth thy glorious way hast ploughed,
> And on the neck of crowned fortune proud
> Has reared God's trophies and his work pursued,
> While Darwen stream with blood of Scots imbrued,
> And Dunbar field resounds thy praises loud,
> And Worcester's laureate wreath; yet much remains
> To conquer still; peace hath her victories

No less renowned than war, new foes arise
Threatening to bind our souls with secular chains:
Help us to save free conscience from the paw
Of hireling wolves whose gospel is their maw.

John reviews confidently, even complacently, Cromwell's military victories over the Scots at Dunbar and over Charles II at Worcester, offering a precise and bloody detail to make his point. The Darwen joins the Ribble near Preston, and it was precisely where Cromwell, joining with Lambert, routed the invading Scottish army under the Duke of Hamilton in August 1648. Only half the Scots army survived. The first ten lines of the sonnet are dominated by this celebration of Cromwell as warrior, ploughing his way to peace and truth by the use of his sword, undeterred by his critics, by 'detractions rude'. Traditionally, sonnets change course after the first eight lines. Here Milton runs over into the ninth line, Cromwell's achievements hurtling the verse forward.

Then comes a telling pause: 'yet much remains'. This is where John Milton challenges Oliver Cromwell. The great military leader may have won the war: can he win the peace? The sonnet has stylistic echoes of the Roman writer Cicero here, but in content it is focused resolutely on contemporary religious politics. Above all Milton argues that the emergent 'new foes' are more dangerous than the Scots or the Royalists. They seek to 'bind our souls with secular chains'. Cromwell must stand firm against these ravening wolves, must save 'free conscience'. The language is similar to that of fifteen years earlier and *Lycidas*, and to eight years earlier and his poem condemning the Presbyterian drive for conformity, but now Milton's aims are bigger. No longer content with reforming the corrupt national Church, with removing the 'blind mouths' who feed off the people's ignorance, he now argues for complete freedom of conscience, the complete separation of Church and State. This beautifully turned, utterly controlled sonnet argues that 'peace hath her victories': was Milton already aware that Cromwell, the great soldier, was not the man to sustain the liberties of the new republic?

Another sonnet, written only a month or so after Milton's son's death, addresses the man he may well have believed *could* do so. Henry Vane had been elected, somewhat reluctantly, to the Council of State shortly after the King's execution (the same King he had served as Treasurer to the Navy in earlier years). On 13 March 1649, he had been appointed to the Committee that John Milton served. Vane's early experience as governor of the colony in Massachusetts was perhaps instrumental in his appointment. There, as a very young man, he had shown himself a wise and sensitive leader, winning the trust of the strict religious communities he joined (despite his long hair and fashionable clothes). Vane was a staunch opponent of the established Church, and, although he had been hesitant in his support of the new regime immediately after the execution of Charles, his initial scepticism about the republic and the revolution was replaced by wholehearted commitment to the people's pre-existent 'natural right' to self-government. In this he was similar to John Milton. Having fully embraced republicanism in the final weeks of the monarchy, Milton was now utterly committed to it as the best form of government for the free English people.

Milton's sonnet to Henry Vane celebrates, crucially, the interconnection between Vane's *civic* virtue and wisdom, and his military ability. As with the sonnet to Cromwell, current events permeate the verse. In Vane's case, it is the war with the Dutch, which had started in 1652 and would continue for two years, and puns on Holland and its threat permeate the poem. There had been a long-standing commercial rivalry between the Dutch and the English; the Navigation Act of October 1651 had taken steps to support English trade, threatened by the Dutch. All imports to England now had to be in English ships, or in the ships of the country from which the imported goods originated. The Dutch were not happy. The commercial rivalry was now being inflamed by perceived religious differences. The Dutch were thoroughly Presbyterian; the English were not, although in 1652 they were not quite sure what they were. Many of the religious radicals urging the war, in particular the Fifth Monarchists, also had sound economic reasons to challenge the Dutch. Fifth Monarchists were often cloth-makers, and the Dutch dominated the cloth market. The war quickly became something of a test of international prestige. Could the new Commonwealth take on its enemies? The answer was that it could, and Vane, Treasurer of the Navy, was one of its heroes.

Milton therefore celebrated Henry Vane for his intelligence in both senses of the word: gathering military information and masterminding operations. The sonnet ends, however, by refocusing on Vane's clear understanding of the necessary separation between Church and State:

> Vane, young in years, but in sage counsel old,
> Than whom a better senator ne'er held
> The helm of Rome, when gowns not arms repelled
> The fierce Epirot and the African bold.
> Whether to settle peace or to unfold
> The drift of hollow states, hard to be spelled,
> Then to advise how war may best, upheld,
> Move by her two main nerves, iron and gold
> In all her equipage; besides to know
> Both spiritual power and civil, what each means,
> What severs each, thou hast learned, which few have done.
> The bounds of either sword to thee we owe;
> Therefore on thy firm hand Religion leans
> In peace, and reckons thee her eldest son.

As Vane's biographer points out, 'the contrast between Milton's sonnets to Vane and Cromwell – unqualified admiration versus apprehensive entreaty – mirrors the growing distance between these statesmen by 1652. Both were anti-formalists who abhorred oppression of godly consciences, yet whereas Cromwell equally detested impious abuses of liberty Vane thought that even the Ranters' "gross mistakes" might be perversions of "true and high discoveries".'[17] The sonnets not only demonstrate the gap between Vane and Cromwell; they demonstrate clearly which side of the gap John Milton stood on. Milton, in 1652, stood for conciliar republican government and for freedom of conscience.

These powerful sonnets not only demonstrate Milton's beliefs at this time but mark a return to poetry. They are the first of his poems produced in total blindness and demonstrate his determination to continue to express his political and religious views despite the obstacles in his way. The obstacles were social and psychological as well as physical. One meaning of 'blind' is 'out of the way, private, obscure'. This is what Milton was determined not to be.

The odds were against him. The majority of disabled people struggled to continue to work and live independently in the seventeenth century. Without earned income, they had to rely on charity or the kindness of friends and family. A survey of the poor taken in the city of Norwich gives a vivid picture of the living conditions of the 'weak, diseased, bed-ridden, lame, crooked'. Perhaps surprisingly, the 'somewhat lunatic' or 'beside themselves' seemed to find it easier to live independently, although they were unable to work. Of ten blind or 'almost' blind men and women, one still worked as a baker, and a woman of fifty managed to knit; the others could do no work. In addition to charity and friendship, individuals made arrangements that enabled them to live. In Norwich, one blind man of fifty was married to an 'unable' woman of ninety-six, the discrepancy in age pointing to a marriage of convenience, marriage as a strategy for survival. Another blind man in his fifties had a fatherless child of twelve to lead him about, and there were other 'symbiotic' relationships of this kind. The blind and the lame often joined forces, as did the blind and the mentally deficient (a phenomenon still prevalent in some cultures today).[18] These Norwich records tell the story of the disabled poor. Milton may not have been poor, and he remained able to work, but he still needed practical support. A snide note in a 1650 edition of *Eikonoklastes* acts as a reminder of this: '. . . the man that wrote this book is now grown blind and is led up and down.'[19]

As we have seen, Milton lived in a world in which any physical disability was viewed as a punishment from God. Despite being prevalent throughout society, disability was invariably represented in demeaning and punitive ways, blindness shown as grotesque disfigurement or as eye sockets covered in bandages. Above all,

Milton's blindness would have increased his everyday vulnerability, as is vividly evoked in an etching by the great Dutch observer of human frailty, Rembrandt. Dating from 1654, it encapsulates the potential for daily humiliations of the blind person. The etching depicts blind Tobit, Tobias's father, a character from an apocryphal Bible story. Tobit's son has been away for years, and when his wife tells him that the son is returned, he rushes to the door to greet him: 'And Tobit went forth toward the door and stumbled' – or, as the Dutch Bible has it, more bluntly, 'And Tobit went to the door and hit himself against it.' More chilling, a ballad of the time told the tale of the man who tamed his nagging, unfaithful wife by blinding her, rendering her thus helpless and dependent. This so-called humorous ditty encapsulated the link between blindness, dependency and, crucially, effeminacy, a deeply troubling combination for any man raised on the ideal of masculine sovereignty, and perhaps particularly troubling to a man such as John Milton who had come so late to a full adult male identity.[20]

Milton's ability to live with his disability, to work with his blindness, not against it, was therefore a struggle against many things, not merely the physical difficulties of existence in a pre-industrial, pre-technological world. His determination to continue with his work is extraordinary and has provoked great admiration through the years. The celebrated campaigner Helen Keller, who was both deaf and blind, was inspired to found the John Milton Society for the Blind, in tribute to Milton's strong Christian faith and his refusal, after the loss of his eyesight, to give up, his determination to continue writing.[21] That he did 'not give up' is, however, particularly illuminating in his own time. His 'strong Christian faith' may have been as much an encouragement to withdraw from the world and consider his sins as it was to persevere in his political battles.

Yet there was a cultural tradition available to Milton, indeed ideally suited to his learning and his temperament, that provided an inspirational model for the blind writer. Whether in ancient Egyptian society, where blind harpists were believed to be in direct communication with the gods through music, or in ancient Greece, which offered the example of Homer, whom legend depicts as blind, or the mythical

Tiresias the blind seer, there was a tradition in which the blind saw more clearly in spiritual matters than the sighted. Closer to Milton's own time, recent philosophical and religious developments had encouraged poets to explore their own, internal perceptions and experiences. As Sir Philip Sidney, one of the most brilliant exponents of poetry in the Elizabethan period, had written in the final line of the first poem in his glittering sonnet sequence *Astrophil and Stella*, '"Fool", said my muse to me; "look in thy heart, and write".' These traditions undoubtedly supported Milton in his blindness and would emerge triumphantly in his later poetry.

Milton the blind bard, looking inward rather than outward, has remained an enduring image into our own time, his disability some-how connected with his greatness, or used to further the notion of the isolated creative genius. Greatness and genius, yes: but no author, least of all John Milton, worked in isolation in the seventeenth century. Like most of his sighted literate contemporaries, Milton employed others to do his writing for him and to read to him. To be read to was an utterly normal way of experiencing a book. There was no need to find someone special for the task: Samuel Pepys, for one, simply has his 'boy' read to him, using whichever (literate) servant happened to be around at the time. All of the later poetry in the Trinity Manuscript, including the sonnets of 1652, is written in a hand other than Milton's. Scholars have spent much time and energy in trying to identify who these copyists were, but they are in agreement that they worked under the close supervision of the author himself. In his work for the Council, efforts were made both by Milton and by those around him to facilitate him in doing his job. Although he described his 'enforced absence' from Whitehall in a letter to John Bradshaw, he also described the way in which work was sent to him, presumably to his house in Petty France. Furthermore he pointed out that, while it was very kind of everyone to suggest that he had an assistant, he really did not need any help: 'I find no encum-brances of that which belongs to me, except it be in point of attendance at Conferences with Ambassadors, which I much confess, in my Condition I am not fit for.'[22]

Having said that, Milton was in fact writing to Bradshaw in February 1653 to recommend the, to his mind, ideal man to be his new assistant: one 'Mr Marvell', a 'man whom both by report, and the converse I have had with him, of singular desert for the state to make use of; who also offers himself, if there be any employment for him'. Both Andrew Marvell's abilities and social background were praised by Milton: the son of a minister in Hull, Marvell had spent four years abroad in Holland, France, Italy and Spain,

> to very good purpose, as I believe, and the gaining of those 4 languages; besides he is a scholar and well read in the Latin and Greek authors, & no doubt of an approved conversation, for he comes now lately out of the house of the Lord Fairfax who was General, where he was entrusted to give some instructions in the Languages to the Lady his Daughter.[23]

(Milton did not mention that Andrew Marvell was already one of the most impressive poets of his generation, author of the complex and beguiling poem *Upon Appleton House*, a homage to the Fairfax family and their estate.)

Marvell was being recommended at a difficult time for Bradshaw, and this may explain why Milton did not get his choice of assistant. Instead, Philip Meadows was appointed to assist him in his Latin translations, on the recommendation of the rising star of the political firmament, John Thurloe. Meadows took the job of Assistant Latin Secretary and ran with it, in ways not open to Milton, in part because of his blindness but in part because of his temperament. By 17 October, Meadows had been promoted to a position in which he assisted Thurloe directly in the management of foreign affairs, with his salary doubled to £200 per annum. By 3 February 1654 he was confirmed as full 'Latin Secretary', with John Milton remaining 'Latin Secretary Extraordinary'.

Meadows would go from strength to strength, heading as envoy to Portugal in 1656 to ratify an Anglo-Portuguese treaty. This was precisely the kind of task, involving foreign travel, that John Milton could not have taken on, certainly since the later 1640s. The Portugal mission was an exciting and dangerous brief; Meadows was shot at while in Lisbon and injured in the hand.[24] Other Commonwealth representatives had been murdered overseas, often by exiled Royalists, as happened to the Commonwealth's man in Madrid (whose letters of credential had been written by Milton, who would also write the letters of remonstration sent after his murder).

Remaining in England, Milton watched as his fears for the republic became realities. In 1652 the Rump Parliament passed an Act of Oblivion, offering those who had refrained from acting against the State since the Battle of Worcester in September 1651 a pardon for their earlier treasons and felonies. By 1653, some exiles were ready to return, even those under sentence of death. Cromwell personally intervened in some cases, such as that of Roger L'Estrange, and nullified the death sentence. The Act of Oblivion was a pragmatic political move, designed to increase political unity, but it was also a sign that it was proving difficult to find a model of representative government that would ensure the survival of the republic.

There was a real danger that if democratic participation was increased, then any newly elected government would actually be hostile to the republic. In September 1652, yet another Committee convened to consider the problem. In a significant move, men such as Henry Vane were excluded from the meetings. Soon the discussion became dominated by the concerns and interests of the increasingly frustrated army officers. The Committee generated many radical suggestions of reform, under pressure from the army veteran Col. Pride (who 'attended at the door while this was in debate'), but still nothing was put into action.

By the spring of 1653, Cromwell himself had grown dissatisfied with the very Parliament that had brought him to power. In 20 April 1653, he took events into his own hands in an extraordinary move. He disbanded the Rump Parliament, calling the MPs whoremasters and drunkards, unfit for government. He ended by saying, '. . . you have been sat too long here for any good you have been doing. Depart, I say, and let us have done with you. In the name of God, go!'[25]

This action was the culmination of years of frustration. The New Model Army, riding high on the success of the Irish and Scottish campaigns, had been putting increasing pressure on Parliament to introduce constitutional, legal and religious reforms. The MPs continued to react slowly, the army ran out of patience, and Cromwell decided to act in his role as army man rather than Member of Parliament. He later claimed that nobody cared very much. The dissolution of the Parliament provoked 'not so much as the barking of a dog'.[26]

Cromwell had, however, by dissolving the Rump Parliament, removed the last vestige of the legally constituted English government.[27] He also took the opportunity to oust many of his colleagues from the palace at Whitehall: John Bradshaw managed to cling on to his official suite of rooms there and continued to serve in the court for relief on articles of war, but he, like the few other survivors, was aware that it was only a matter of time before he would be removed from the centre of government.

The millenarians were now in control, led by army men such as Col. Thomas Harrison, and authorised by Cromwell, who had reached the high tide of his own millenarian beliefs. Cromwell now saw himself as a second Moses, initiating the rule of the saints. The Dutch had betrayed the cause; Rome would indeed fall. These religious radicals were actively preparing for the Second Coming. Their primary aim was to establish the Kingdom of Christ, and to that end, letters were sent out to congregational churches asking them to nominate men fit to serve in this Parliament. The result of the consultation was known popularly as the Barebones Parliament, after one of its members, Praise-God Barbon, a London merchant and religious independent. The Royalist historian Edward Hyde, Lord Clarendon would later damn the Barebones MPs as 'inferior persons of no quality or name, artificers of the meanest trades, known only by their gifts in praying and preaching . . . they were a pack of weak, senseless fellows'.[28] Clarendon was certainly a hostile witness, but not many people rushed to praise this new, unelected Nominated Parliament of the Saints.

The Barebones Parliament did actually take some small steps towards reform, at least in the matter of religious government. At last tithes were abolished, as well as one of the most hated courts of law, Chancery. But soon the Parliament began to seem threatening to Cromwell himself, and to those who shared his values. Its small radical victories actually ensured its destruction: people began to fear that 'property and society as they knew it were in danger.'[29] Cromwell himself was alarmed by the very men he had chosen to further the Reformation of Church and State, fearing (or so he said later) 'the confusion of all things'. In getting rid of the Rump Parliament, he had been forced to choose between the political moderates and the more radical army. The political reality was, however, that the army was not happy with the Barebones Parliament either. There seemed only one way forward. On 16 December 1653, Oliver Cromwell, Commander-in-Chief of the Army, was installed as Lord Protector of the Commonwealth. In a sign of the times, he and his successors were given Whitehall for 'the maintenance of his and their state and dignity'. By 1654, the Privy Gallery, which had been used for committees, had been cleared, and reverted to its traditional monarchical style of use.[30]

The free English Commonwealth, governed by Parliament and Council, had lasted not much more than four years, and in those years John Milton had lost his wife, his only son and his sight. For some, the demise of the Commonwealth marked the end of their political lives, at least for a time. Henry Vane for one, admired by Milton, could not support Cromwell as Protector and withdrew completely from public life. Milton, however, did not. And in private, he found a way to express his despair for his country and for himself.

In the summer of 1653, Milton returned to the Psalms, penning a series of translations which demonstrate his ability to experiment, confidently, with a variety of different metres. But these Psalm translations are much more than metrical exercises. Milton noted the day and the month of each one: they are like a diary of his pain. He even inserted his own blindness into the Psalms, adding the phrase 'and dark' to the Hebrew original:

> My bed I water with my tears; mine eye
> Through grief consumes, is waxen old and dark
> I' the midst of all mine enemies that mark.
>
> *(Psalm VI*, ll. 13–15)

Milton *is* the psalmist, pleading with God to hear him, beset with enemies, mourning the destruction of his nation. There is some hope: the sense that the 'blessed man' studies Jehovah's law 'day and night' in 'delight' (*Psalm I*), the belief that God will 'laugh', that the Lord 'shall scoff', at earthly tyrants. But there is more confusion and fear. *Psalm II* asks why there is tumult, war and arrogant kings; *Psalm IV* complains that others who 'prize / Things false and vain and nothing else but lies' are successful; and *Psalm III* complains 'Lord how many are my foes.'

Above all, however, there is a beautifully expressed dependence on God's love, a fantasy of peaceful rest, of safety in the protection of the Lord: 'But thou Lord art my shield and glory' (*Psalm III*). *Psalm IV* ends:

> In peace at once will I
> Both lay me down and sleep
> For thou alone dost keep
> Me safe where'er I lie
> As in a rocky cell
> Thou Lord alone in safety mak'st me dwell.
>
> (ll. 37–42)

Psalm VII, dated 14 August 1653, makes the request for God's protection even more explicit and emotional:

> Lord my God to thee I fly
> Save me and secure me under
> Thy protection while I cry.
>
> (ll. 1–3)

FOURTEEN

DEFENCE

1654

I N A LETTER TO A FRIEND just over a year later, Milton continued to bear witness to the pain, both psychological and physical, that he had experienced over ten years of weakening sight. He was explicit, as he was nowhere else, about his bodily symptoms (his spleen and his viscera were 'burdened and shaken with flatulence') and the progress of his disability:

> . . . while considerable sight still remained, when I would first go to bed and lie on one side or the other, abundant light would dart from my closed eyes; then as sight daily diminished, colours proportionately darker would burst forth with violence and a sort of crash from within.[1]

Now, in 1654, 'permanent vapours seem to have settled upon my entire forehead and temples, which press and oppress my eyes with a sort of heavy sleepiness, especially from mealtime to evening.' At first he was able to see a little, mistily, but now all was 'pure black, marked as if with extinguished or ashy light'.

Milton wrote in such graphic detail about himself only because his friend, Leonard Philaras, had begged him to describe his symptoms. Philaras knew a doctor who might help. Milton still carried a desperate hope, since a 'minute quantity of light' entered his eye when moved in a certain way, 'as if through a crack'. Perhaps, he wrote, Philaras's offer of help was an expression of divine purpose. Perhaps his blindness could be cured.

The hope was as faint as the glimmer entering Milton's eye, and he knew it. The rest of this remarkable letter is dominated by a moving explanation of his acceptance of the incurability of his condition:

> Although some glimmer of hope too may radiate from that physician, I prepare and resign myself as if the case were quite incurable; and I often reflect that since many days of darkness are destined to everyone, as the wise man warns, mine thus far, by the signal kindness of Providence, between leisure and study, and the voices and visits of friends, are much more mild than those lethal ones . . . [I am] capable of seeing, not by [my] eyes alone, but sufficiently by God's leading and providence. Indeed while He himself looks out for me and provides for me, which He does, and takes me as if by the hand and leads me throughout life, surely, since it has pleased Him, I shall be pleased to grant my eyes a holiday.[2]

The 'voices and visits of friends' were crucial to the process that enabled Milton, a year later, to place all of his troubles firmly in the past: '. . . at that time especially, infirm health, distress over two deaths in my family, and the complete failure of my sight beset me with troubles,' he could write assuredly in a pamphlet of August 1655.[3]

Many of Milton's friends from the mid-1650s were political insiders. Edward Lawrence was, for example, the son of the leader of the Council from early 1654 (as Milton pointed out in the opening line of a sonnet addressed to him), and an MP himself from 1656. Andrew Marvell would have meetings with John Bradshaw and convey the latter's message of 'all respect to your person' to Milton.[4] Another friend, both of Milton and Edward Lawrence, was a diplomat from Germany, Henry Oldenburg, who by 1656 had entered Oxford and become tutor to Richard Jones, one of Milton's ex-pupils in the Aldersgate house.

Through his later forties, friendship was one of the most important themes explored in Milton's poetry, alongside his own blindness and the political situation. It is both surprising and somewhat cheering to see the return of a language of playful familiarity, with echoes of his poetry of some thirty years earlier. Suddenly, he seems surrounded by young friends, talented, educated, politically engaged men he has met through his teaching or his government work. Not quite a circle, these men often knew each other, and they cared for Milton. Marvell wrote to him, for example, that he was glad that Cyriack Skinner had 'got near to' him in London.[5] Equally important, letters show Milton sending these friends his latest works, and they in turn offer him support and encouragement. Marvell, developing into one of the great poets of the seventeenth century, was effusive in his praise of his new friend's prose, writing that he 'shall now study' Milton's latest work 'even to the getting of it by heart'.[6]

To these friends, Milton wrote sonnets that, while celebrating the men's lineage (as he was wont to do), also seem determined to have fun. To Cyriack Skinner, Milton wrote that he intended to 'drench in mirth' 'deep thoughts'; he was going to put aside Euclid and Archimedes, stop worrying about the Swedes and the French. The sonnet was a reminder, partly to Skinner, partly to himself, that it is important to relax: 'care' burdens the day, so 'when God sends a cheerful hour', enjoy yourself! To Edward Lawrence, an upwardly mobile figure in the political hierarchy and only in his early twenties, Milton wrote a sonnet of friendship expressed in a relaxed, pastoral mode ('Lawrence of virtuous father'). The weather was terrible, 'now that the fields are dank, and ways are mire': how on earth were they going to meet up? As with his earlier Latin poetry, Milton was both imitating a Classical form (this time Horace) and also referring to the actual conditions of his life in rainy England. He looked forward to summer when a

> neat repast shall feast us, light and choice,
> Of Attic taste, with wine, whence we may rise
> To hear the lute well touched, or artful voice
> Warble immortal notes and Tuscan air?
> He who of those delights can judge, and spare
> To interpose them oft, is not unwise.
>
> (ll. 9–12)

Again, Milton was advocating indulgence in the good life, as he did to Skinner. Typically, however, the use of the ambiguous word *spare* in the penultimate line offers the reader a choice: the wise man either knows how to spare time for pleasures in his busy life, or knows how to indulge himself sparingly. Either way, there is room in life for wine, music and good food, even perhaps for that long-suppressed aspiration, 'Attic' salt.

Women are not present in these poems, and there is no reason for them to be so. As ever, it seems that men provided most, if not all, of the emotional life John Milton needed. As with his writings and experiences as a young man, it is impossible to know whether these friendships of his later middle age had a sexual element. Certainly nothing had changed in English society to have made it more acceptable had they done so.

Lack of proof did not stop his enemies, however. The steady stream of hostile responses to the English Commonwealth had continued unabated, and in early 1653, Milton's simmering feud with Salmasius turned truly nasty. Salmasius claimed in January that Milton had worked as a male prostitute during his time in Italy, 'selling his buttocks for a few pence' (*Paucis nummis nates prostituisse*).[7] One of Milton's European friends (at this period at least), Nicholas Heinsius, leapt to deny the allegation, but the fire had been started. By May 1654, John Bramhall, a Royalist ex-bishop in exile, was claiming that Milton had been sent down from Cambridge for unnatural practices, so shameful that he would kill himself if known.[8] Throughout this period, the sexual body and sexual acts were used as metaphors for political engagements and transgressions, and of course Milton himself used this language when attacking his opponents. What is interesting about the attacks on Milton was that he was being accused of having sex with men.

Milton's response to these and the numerous other attacks at home and abroad was to defend himself and his country. In a letter to his friend Henry Oldenburg, dated 6 July 1654 and written from West-minster, he describes the value of his writings: '. . . what among human endeavours can be nobler or more useful than the protection of liberty?' He tells Oldenburg that he is continuing to work despite 'illness', despite 'this blindness, which is more oppressive than the whole of old age' and despite 'the cries' of 'such brawlers'.[9]

The noble and useful work that 'John Milton an Englishman' (as the title page put it) had been working on was a government-commissioned response to an anonymous Royalist publication, *Regii sanguinis clamor ad coelum* (The Cry of the Royal Blood to Heaven). As Milton himself pointed out, he was still the man for the job. His task in his first *Defence* had been to 'defend publicly (if any one ever did) the cause of the people of England, and thus of liberty itself'. He had not disappointed since his opponent, Salmasius, had been 'routed' and retired, his reputation in shreds. Milton's *Pro Populo Anglicano Defensio Secundo* (Second Defence of the English People) continued the work but also gave its author a chance to defend himself against his attackers.

First and foremost, however, the *Second Defence* was propaganda for the Protectorate and its Protector. The praise for Cromwell is extensive and precise, focusing on his military abilities and his religious conviction. As a soldier, he was 'above all others the most exercised in the knowledge of himself; he had either destroyed, or reduced to his own control, all enemies within his own breast – vain hopes, fears, desires'. Milton ended the tract by addressing Cromwell directly: '. . . you, who are the greatest and most glorious of our citizens, the director of public counsels, the leader of the bravest of armies, the father of your country'. To the English people, Milton had an equally clear message: Cromwell was 'your country's deliverer, the founder of our liberty, and at the same time its protector'.

The *Second Defence* is a rousing celebration of the new England of liberty in civil life and divine worship, and it refuses to concede an inch to Royalist opponents. The Protectorate is paraded as a model of tolerant government. Milton, responding to the fact that his own works have been burned in Paris, points out that the English *could* have burned Salmasius' books in London but simply did not do that kind of thing. With casual insouciance (and a telling conflation of book and author), Milton observes, 'I find I have also been burned at

*Joannis Milton*I

ANGLI

PRO

POPULO ANGLICANO

DEFENSIO

SECUNDA.

Contra infamem libellum anonymum
cui titulus,

Regii sanguinis clamor ad
cœlum adversus parri-
cidas Anglicanos.

LONDINI,
Typis Neucomianis, 1654.

Toulouse.' The *Second Defence* is a resolutely confident work, dominated by Milton's presentation of himself as *the* author for this
moment when the people of England had thrown off 'a most debasing
thraldom'.

On the other hand, the work is coloured by Milton's misunderstand-
ing of the authorship of the work he is attacking. He believed that one
Alexander More (who had actually only contributed the preface and
then taken the work along to the printers) was the author. More made
an easy, if inaccurate, target. Yet another of the brilliant European
intellectuals of the time (born in France the son of a Scottish clergyman
and a French mother), he was a man dogged by controversy, whether
over his religious beliefs, not strict enough for some, or his sexual
behaviour, too lax for most. Crucially, More was a friend of Salmasius.
Indeed, it was in Salmasius' house, and possibly in his garden shed, that
More had inseminated a servant, Elizabeth Guerret, who then claimed
that he had promised her marriage, a claim he vigorously denied.

In the *Second Defence* Milton used every trick in the book to demean,
ridicule and dismiss his opponent.[10] He fused the *sal et lepos* of his Latin
works with the satiric energy of his early prose tracts, throwing More
out of the community of urbane scholars and into the garden shed with
his numerous mistresses. Predictably, More responded with *Fides
publica contra calumnias Joannis Miltoni* (A Faithful Statement against
the False Accusations of John Milton), exposing inaccuracies in
Milton's tract and condemning the outrageous obscenities in the
attack upon him. Milton in his turn replied again, this time with
Defensio Pro Se (Defence of Himself).

In the *Second Defence*, Milton only dropped his abuse of More when
he wanted to create space to attack Salmasius, 'or Salmasia (for of what
sex he was, was rendered extremely doubtful, from his being plainly
ruled by his wife, alike in matters regarding his reputation, and in his
domestic concerns)'. It could all get very silly. Milton created a little
Latin poem about herrings, which begins '*Gaudete scombri . . .*' (Mackerels rejoice . . .), and went on to imagine fish dressed in the kit, as it
were, of the Salmasius team. As the Victorian Milton scholar Mark
Pattison wrote with stern disapproval, the majestic Milton 'descends

from the empyrean throne of contemplation to use the language of the gutter or the fish-market'. It is precisely these qualities that make the work so enjoyable.

Salmasius was, however, dead by the time Milton wrote his *Second Defence*, and Milton seized on this to score a heartfelt point: 'I will not impute to him his death as a crime, as he did to me my blindness.' Milton's enemies (and even some of his supporters) had argued that his blindness was a punishment, inflicted by God. It was time to fight back: 'Let us come now to the charges against me. Is there anything in my life of character which he could criticize? Nothing, certainly. What then? He does what no one but a brute and a barbarian would have done – casts up to me my appearance and my blindness.'[11] Before tackling his blindness, however, Milton needed to address some other slanders, ranging from his lowly social background to his sexual predilections, from his shortness of height to his lack of ability with a sword. So the reader learns he was born in London, of respectable parents; that his father was a man of integrity, his mother a woman of charity; that he was brought up by his parents for study of literature, languages and philosophy; and that he spent his youth at his father's country house, 'completely at leisure'. It is a lovely vision of a man from the leisured, even noble classes: some of it is even true.

Beset by accusations of unchastity, particularly with men, Milton insisted that even in Geneva, 'where so much licence exists, I lived free and untouched by the slightest sin or reproach'. Accused of being short and ugly, he pointed out that he was no such thing. His complexion was superb, and although he was 'past forty' (he was forty-five), 'there is scarcely any one to whom I do not seem younger by nearly ten years.' Admittedly, he was not tall, but he was not short, and in any case, even if he were short, it would not be a problem. Accused of cowardice, having not actually taken up arms for the Commonwealth or Protectorate, he pointed out that he had been toiling for his 'fellow-citizens in another way, with much greater utility, and with no less peril'. In any case, Milton remembered that 'I was not ignorant of how to handle or unsheathe a sword, nor unpractised in using it every day: girded with my sword, as I generally was, I thought myself equal to anyone, though he was far more sturdy.' He insisted that even 'at this day, I have the same spirit, the same strength, but not the same eyes. And yet they have as much the appearance of being uninjured, and are as clear and bright, without a cloud, as the eyes of men who see most keenly.'[12]

This of course is the problem that Milton cannot dismiss, as he all too painfully recognises. He can deny that he is unchaste, ugly and cowardly, but he cannot deny he is blind: 'Would it were equally in my power to confute this inhuman adversary on the subject of my blindness! but, it is not.' The next sentence epitomises Milton's eloquent courage, both in standing against his enemies and in facing his own predicament: 'Then, let us bear it. To be blind is not miserable; not to be able to bear blindness, that is miserable.'

This was a hard-won acceptance and achieved in the face of an overwhelmingly negative view and experience of blindness in Milton's own time, as is evident in his letter to his friend Philaras about his symptoms, in which he thanks him particularly for his kindness to 'one who could not see', whose misfortune 'has made me more respectable to none, more despicable perhaps to many'.

In the writings of the mid-1650s, Milton took on almost all aspects of his disability and transformed their meaning. He refashioned his need for support as a chance to demonstrate exemplary friendship instead of a demeaning dependency on, say, a mentally deficient servant as guide. His friends were such good friends that they would physically guide him; Euripides was brought in to express the ideal: 'Give your hand to your friend and helper. Throw your arm about my neck, and I will be your guide.' Milton knew that most blind people could not work. In his case, he pointed out, the government had continued to employ him: they might 'readily grant me exemption and retirement', but they had instead maintained his dignity and public office, and paid his salary. Milton knew that blind people were invariably represented as grotesques, and he made clear, therefore, that he was not disfigured by his blindness. (A sonnet to Cyriack Skinner expresses relief that others cannot tell that he is blind.) Milton knew that blindness could be interpreted as a punishment from

God, so he suggested that it was the *natural* consequence of his overzealous studies when a child, when he did not leave his books 'for my bed before the hour of midnight'. Milton knew what he was up against, and in his writings at this time, he systematically responded to and challenged his enemies' and his society's view of his disability.

First, however, he had to deal with his own sense of loss and despair. One of his most famous poems, the sonnet that begins 'When I consider how my light is spent', dramatises the ongoing struggle. The 'light' of the opening is most obviously his blindness but also could refer to his fragile sense of purpose, and the following lines are confused by tortuous syntax and a puzzling reference to the passing of 'half my days'. (Milton was at least forty when he wrote the poem, probably nearer fifty, but perhaps he hoped that people really did think he was ten years younger, halfway to his threescore years and ten. Or perhaps he considered the lifespan of his own father, who lived into his mid-eighties.)

> When I consider how my light is spent,
> Ere half my days, in this dark world and wide,
> And that one talent which is death to hide,
> Lodged with me useless . . .
>
> (ll. 1–4)

The convolution may be the whole point: Milton, considering his uselessness, gets tangled up in complexity. The sonnet itself, as it turns, suggests that the questions are asked 'fondly' (i.e., stupidly, innocently). Patience, who responds to these fond questions, is clear in her response: they 'serve him best' who bear God's mild yoke. The poem ends, famously, with Patience's description of those who serve God:

> Thousands at his bidding speed
> And post o'er land and ocean without rest:
> They also serve who only stand and wait.
>
> (ll. 12–14)

Milton can, as a blind man, still serve God: his light is not spent. The assurance that 'they also serve who only stand and wait' relies for its subtle consolation on both a passive and an active understanding of the verb 'to stand'. Milton is required both to accept the necessity for stillness and to stand firm.

Another less well-known, but equally touching, sonnet offers a slightly different response to blindness, one which seems more active, certainly more politically engaged. In a poem addressed to his student and friend Cyriack Skinner, Milton recounts three years of complete blindness. His eyes, now 'idle orbs', are 'bereft of light their seeing have forgot'. Again, the psychological struggle is allowed into the poem: the horror of idleness, the grief at the forgetting of the visual world, whether 'sun or moon or star', 'man or woman'. But the fear and bereavement are firmly put aside. Milton does not argue with heaven but vows to 'bear up and steer / Right onward':

> What supports me dost thou ask?
> The conscience, friend, to have lost them overplied
> In liberty's defence, my noble task,
> Of which all Europe talks from side to side.
> This thought might lead me through the world's vain mask
> Content though blind, had I no better guide.
>
> (ll. 9–14)

Now Milton is arguing that it is in the defence of liberty, the 'noble task' 'of which all Europe talks', that he has lost his sight. Blindness becomes almost an injury sustained in war.

These kinds of arguments are, in the *Second Defence*, superseded by a third narrative, and a much more explicitly religious one. John Milton has heard the voice of God. Asked by his God to do more, in the full knowledge that it would hasten his blindness, he has chosen God's work. His 'two destinies' are linked: blindness and duty. Milton writes that he neither believes nor has found 'that God is angry'. Instead God has shown mercy and paternal goodness towards him. Milton acknowledges that he is classed with 'the afflicted, with the sorrowful, with the weak', but he also knows that 'there is a way, and the Apostle is my authority, through weakness to the greatest strength': '. . . thus, through this infirmity should I be consummated, perfected.'

Yet the *Second Defence*, for all these incidents of eloquent confidence in self and nation, has a number of politically jarring moments. Alongside the praise of Cromwell, Milton offers praise of John Bradshaw (sprung, inevitably, from a 'noble family'), who, as we have seen, was struggling politically at precisely this time. Bradshaw is applauded as a defender of liberty and in very personal terms:

> More tireless than any other in counsel and labour for the public good, he is by himself equal to a host. At home he, as much as any man, is hospitable and generous according to his means, the most faithful of friends and the most worthy of trust in every kind of fortune. No man more quickly and freely recognises those who deserve well of him, whoever they may be, nor pursues them with greater kindness.[13]

Other military and civic leaders who had fallen away from power are also praised in the *Second Defence*: men such as Gen. Lord Fairfax, admired for his courage, modesty and sanctity of life. The presence of these tributes hints at least at some criticism of Cromwell's rule, compounded by the suggestion that although the monarchy has been removed, the establishment of true civic and religious liberty is faltering.

Milton felt it necessary to rouse his nation to action, fearful, as he had been as early as the spring of 1649, that the English people were not capable of sustaining liberty. Did they really want to be slaves in their hearts? If so, however hard they fought, they would never succeed in attaining true liberty. Earlier Milton had written that the English needed courage, and not just in battle: 'every species of fear' needed to be overcome. Indeed, the English needed *more* courage than the Romans and Greeks who successfully overcame tyrants, because modern-day tyrants linked their power to their claim to be 'vicars of Christ'. The lower orders had been 'stupefied by the wicked arts of priests', and the civilised world had *made* their leaders into gods, 'deifying the pests of the human race for their own destruction'. The English people had to learn to be masters of themselves, remain 'aloof from factions, hatreds, superstitions, injuries, lusts, and plunders'. If they did not, they would have failed themselves and their nation, and future generations would judge them harshly.

> The foundations were soundly laid, the beginnings, in fact more than the beginnings were splendid, but posterity will look in vain, not without a certain distress, for those who were to complete the work, who were to put the pediment in place. It will be a source of grief that to such great undertakings, such great virtues, perseverance was lacking.[14]

Perseverance would not be wanting if the people listened to John Milton, nor would the praise of future generations. It was Milton who would 'exhort' and 'encourage', Milton too who would 'adorn, and celebrate, in praises destined to endure forever, the transcendent deeds, and those who performed them'.

In his *Second Defence of the English People* Milton offered a dazzling celebration of his own authority, and of the power of the printed word to reach people, cross borders, bring nations together in liberty, to spread 'the restored culture of citizenship and freedom of life'. Milton, physically trapped by his own blindness in a house in Petty France, could travel the world, conflating book and man as he did so powerfully in *Areopagitica*:

> I imagine myself to have set out upon my travels, and that I behold from on high, tracts beyond the seas, and wide-extended regions; that I behold countenances strange and numberless, and all, in feelings of mind, my closest friends and neighbours . . . from the columns of Hercules to the farthest borders of India, that throughout this vast expanse, I am bringing back, bringing home to every nation, liberty, so long driven out, so long an exile.[15]

It is a tremendous performance. Only after a few moments does the reader realise that Milton has also defended the political status quo (Cromwell as Lord Protector) without making clear exactly how Cromwell was creating the land of civic and religious liberty to which the *Second Defence* aspired.

In reality, Cromwell's government was lurching towards dictatorship. The internal threat from Royalists was increasingly insignificant. A Royalist rising in Wiltshire in March 1655 was easily crushed, and Cromwell's Secretary to the Council, John Thurloe, had now become an astute chief of intelligence, even infiltrating Charles Stuart's entourage in exile. Any opposition to Cromwell was coming from what had been his own side. Bradshaw and his allies, now 'Commonwealthmen', might criticise the formation of the Protectorate, but their voices carried no political or military weight. MPs in the short-lived First Protectorate Parliament were forced to sign a Recognition of the new constitution (the Instrument of Government) which legitimised Cromwell's rule, or resign. The same year, Cromwell tightened up the licensing system, focusing on the dissemination of news.[16] He moved to suppress all newspapers except official publications like *Mercurius Politicus*.

John Milton's gory sonnet 'On the late Massacre in Piedmont', written during this period, suggests, at first sight, that he was still very much Cromwell's man, despite these political moves. The poem was a direct product of Milton's involvement with the construction of the diplomatic letters that were written in response to this massacre. Piedmont (on the borders of France and Italy) was the home of the Vaudois community, which had been excommunicated by the Church as early as 1215, and whose members were thus viewed as natural allies to the Protestant English, who had left the Catholic Church three hundred years or so earlier. Since 1561, the religion and lives of the quasi-Protestant Vaudois had been protected by a treaty with the Duke of Savoy, but in 1655 the current duke sought to expel them from his territories. The Vaudois attempted to escape to the mountains but were pursued. They were either massacred or died in the snow. The number of dead was estimated by the Vaudois themselves at

1,712. Cromwell was personally interested in their cause, and Milton was instructed to write letters of protest to various European leaders, on 25 May, and to write (or most likely translate) an address to be delivered to the Duke of Savoy by Sir Samuel Morland, Cromwell's special ambassador. The day itself was proclaimed 'a day of solemn fasting and humiliation' for all of England, and parishes were directed to take up a special collection to assist the survivors. In all, an impressive £38,000 was raised, including £2,000 from Cromwell himself.

This was the moment at which Milton wrote his poem. The opening five lines take no prisoners, commanding God with autocratic verbs to wreak vengeance ('Avenge O Lord thy slaughtered saints') and to register the crime: 'Forget not: in thy book record their groans.' The 'book' here is the one mentioned in the Book of Revelation 5:1 ('I saw in the right hand of him that sat on the throne a book'), Milton invoking the most apocalyptic text in the New Testament. The poem continues with a graphic description of the massacre: the soldiers 'rolled / Mother with infant down the rocks'. He was not being gratuitous. One account of the massacre included three different women who were hurled down a precipice with their children. In one case, incredibly, the baby survived. The blood of the innocent will, the sonnet envisions, be sown throughout 'the Italian fields' controlled by the 'triple Tyrant', an allusion to the Pope's three-tiered crown. Milton combines the legend of the dragon's teeth and the biblical parable of the sower to create an image of Reformed religion springing up at the heart of Roman Catholicism. He had cut his Protestant teeth on opposition to Catholicism and then Laudianism, so it was entirely consistent to espouse this view in the 1650s. It helped, of course, that Milton was echoing the language and beliefs of his leader, Cromwell.

Millenarianism could, however, threaten as well as support Cromwell's rule. On 7 January 1654, a Fifth Monarchist called Anna Trapnel was 'seized upon by the Lord' in a room in Whitehall, and began praying and singing. Her friends took her to a room in a nearby inn where she stayed for twelve days, neither eating nor drinking for the first five, then drinking some small beer, and eating a little toast, once a day. Lying rigid in bed, she alternated prose prayers and verse songs in ballad or common hymn metre in sessions lasting from two to five hours.[17]

Trapnel was visited at the inn by at least eight members of the disbanded Barebones Parliament, as well as many hundreds who did 'daily come to see and hear'. She was saying some very strange things, but embedded in her rambling words were apocalyptic threats:

> Write how that Protectors shall go
> And into graves there lie;
> Let pens make known what is said, that
> They shall expire and die.[18]

On the last day of her prophesying, the Council of State, severely worried, published an ordinance that made it treasonable 'to compass or imagine the death of the Lord Protector' or to declare his government tyrannical or illegitimate.[19] Marchamont Nedham, editor of *Mercurius Politicus* and a man with his finger on the pulse of print culture, remained concerned. He wrote to Cromwell warning the Protector that there were plans to print Trapnel's 'discourses and hymns' and to send her out into the country to proclaim them. Trapnel was doing a 'world of mischief' in London. Her prophecies might be nonsense, but they might influence 'the vulgar'. Nedham promised Cromwell that he would move swiftly and seize copies of the prophecies, and show them to him: '. . . they would make 14 or 15 sheets in print.'[20] Eventually, Trapnel was sent to Bridewell and imprisoned in a cell infested with sewage and rats.[21]

Anna Trapnel's fate epitomised the stranglehold that Cromwell had on rule at home, if also suggesting some of the tensions generated by that rule, most obviously that between his religious radicalism and his social and political conservatism. The latter ensured that viewpoints such as the Levellers' would remain intolerable, and that Cromwell's view of the people and their power would remain politically conservative. His confidence and pragmatism were fuelled not by political ideology but by his sense that he was doing God's work.

In the following year, news came from abroad that made this deeply religious man question his own actions, precipitating yet further political change. When the Protectorate's forces were defeated in the Caribbean, Cromwell took it as a sign of God's displeasure. He became depressed and upset, and then fuelled by renewed religious zeal. The Reformation needed to progress more swiftly; the suppression of vice and the encouragement of virtue, which were the very purposes of magistracy, needed to be attended to, and urgently.[22] This belief precipitated his next step, the establishment of open military government led by the Major-Generals, who would enforce the godly Reformation throughout the country, something that successive parliaments had been unable to deliver. (The Major-Generals also enforced a 'decimation' tax whereby 10 per cent of the value of the estates of known Royalists worth over £100 per annum in land, and £1,500 per annum in goods, came to the government. It all helped to pay Cromwell's armies and avoided taxing the rest of the predominantly neutral if not loyal gentry.) Cromwell ordered his Major-Generals to put into effect the 'Laws against Drunkenness, Blasphemy, and taking the name of God in vain, by swearing and cursing, Plays and interludes, and prophaning of the Lord's day, and such like wickedness and abominations'.[23] They were to control ale houses, gaming houses and brothels.

These were the unprecedented conditions in which there was talk of readmitting the Jews, expelled back in 1290, to England. Radical millenarians knew that one condition for the Second Coming of Christ was the conversion of the Jews: it would help if there were Jews to convert. (There would also be some useful economic side-effects, the Jewish community being thought to offer the prospect of business acumen and capital unrivalled in the period.)[24] Any readmission would be an astonishing step, on the surface at least challenging the entrenched anti-Semitism of English Christian culture.[25] Even for those Christians who wanted the Jews to return, the desire caused anxiety since it went so profoundly against the grain of their beliefs and practices. A conference was convened by the Council of State to discuss the issues, and the leader of the Dutch Jewish community,

Menasseh ben Israel, travelled to England to discuss the prospect of readmission.[26] In the end, nothing official was decided; no formal readmission occurred. Both the original suggestion, and the inability to come to a decision, signalled the crisis in government.

Cromwell himself was unable to see a way forward. Tellingly, his strength and his vulnerability lay in his religion, not definable by denomination (and in this similar to Milton's) but nevertheless of vital importance to him. His belief in 'remarkable providences' meant that when things were going well, he knew God was with him. Back in 1648 this attitude had inspired and justified military victory. But in the mid-1650s, with things going wrong, whether a military defeat, or the loss of his beloved daughter Elizabeth to cancer, or the impasse over the readmission of the Jews, God's purposes were less clear.

In March 1656 Cromwell appeared utterly perplexed as to the way forward for the country, or at least he announced that he was, publishing a fast-day declaration announcing that he awaited 'a conviction' enabling him to see the way forward, and the recovery of God's 'blessed presence'. He appeared to be offering an invitation to politicians and religious figures to offer their counsel. Henry Vane, for one, emerged from political retirement to urge representative government, where the 'whole body of the good People' should exercise their 'right of natural sovereignty'. Another response came from James Harrington, the leading English republican political theorist, who published *The Commonwealth of Oceana* in 1656: '. . . his proposed republic entailed regular elections for all public offices and secret ballots among a citizenry of independent gentlemen.' Harrington's republicanism would be profoundly influential on the constitutions of the early American colonies, and on the rebels of 1776.[27]

But in 1656 Cromwell was not really listening to anyone but God. Instead, arguing (as is so often done at these moments in history) that the English people were under threat from their 'great enemy' the Spaniard, he assumed absolute power. He was starting to look very much like a King. Nedham's newspaper, *Mercurius Politicus*, reported obsequiously on something akin to a royal wedding: '. . . yesterday afternoon his Highness went to Hampton Court, and this day the most illustrous Lady, the Lady Mary Cromwell, third daughter of his Highness the Lord Protector, was there married to the most noble Lord, the Lord Falconbridge, in the presence of their Highnesses and many noble persons.'[28] Whitehall and Hampton Court became in effect the courts of the Protector, still decorated with the remnants of Royal collections, still serving very similar functions. A historian of dress notes the phenomenon whereby official portraits of the 1650s 'frequently copied Van Dyck's paintings of the courtly regime, simply substituting new parliamentary heads for old royalist ones. Thus despite the disruptions of political and social life, the visual appearance of the elite remained unbroken until the 1660s'.[29] The evidence of the portraits and the palaces was only one aspect of Cromwell's rule. The same religious faith that brought him to such power and glory also ensured that Cromwell would *not* be King. When offered the title of monarch he said no, because he would not 'seek to set up that that providence hath destroyed and laid in the dust'.[30]

This was the highly charged political world in which John Milton continued to work, the volatile government he continued to serve. There was still no retreat from public life. He continued with many of his duties, producing a steady stream of correspondence, whether on the subject of foreign shipping, the political situation in Algiers or introducing the new English Resident to France (a process that took many, many months). As the Protectorate moved to ban or even to burn books of 'prophane and obscene matter' (a book ordered to be burned in April 1656, a poetic miscellany full of sportive wit or, as the Council saw it, 'scandalous, lascivious, scurrilous, and prophane matter', was actually edited by Milton's own nephew, John Phillips), the ideals of *Areopagitica* seemed a far-off dream.

For most people, however, *Areopagitica* was long forgotten. John Milton remained in the bookstalls but most notably as a defender of the Commonwealth and Protectorate, most notoriously as the defender of divorce and, in some quarters, as a poet. In the heart of government, Westminster, Milton, Latin Secretary to the Council, remained actively involved in sustaining the international prestige of his country and its leaders. Day by day he composed 'some of the

soaring Latin letters with which Cromwell hoped to rally the Protestant powers of Europe', and for Milton scholar Stephen Fallon,
much of the ardour of these letters is Milton's own, as in the following
plea to the Dutch on behalf of the Vaudois:

> You have already been informed of the Duke of Savoy's Edict, set
> forth against his subjects inhabiting the valleys at the feet of the
> Alps, ancient professors of the orthodox faith; by which Edict they
> are commanded to abandon their native habitations . . . and with
> what cruelty the authority of this Edict has raged against a needy
> and harmless people, many being slain by the soldiers, the rest
> plundered and driven from their houses together with their wives
> and children, to combat cold and hunger among desert mountains,
> and perpetual snow.[31]

The letter to the Dutch was one of a series, using similar rhetoric but
adapted for each recipient, ranging from the Evangelical Cities of
Switzerland and the Most Serene Prince of Transylvania (likely
supporters) to the King of France and Cardinal Mazarin (likely
opponents). The most crucial was the one to the Duke of Savoy
himself:

> *Partem tamen exercitus vestri in eos impetum fecisse multos crudelissime*
> *trucidasse, alios vinculis mandasse, reliquos in deserta loca montesque nivibus*
> *coopertos expulisse, ubi familiarum aliquot centuriae, eo loci rediguntur ut sit*
> *metuendum ne frigore & fame, brevi sint misere omnes periturae.*

> (25 May 1655, from Our Hall at Westminster)

> A part of your army fell upon 'em, most cruelly slew several, put
> others in chains, and compelled the rest to fly into desert places and
> to the mountains covered with snow, where some hundreds of
> families are reduced to such distress, that 'tis greatly to be feared,
> they will in a short time all miserably perish through cold and
> hunger.[32]

Did Milton relish the opportunity to give voice to Cromwell's vision, which, put most generously, involved a passionate commitment to Protestant unity, urged as a holy cause?[33] He was certainly complicit with the defence of these policies, and indeed the defence of the more pragmatic moments in Cromwell's foreign policy, when England made alliances with Catholic powers and waged war on her fellow-Protestants.

Political pragmatism, if that is the best way to describe Milton's activities at this time, was a common feature of life under Cromwell, is indeed under any system of government. Having said that, Milton did not *need* to work for Cromwell's government: it seems he chose to do so. He was still living in Petty France, presumably with his daughters, Anne, Mary and Deborah, who celebrated their ninth, seventh and third birthdays respectively in 1655. Milton himself would be forty-seven in the December of that year. He had time to turn to his private studies, starting work on a Latin and then a Greek dictionary. In May 1656, he wrote fairly happily to friends about his time at Cambridge, about people they knew at Oxford, about mutual friends travelling between England and the continent. Presumably he had servants who kept house for him, and probably a woman who cared for the girls. Money was not a problem at this time, although it seems to have been for Milton's mother-in-law, who sued again for war reparations in January 1656, again without success. Other legal cases involved Milton, predominantly concerning the estate in Oxfordshire, but there was little threat either to his ownership of the land or to his income from it. As he acknowledged in the *Second Defence*, he was permitted a substitute for the work he could no longer do, with a concomitant reduction in salary to £150, but this was guaranteed as a pension for life. It is probable, given his financial astuteness, that he did not need this £150.

Perhaps his continued service to the government reflected his belief that he was in a good position to influence events, able to offer guarded criticisms of Cromwell carefully couched in the form of comparisons or advice from his position as political insider. There is a prevailing sense in Milton's writing that Cromwell knew how to win battles but not how to govern. Even in the Piedmont sonnet, which seems so bloodthirsty and apocalyptic, the lesson for future generations (in Milton's eyes at least) is to be more wary, to flee before your enemy gets you: 'who having learnt thy way / Early may fly the Babylonian woe.' In contrast, Cromwell was not someone to advocate pre-emptive flight. Similarly, in the *Second Defence* the praise of Bradshaw's hospitality and assiduity in Council stands in contrast to Cromwell's ruthless military energy. Also Milton praises Robert Overton, a man interrogated and imprisoned by Cromwell shortly after the work's publication, and a figure who became synonymous with protest. Overton was a hero to Milton, 'who for many years [had] been linked with a more than fraternal harmony, by reason of the likeness of our tastes and the sweetness of your disposition'.[34] These were not the kind of terms John Milton used of Oliver Cromwell.

Meanwhile, others who were wont to express oblique disapproval of Cromwell, such as Andrew Marvell, elected MP for his home constituency of Hull in 1659, nevertheless took posts in his government. So did John Dryden, another famous poet. Unlike Dryden, and to some extent Marvell, Milton did not subsequently turn his back on the republican ideal. Milton's support of Cromwell's regime was not mere political time-serving. Even in the mid-1650s, he believed that the civic and religious liberties he desired were most likely to be delivered by Cromwell, whether through the form of Council, Parliament or the rule of the Major-Generals. Above all, Cromwell was committed to religious toleration and to the separation of Church and State. These were the two fundamentals for John Milton.

In 1656, he had the opportunity to enact, in a small way, one of his ideals. He had argued through the 1640s that the ministers of the Church had no right to involve themselves in the nuptial contract. So, when on 12 November John married Mistress Katherine Woodcock of the parish of Aldermanbury, spinster, in a civil ceremony presided over by a Justice of the Peace, with the Church no longer involved at any stage in the proceedings, his marriage was conducted according to his religious and political ideal.

The new Mrs Milton came from a relatively modest background. Katherine's father, killed in the wars in Scotland, had been a seller of leather and, occasionally, of books before going for a soldier. He had demonstrated such 'improvidence' in financial matters that when Katherine's mother, Elizabeth, was bequeathed £10 by her step-mother it was stipulated that the money should be 'paid unto her and not to her husband upon her own acquittance'. This prudent woman also willed that her executors 'be kind and loving to my said daughter Elizabeth Woodcock, so that she may have as free entertain-ment in my now dwelling house as now and hitherto she hath had . . . And I do give and bequeath unto my grandchild Katherine Woodcock a feather-bed and bolster and also a little chest with all things to be found therein, the key of which chest I have already delivered to her'.[35] Presumably, Katherine brought this furniture to the house in Petty France on her marriage to John.[36]

John Milton did not need a wealthy bride. He still had spare cash to buy books from Europe, and continued to acquire property and make loans. But he had three daughters to care for. A wife might be helpful in the raising of daughters; remarriage was nevertheless a serious step. When Oliver Heywood, he who had mourned his wife so much and congratulated himself on finding the ideal maid to help care for his young children, considered marrying again, it provoked much soul-searching: '. . . now at last I am thinking of changing my condition, and have been spending part of this day in solemn fasting and prayer to mourn for my sins and beg mercy.' The solemn fasting and prayer reassured him, and he reported happily that he was 'abundantly satisfied in my gracious yoke-fellow'.[37] Heywood was concerned in part because his first marriage had been so happy, but commentators also pointed out that those who had been unhappily married could have hopelessly high expectations of a second wife or husband. They might even seek 'jollity, and a braver and fuller life, then formerly they were content with'.[38] And, of course, sex. Despite, or perhaps because of, anxieties about the carnality or wastefulness of sexual acts, couples were increasingly encouraged to 'mutually delight' in each other. This advice was partly based on attitudes towards women's health. 'The use of venery is exceeding wholesome,' advised a book called *The Woman's Doctor* in 1658, so much so that widows who were not having sex were encouraged to ejaculate seed (as the female orgasm was understood to do) with the aid of 'a skilful Midwife and a convenient ointment'. More important, however, sexual pleasure was viewed as essential to conception'.[39]

While it is pleasant to think that Milton did experience 'jollity and a braver and fuller life', and while it is certain that he did have sex with his new wife, he could just as easily have had few or no expectations of personal happiness, or indeed been disappointed if the fuller life he hoped for did not materialise. It is impossible to know since once again the personal documents simply do not exist.

What is known is that Katherine was twenty years her new husband's junior, twenty-eight to John's forty-eight. This is no surprise. Older men of Milton's generation were far more likely to remarry than older women (90 per cent of men over sixty were married, only 25 per cent of women of that age) and two-thirds of these 'elderly' married men had wives who were more than ten years younger than themselves. The strategy was all part of a determination on the part of widowers to guard against destitution or neglect. Their young and active wives would provide some protection.

John Milton's young and active second wife took on the responsibility of caring not only for an older, disabled husband but also for his three daughters. There is no indication of the girls' response to their new mother, although one John Ward, making notes about Milton, wrote that she was 'very indulgent to her children in law', as stepchildren were referred to at the time.[40] Within only three months of her marriage, Katherine was pregnant. On 19 October 1657, John Milton's fifth child, and his new wife's first, was born, a baby girl named Katherine for her mother.

Little else is known about Katherine Woodcock Milton. Nevertheless, for some reason, this second marriage is invariably represented, even by the most hard-headed of biographers, as an idyll, a rare period of happiness in Milton's emotional life. There is, however, absolutely no evidence that this was the case. That Milton did not complete any translation work for the government between January and July of 1657 may indicate his focus on domestic life, but it may also have been a product of the acute political uncertainties at the time. During this period, Cromwell abandoned the constitution that had, to some extent, legitimised and provided a curb on his powers, the Instrument of Government, and the reign of the Major-Generals was also halted. Rejecting the title of King in April, by June Cromwell was restored as Lord Protector and granted £1.3 million to run the country.

Whatever its nature, the new Milton family unit would be as short-lived as Cromwell's experiments in government. Just over three months after giving birth to baby Katherine, Katherine Woodcock Milton died, probably of tuberculosis. She was only one month short of her thirtieth birthday. Anne Milton was twelve, Mary nine, Deborah five: Katherine Woodcock Milton had been a mother to the girls for only fourteen months, and now she left behind a new baby girl as well. Baby Katherine would not live much longer than her mother, dying before she reached five months old. If Milton's strategy had been to provide for his old age and disability, then things had not worked out as planned. If there had been a sincere commitment to Katherine, as seems possible, the damage was more long-lasting. John Milton had been emotionally courageous enough to marry again, but he had now lost the one woman he had loved, and her only child.

He certainly gave Katherine a good funeral, providing a very public statement of his family's status. She was buried in St Margaret's Church, Westminster, the parliamentarians' church. The bill for the ceremony survives, because this was a State funeral, if on a very small scale:

Work done for the funeral of Secretary Milton his wife her name Woodcock

Item for eight Taffaty escouti [taffata escutcheons]	02–13–4
Item for one dozen Buck escou	01–10–00
Item for a pall	01–00–00
	—————
	05–03–4[41]

This was a fine funeral for Secretary Milton's wife.[42] The note of expenses carried a parted shield, with the Milton arms (the spread eagle, originally the sign over the Milton family business) on one side and the Woodcock arms on the other. The spread eagle proclaimed Milton a gentleman. A story went that 'when Mr Milton buried his wife he had the coffin shut down with 12 several keys, and that he gave the keys to 12 several friends, and desired the coffin might not be open'd till they all met together'. True or not, the story speaks to the apocalyptic flavour of the Cromwellian establishment.[43]

The funeral is yet another piece of evidence that Milton was more than a mere cog in the government, and it also demonstrates his desire to celebrate his wife's life publicly.[44] One of Milton's most expressive and powerful poems offers a glimpse of the emotional, spiritual and psychological impact of a wife's death. In this sonnet, all the grief of the widower emerges. He dreams of his dead wife. In his 'fancied sight', she appears to him; she shows him that she is with God, redeemed, out of pain. He believes that he will have 'full sight of her in heaven without restraint'. Surely this is a consolation? But in a devastating final line, Milton writes, 'I waked, she fled, and day brought back my night.'

Yet, tantalisingly, the evidence resists any certain connection between this poem and Katherine. It may well have been composed at the death of Mary Powell Milton. Katherine did not die in childbirth (the wife in the poem does), whereas Mary did. The belief, rehearsed in almost all modern biographies, that Katherine was John's true love, and Mary his merely functional wife, forces Katherine into the poem.

None of this matters. The sonnet is a quite brilliant evocation of grief. Here, at last, the Classical allusions do not merely lend elegance or distance to the poem: they generate an emotional charge. The dead woman is both like Alcestis, who in Euripides' play gave her life for her husband's, and not like her: Alcestis was brought back from the grave by Hercules; Milton's wife remains lost. Milton is both like Odysseus, who sought to clasp his mother's shadow, and not like him, because in Milton's poem there is only one doomed attempt to clasp his wife, while his Classical sources allow Odysseus the luxury of three. Above all, here, at last, Milton uses a twist at the end of a poem to intensify the emotion rather than to diffuse or complicate the reader's experience. In simple monosyllables the agony of bereavement is expressed, all the more starkly in contrast with the convoluted syntax of the previous thirteen lines. 'I waked, she fled, and day brought back my night': the pain of his bereavement and the experience of blindness are fused in that one desolate line. Consolation is fantasy. Consciousness is darkness.

FIFTEEN

CRISIS

1659

A NOTHER DEATH WOULD come soon after Katherine's, and this time the impact would be felt nationally. In the summer of 1658, however, all looked calm. For those who supported Cromwell, and in particular his foreign policy, June brought a much-needed triumph. Across the English Channel, Dunkirk was captured, marking the reversal of centuries of strategic losses on the continent. The victory was the successful conclusion of a tactical military alliance with France against the Spanish, who had previously controlled the town. Some 30,000 English Royalist troops, commanded by James, the younger son of Charles I, were serving in the Spanish armies, so the victory was even sweeter. As one historian of the period suggests, things were looking good for the Protectorate in the summer of 1658:

> Many were impressed that Cromwell's foreign policy was more to the credit of a Protestant nation than that of the Stuarts, and many were coming to recognize that in significant respects the experience of Cromwellian rule was more liberal and humane than that of Charles I, particularly in its quite exceptionally generous policy of religious toleration, its allowance of an unusual degree of freedom to the press, and its aspiration to reform the law. All the indications were that the Protectorate would survive.[1]

It did not.

The most important factor in the demise of the Protectorate was the death of Oliver Cromwell on the afternoon of 3 September 1658 in the Palace of Whitehall. The Council moved quickly in response, organising a lengthy lying-in-state at Somerset House and an impressive State funeral on 23 November. Despite these rituals, rumours began circulating almost immediately that Cromwell's corpse had been buried privately elsewhere, that the death was suspicious, that God had at last punished an evil man. There were whispers that his corrupt body, despite the best efforts of spices and cerecloth and lead and wood, had 'purged and wrought through all', necessitating an early, private burial.

John Milton, for one, was prepared for this dangerous moment in the progress of the 1649 revolution. In October 1658, between Cromwell's death and his funeral, Milton published a revised edition of the *Defence of the English People*, with the subtitle *John Milton Englishman's Defence*. As he had done in 1651, he wanted to remind his audience that it was one thing to triumph, another to know 'the purpose and reason of winning'. He had not changed his views in the intervening years; it was simply that his country needed to hear them once again, and particularly at this potentially critical moment.[2]

At first, however, the expected crisis did not materialise. 'All men wondered to see all so quiet, in so dangerous a time,' wrote one minister. 'There is not a dog that wags his tongue, so great a calm are we in,' commented John Thurloe complacently, still Secretary of State.[3] Mimicking monarchic practice, Richard Cromwell, Oliver's son, took charge of the Second Protectorate. Men such as John Dryden, Milton's colleague in the Foreign Office, found time to write poems in celebration of Oliver Cromwell's achievements. His *Heroic Stanzas*, printed in 1659, praised Cromwell as a strong and intelligent ruler.

Political unity held together until Cromwell's funeral but then swiftly unravelled. A large part of the problem was Richard Cromwell himself. Born in 1626, his elder brother had died, leaving Richard as his father's heir. Yet Richard's experiences up to 1659 had done little to prepare him for government. He did not have a military career, and even when Oliver Cromwell became Lord Protector, he did not offer his eldest son a role. Indeed, Oliver was one of Richard's sternest critics, regularly upbraiding him for his idleness and lack of godly zeal. Only in 1657 was Richard given any governmental responsibility, and by then it was too little, too late. Through 1659 Richard's failings as a leader became starkly visible, and the army began flexing its muscles. The army was not only more republican in politics and more enthusiastic in religion than Richard Cromwell, it was also more ready for a fight. Stuck in the middle was Parliament. The English nation began to look, increasingly desperately, for a new constitutional settlement.

For Milton, it was time to write again, in his own name and for his own cause: religious liberty. He had been thinking ahead, conscious that the moment would come when he would have to speak out. He wrote to Parliament that he had 'prepared, supreme council, against the much expected time of your sitting, this treatise': this treatise was *Of Civil Power in Ecclesiastical Causes; Showing That it Is Not Lawful For Any Power on Earth to Compel in Matters of Religion*, published on 16 February 1659, and sold in Paul's Churchyard, Fleet Street and Westminster. Only the author's initials were put on the published work, but the advertisement for it in *Mercurius Politicus* assured the reader that it was 'written by Mr Milton'.

The tract's authority depended on Milton's representation of himself as a government insider, a man who knew the realities of life at Whitehall, who had 'heard often for several years' exemplary Council discussions 'so well joining religion with civil prudence, and yet so well distinguishing the different power of either'. Anyone present at meetings, as Milton was, would have been 'a convert in that point'. Here the Council of State was the champion of religious liberty, the eloquent guardian of the necessary separation between religious and civic power. Milton was positive, but more tentatively, about the overall achievements of the 'governors of this common-wealth, since the rooting out of prelates'; they had made 'least use of force in religion, and most have favoured Christian liberty of any in this island'.

Complementing this somewhat rose-tinted view of the previous fifteen years or so is a frightening vision of a future in which religious liberty is *not* present: '. . . nothing but troubles, persecutions, commotions can be expected; the inward decay of true religion among ourselves, and the utter overthrow at last by a common enemy'. Religion is, however, never considered in isolation. A government that neglects freedom of conscience will also never respect 'our civil rights'.

In this tract Milton articulated his long-held beliefs with clarity and precision:

> Two things there be which have been ever found working much mischief to the church of God and the advancement of truth: force on one side restraining, and hire on the other side corrupting the teachers thereof . . . For belief or practice in religion according to this conscientious persuasion, no man ought to be punished or molested by any outward force on earth whatsoever.[4]

He explained, clearly, why it was both wrong and futile to impose by force controls upon an individual's religious beliefs or practice. Faith was defined as 'things as belong chiefly to the knowledge and service of God', these things were 'liable to be variously understood by human reason'. Moreover, all human beings needed revelation to understand God, but that revelation would be variously understood by different people. Further still, since Scripture was the only true authority, and Scripture could only be understood by divine illumination, 'it follows clearly that no man or body of men in these times can be the infallible judges or determiners in matters of religion to any other men's consciences but their own.'

Six months later, in August 1659, Milton returned to his theme in his *Considerations Touching the Likeliest Means to Remove Hirelings out of the Church*. The hirelings he sought to remove were those men who took 'hire' – payment – for their ministry. (This work, too, was advertised in *Mercurius Politicus*.) At the same time, Milton reiterated his belief that ministers should not meddle with marriage, celebrating the achievement of Parliament in recovering 'the civil liberty of marriage' and raising the spectre of 'Milton the Divorcer' of the 1640s. Milton's vision of an uncorrupted lay clergy is rather touching and transparently reveals his own concerns. If a minister needed books, he could get the necessary library for a mere £60: perhaps Milton actually did the maths. Then again, 'if any man for his own curiosity or delight be in books further expensive, that is not to be reckoned as necessary to his ministerial either breeding or function.' These 'further expensive' books might not be *necessary*, but Milton could not quite forget them, and suggested that perhaps, in an ideal world, the State could provide libraries and schools from which they could be borrowed. These suggestions may be touching, but the point Milton was making was, and indeed remains, a radical one: that a professional ministry, particularly one appointed and controlled by a State Church, was not compatible with true religious freedom.

As with his previous tract, Milton reminded Parliament of its achievements to date, spurring the institution on. They had 'freed the nation from the double tyranny of crown and prelates', king and bishops. He also reminded Parliament of his *own* achievements as their propagandist since 1649. He had been 'so far approved as to have been trusted with the representment and defence of your actions to all Christendom against an adversary of no mean repute' – a glance at Salmasius. But, as with the previous tract, *Hirelings* ends with a warning. If Milton was not listened to, 'infinite disturbances in the state' would ensue: 'If I be not heard nor believed, the event will bear me witness to have spoken truth; and I in the meanwhile have borne my witness, not out of season, to the Church and to my country.'

John Milton's language of bearing witness was profoundly signifi-cant at this critical moment for his country. *Hirelings* explicitly celebrates a culture of tolerance in which individuals can speak out. Milton placed himself firmly within that culture and reminded Parlia-ment that it was through their 'protection, supreme senate' that 'this liberty of writing which I have used these eighteen years on all occasions to assert the just rights and freedoms both of Church and state' had been permitted. This is a little disingenuous, given that the Presbyterian parliaments of the 1640s had not exactly encouraged Milton's tracts, so much so that many had been published without licence, but it is effective rhetoric. The unbreakable link between

religious and political 'just rights and freedoms' and freedom of speech
is once again asserted. The question was, could Milton's eloquent
vision ever become political reality?

It would need the support of men such as Henry Vane, who re-
entered public life at this time, joining a group of 'Commonwealthmen'
made up of similarly minded parliamentary colleagues, disaffected
former army officers and loyal Cromwellians, such as John Lambert.[5]
This rising tide of nostalgic propaganda for the 'Good Old Cause', the
republic that had flourished between 1649 and 1653, fed not only the
political aspirations of the Commonwealthmen but also the frustra-
tions of the religious and political radicals in London (most notably
the Fifth Monarchists, still preparing for Christ's Second Coming) and
the grievances of a discontented army. By mid-February, *The Humble
Petition of Many Thousand Citizens and inhabitants in and about the City of
London to the Parliament of the Common-wealth of England* and a series of
subsequent tracts were calling for supreme authority to be returned to
Parliament in language characterised by a 'heady and inflammatory
mix of biblical oracles, apocalyptic imagery, millenarian expectancy
and Fifth Monarchist fervour'.[6] Elsewhere in London, wealthier
citizens discussed the need for republican government over the
new and fashionable drink, coffee. The 'Rota', named for the theory
of its foremost member, James Harrington, who argued for a rotating
senate system that would ensure fair and impartial government, met
in a pub, the Turk's Head, in New Palace Yard right by Westminster.
The diarist John Aubrey, who attended the meetings along with
Milton's friend Cyriack Skinner and a young Samuel Pepys, described
the atmosphere in vivid detail:

> Every night a meeting at the (then) Turk's Head – in the new
> palace-yard – where they take water, the next house to the stairs,
> at one Miles's – where was made purposely a large oval table,
> with a passage in the middle for Miles to deliver his coffee. About
> it sat his disciples and the virtuosi. The discourses in this kind
> were the most ingenious and smart that ever I heard or expect to
> hear, and bandied with great eagerness: the arguments in the

Parliament house were but flat to it . . . We many times adjourned
to the Rhenish wine-house . . . The doctrine was very taking, and
the more because, as to human foresight, there was no possibility
of the King's return.[7]

These republican doctrines were indeed 'very taking', at least to John
Milton, and in the early months of 1659 it seemed that they might
become reality. It was the army, however, that delivered the change in
government. Henry Vane had predicted the next step in the nation's
collapse into anarchy. He had recommended that the army's grievances should be dealt with promptly so as to neutralise their power,
but it was already too late. On 6 April 1659, in another *Humble Petition*
but this time of the *General Council of the Officers of the Armies of
England, Scotland and Ireland*, Richard Cromwell was asked to support
the 'Good Old Cause', to act against prominent Royalists in London
and to meet the army's pay arrears. There was little humble in the
army's demands: they knew they had the firepower to enforce their
wishes. By 22 April, Richard Cromwell was fully in the army's control,
dissolving Parliament only a day after he had been instructed to do so
by army officers.

By the end of the month, the army was the only significant power in
the country. It would intervene no fewer than four times during 1659
and 1660: political thinking simply did not, could not, keep up with
events. The discussions over coffee, the tracts in defence of religious
toleration, even the parliamentary debates, meant nothing in comparison to men with guns.

Even a country squire, William Lawrence of Shurdington, who rarely
commented on political matters (the editor of his letters describes him as
'an observer of the events of his time but never involved') was moved to
lament the state of the nation on 30 May 1659:

The Nation is so trampled upon by Troopers, and so submissive to
the force of powder, that every single nine-penny Redcoat thinks he
can discharge parliament with as much ease as his musket.

There have been of late years so many changes and such antipodes
in government, that I think no age or nation hath been so eminently
wicked as to be able to produce a parallel.[8]

This diarist was moved to his observation partly out of fear (of the
men and muskets) and partly out of despair at the apparently never-
ending revolutions in government. His response was typical of many
bemused and frightened by the conditions of 1659.

Yet, out of the near anarchy of the preceding months there emerged
the form of government most admired by John Milton. Republicanism
was being restored by the men with guns. In an extraordinary move,
forty-two of the MPs who had served between 1649 and 1653 were
recalled, a rump of the Rump. These men were the embodiment of the
radical, religious republican movement. Two weeks later, on 24 May
1659, Richard Cromwell abdicated. When a Royalist insurrection was
crushed, easily, by Lambert, Milton saw 'such a signal victory' as a
sign from God, when 'so great a part of the nation were desperately
conspired to call back again their Egyptian bondage'. If God could
give a victory now, then 'God was pleased' with the restoration of the
Rump.[9]

For some scholars, the crisis of this time precipitated Milton
towards fully fledged republicanism. They argue that 'only in
1659–60 did he unambiguously renounce monarchy of any kind.'[10]
Even if this late arrival at such a position is accepted, it only serves
to underline the passionate commitment John Milton now had to
this form of government, a form of government he felt could not
survive under what he called the 'deluge of this epidemic madness'.[11]
Because he, unlike John Aubrey, who believed there was no possibility of the King's return, was horribly certain 'Egyptian bondage'
would not only be restored but welcomed by the weak English
people. Milton believed that he was now supporting a lost cause. Still
a servant of government (paid on 22 October 1659, for example, and
writing letters for the Rump Parliament in May 1659), he may have
had a better sense than many of the precariousness of the political
situation.

The threat would come from within rather than without. Lambert, the crusher of Royalist rebellion, moved now to crush the Rump Parliament in a shocking coup d'état. Milton was not too dismayed. Again, he responded to events in writing. This time, it was a letter to an (anonymous) friend, someone with whom he had discussed the nation's predicament.[12] This letter may well be a fiction, the equivalent of the 'humble petitions' and 'addresses' of the period. In it, Milton tells his correspondent, real or imagined, that he can do what he pleases with the document: 'put out, put in, communicate or suppress'. Milton's only concern is 'to offer something which might be of some use in this great time of need'. Dated 20 October 1659, the letter admits that Milton has not yet got the full details in part because he is housebound ('I speak only what it appears to us within doors . . .') but reiterates his desire for 'full liberty of conscience and the abjuration of monarchy'. In this state of political emergency, his thinking has become more radical. He espouses 'a perfect democracy' with committees from each county. The letter was not 'put out' in his lifetime, perhaps yet another sign of the inhospitable political territory in which he was now operating.

He had good reason to fear for his future. If indeed 'so great a part of the nation were desperately conspired to call back again their Egyptian bondage,' then that great part of the nation would have little time for John Milton, apologist for the regicides, religious independent and republican. It is no coincidence that at precisely this time, he moved to ensure that copies were made of many of the documents he had produced in the service of the government. He knew full well that if he was removed from his post, he would have to hand over his papers, even to a benign successor. Did he want simply to preserve a record for himself or to publish his papers, so that posterity could witness republican government in action? Perhaps he had both aims in mind, but what is clear is that the copying was done in some haste, suggesting urgency, even panic. The very manuscript into which key letters were copied was simply seized for the occasion: 'It is a crudely bound notebook of unusual size (6.5 inches by 15 inches), which quite obviously belonged to *someone else*. The first nineteen pages are a commonplace book consisting of entries, mostly on political matters, in which Milton could have had little interest'.[13] Whose notebook Milton (or whichever ally helped him) took is a mystery, but its very appearance suggests the impromptu, improvised nature of the effort.

Milton's religious beliefs were as potentially damning as his political writings. In the preceding decades, his thinking had become more radical and less orthodox. He was, for example, sympathetic to Jewish thought, and his Hebrew, certainly fine enough to translate the Psalms, also allowed him to study the Talmud, Midrash and Maimonides.[14] More startling than this evidence of philo-Semitism are the contents of a long manuscript that provides a startling account of profoundly heterodox religious beliefs. Known as *De Doctrina Christiana* (Of Christian Doctrine), it was compiled over a number of years, in Latin, and possibly begun with an eye to publication in Europe (although it is hard to imagine it finding a publisher). It contains highly inflammatory challenges to core Christian beliefs, questioning, for example, the idea of the Trinity, or defending the practice of polygamy. *Of Christian Doctrine* remained well hidden for hundreds of years, only surfacing in the nineteenth century, since when it has been a bone of contention among Milton scholars, some of whom still do not accept it as his work.[15]

In 1659, Milton's concern was to preserve his political legacy, and his collection of State letters was made only just in time. Lambert's rule proved as short-lived as all the other forms of government since the death of Oliver Cromwell. People looked further back – when had there been stability in the country? By late February 1660, there was open talk of a return of monarchy. Even in the last months of 1659, this kind of talk had been conducted in whispers, if at all. Royalist sympathisers, men such as Roger L'Estrange, re-admitted to England due to Cromwell's Act of Indemnity back in 1653, may have advocated the dismissal of the Rump Parliament and the calling of a free Parliament, but they did not call for the restoration of King Charles II. Now suddenly all was changed. Aubrey, writing about the discussions of republican government in the coffee-house meetings, said that they continued 'till 20 or 21 February and then, upon the unexpected turn upon General Monck's coming in, all these airy models vanished. Then 'twas not fit, nay treason, to have done such'.[16]

Gen. Monck had been one of Cromwell's best military leaders, victorious against the Dutch at sea back in 1653 and then put in military command in Scotland. His success there was based on his determination to root out religious extremists, such as Levellers or Quakers, from the army. But on 1 January 1660, he led his part of what had been the New Model Army across the River Tweed and into England. The army now supported the claim of Charles Stuart, the son of Charles I. The irony was that Monck was driven to restore the King because of his hatred of military government: 'I am engaged in conscience and honour to see my country freed . . . from that intolerable slavery of a sword government, and I know England cannot, nay, will not, endure it.'[17] Monck had, cannily, sent his personal messenger to Charles, unwilling to trust negotiations to a letter that could be intercepted. He offered three pieces of advice to the man who would be King. Charles should offer a 'free and general pardon' to all, except a few exempted individuals. He should sell public lands in order to pay his soldiers. And the King should support an Act for the toleration of 'Liberty of Conscience to all his Subjects'. There was also the politic suggestion that he move his European base from the Roman Catholic Spanish Netherlands to the Protestant United Provinces before returning to England. This change in the political tide was vividly illustrated in the proceedings at the Palace of Whitehall at this time. In 1659, the palace had been put up for sale, the money intended to finance the payment of long-overdue wages for the army. The sale was, however, abandoned in February 1660 with the arrival of Gen. Monck, who was promptly assigned lodgings in the palace right at the waterside.

By the time Monck arrived in Whitehall and Westminster, the blind John Milton had already been mocked in a pamphlet, *The Outcry of London Prentices.* On 16 February, Monck called for a free Parliament. Five days later, the Rump Parliament was (yet again) restored, this time with the Presbyterian members who had been excluded twelve years earlier re-admitted. The newly re-formed Rump looked rather like the Long Parliament of the 1640s. Everything seemed set for the return of Charles Stuart. John Evelyn could now write that everyone was hoping and desiring that the government would be established once again 'on its ancient and right basis'.[18] By 6 March, Pepys was noting that 'everybody now drinks the King's health without fear, whereas before it was very private that a man dare do it.'[19] In mid-March, Parliament dissolved itself 'very cheerfully' (Pepys again), and by April, the King's arms were appearing everywhere. It had all happened very quickly.[20]

Milton responded to events as they happened, writing with an awe-inspiring urgency, desperation and courage. As Parliament was being recalled, he penned *The Readie & Easie Way to Establish a Free Commonwealth*, ready for publication just as the new Parliament convened. The author and printer are only identified by initials, but the book-seller was announced as Livewell Chapman at the Crown in Popes-Head Alley.[21] A week later, the Rump or Long Parliament dissolved itself, and Milton returned even more urgently to his work, revising his tract in time for the elections at the start of April. He clearly sensed that the English nation would choose a King again.

This second edition of the *Readie & Easie Way* is astonishing for the sense it gives of Milton responding, almost day by day, to the debates around him. He is still insistent on the moral difference between republicanism and kingly rule, but he is less insistent in his support for a grand Council, up to this point his ideal regime. As with his *Letter to a Friend*, pressed by circumstances, criticism and rival schemes, Milton now imagines a more democratic kind of government, and advocates, pragmatically, a more popular assembly to complement the noble senate or Council. His politics remain both patrician (the people need to be saved from themselves and compelled to liberty) and visionary, imagining a free Commonwealth whose leaders 'walk the streets as other men, may be spoken to freely, familiarly, friendly, without adoration'. He restates his profound conviction that the 'whole free-dom of man consists either in spiritual or civil liberty'. The former is achieved when an individual is at 'liberty to serve God and to save his own soul, according to the best light which God hath planted in him to that purpose'. The latter is most likely to occur in a Commonwealth, which will ensure 'the civil rights and advancements of every person according to his merit'. The final pages of the work are deeply moving in their desperate sense that this vision will never become reality: Milton is speaking to the stones, like the prophet Jeremiah, because he has 'none to cry to'. Still, he must speak out, these 'last words of our expiring liberty'. There is a faint hope: 'I trust I shall have spoken persuasion to abundance of sensible and ingenuous men: to some perhaps whom God may raise of these stones to become children of reviving liberty.'[22] This hope is countered by the final phrases, which raise the spectre of a nation, a 'misguided and abused multitude', gripped by an epidemic madness.

Milton's *Brief Notes Upon a Late Sermon*, which followed soon after, was equally and absolutely rooted in this politically charged moment, when fear of complete anarchy or popular revolution gripped the nation. A Royalist clergyman had preached a sermon gloating over what he saw as the imminent return of the King and the destruction of his enemies. Royalist leaders behind the scenes, desperate to keep the political temperature down, were not happy. To preach the sermon was merely inflammatory. To publish it, dedicated to Gen. Monck, was positively dangerous. The clergyman ended up in prison, but he had provoked Milton into a response: a short, unregistered work (perhaps because time was short, perhaps because the situation was getting dangerous for these kinds of gestures) that reminded Monck of his republican promises. *Brief Notes* offers desperate arguments for desperate times. Milton seems to have accepted that the English people wanted monarchy, God help them, but if they wanted a monarch, they should at least choose the best man for the job: Gen. Monck over Charles Stuart. (The man to whom Milton might have turned at this time, John Bradshaw, had died in October 1659.)

All that the *Brief Notes* did was to draw attention to Milton. Roger L'Estrange, relishing the political moment, satirised him in *No Blinde Guides*, in which the calculated insult of the title was exacerbated by the motto, 'If the blind lead the blind, both shall fall into the ditch' (from Matthew 15:14). Nothing would stem the tide of support for Charles Stuart. The events of 1 May 1660 are recorded by Pepys in his diary: '. . . great joy all yesterday at London; and at night more bonfires than ever and ringing of bells and drinking of the King's health upon their knees in the streets.'[23] The previous day the Parliament in session since 25 April had voted that the 'fundamental laws' of the nation meant that the government of England was by King, Lords and Commons. There had been little or no bloodshed. In just a few short months, the English republic had gone forever, consigned to the history books as the 'Interregnum', the mere interruption of centuries of monarchy.

Good times had come again for men like Richard Powell, Mary Powell Milton's brother, who on 28 April 1660 was listed among the gentry of Oxfordshire who had remained loyal to Charles I. Another of Milton's brothers-in-law, Thomas Agar, had suffered under the Cromwellian regime. In 1660 he regained his post and even added a new position to his portfolio: Clerk of Appeals. John Dryden, like many of his contemporaries who were quickly abandoning their politically incorrect republican beliefs, forgot that he had followed Cromwell's funeral cortege, and greeted the returning King with an elegant poem, *Astraea redux* (Justice restored), which represented Charles Stuart as a second Augustus. Even John Thurloe, Cromwell's much-feared head of intelligence, became a servant of the new government and thus survived the regime change. Milton's old adversary Bishop Bramhall was back in town, at Westminster on 15 June: he was appointed Primate of Ireland on 1 August 1660.

In sharp contrast, these were perilous months for Milton himself. Repeatedly vituperated and threatened in print, it was claimed that he had been struck blind by God as he wrote the second word of *Eikonoklastes*. It was only a matter of time before words would become deeds. Milton prepared for the inevitable retribution. He had been calling in debts for some months. Somewhat surprisingly, a document from November 1659, signed by Milton himself with a sprawling signature, acknowledges the repayment of the £500 loaned to Richard Powell back in 1627. In December, an extra £10 was added to what was an emergency fund, when John Bradshaw left Milton the amount in his will. In the early months of 1660, Milton continued to raise cash by offloading assets.[24]

And then, on 29 May 1660, King Charles II entered London in triumph. The monarchy was officially restored in England, where it continues to this day. The celebrations were, it seemed, unanimous: 'upon this King's most happy Restoration', all had hearts full of reverence and obedience 'to his sacred person'. How lucky the English people were to be born his 'subjects'.[25] One sceptical diarist noted tersely 'King crowned, great joy, much sin, the Lord pardon. 'Twas a very wet evening.'[26] There were others who were more explicit, at least in private, in their dismay at the return of the King. Lucy Hutchinson, the widow of one of Oliver Cromwell's officers, wrote a history of the times, commenting that it was wonderful (that is, full of wonders), 'to see the mutability of some, and the hypocrisy of others, and the servile flattery of all'.[27]

Not of all. John Milton had maintained his position of opposition to the monarchy, his support of religious tolerance, until the wheels of the King's carriage could be heard entering London. But by the time Charles arrived in the city, Milton was in hiding. How he survived during these months, where he hid, how he lived, remain well-kept secrets.[28] Other mysteries remain. What happened to his daughters? The regicide Henry Marten's letters from this period, when he was on trial, reveal a deep concern for the welfare and future of his three young children. His solution was to send them to be cared for by his mistress. Nowhere does Milton express any opinion, caring or un-caring, about his daughters (and few biographers then or now have seemed interested in the girls, now aged fifteen, twelve and nearly nine). It is probable that they stayed with their grandmother, Anne Powell, still living in London at this time and, crucially, now the elderly matriarch of a Royalist family.

Whoever sheltered the girls' father was running a huge risk. Milton's name was on the list of those being considered for the death penalty. Many others were safe, covered by the general amnesty proclaimed by Charles II, but not Milton. On 16 June 1660, proceedings for his arrest began. On the same day, in Oxford, the historian Anthony Wood noted that Milton's books were being removed from the 'public library' – that is, the Bodleian.[29]

Milton's choice of hiding place needed to be good, and it was. (His nephew later speculated that he had hidden in St Bartholomew Close, near St Paul's.) Meanwhile, the vilification in print continued, with yet further variations on the theme of being struck blind by God in punishment alongside attacks on Milton, the blind beetle, the mercenary hack. By early July, there were rumours that his books had been burned and he summarily hanged. In mid-August, a step further was taken towards making these rumours reality.

A proclamation against *The Defence of the English People* and *Eikonoklastes* was issued on 13 August 1660. The proclamation announced that all books by John Milton were to be called in and burned. There would have been raids on stationers' shops (Milton's *Treatise of Civil Power* had appeared in a catalogue of new books as late as 31 May 1660) and on private houses. Others perhaps handed over their copies to the authorities, eager to show evidence of conformity. On 27 August 1660, Milton's books were publicly burned by the hangman at the Old Bailey. It is impossible to forget the poet's lines from *Areopagitica*, 'as good almost kill a Man as kill a good Book', his warning to be wary of the spilling of 'that season'd life of man preserved and stored up in books: since we see a kind of homicide may be thus committed, sometimes a martyrdom, and if it extend to the whole impression, a kind of massacre' in which is slain 'the breath of reason it self . . . an immortality rather then a life'.

This same proclamation that called for the burning of Milton's books contained the admission that the authorities could not find the man himself. He had 'fled, or so obscured' himself that 'no endeavours used' to track him down had worked. It was, however, surely only a matter of time before he was tracked down and executed.

Yet, just two days after the book-burning, the Act of Free and General Pardon, Indemnity and Oblivion was given Royal assent, and, astonishingly, Milton was *not* on the list of those sentenced to death. Others were not so lucky. The list of those 'excepted' from pardon included both the living and the dead: Cromwell, Bradshaw and other regicides would suffer retribution beyond the grave. Other allies had already suffered. As early as 9 January, Henry Vane had been summoned to face charges of 'Crimes, Miscarriages and Misdemeanours' committed during 'the interruption'. Vane was banished from London, his regiment disbanded, and then he was arrested.[30]

Who ensured that Milton's name was taken off the list of those who would die? It may well have been friends such as Andrew Marvell. Marvell appeared to modify his own political beliefs and behaviour in light of the regime change, yet he remained loyal to Milton, who would not do so. Or it may have been the wider Milton family. Three close male family members, John's brother, Christopher, and two of his brothers-in-law, Richard Powell and Thomas Agar, were all avowed Royalists. Christopher in particular was thriving in the new conditions, reaping the long-awaited rewards for his loyalty to the King's cause back in the 1640s. On 25 November 1660, he was called to the Bench of the Inner Temple. Christopher, Richard and Thomas may have exerted pressure on Parliament to spare their wrong-headed brother's life, just as Milton had protected the Powells in their time of trouble in the 1640s.

Exempted from the death penalty, John Milton emerged from hiding. He rented a house in Holborn, in St Giles-in-the-Fields, on the semi-rural outskirts of London. He was immediately greeted by a voice from the past: the publication of a posthumous work from his old enemy Salmasius, complete with dedication to Charles II penned by Salmasius' son. John Milton was still a European cause célèbre, his fight with Salmasius very much in the public mind. It is possible that he was tempted to respond, but there was no time. Just as he may have believed that the period of acute danger was over, he was arrested and imprisoned late in 1660.

Part Three

POET AND PROPHET

SIXTEEN

DEFEAT

1660

I T SEEMS THE new regime merely wished to humiliate or intimi-
date Milton, for he was permitted to leave prison on 15 December
1660, after probably two months of imprisonment. Like all prisoners,
he paid his own jail fees as he left. He was fifty-two years old, blind,
and a social and political outcast.

The new year brought only more misery. The government ordered
the exhumation and posthumous execution of key leaders from the
republican years. There were rumours even at the time that they had
not got the right bodies (the corpses hung in their shrouds from the
gallows in order to prevent the revelation, people said), but it did not
really matter. The mood was one of retribution, and the moment was
enjoyed by all those who had suffered under Cromwell's regime.

> On Monday night Cromwell and Ireton, on two several carts, were
> drawn to Holborn from Westminster, after they were digged up on
> Saturday last, and the next morning Bradshaw; today they were drawn
> upon sledges to Tyburn, all the way (as before from Westminster) the
> universal outcry of the people went along with them. When these their
> Carcasses were at Tyburn, they were pulled out of their coffins, and
> hanged at the several angles of that triple tree, where they hung till the
> sun was set; after which they were taken down, their heads cut off, and
> their loathsome trunks thrown into a deep hole under the gallows.[1]

The regicides' heads were displayed on poles above Westminster Hall
until 1684. This very public ritual was designed to demonstrate the

complete overthrow of the previous regime and the triumph of the restoration of the monarchy, but in reality, there was much still to do to achieve political and social stability. First the New Model Army was disbanded, and the soldiers paid off. King Charles II and his supporters had one less thing to worry about: '. . . the court was at great quiet when they got rid of so uneasy a burden as lay on them from the fear of such a body of men,' wrote one contemporary.[2]

With the army disbanded and dispersed, the government moved to enforce political and religious conformity. There would be no return to the chaos of competing views that had characterised so much of the preceding decade of civil and religious government. The Church of England was re-established, and compliance with its doctrine and practice enforced by an Act of Uniformity. A draconian Licensing Act was brought in to control the press. No carpenter could construct a press, no ironmonger could found type, without the permission of the Stationers Company. Pre-publication censorship (the kind of censorship that Milton had so strongly opposed in *Areopagitica*) was re-introduced and involved a two-tier process, with government censors and the Stationers Company both given more aggressive powers actively to search out seditious material.

Roger L'Estrange, one of the most outspoken and vindictive of the Royalists, a man fiercely critical of the new government's apparent determination if not to forgive, then to forget, came to dominate the world of the press. The extremism of men like L'Estrange was embarrassing to more moderate members of the Royal court and government, including the King himself, but it was L'Estrange who demanded and got tougher laws and powers to stamp out the publishing underground. Appointed in 1663 as Surveyor of the Press, he was granted formidable powers to search for unlicensed books, illegal presses and all those involved in the production of illicit material.[3] Dawn raids, rewards for informers and imprisonment without trial characterised his rule.

The punishments for authors and printers could be severe. On 20 February 1664, the printer John Twyn was executed for printing an anonymous book (*Treatise of the Execution of Justice*) which echoed

Milton's own *Tenure of Kings and Magistrates*, although instead of Milton's discussion of the legal basis for the execution of tyrants, the offending *Treatise* was a terrorist's appeal, urging the assassination of Charles II and his family. The suppression of opposition generally took less brutal, but perhaps more insidious, forms. In London, the coffee house became the place to talk politics. Unable to stop new coffee houses opening, Charles II enlisted coffee merchants to act as spies for the State, reporting on any person who made criticisms of the government.

From pulpit to coffee house, it was all part of the restored monarchy's attempts to secure its authority, and predictably many of those who had previously seemed content with republican government were quick to see the error of their ways. Some, such as John Dryden, developed a theory of human nature that explained his change of heart: 'As I am a Man, I must be changeable . . . An ill dream, or a Cloudy day, has power to change this wretched Creature, who is so proud of a reasonable Soul, and make him think what he thought not yesterday.'[4] Yesterday, as it were, he had celebrated Oliver Cromwell in *Heroic Stanzas*. Today, he was writing *To His Sacred Majesty, a Panegyric on his Coronation* (which had taken place on St George's Day 1661).

Others who had supported the monarchy even during the years of republican government continued to flourish. On 30 October 1661, Christopher Milton's son, also Christopher, entered the Inner Temple at the request of his father, who himself was continuing in his exemplary legal career. Fifteen months later, Richard Powell, Mary Powell Milton's brother, was called to the Bench. But John Milton was not for turning. His stance is an exceptional one. Back in the early years of the seventeenth century, there had been very few people in England who had described themselves as republicans, but by the time Milton became republican himself, in the late 1640s, he was joining a significant but powerful minority. This was unremarkable in itself. What is striking is that he remained so through the 1650s, despite the failure of republican government to deliver the political and religious reforms he hoped for. What is astonishing and truly rare is that he remained a republican after the restoration of monarchy – and that he remained in England. The majority of his republican contemporaries, such as they were, either left the country for continental Europe or the New World, or, if they remained, were only too happy to forget that they had ever been so.

His commitment to the cause was signalled by the publication of one of his poems in 1662, a sonnet written years earlier in praise of Henry Vane. Milton had admired Vane then, praising him as the ideal senator, and admiring his belief in the separation of spiritual and civil power, and he still admired him now. But Vane was one of the casualties of the restoration of the monarchy. On 14 June 1662, he was executed, the victim of Parliament's desire for regicide blood and his own refusal to renounce his political beliefs. Indeed, adversity seems only to have strengthened Vane's confidence in the cause, even as he became perplexed by the 'black shade which God hath drawn over his work', the godly republic.[5] Vane, like Milton, saw the failure to establish true religion and government as the result of misman-agement by humans rather than a sign that the project itself was inherently evil. Three weeks after Vane's execution, on 3 July 1662, Milton sent his sonnet tribute to Vane's biographer, George Sikes. Two months later Sikes's *Life and Death of Sir Henry Vane* was published.

The re-publication of the sonnet in Vane's honour was an early indication that Milton would not retreat into silence after the Re-storation. It also indicated that it was possible, if fraught with danger, to publish, and that Milton still had good connections with the radical press of the City. But it was not a world that made him very welcome. His divorce tracts were still causing problems at home and abroad, as were the more obvious politically incorrect works such as *Eikonok-lastes*. Milton's battle with Salmasius still had people talking, as we have seen. On 30 January 1663, a sermon against Milton was preached at court, in the presence of King Charles II, where he was described as a 'blind Adder' who had spat 'Poison on the King's Person and Cause'. The year 1664 opened with a satire on 'blind Milton' in the popular almanac *Poor Robin*.[6]

In more general terms, Milton was out of step with the new consumer society, with its new fashions, new foods, new styles of living. The term *Restoration* suggests, obviously, a return to a previous order. To some extent, this was the case. Rituals such as the celebrations surrounding Twelfth Night were revived, having lapsed during the Civil War and beyond, with Samuel Pepys describing, for example, in 1661 the baking of a great cake with a solitary bean hidden in it. The person who found the bean became King for the day. But the early years of the 1660s saw not just the revival of long-abandoned social practices but a startling revolution in daily life. Pepys's diary gives a vivid account of the new London lifestyle. It is hard, for example, to imagine John Milton heading out on a gastronomic expedition, as Pepys did with his wife, all the way to Islington Fields in order to taste a cheesecake from the famous cheesecake house.[7]

The changes were fuelled by the experiences of the returning Royalist exiles. Many of those now in power had spent many years abroad, particularly in France, and brought back with them French tastes in cooking and fashion. They were eating ragouts (sauces of broth, herbs and onions) and fricassées (fried meat with cream sauce), and wearing clothes with an exaggerated fullness, bedecked with ribbons. Women's forearms were being revealed for the first time in hundreds of years, and the viewer's eye directed to the hips, supplemented by hip pads, in a world in which the ideal woman had a kind of 'soft massivity', in the words of one historian of clothing.[8] In these new clothes, men and women would go to new places, whether the fashionable coffee houses (tea and coffee replaced beer and ale as the national beverages, at least in London) or the reopened theatres. The drama of the time was performed by actresses, another idea imported from continental Europe, and the plays (what is now known as Restoration Comedy) were witty and ebullient, as well as amoral and cynical. Theatre was inextricably linked with the culture of the court, and John Milton's old home at Whitehall was now the scene of sophisticated sexual intrigue, both real and on stage. Actresses became the mistresses of noblemen and the King himself. So John Dryden's first play, *The Wild Gallant*, which opened at the

Theatre Royal in February 1663, was being performed a couple of weeks later 'at court', probably at Whitehall, and almost definitely through the influence of the King's mistress Lady Castlemaine. Sadly for Dryden, his attempt to represent debauchery to a court already renowned for its dissipation was not successful. Pepys commented that *The Wild Gallant* 'was ill acted and the play so poor a thing as I never saw in my life almost, and so little answering the name, that from beginning to end I could not, nor can at this time, tell certainly which was the wild gallant'.[9]

It seems highly unlikely that, in this changed world, John Milton ever considered reinventing himself as the writer of sex comedies or panegyrics on the coronation. Two early biographers, Edward Phillips and John Aubrey, suggest instead that he had returned, during the fraught closing months of the 1650s and through the early years of the 1660s, to ideas he had first explored twenty or even thirty years earlier. In the Trinity Manuscript back in 1640, Milton had produced rough notes for a tragic drama that would tell the story of Adam's expulsion from Eden. Earlier still, in his writings from the late 1620s (such as *At a Vacation Exercise*) and then on into the early 1640s, he had expressed a desire to write a patriotic heroic epic, using the history of Britain as his material. Now, at a time of acute crisis in his own life and that of his country, the two prospective literary endeavours came together. Milton began writing a biblical epic.

Whether he was expressing his apocalyptic hopes by returning to the Bible, or showing a canny awareness that a national, historical epic would not be published in a volatile political climate, or whether the death of Katherine Woodcock Milton spurred him into action remains unclear.[10] Whatever the impetus, and whichever was the precise moment he turned back to poetry, Milton's living conditions were not conducive to relaxed composition. He was just about surviving, staying in lodgings in Jewin Street off Aldersgate, the street where he and Mary Powell Milton had lived and in which his first two daughters had been born. John's middle daughter Mary, fourteen in 1661, was almost of an age to take over some of the household responsibilities, but Anne, with her disability, was less well placed to take on the arduous physical business of running a home in the 1660s. Their father's gender, as much as his own disability, ensured he would stay well away from the rigidly defined domestic, and thus female, spaces in seventeenth-century houses. It was deemed shameful for a man to enter the woman's domain. If he did, he was a 'cotquean', effeminate.

In Jewin Street, Milton was back on the edge of a dangerous and restive city that was growing all the time. In his own parish there were ever-increasing numbers of leather-workers, smiths, cutlers, tailors and weavers, bakers and butchers and cobblers and glovers, and there was little support for the newly restored monarchy among such men. As early as March of 1661, elections in the City of London returned two Presbyterian and two Independent members, with much chanting of slogans: 'no bishops, no lord bishops'. Two months earlier, the Fifth Monarchists, led by Thomas Venner, rose up in London, their cry 'King Jesus, and the heads upon the gates'. At least fifty Fifth Monarchists threw the City into a panic, but the trained bands finally defeated them. Venner and his comrade Roger Hodgkin were hanged, drawn and quartered in Swan Alley, the location of Venner's congregation, and hung in pieces on the city gates and London Bridge.

This fear of radicals drove not just the Act of Uniformity of 1662 but also the Conventicle Act of May 1664, which forbade meetings of more than five people except in private households, and the Five-Mile Act of 1665, which forbade any Noncomformist preacher or teacher to come within 5 miles of a city or corporate town where he had served as minister. If Milton had wanted to engage in any collective action in defence of his religious or political views, it would have been very difficult to do so.

Yet these Acts were a tacit recognition that Protestant Noncon-formity had survived despite the re-establishment of the Church of England, and despite the vicious efforts to eradicate it. Catholics also suffered from the new tests of belief, but they at least had the support (ineffectual at times) of the King. Again, King and Parliament were not in agreement, with Charles II offering toleration to Dissenters in

1662, only to have Parliament force him to withdraw the short-lived Declaration of Indulgence the following year.

Protestant Nonconformity nevertheless survived and was prevalent in Milton's own area of the City. Jewin Street itself was crammed with Dissenting meeting houses, the area something of a haven for Huguenots, French Protestants escaping persecution in their Catholic homeland. Grub Street, close to Jewin Street, was a centre for radical religious groups and their equally radical pamphlets.[11] Despite the best efforts of L'Estrange and men like him, London remained alive with news, whether circulated in print or by word of mouth in the coffee houses. As one contemporary commented, '. . . you cannot imagine to what a disease the itch of news is grown.'[12] Milton's nephew John Phillips lived in the area, probably because of its proximity to the printing industry. Phillips had been a prolific author from 1655 onwards, something of a literary hack, willing to write on almost any subject and with a penchant for burlesque, but not exclusively so, since he also produced a vigorous translation of *Don Quixote*.[13] His brother Edward was in contrast a committed Royalist. When John Evelyn found out that Edward Phillips had become his son's preceptor (teacher) he was understandably a little worried to find that 'this gentleman was nephew to Milton, who wrote against Salmasius' *Defensio*.' He was heartily relieved, however, to find that Edward 'was not at all infected with his principles, though brought up by him'.[14] This suggests either that Milton was ineffectual as a teacher or, a kinder interpretation, that he did not impose his political or religious views on those he taught.

What of Milton's daughters? Although there is little hard evidence, it seems that the experiences of these years had stretched the relationship between them and their father to breaking point. It cannot have helped that, probably for the first time in his life, Milton was struggling financially. On his release from jail, he had protested (assisted by Andrew Marvell, according to Edward Phillips) at the 'excessive' fees he had been forced to pay for his own incarceration: £150. This was a small loss compared to the £2,000 he had lost, also according to Phillips, in the collapse of the Excise Bank.[15] Putting aside the issues particular to the family of Milton's political ruin – his financial problems, his blindness and the lack of a mother for the girls – the bond between a father and his daughters was a notoriously problematic one, the crux invariably the issue of obedience. Distance between fathers and daughters was created by the marriage strategies of the time, which took daughters to new families; straightforward conflict between different generations; and, above all, the ideal of the authoritarian father figure, which meant that even close relationships could be threatened by signs of female independence.[16]

The ideal father's behaviour was modelled on God the Father, who may love his children to an infinite degree but also has a duty to punish them. John Milton, advocate of religious toleration, expresser of Nonconformist religious beliefs, surrounded by Nonconformist congregations, may well have found dissent in his own female children to be an intolerable threat to his manhood. Within his own household it was yet another sign of his emasculation and weakness. Whatever waves of political and religious radicalism were surging through England at this time, very few people paused to review the gender hierarchy. Even the proto-communist Winstanley, who did at least consider the plight of abandoned wives in a culture of free sex, argued consistently that fathers and husbands were the first link in the 'chain of magistracy'.[17] So long as the daughter was obedient – the most highly valued quality in a woman – then the girl was a comfort. But, with sadness, many commentators noted a decline in standards of discipline: things definitely weren't what they used to be, both a cause and a result of the breakdown in social and political consensus.[18]

Adult daughters, as Anne and Mary soon would be, were often seen as burdens and obligations to their parents, who usually solved the problem of an expensive drain on family resources by marrying their daughters off, at which point (and once the jointure arrangements were made) they became part of a new family. The Milton girls had lost both their birth mother and their stepmother, so the mother/ daughter bond was not going to make their parting from their father's house difficult, as it was for many mothers and daughters.[19] On the other hand, Milton does not seem to have made any attempt to implement a 'gentry marriage strategy' for his daughters over the coming years. Something seems to have been wrong throughout: a sense that neither daughters nor father knew what they should be doing in this altered world.

The strained bond between father and daughters was not helped by Milton's next act. He married for the third time, and (admittedly the comment comes from a hostile witness) he did not even tell his daughters that he was about to do so.[20] On 11 February 1663, he signed, with his own hand, a declaration of intention to marry Elizabeth Minshull. Milton was 'of the parish of St Giles, Cripplegate, London, Gentleman, aged about fifty years and a widower'. In reality, he had reached fifty-four years the previous December. Elizabeth's age was given as twenty-five and she was 'of her own disposing'. She had in fact just celebrated her twenty-fourth birthday. Both parties may have wanted to minimise the age gap.[21]

The third Mrs Milton had been born in Cheshire in 1638. War and ever-changing political regimes had been all she would have known until she reached full adulthood. Although it is unclear why she had come to London, her introduction to Milton had been through a relative, Nathan Paget, a friend of Milton's and probably his physician. Paget 'recommended' – in the words of Edward Phillips – the twenty-four-year-old Minshull to the fifty-four-year-old Milton.[22] The recommendation seems to be evidence that his godly friends were seeking out a suitable young woman for him in his time of trial. The marriage led to another house move, to Artillery Walk by Bunhill Fields.

Most biographies have presented a rosy picture of this third marriage. What began as a marriage of convenience for both parties became a cosy existence. Barbara Lewalski's verdict is typical. Betty Minshull Milton crucially brought 'order and domestic comfort' to her husband's life. With the 'attentive care of his wife', John could be busy and productive.[23] The impression (reinforced in her own time by Betty) is that the new Mrs Milton provided much valued personal stability and some good home cooking.[24]

The most significant friendship from these years began, however, in 1662, when Milton met the young Thomas Ellwood, a Quaker. The term *Quaker*, like *Leveller* before it, was a term of abuse: Ellwood called himself a Friend. Many Friends had suffered persecution far more extreme than anything that Milton had experienced, primarily because they were explicitly antinomian – that is, they replaced an external moral law with an internal spiritual one. So, for example, the Quaker James Nayler was convicted of 'horrid blasphemy', the skin flayed from his back by more than 300 lashes, his forehead branded with 'B', and his tongue bored through with a red-hot iron. He spent the next three years in solitary confinement in Bridewell. Released on a general amnesty in 1659, Nayler died the following year, after being robbed and probably beaten while attempting to travel back to his home in Yorkshire. Although he was at the extreme edge of the movement (his blasphemy was to ride into the city of Bristol on an ass, backwards, thereby appearing to imitate Christ), he summarised well their predicament. Quakers, he argued, 'as thou scornfully calls us', were a 'poor, despised, persecuted, reproached people, whom God hath called out of the world's ways, words, works, worship, riches and pleasures, and so are become strangers and wanderers to and fro'. Proverbs 3:2 lay at the heart of his belief, that God 'giveth grace to the lowly'.[25]

Milton's new friend Ellwood had met Nayler just after his release from prison and admired him. Ellwood met Milton a couple of years later, and his account of the start of the relationship further illustrates the realities of persecution and camaraderie among Friends. At the time, Ellwood had only just been released from prison himself, and his various accounts of imprisonment suggest wide discrepancies in practice. Some prisons were thoroughly porous.[26] Ellwood described some of his fellow Nonconformists being allowed to go home at night, 'a great conveniency to men of trade and business', a kind of 'easy restraint'. And even when in prison, work could go on, with tables serving 'the tailors for shop-boards'. Newgate in the City of London was, in contrast, a scene of horror, a 'type of hell upon earth'. Ellwood found himself there because of a political 'storm in the city'. Three men had been executed already, and their 'bloody' quartered bodies lay in a room near the prisoners. The dead men's families were desperately seeking the bodies for burial; they were permitted, at last, the bodies, not the heads. The heads, wrote Ellwood,

> were ordered to be set up in some parts of the city. I saw the heads when they were brought up to be boiled. The hangman fetch'd them in a dirty dust basket out of some by place, and setting them down amongst the felons, he and they made sport with them. They took them by the hair, flouting, jeering and laughing at them; and then giving them some ill names, box'd them on the ears and cheeks. Which done the hangman put them into his kettle and parboiled them with bay salt and cumin seed; *that* to keep them from putrefaction, and *this* to keep off the fowls from seizing on them.[27]

This 'loathsome' experience made Ellwood even more determined to visit his fellow-Friends when they were incarcerated, and it was this desire that delayed his planned studies with 'Master Milton'. Ellwood was then further 'moved' to visit the Pennington family in Buckinghamshire 'with other friends in that country', so walked the 22 miles or so to Buckinghamshire in one day, 'the weather being frosty, and the ways by that means clean and good'. He fully intended to return to London and his studies but stayed to become Latin tutor to Pennington's children. It seemed to be God's will. At last, however, he was free to return to London and his long-awaited lessons with Master Milton.

The link with Ellwood and his circle would prove crucial to Milton. In the hostile climate of the 1660s, Ellwood provided access to an extraordinary underground network. Print was the network's life-blood, making him a valuable ally.

> Most persistent in their evasion of the curbs on the press, and most thoroughly organised as a group, were the Quakers, whose publications were very rarely licensed. Quakers did not recognise the state's right to silence the printed, any more than the spoken, word: "our mouths were not opened by nor can they be shut by the will of man" wrote Edward Billing . . . Determined to continue their

mission, the Quakers established a press organization and print culture wholly independent of the state.[28]

Having got to London, Ellwood took lodgings near Milton in Jewin Street, 'and from thenceforth went every day in the afternoon (except on the first-days [the Quaker term for Sundays] of the week) and sitting by him in his dining room, read to him in such books in the Latin tongue, as he pleased to hear me read'.[29] It seems a pleasant image of scholarly retirement, and both men may well have gained much pleasure from the exchange. But, as ever, books were not there merely to be enjoyed; they were not merely 'dead things' but alive and to be used. Like all readers in their century, Ellwood and Milton were reading for action.

What that action would be depended on the political and religious climate. By the mid-1660s, the country seemed to be descending once again into crisis. Those who had believed that the return of Charles II promised political stability were to be disappointed. As early as January 1661, when official celebrations for the anniversary of his return took place, opponents were pleased to note that 'the public meetings were very thin.'[30] Some things were going well, such as Milton's old brief of foreign affairs, but there was a good base to build upon: Cromwell's military achievements, for right or wrong, were indisputable. The English successfully captured New Amsterdam from the Dutch in August 1664, renaming the city New York in honour of its new leader, James, Duke of York, brother of King Charles II. Unfortunately, Parliament had underestimated just how much this war with the Dutch would cost: the budget had been £500,000, but it would cost ten times this amount. The Restoration had brought only further rifts in religion and serious financial problems to the nation.

Then came natural disaster: the plague. Of course, to the seventeenth-century mind, the plague was not merely a natural disaster. Every event demonstrated God's active involvement in the world. When the winter of 1661–2 was particularly severe, the government ordered a 'general fast' throughout the nation. John Evelyn reported in January that the fast was being 'now celebrated at London, to avert God's heavy judgement on this land, there having fallen so great rain without any frost or seasonable cold', and went on happily to note that 'the effect of this fast appeared, in an immediate change of wind and season: so as our fleet set sail this every afternoon, having lain wind-bound a month.'[31] God had been placated. Now, in 1665, he had sent the plague as a providential punishment to castigate the English people for their evil ways.

Faced with a God-given plague and with no understanding of its natural causes, there were really only two scenarios for Londoners. If identified as a plague sufferer, the victim would be 'shut up' in their house to die. Anyone nursing the sick person would also be 'shut up' and would most likely die too. It was a brutal way to try to control the epidemic. The only escape was to get out of town, and for that one needed a pass indicating good health, financial resources and somewhere to go to. It is estimated that only one in six people were in a position to leave, even in relatively wealthy Westminster. Milton and his family in crowded Artillery Walk were lucky. When plague struck, Thomas Ellwood arranged for them to move to Chalfont St Giles in Buckinghamshire.

During this period of political repression, economic crisis and virulent plague, it is perhaps no surprise that there was silence from John Milton. His enemies were also strangely quiet. There are only three surviving references to Milton's work in 1665, referring to *Eikonoklastes*, the divorce tracts and his links with the Quakers.

Milton's retreat from the political and literary centre of the nation was not, however, a pleasant sojourn in the country for an elderly, tired man in search of rural tranquillity. It was a desperate flight from a city of death, helped by a religious radical and his network. Chalfont St Giles, and its surrounding villages and towns, are now an affluent commuterland. In the 1660s, the area was a hotbed of religious radicalism. The house that Ellwood rented for Milton was owned by Anne Fleetwood, daughter of the regicide George Fleetwood. The Fleetwood family owned a large house nearby, The Vache, which provided protection for Nonconformist ministers. The reality of Quaker life was revealed when, just after the Miltons' arrival, Ellwood was imprisoned once again, this time in Aylesbury, for about a month. On his release, he visited his friend Milton, and during this visit, in

August 1665, Ellwood was shown a manuscript of what he described as an 'excellent poem'. This manuscript revealed that the apparent silence of these years had been an illusion, and that Milton had in reality been engaged in a phenomenal burst of literary activity. The poem was Milton's biblical epic, *Paradise Lost*.

Paradise Lost brought together the two phases of his life to date. As a young man, he had explored his talents for the literary and the poetic, without much sense of the cause to which those talents should be devoted. In his middle age, the military and political conditions in his country had thrust him into the role of polemicist and propagandist. Through the 1640s and 1650s, Milton was usually certain of his cause and honed his writings in prose accordingly, with only occasional ventures into poetry. Now he returned wholeheartedly to poetry, but a poetry that would explore the events, and celebrate the causes, that had dominated his life over the preceding two decades of activism.

Paradise Lost is a great achievement in itself but an even more remarkable one for an elderly, blind man living in a world of persecution and plague. According to Milton's nephew, the epic was composed in his uncle's mind, often in the early hours of the morning, and then, the day begun, the new lines were dictated to anyone who could write the words.[32] Ever since he was a child, John had developed remarkable powers of memory, yet his ability to hold in his mind the ten books of *Paradise Lost*, with all the subtle interconnections and interplays of language that characterise his art, is astonishing. No matter that he claims that the work was dictated to him 'slumbering', and that his 'celestial patroness' 'inspires / Easy my unpremeditated work' (*Paradise Lost*, IX: 22–4): the reality simply cannot have been so easy. Even if his own account of effortless nighttime inspiration is accepted, there remained the challenges of preparing and editing a fair copy of the manuscript, and the potentially vexing issue of publication. The great work deserved an audience, but how to get it published when its author was who he was?

Milton's response to the last known letter to him indicates his state of mind at this crucial time. Scholars have been harsh in their judgements upon his correspondent, one Heimbach, who managed

Paradise lost.

A
POEM
Written in
TEN BOOKS

By *JOHN MILTON*.

Licensed and Entred according
to Order.

LONDON

Printed, and are to be sold by *Peter Parker*
under *Creed* Church neer *Aldgate*; And by
Robert Boulter at the *Turks Head* in *Bishopsgate-street*;
And *Matthias Walker*, under St. *Dunstons* Church
in Fleet-street, 1667.

to be both obsequious and patronising, and whose Latin was apparently 'dreadful, with false case-constructions and a syntax defying analysis'.[33] Milton in response apologised to Heimbach for any errors in *his* Latin. If mistakes appeared, then 'blame it on the boy who wrote this down while utterly ignorant of Latin, for I was forced while dictating – and not without some difficulty – to completely spell out every single letter.' This is a fascinating revelation of the challenging conditions (for both boy and Milton) in which the letter was produced. It offers a glimpse of the sheer labour of production involved in a work such as *Paradise Lost*, which, although not in Latin, is nevertheless of startling complexity.

The deeper interest of this letter lies, however, in Milton's sense of self. Heimbach had expressed the fear that Milton had died of the plague. He had also compared him to Simeon, a biblical figure renowned only for his quietism and the fact that, having once held the baby Jesus, he could die happy. Milton is having none of it. He is very much alive, and he is no Simeon: '. . . by the blessing of God, who had prepared a safe place for me in the country, I am both alive and well. Let me not be useless, whatever remains for me in this life.' It is a moving and heartfelt expression of religious faith and a plea for purpose in an otherwise urbane letter.

'Let me not be useless, whatever remains for me in this life.' Milton would not be useless, and much did indeed remain for him in this life. The place to do it was London, still by far the most important city in England with a population of half a million. In fact Milton was back in the City at the time of this letter, August 1666, possibly making attempts to get his great poem published. Then further disaster struck the capital: the Great Fire. Although there are records of only five deaths due to the fire's slow-moving nature, the City was destroyed in the space of four days, between 2 and 6 September 1666.

For a man who loved the City, who needed the City, the plague and the fire were horrifyingly destructive of a familiar world. In 1665 more than seven thousand people had died in one week alone from bubonic plague. The next year, in less than five days, the Great Fire destroyed the City between the Tower and the Temple. This was Milton's

London and it was gone forever. Even the most urbane of his contemporaries, John Evelyn, saw the fire as an apocalyptic event:

> . . . the noise and cracking and thunder of the impetuous flames, the shrieking of women and children, the hurry of people, the fall of towers, houses and churches, was like a hideous storm, and the air all about so hot and inflamed that at the last one was not able to approach it, so as they were forced to stand still . . . Thus I left it, this afternoon burning, a resemblance of Sodom or the Last Day.[34]

Almost every commentator saw God in the flames.

The fire precipitated all kinds of crises, not least the plight of the thousands of people made homeless, living in makeshift shelters, or camped in fields. Although the City bankers of Lombard Street had removed their assets in good time, many of their creditors had lost everything. King Charles, already in financial trouble, was one of the worst hit, the Crown's income from customs duties decimated by the loss in trade revenue. Charles, unsurprisingly, was one of the prime movers in the regeneration of the City, laying the first stone in the Royal Exchange and pushing for the reconstruction of the Custom House. (They opened three years later, in 1669.)

Although the fire had not reached John Milton's own neighbourhood around Bunhill Fields, it had implications for him as an author because of its catastrophic effect on the book trade. In a tragic misjudgement exacerbated by clerical greed, the book-sellers of the area around St Paul's stored their stock in the cathedral (charged for the pleasure by the Bishop of London). St Paul's burned to the ground, and with it the stock of many stationers and printers. Approximately £200,000 worth of books and papers were lost, and many in the book trade never recovered.

Two London book-sellers were, for example, forced into writing to an Antwerp publishing house in the aftermath of the Great Fire:

> You have no doubt heard of the terrible desolation of this city. Nine tenths of what lies within the walls has been burned to a cinder.

Eighty churches lie in ruins, the Exchange, the Town Hall and almost all the main public spaces. Among others, the Church of St Paul's and with it almost all the bookshops.[35]

They had set up their new shop in Little Britain and were asking the Antwerp publishers for cheap stock to sell. Sadly for the book-sellers, Antwerp wanted payment in advance, and in the current economic climate, this was too much of a risk.

It was not an ideal time to seek a publisher, but Milton continued to do so. At last, on 27 April 1667, he signed a contract with Samuel Simmons for the publication of *Paradise Lost*. Simmons was very much part of the London print world, the son of printers and book-sellers, growing up a neighbour of Milton's in Aldersgate Street in the 1640s and 1650s. His parents, Matthew and Mary Simmons, ran the family printing business, their various premises over the years offering a gazetteer of the London publishing trade as they moved from Moorgate, to the Golden Lion in Duck Lane, to the Barbican near the Red Cross, to Goldsmiths' Alley. Mary Simmons now ran the main business and was doing well: the Hearth Tax of 1666 (whereby individuals were taxed for the number of fireplaces they had in their houses) noted that her establishment had thirteen hearths, making her printing house the largest such recorded on the tax roll.

Thirteen hearths or no, the publication of *Paradise Lost* was a bold step for her son Samuel, the first work that he was to register under his own name. It was also a sign of remarkable loyalty to an author on the part of a printer-publisher. Matthew Simmons had printed Milton's work in the far-off days of the 1640s, including his most radical (and condemned) works, such as the *Doctrine and Discipline of Divorce, Eikonoklastes* and *The Tenure of Kings and Magistrates*. Other unlicensed works from the period such as *Areopagitica* may also have come from the Simmonses' press. *Paradise Lost* would, however, be the first work by Milton that the Simmonses had published for nearly twenty years.

Milton's contract with Simmons survives, the earliest formal agreement of its kind to do so. Milton would receive £5 on the signing of the contract, and then £5 and 200 copies of the work when each print run, or impression, sold out. Each impression was guaranteed not to run to more than 1,500 copies, ensuring a reprint and more money for the author.[36] The contract shows Milton to have been a new breed of author in a newly developing market-oriented literary system: perhaps unsurprisingly, given his financial astuteness, he also struck quite a good deal and insisted on his intellectual property rights, something extremely rare at the time. The quality of the printing and the distribution of the poem would be, however, as important as the financial arrangements, and Simmons did well by his author. The 1667 printed text of *Paradise Lost* was by seventeenth-century standards rather good, carefully prepared and well presented, neatly printed and without major errors. What is more, Simmons made arrangements for the sale of the poem with no fewer than six book-sellers to assure proper distribution of the first edition. This may well have been motivated by a desire to share risk in the venture, but it was a constructive move.

John Milton and Samuel Simmons had done what they could. Now came the really difficult task: getting the work past the censors. Milton's regicide tracts were still very much in the public mind, and the very title of *Paradise Lost* could quite easily be seen to refer to the political paradise that the republic might have been. Milton had to tread very carefully: any explicit criticism of the Stuart monarchy, any impassioned plea for republicanism, and the work would never reach the book-sellers.[37] Trouble indeed came, according to John Toland, one of the work's later publishers. The stumbling block from the censor's point of view was an allusion to the overthrow of Charles II, what Toland described as the 'imaginary treason' of the following lines:

> . . . as when the sun new ris'n
> Looks through the horizontal misty air
> Shorn of his beams, or from behind the moon
> In dim eclipse disastrous twilight sheds
> On half the nations, and with fear of change
> Perplexes monarchs.
>
>   (I:594–9)

Milton's mention of eclipses, perplexed monarchs and change all set off alarm bells. Throughout the period, the Church was worried about radical dissenters interpreting natural phenomena as signs of providential intervention. There were stark warnings about the dangers of astrological readings, of interpreting comets and solar eclipses. Those who saw these natural phenomena as signs of God's purposes were, argued Church and censors, guilty of scaremongering, and authors who looked for omens and signs only served to 'dishearten' or 'inflame' the people. And it was no time for scaremongering with the threat posed by a Second Anglo-Dutch War, a threat which in the view of the licenser necessitated the maintenance of unity at home.

In the light of all this, it is somewhat surprising that *Paradise Lost* did get past the censor.[38] This can be attributed, in part, to the poem's style. It was easy to view *Paradise Lost* as high culture, beyond the grasp of the wider readership that the censor had a duty to protect.[39] Nevertheless, it was a slow process. Four months after signing the contract with Simmons, the poem was registered for publication. Another two months passed before the first small, quarto edition appeared, sometime in October 1667.[40]

That Milton emerged alive from the regime change of 1660 is noteworthy. As one opponent pointed out, in a note on a copy of *Eikonoklastes*, 'Old, Sickly, Poor, Stark Blind, thou writ'st for Bread', going on to suggest that Milton would have been better off if Charles II *had* executed him. That Milton, who was indeed old, sickly, poor and 'stark blind', entered into one of the most creative phases of his life is surprising. That he found a way to make his voice heard in the new conditions is nothing less than extraordinary. In October 1667, it was reported that one Sir John Denham rushed into the House of Commons one morning with a sheet of *Paradise Lost* 'wet from the press, in his hand'. To the assembled MPs, Denham announced that what he had in his hand was 'part of the noblest poem that ever was wrote in any language or any age'.[41] John Milton was back.

SEVENTEEN

EPIC

1667

*P*ARADISE LOST is the creative distillation and passionate expression of John Milton's religious and political vision, the culmination of his literary ambitions since he was a very young man. The epic stands as a remarkable coalescence of his highly developed talent with languages; his wide-ranging personal and political experiences, for good and for bad; and, above all, his fertile, visionary imagination. The poem acts both as the ultimate expression of Milton's sense of his own Englishness and the state of his nation, and as a lament for *and* a celebration of all of humanity that transcends both time and place.[1]

Milton chose to create his epic from the opening chapters of the Old Testament, the account in the Book of Genesis of the expulsion of Adam and Eve from the Garden of Eden. Back in the period after his return from Italy, he had considered shaping these materials into a drama, but now he decided that he was ready to create an epic, rejecting the usual subject of the genre ('Wars, hitherto the only argument / Heroic deemed') and determined instead to celebrate other heroic virtues:

> The better fortitude
> Of patience and heroic martyrdom
> Unsung.
>
> (IX:31–3)[2]

The story of Adam and Eve may have been 'unsung' in epic, but it was a story, a history, with which all Milton's readers would be familiar.

In the beginning God created the heaven and the earth. And the
earth was without form, and void; and darkness was upon the face of
the deep. And the Spirit of God moved upon the face of the waters.
And God said, Let there be light: and there was light.

(Genesis 1:1–3)

Next, God created humanity, Adam and Eve, and set one prohibition
on them:

So God created man in his own image, in the image of God created
he him; male and female created he them.

(Genesis 1:27)

And the LORD God commanded the man, saying, Of every tree of
the garden thou mayest freely eat. But of the tree of the knowledge
of good and evil, thou shalt not eat of it: for in the day that thou
eatest thereof thou shalt surely die.

(Genesis 2:16–17)

Every one of Milton's readers knew who had failed to obey God's
command, who had been tempted by the serpent, and who had thus
brought sin and death into the world.

And when the woman saw that the tree was good for food, and that
it was pleasant to the eyes, and a tree to be desired to make one wise,
she took of the fruit thereof, and did eat, and gave also unto her
husband with her; and he did eat.

(Genesis 3:6)

The foundation of Milton's epic is this familiar, fundamental story.
The biblical materials are, however, refashioned in radical ways, in
Milton's struggle to understand, and to help his readers understand,
his God and themselves.

The scope, the ambition, of *Paradise Lost* are awe-inspiring. It, more
than perhaps any other work of poetry in the English language, takes

on the big questions, as is fitting for an epic. Margaret Kean, in a superb guide to the work written for the first-time reader, shows how Milton took the profound questions asked by the epic and added yet more:

> What is man's relationship to the divine? What is community? Is the individual's fate predetermined? Is fame a sufficient recompense for an early death on the battlefield? What constitutes a hero? What constitutes a foe? What is our destiny? *Paradise Lost* inquires into all these areas of fundamental human concern but it sets a new question of its own: What constitutes human liberty and how can it best be supported?[3]

As he had done with so many of his previous writings, whether creating a complex moral landscape in his *Maske* or turning sonnets, traditionally studies of unrequited love, into searching explorations of individual and national political identities, Milton picked up a familiar genre and developed it in radical ways.

Not content with merely exploring the reasons for humanity's fall, Milton takes the reader from the very beginnings of the universe to the very end of time: the Son of God's second coming. Spatially, *Paradise Lost* is not confined to Eden but ranges across the universe, from heaven to hell, through the wastes of chaos and back down to our own earth. Alongside these truly epic movements within space and time, there is an examination, on a very human, accessible level, of the psychology of evil and of love. Almost every line is informed by Milton's decades of study, his phenomenally wide reading in the Classical, biblical and contemporary traditions. So, when he writes that Satan

> Stood
> Unterrified, and like a comet burned,
> That fires the length of Ophiucus huge
> In the Arctic sky . . .
>
>   (II:707–10)

he is asking the reader to remember Virgil's comparison of Aeneas to a comet (and perhaps to measure Satan's heroism against that of Aeneas, to measure Milton's moral epic against Virgil's epic of war); he is asking his reader to think about the relation between Ophiucus (the constellation depicted as a man carrying a serpent) and Satan, while nodding towards Ovid, who wrote of the serpent constellation lying nearest the icy pole.[4] The reader is asked to reach out to other works, other writers, to find the consonances and dissonances between Milton's art and that of the other writers he invokes. Equally challenging is the way in which he invokes multiple meanings in single words. This polysemicity is apparent throughout: when Satan bemoans that he is 'condemned / In this abhorred deep to utter woe', 'utter' can function as an adjective ('total' or 'complete') or as a verb ('to give voice'), and still have the connotation of 'outer'. Just two lines later, Satan complains that the 'pain of unextinguishable fire / Must exercise us without hope of end': in this case, apart from remembering that the 'inextinguishable fire' is taken from Isaiah 66:15–16, Milton brings in the Latin meaning of *exerceo*, allowing 'exercise' to suggest the sense 'to vex and trouble' as well as 'to practise and employ'.

Milton's 'grand style' is well known, but the phrase does not tell the whole story. Alongside the long verse paragraphs, the epic similes, the Latinate constructions, the subtle allusions and the polysemic diction, Milton places phrases of compelling simplicity. Indeed, the epic as a whole seems to encourage the reader to value these moments of plain expression more highly than all the elaborate arguments. Throughout the work there are many examples of simple, sensuous, passionate writing, just as Milton wanted poetry to be: '. . . what glorious and magnificient use might be made of poetry both in divine and human things,' he had enthused, back in 1644.[5]

Paradise Lost excites, however, not only because of its exceptional effects of language, but because it is a high-risk poem in which Milton, and his readers, confront their demons. The first character the reader meets is Satan, who, having led a rebellion against God in heaven, has just been defeated in battle and cast down into hell. Later the reader will learn about the war in heaven; Milton, uniquely, will make the battle evenly matched, a civil war, not merely a rout, an example of just how close the battle between good and evil can be.[6] That war is, however, won by God and the Son: but as Milton had learned when watching Cromwell, the real dangers lie in handling the peace. So, in the opening books of the epic, the focus is exclusively on Satan and, more importantly, a Satan who has been defeated in battle.

It is a high-risk strategy, to begin by focusing on the demonic. Yet, for the poem to have the most power, it is necessary to be seduced by Satan, just as Eve will be in the Garden of Eden. Only in understanding Satan's power, only in understanding the workings of evil, might it be possible, perhaps, to overcome evil.

Milton poured all his dramatic talents into writing his Satan, the greatest anti-hero of them all. This charismatic, intelligent, ruthless figure has fascinated generations of readers and led many (most notably the poet William Blake) to argue that the character got away from his author, that Milton was 'of the devil's party' but did not know it. In recent years, another argument has been put forward that takes this response into account, but suggests that Milton was encouraging precisely this sympathy with Satan in order to provoke a religious or moral awakening. The reader identifies with Satan; the reader resents God. The reader is impressed by Satan's rhetoric, knowing full well the implications of this naive response. Humanity will fall, death will come into the world. In this reading, Milton, far from losing control of his anti-hero, has designed him so that the reader falls for Satan's lies, is solicitous for his psychological torment and is seduced by his charisma. Only at the end of the poem does the reader, shamefacedly, realise that this has been a misreading. That moment of realisation is also a moment in which the reader recognises his or her own sin. *Paradise Lost*'s entrapment of the reader is, however, no negative game but one that encourages readers to learn from their responses, and thus to renew their moral vigilance.

The trap is well baited. Even in hell, defeated, Satan remains an inspirational leader, rousing his dejected followers with superb rhetoric. He is the master of the sound-bite: 'What though the field be lost? All is not lost . . .'; 'Better to reign in hell, than serve in heaven.' He is the consummate politician who, surveying the horrors of hell, can still argue to his followers, and crucially be believed, at least so long as he speaks, that 'Here at least we shall be free . . .' 'Here', in hell, Satan can for a moment *look* like the great military leader he is not.

Satan, who is nothing if not intelligent, knows the reality. The military option has failed, so now he plans to 'work in close design, by fraud or guile / What force effected not'. When the rebel angels have a council of war to formulate their strategy in the face of defeat (a process that looks suspiciously like a parliamentary debate), Milton shows that, for all the impression of genuine discussion, Satan remains in control. He is already clear that 'some easier enterprise' should be undertaken, having sensibly determined that in a war with God, there is only ever going to be one winner.

Satan's new target, the easier enterprise, is 'some new race called Man', which, much to his disgust, is favoured by God. The only problem is the danger of the cosmic journey from hell to the new created earth. Who will undertake this great journey since 'long is the way and hard'? To no one's surprise, least of all the reader, Satan offers himself for the task:

> I abroad
> Through all the coasts of dark destruction seek
> Deliverance for us all: this enterprise
> None shall partake with me.
>
> (II:463–6)

He has convinced his wavering supporters, tempted by arguments (for open war, for appeasement, for inaction) from other rebel angels, that his is the way and that he is their hero, their deliverer.

As with the war in heaven, Satan's sophisticated tyranny clearly works as a political allegory for Milton's own time. But Milton does something more: he takes the reader into the mind of Satan, allowing identification and understanding of his appalling position, his psychological torment. For Satan suffers: he is 'racked with deep despair', constantly attempting to assuage his pain, never succeeding. There is something dynamic and compelling about his defiance. He tells himself that there is no going back (even when *Paradise Lost* as a whole suggests that he could do so – one of the fallen angels, Abdiel, does indeed repent and return to heaven). Satan refuses to change and makes his obduracy into a perverse virtue, as when he greets his new home, hell:

> Receive thy new possessor: one who brings
> A mind not to be changed by place or time.
> The mind is its own place, and in itself
> Can make a heaven of hell, a hell of heaven.
>
> (I:252–5)

It is a powerful expression of the power of the individual to make his own reality, or the power of the mind to stand firm in the face of onslaught, with echoes of the Lady in the *Maske* insisting that 'thou canst not touch the freedom of my mind.' *Paradise Lost* returns to this idea, of the paradise within, much later, when Adam and Eve are confronting a world of evil, but here, in hell, without grace, Satan's adoption of the stance is proven to be horribly insufficient. When their council of war breaks up, the rebel angels wander off. After the diversion of the debate, they are lost again, seeking desperately for ways to distract themselves from the horrors of hell. Whatever they do, they find 'no rest'. Wherever they look, there is no new world to run to. They inhabit a 'universe of death'.

For Satan, the situation is even worse. Even when he succeeds in physically leaving hell, even when he reaches Eden, there is no escape from the agonies of damnation, because those horrors are contained within him.

> . . . horror and doubt distract
> His troubled thoughts, and from the bottom stir
> The hell within him, for within him hell
> He brings, and round about him, nor from hell
> One step no more than from himself can fly
> By change of place.
>
> (IV:18–23)

Perhaps most remarkable is the fact that readers respond so positively to Satan even in the face of Milton's relentless reminders, both subtle and unsubtle, of his sheer nastiness, the emptiness of his promises, and, above all, his dismal insufficiency, failure, and defeat. Satan can't even raise his head unless God lets him do so; Satan's malice 'served but to bring forth / Infinite goodness, grace and mercy' towards man; Satan will suffer 'treble confusion, wrath and vengeance poured' upon him; his followers are reduced to the size of 'faerie elves' just at the moment when they have built Pandemonium, their 'high capital'. Other effects are much more subtle, based on hardly perceptible linguistic hints, as here in a passage from the start of Book II:

> High on a throne of royal state, which far
> Outshone the wealth of Ormus and of Ind,
> Or where the gorgeous East with richest hand
> Showers on her kings barbaric pearl and gold,
> Satan exalted sat, by merit raised
> To that bad eminence; and from despair
> Thus high uplifted beyond hope, aspires
> Beyond thus high, insatiate to pursue
> Vain war with heaven, and by success untaught
> His proud imaginations thus displayed.
>
> (II:1–10)

The critic John Leonard has superbly demonstrated the subtle games Milton is playing with language. 'Merit' can mean 'deserving either good or evil': Satan thinks he deserves good, but 'bad eminence' suggests otherwise. 'High uplifted beyond hope' can mean that he has climbed higher than he had hoped but cannot quite escape the alternative construction: 'lifted high, but in a place so low as to be beyond all reach of hope'. As Leonard shows, after this, 'success' must mean 'ill success', 'failure':

> But the positive sense is not just absent. Milton aggressively withholds it – dangles it, as it were, under Satan's nose. Satan is

'by success untaught' because he has learned nothing from defeat, and because he has no victory from which to learn. The twist of the knife is 'imaginations', which here means 'schemes, plots' but also hints at Satan's proud delusion.[7]

The devil truly is in the detail. But for all the narrative belittling Satan remains dangerous, and for one overriding reason, glimpsed when he travels to earth to make his first attempt on his easy target, man. God, being a wise commander, has positioned guards, archangels, at the four corners of the universe, yet Satan talks his way past the archangel Uriel. How does he do so?

> So spake the false dissembler unperceived;
> For neither man nor angel can discern
> Hypocrisy, the only evil that walks
> Invisible, except to God alone,
> By his permissive will, through heaven and earth.
>
> (III:681–5)

This is Satan's ultimate threat to man. He is a hypocrite, and even angels cannot discern hypocrisy: only God can.

This offers a key to the experience of reading *Paradise Lost*. Repeatedly the reader is asked to attend to arguments in their context, attend to who is saying what to whom, and why. Milton regularly offers different versions of the same event, so that the reader becomes more alert to bias and rhetoric. This is a political training as much as a moral or religious training, delivered by an author who still, maybe more than ever, believed that the basis of a free state was free speech and freedom of conscience. But free speech and indeed freedom of conscience relied on the ability of individuals to sift truth from lies for themselves. Without this ability, the people would fall for any religious or political demagogue with a good line in rhetoric. The people would fall for Satan.

Book II concludes with Satan's magnificent, thrilling journey out of hell and across the cosmos. The final image is of the earth:

> And fast by hanging in a golden chain
> This pendent world, in bigness as a star
> Of smallest magnitude close by the moon.
>
> (II:1051–3)

'This pendent world' is the created universe, as described in Genesis. In a typical moment of linguistic play, Milton uses 'pendent' in two meanings. The earth is physically hanging by a golden chain (as was still believed by some), but the earth's fate is also in the balance, undecided, as Satan arrives on his mission. The most important word, however, is not 'pendent' but 'this': Milton is talking about the world, our world, in which his readers, we, are reading the poem.

Paradise Lost does not permit its readers the luxury of detachment. Yes, the plot is known before the start: Eve will eat the apple in the Garden of Eden. Yes, the Christian reader knows (unlike characters like Satan) where the Fall sits on the timeline of human history, giving the reader a god-like perspective on events. Yet Milton never allows his readers to settle into a complacent historical perspective. This is history that does matter, to everyone, now. Indeed, events unfold as if in the present ('now' Milton will write, again and again) and the reader experiences events at the same time as the characters.

Indeed, other vital characters in the epic are introduced to the reader through Satan's eyes. God, for example, actually appears in Book III, but over the course of the preceding two books God has been variously described as anything from a tyrant to the angry victor. Many readers have concurred with Satan's negative assessment of Milton's God, and much, probably too much, critical ink has been expended both defending God and criticising him. What is certain is that one of the things that makes *Paradise Lost* 'one of the most serious epics ever written is partly its refusal to take the divine protagonist's character for granted', a point made by Alistair Fowler, the eminent editor of *Paradise Lost*.[8]

More important, Milton uses the scenes in heaven to explain to his readers the most significant theological idea in the whole poem: free will. Put simply (and he does put it simply), God is all-powerful and all-knowing, as might be expected. God knows that humanity will fall, that Eve will listen to Satan's lies, and he knows that Satan's revenge will rebound upon him. The question often asked, therefore, is: If God knows that this will happen, why does God not stop it? The answer lies in God's insistence on free will in all creation. God does not want passive obedience from his creations; he does not want forced obedience from necessity. Instead, true freedom is the freedom to err: men and women are 'authors to themselves'. As God says, 'I formed them free, and free they must remain,' even if they choose to fall. As the narrator says, 'Freely they stood who stood, and fell who fell.'

The God of *Paradise Lost* understands, however, that there is a crucial difference between the fall of the rebel angels and that of humanity. Satan and his followers fell 'by their own suggestion';

> Self-tempted, self-depraved; man falls deceived
> By the other first: man therefore shall find grace,
> The other none.
>
> (III:130–33)

God in his mercy will make sure that humanity is not quite lost. On the other hand, ungrateful ('ingrate') humans will know very well who has saved them,

> that he may know how frail
> His fallen condition is, and to me owe
> All his deliverance, and to none but me.
>
> (III:180–82)

As so often in *Paradise Lost*, the reader is asked to discriminate carefully between God's offer of 'deliverance' and Satan's, to spot the difference between God's righteous anger and Satan's spite. Sometimes, they can look rather similar.

The difference is there, however, and revealed shortly after God's rigid pronouncement, on hearing of the Fall, that man must die, or justice will die. There is only one other option:

> . . . unless for him
> Some other able, and as willing, pay
> The rigid satisfaction, death for death.
> Say heavenly powers, where shall we find such love,
> Which of ye will be mortal to redeem
> Man's mortal crime, and just the unjust to save,
> Dwells in all heaven charity so dear?
>
> (III:210–16)

'Where shall we find such love?': one of those simple, stark questions, delivered in monosyllables that are as characteristic of John Milton's writing as the Latinate constructions, and a question that goes to the heart of his Christian faith.

After a dramatic moment of silence in the poem, 'such love' is offered, freely, by the Son of God, who willingly goes to his terrible death so that 'man shall find grace.' Again, using plain words, the Son recognises the justice of God's wrath but takes it upon himself: '. . . on me let thine anger fall; Account me man.' The offer is, however, made in faith. The Son knows that God will not abandon him. He will rise victorious, destroy death, and lead 'the multitude of my redeemed' to heaven 'long absent, and return'.

It is a reassuring moment before the reader returns to the narrative of the Fall, and returns to the consciousness of Satan, still tormented, and eloquent about his torment. One thing remains stable, his hatred of God. In a brilliant psychological insight, it is God's goodness that Satan cannot bear. Satan hates being grateful to God: 'the debt immense of endless gratitude / So burdensome still paying, still to owe'. Intelligent as ever, self-knowing as ever, he can see his response as flawed:

> . . . a grateful mind
> By owing owes not, but still pays, at once
> Indebted and discharged.
>
> (IV:55–7)

His insight cannot help him to change.

Which way shall I fly
Infinite wrath, and infinite despair?
Which way I fly is hell; my self am hell.

(IV:73–5)

These moments of self-awareness culminate in Satan using his own glib rhetoric upon himself: 'Farewell remorse: all good to me is lost; / Evil be thou my good.' (IV:109–10) Satan remains fascinating, despite or because of his obvious flaws, and Milton insists that the reader stays within his consciousness, sees with his eyes, as the humans Adam and Eve are introduced to the poem.

Throughout the Edenic couple's first scenes, Satan the voyeur watches, as mesmerised by their naked beauty and happiness as the reader is by his complex evil. In a masterstroke of psychological realism, Satan is overcome by the desire to join with Adam and Eve:

. . . league with you I seek,
And mutual amity so strait, so close,
That I with you must dwell, or you with me
Henceforth.

(IV:375–8)

But to join with them, he must destroy them first. The politician in him suppresses the pain of despair and fluently justifies his desire for their destruction: he has 'public reason just', of course.

It is no wonder that John Milton has been described as one of the devil's party, so well did the author of *Paradise Lost* understand his creation, Satan. But Milton could also write paradise; he could make the reader understand, to feel, what Satan was drawn to destroy.

What does Satan see? At first sight, both to Satan and the reader, Adam and Eve appear to conform to every stereotype of gender available to Milton in the seventeenth century. Adam is bigger, stronger, more intelligent and has hair only down to his broad shoulders: he thus has 'absolute rule' over Eve and can directly relate to God. Eve is smaller, softer, more beautiful, less intelligent and has

wanton ringlets hanging down to her waist. She is thus subject to
Adam and will understand God through him.

> . . . though both
> Not equal, as their sex not equal seemed;
> For contemplation he and valour formed,
> For softness she and sweet attractive grace,
> He for God only, she for God in him.
>
> (IV:295–9)

Yet Milton has a surprise for his readers. Eve's 'wanton ringlets' offer a
clue. *Wanton* is a pejorative term, a term that might be used for a sexually
loose woman, but here Eve, in Eden, has 'wanton ringlets'. Milton is
rehabilitating the word, refusing the reader its current, fallen, meaning,
and thus perhaps even reclaiming female sexuality as a positive thing.[9]

Milton's vision of Eden is an erotic world of sensuous pleasures,
where man and woman are fascinatingly different from each other.
Adam and Eve walk through Eden, hand in hand, those 'wanton
ringlets' waving as she moves, every step a kind of foreplay. Eve 'half
embracing' leans on Adam:

> . . . half her swelling breast
> Naked met his under the flowing gold
> Of her loose tresses hid.
>
> (IV:495–7)

The lovers 'enjoy their fill / Of bliss on bliss'.

Milton, unlike many religious commentators, unlike his younger
self, is quite comfortable with the idea that there was sex, and good
sex, before the Fall. But it has to be sex with love rather than

> the bought smile
> Of harlots, loveless, joyless, unendeared.
> Casual fruition . . .
>
> (IV:765–7)

No 'casual fruition' for Adam and Eve; instead, 'mutual bliss', and then a delightful sleep as rose-petals fall upon their naked bodies. They

> lulled by nightingales embracing slept,
> And on their naked limbs the flowery roof
> Showered roses . . .
>
> (IV:771–3)

This is what humanity has lost. Once Adam and Eve fall, they 'burn' in lust. Later, having eaten the apple, they are permitted one intense sexual experience on a bed of flowers, after which they sleep exhausted. It is now, however, a sleep of 'unrest': on waking they feel guilt, shame, anger, blame and a desire to hide. Now they are like Satan, who can never be satiated, because he is compelled by fierce desire, not love: desire which, even when achieved, leaves one craving for more, always unfulfilled.

Milton's Edenic vision of ideal heterosexual love, expressed both physically and emotionally, is an extraordinary development in his writing, indeed in his life. He had struggled since his teens to ensure that he would not be contaminated by desire, whether textual or lived. Now he can, at last, imagine sex between men and women without recoiling in horror. Although in *Paradise Lost*, homosexual desire is almost entirely demonised, quite literally in the representation of the devil Belial, Milton's language has echoes of his earlier celebrations of love between men.[10] Adam and Eve, in Eden, express a love founded in reason, and this remains sharply separated from the merely physical form of sex that is held in contempt. Milton, in the past, had elevated rational, probably sexless, male/male love far beyond the animalistic sex between men and women, which remained 'carnal performance' or 'servile copulation'.

Yet Milton's celebration of male/female love and sex was a fragile achievement. Elsewhere in *Paradise Lost*, he still wrote with the venom of his divorce pamphlets about sex and the body, particularly the female body. Book II, for example, ends with a grotesque encounter between Satan, Sin and Death, the latter pair guarding the gates of hell. At these moments, for all its psychological and moral complexities, *Paradise Lost* can be a straightforwardly violent and nasty piece of work.[11] Milton describes with relish the incestuous anti-Trinity, the Father Satan, his daughter Sin, their child Death. This is a child who, having torn through his mother's entrails 'with fear and pain', rapes her and so produces the hell hounds that are

> hourly conceived
> And hourly born, with sorrow infinite
> To me, for when they list into the womb
> That bred them they return, and howl and gnaw
> My bowels, their repast.
>
> (II:796–800)

Sin and Death are just waiting for Satan to succeed.

To succeed, to bring sin and death into the world, God's perfect creation Eve must eat the apple from the Tree of Knowledge, and also give it to Adam. *Paradise Lost* has already explained, and will explain again, the doctrine of free will. Once created, Adam and Eve make their own decisions, and they are 'sufficient to have stood' – they are fully armed against the foe.[12] The problem remains that Eve chooses, of her own free will, to eat the apple. Why?

Paradise Lost offers no simple answers, but one way of understanding Eve's action is to remember that she is 'not equal', and she knows it. Therefore, practically and psychologically, is Eve 'sufficient to have stood' without Adam? Is *she* fully armed against the foe?

Eve herself appears to revel in her own subjection, indeed her ignorance, saying early on in the poem, to Adam,

> My author and disposer, what thou bid'st
> Unargued I obey; so God ordains,
> God is thy law, thou mine: to know no more
> Is woman's happiest knowledge and her praise.
>
> (IV:635–8)

But, significantly, during crucial conversations between Adam and the visiting archangel Raphael, Eve is not there. Most notably, she decides that they are talking about difficult things and goes off to do some more gardening. She looks forward to hearing the information from Adam's lips, complete with conjugal caresses.

This is all very well, but it puts a burden of responsibility upon Adam, a burden that he fails, ultimately, to carry. Again, the reader is faced with divided responses. Adam loves Eve intensely. From the moment that he dreams of a creature 'Manlike'

> But different sex, so lovely fair,
> That what seemed fair in all the world, seemed now
> Mean
>
> (VIII:471–3)

he is desperate for this vision to be made reality. In a clear echo of Milton's own sonnet on the death of his wife, Adam describes the moment of waking:

> She disappeared, and left me dark, I waked
> To find her, or for ever to deplore
> Her loss, and other pleasures all abjure.
>
> (VIII:478–81)

Eve in reality is even better. Sex is a revelation to Adam, a 'commotion strange', the moment when 'passion first I felt'. Adam *knows* that Eve is 'of inward less exact', that she *is* inferior to him, but when he comes near to her, he forgets it all, since

> so absolute she seems
> And in her self complete, so well to know
> Her own, that what she wills to do or say,
> Seems wisest, virtuousest, discreetest, best.
>
> (VIII:547–50)

When Raphael hears Adam saying these things, he insists that he pull himself together. In a glorious exchange, Adam responds indignantly: it is not just the sex but the 'thousand decencies that daily flow', the 'delights', and in any case, how can Raphael understand sex, he's an angel! Raphael has a trump card: angels have sex too. They may not have bodies, but they enjoy it

> In eminence, and obstacle find none
> Of membrane, joint, or limb, exclusive bars:
> Easier than air with air, if spirits embrace,
> Total they mix, union of pure with pure
> Desiring: nor restrained conveyance need
> As flesh to mix with flesh, or soul with soul.
>   (VIII:624–9)

Adam is duly chastised at this revelation of the sexual practices of angels and promises to take his responsibilities towards Eve seriously. Raphael warns him that Satan is plotting against him and Eve 'now': Adam must 'warn thy weaker'. Eve, the weaker, needs Adam's protection and guidance. She is not, and never will be, 'in her self complete'.

So when Eve suggests that she and Adam could get more gardening done if they separated for a while, and Adam lets her go, he is offering up a weak victim to Satan. No matter that Eve's arguments resonate with Milton's own many years earlier in *Areopagitica*, perhaps earlier still in the *Maske*, that a society based on fear is no society, that cloistered virtue, 'unexercised and unbreathed', is no virtue.

> How are we happy, still in fear of harm?
> And what is faith, love, virtue unassayed
> [. . .]
> Alone, without exterior help sustained?
>   (IX:326, 335–6)

asks Eve, and she concludes, in a highly competent rhetorical flourish, that 'Frail is our happiness, if this be so, / And Eden were no Eden thus exposed.'

The spirit shown by Eve here is all part of Milton's fascinating insight into her psychology, evident from the very moment of her creation. Eve had previously described her own creation as waking from a dream. In Book IV she recounts looking into a pool and loving what she sees, herself. A voice, one of the many voices, both good and evil, that lead Eve in *Paradise Lost*, informs her that she can do better, she can find someone she can actually touch, someone with whom she can bear children, become the 'Mother of human race', come to embody her very name. In a statement that will become Eve's signature, she follows: 'What could I do / But follow straight, invisibly thus led?'

She is being led to Adam, but, perhaps surprisingly, when she sees him she is not sure she wants him. She turns away, only to be called back, indeed 'seized' by Adam:

> I yielded, and from that time see
> How beauty is excelled by manly grace
> And wisdom which alone is truly fair.
> (IV:489–91)

Eve's gazing into the water and falling in love with her own reflection echo the Narcissus myth from Ovid, in which proud, beautiful Narcissus is punished for being scornful by being made to fall in love with his own reflection. Narcissus pines away because it is impossible to reach his desire. What is the significance of Eve's gazing upon herself, and her initial dislike of Adam? Milton shows Eve having to be trained out of her newborn psyche, in which self-love, possibly even homoerotic desire for the female, predominates.

She will, of course, become Adam's wife, and mother of humankind, not equal, he for God only, she for God in him. But the desire was there, and fascinatingly, Milton takes the idea and builds upon it. Satan's plan is to soften up his enemy. So, while Eve sleeps, he whispers in her ear, trying to reach 'the organs of her fancy'. He succeeds, and Eve dreams that she hears Adam's voice, that she follows him to the Tree of Knowledge, that she sees an angel tasting the fruit ('He plucked, he tasted'), that he holds the fruit to her mouth, that she 'could not but taste', that she flies up – and then she falls and wakes.

No wonder that Adam is slightly perturbed and gives Eve a lecture about the difference between proper imagination, 'fancy' controlled by reason, and 'mimic fancy', which produces 'wild work'. The latter is what Eve is suffering from, but Eve's fantasies, instilled by Satan, are not so easily dismissed.

It is these fantasies that Satan works upon when he tempts the solitary Eve. He flatters her (she is Empress, Queen of this Universe); he deceives her, claiming to have eaten the fruit already and to be absolutely fine; and he offers her power, while diminishing God's, who becomes the Threatener. Above all he relies on Eve's propensity to be led ('Lead then . . .' she says, following him to the Tree) and her inability to spot the flaws in his admittedly brilliantly constructed, highly elliptical arguments. As Satan says, Eve will gain the knowledge of good and evil: how can that be bad?

> Of good, how just? Of evil, if what is evil
> Be real, why not known, since easier shunned?
> God therefore cannot hurt ye, and be just;
> Not just, not God; not feared then, nor obeyed.
> (IX:698–701)

The narrator condemns Eve (Satan's arguments 'into her heart too easy entrance won'), but surely the social and psychological odds are stacked against her. She is 'not equal', by both nature and nurture, and therefore not equal to the challenge presented by Satan. She attempts to reason it out but merely ends up questioning her own fear, born she believes of her own ignorance, the ignorance of which she has been constantly reminded: 'What hinder then / To reach, and feed at once both body and mind?'

> So saying, her rash hand in evil hour
> Forth reaching to the fruit, she plucked, she ate:
> Earth felt the wound, and nature from her seat
> Sighing through all her works gave signs of woe,
> That all was lost.
>
> (IX:780–84)

> Greedily she engorged without restraint,
> And knew not eating death.
>
> (IX:791–2)

Significantly, one of Eve's first desires on eating the fruit, one of her first Fallen responses, is to challenge the gender hierarchy in Eden. Perhaps eating the fruit will

> render me more equal, and perhaps,
> A thing not undesirable, sometime
> Superior: for inferior who is free?
>
> (IX:823–5)

She is ruthless in her ambition now:

> Adam shall share with me in bliss or woe:
> So dear I love him, that with him all deaths
> I could endure, without him live no life.
>
> (IX:831–3)

These are painfully intense moments in the poem. Adam's utter shock is itself shocking to the reader. He,

> soon as he heard
> The fatal trespass done by Eve, amazed,
> Astonied stood and blank, while horror chill
> Ran through his veins, and all his joints relaxed;

From his slack hand the garland wreathed for Eve
Down dropped, and all the faded roses shed.
                                      (IX:888–93)

Adam has an appalling choice, whether to eat the apple offered to him
by fallen Eve, or to reject it and her. He hardly hesitates. He cannot
live without Eve, 'flesh of flesh / Bone of my bone'. Adam eats the
fruit, in full knowledge of the implications of his actions, 'not deceived'
as Eve was. He eats because he loves Eve, announcing simply, powerfully, tragically: 'Our state cannot be severed, we are one, / One flesh;
to lose thee were to lose myself.' (IX:958–9) What he loses, though, is
'the sweet converse and love'.

Now, Adam and Eve become like any dysfunctional, unhappily
married couple, demonstrating that it is not only Satan who is
rendered with psychological accuracy by Milton. Book IX, the book
of the Fall, ends with a numbing vision of their destructive relationship:

Thus they in mutual accusation spent
The fruitless hours, but neither self-condemning,
And of their vain contest appeared no end.
                                      (IX:1187–9)

John Milton's literary treatment of Eve moves far beyond the traditional gender politics of the seventeenth century, in which her inherent
sinfulness was the simple justification for the suppression of all women,
daughters of Eve. Stranger still, as *Paradise Lost* progresses, Milton
himself seems to move past his own misogyny (though for some readers,
not far enough). He had, in the kindest of interpretations, struggled in
his relationships with women. But in *Paradise Lost*, he gives his Eve
considerable, and increasing, textual and emotional power and significance, making her psychologically real, exploring her place in the
society of Eden and, finally, celebrating her womanhood.

Does this make the reader understand why Adam, when confronted
with the loss of Eve, decides to share death with her rather than lose

her? This is precisely the effeminate subjection to a woman that the archangel Raphael has warned him against. Yet when he tells Eve, '. . . we are one, / One flesh; to lose thee were to lose my self,' his statement is profoundly moving.

More strange still, when Adam utterly rejects Eve after the Fall, *Paradise Lost* does not seem to share his disgust. When he shouts '. . . out of my sight, thou serpent,' Eve refuses to descend to his level. Instead, it is Eve who makes peace with Adam, knowing better than he that they will be judged for their sin: 'While we yet live, scarce one short hour perhaps / Between us two let there be peace.' (X:923–4)

When the Son of God is sent to judge Adam and Eve, they are full of guilt and shame, fearful and in hiding. But Adam goes a step further, blaming Eve, 'this woman': 'She gave me of the tree and I did eat.' The Son is having none of it, sternly asking Adam whether Eve was his God, insisting that in taking the apple Adam had resigned his own manhood, that loving Eve did not mean putting himself into her power. Adam was the one supposed to rule 'hadst thou known thy self aright'.

In contrast, when asked to account for herself, Eve says simply, '. . . the serpent me beguiled and I did eat.' There is no self-justification, no blame, merely an honest admission of failure.[13] Book X, the book of judgement, both of Adam and Eve and of Satan, ends in stark contrast to Book IX. Eve has been punished with pain in childbirth and subjection to her husband: '. . . and to thy husband's will / Thine shall submit, he over thee shall rule' (although some might argue that the latter merely describes the status quo in Eden). Adam will now have to labour to gain food. Most important, humanity becomes mortal, 'for dust thou art, and shalt to dust return'.

Eve is not demonised after the Fall. If anything Milton tries to make the reader understand the reasons for her actions and demonstrates her quiet heroism. He is still very much of his time in his representation of her, and he is still the man who had been for years capable of excluding women from his life, sexually, emotionally and practically. But even if the reader does not recognise the attempts made in *Paradise Lost* to counter the standard seventeenth-century misogynistic views of Eve, there is a broader issue at stake. Milton's language works consistently against making simple judgements about characters and events, whether through the choice of words or the placing of them. The difficult questions that Milton believed literature should ask are asked as much of Eve as of any other character. So, presentation of Eve remains open to interpretation, in itself a brave and important step in his writing.

If the interpretation of Eve opens up as *Paradise Lost* progresses, then the opposite process occurs with Satan. Milton's anti-hero is celebrating in Book X. Satan returns to hell, the all-conquering hero, telling his followers that he is 'now returned / Successful beyond hope'. Satan will lead them out of this 'dungeon' created by God the 'tyrant' to a new world. He does not stint on the details of his own heroics:

> Long were to tell
> What I have done, what suffered, with what pain
> Voyaged the unreal, vast, unbounded deep . . .
>
> (X:469–71)

His performance culminates with a rousing call to action: '. . . what remains, ye gods, / But up and enter now into full bliss.' (X:502–3)

In a wonderfully theatrical coup, Milton pulls the rug from under Satan's feet. He stands there, expecting his followers' applause and cheers, but all he hears is 'a dismal universal hiss'. At precisely this moment he himself is transformed, with agonising slowness, into a snake. So are all the other rebel angels. But Milton has saved the best till last. The hell snakes now see a vision of fruit trees. They are desperate with 'scalding thirst and hunger fierce'. They eat the fruit, but 'instead of fruit / Chewed bitter ashes'. In a final twist, the devils cannot stop coming back for more, addicted (the word *drugged* is used), deluded, falling into the 'same illusion' over and over again.

In contrast, Adam and Eve only fell once and are now contrite. They must, however, still leave Eden, and their expulsion is described in the closing two books of *Paradise Lost*. Adam at least is prepared for their journey into the fallen world by a vision of what is to come given to him by the archangel Michael. From the start there is little of comfort. The first scene shown by Michael is the murder of Abel by Cain, and others of horror, violence and tyranny follow in a visual education in death: '. . . what heart of rock could long / Dry-eyed behold?' Indeed, 'Adam could not, but wept.' Michael is insistent on the reason for Adam's tears. The misery has been brought about by the 'inabstinence of Eve', by 'the sin of Eve'. Many of the subtleties of *Paradise Lost* as a whole are countered by these profoundly (and in Michael's view, correctly) misogynistic statements in Book XI.

Yet, overall *Paradise Lost* does not confirm either the pessimism of Michael's visions in Book XI or indeed this view of Eve. Throughout the earlier books, much of the power of the poetry lies in Milton's ability to create a futile narrative hope, akin to the experience of watching a great tragedy unfold. Maybe, this time, things will not turn out so terribly. This foolish yet natural reaction is evoked and then dashed through the poem. In the final books of his epic, however, John Milton induces a very different kind of hope.

Not only is there the hope of the new Covenant with God, represented by the symbol of a bow in the sky after the Flood (in which is destroyed the 'whole earth filled with violence, and all flesh / Corrupting each their way', except for Noah and his family), but there is further promise. The Son of God will be born to Mary, descendant of Eve, and crush the serpent in battle. At this Adam weeps once more, this time in joy, believing that this Son will fight Satan in a new war. No, says Michael, 'Dream not of their fight / As of a duel . . .' Michael explains, carefully, at length, how the Son of God will fulfil the law of God 'by obedience and by love, though love / Alone fulfill the law'.

The love shown by the Son of God, in his willingness to be 'nailed to the cross / By his own nation', dominates the closing pages of *Paradise Lost*. And the word *love* lies at the heart of Michael's final instructions to Adam:

> Only add
> Deeds to thy knowledge answerable, add faith,
> Add virtue, patience, temperance, add love.
>
> (XII:581–3)

If he can do that, Michael tells him, then he will 'possess / A paradise within thee, happier far'.

Eve is a part of this hope. By focusing on her responses (her eloquent expression of her love of gardening in Book XI could be bathetic but is instead deeply touching) and her relationship with Adam at the end of Book XII, the epic returns to a human scale of experience. The writing demands an emotional response from the reader, which in turn serves to complicate Michael's earlier, necessarily reductive judgements. Although Eve slept while Adam received his visions of the future from Michael, she experienced similar visions in a dream. She knows that she is the mother of humankind, that one day her descendant will bear the Son of God. The final words spoken in the poem are Eve's, and now Adam simply listens:

> By me the promised seed shall all restore.
> So spake our mother Eve, and Adam heard
> Well pleased, but answered not.
>
> (XII:623–5)

Despite the recognition that Sin, Death and Satan are at work in the world now, in this world, *Paradise Lost* is not a despairing poem. Satan has triumphed, but not only is there the extraordinary promise of redemption (through the Son of God, who will prove 'above heroic' in his offer of his own life to redeem humankind), but there is the equally striking, deeply moving vision of Adam and Eve leaving Eden, hand in hand:

> Some natural tears they dropped, but wiped them soon;
> The world was all before them, where to choose
> Their place of rest, and providence their guide:
> They hand in hand with wandering steps and slow,
> Through Eden took their solitary way.

EIGHTEEN

REVELATION

1667

*P*ARADISE LOST, in its first appearance, was extremely plain in design. A reader in 1667 would have expected epistles, poems, portraits and prefaces, invariably written by someone other than the author, whether friend, patron or printer, all drawing attention to the extended community within which any book was produced. The first edition of *Paradise Lost*, with its stark transition from simple title page to poem, therefore draws attention to John Milton's isolation as author, an isolation from which he makes literary capital within the poem.

Ironically, however, the two stark title words, *Paradise Lost*, lacking explanation, entice the reader into the poem. Without the usual fulsome explanations of content and purpose, a reader would wonder what was to be found within the pages. What would Milton the well-known defender of regicide have to say about loss? What would he have to say about paradise? These questions place immense pressure on the opening lines of the poem, which allow the reader to begin determining whether they are holding an allegorical fantasy, a Christian poem or a political satire.[1]

Of course, the reader is holding all three of these things, and more. The opening lines of *Paradise Lost* promise the reader a brief history of time, as understood by Christians in the seventeenth century, from the very beginnings of the universe to the last days, from 'man's first disobedience' to the moment that 'one greater man', the Son of God, will 'restore us' through his sacrifice. The verb (*sing*) is withheld until the thirty-ninth word of the sentence, thus setting the poem in the heroic mode, stating 'the magnitude of the poem's subject and so the magnitude of its task, while still insisting that this vastness is within the poet's compass'.[2]

> Of man's first disobedience, and the fruit
> Of that forbidden tree, whose mortal taste
> Brought death into the world, and all our woe,
> With loss of Eden, till one greater man
> Restore us, and regain the blissful seat,
> Sing heavenly Muse . . .
>
> (I:1–6)

All of history is there, but so is John Milton. As the passage continues, the narrator becomes identified with Moses: both men are possessed by the same spirit of creation.[3] This God-given confidence appears throughout *Paradise Lost*, and culminates in the opening passages of Book IX, when the epic turns to the Fall itself. Dismissing 'Wars, hitherto the only argument / Heroic deemed', Milton asserts that he is boldly entering new territory for the epic form, where he will describe the 'better fortitude' of 'patience and heroic martyrdom unsung', a 'higher argument'.

Yet these confident gestures are compromised by anxieties about the author's own position in place and time. Perhaps he writes 'an age too late', perhaps he is writing in too cold a climate (a nod to his belief that the great Classical writers were born and bred in the Mediterranean), perhaps he is too old. This tension between confidence and anxiety runs through Milton's self-presentation in *Paradise Lost*. On one level, the poem acts to celebrate his own heroic feat of authorship. So at the start of Book III, having just heard about Satan's grand journeys through the cosmos, the reader is reminded that the narrator is on a dangerous and arduous journey too. He has descended to hell and is now safely back with his muse: '. . . thee I revisit safe.' On another level, however, *Paradise Lost* acknowledges explicitly its author's physical disability and his political defeat, with some of the most famous lines in the poem expressing a fundamental dependence on God. Milton asserts that he is creating 'things unattempted yet in prose and rhyme' and asks for help in his task:

> . . . what in me is dark
> Illumine, what is low raise and support;
> That to the highth of this great argument
> I may assert eternal providence
> And justify the ways of God to men.
>
> (I:22–6)

That word *dark* hints at the reality of writing for the blind John Milton: his darkness can only be illumined by the imagination, by his muse, by faith. Some exquisite passages in the third book of *Paradise Lost* reveal the loneliness of blindness in painful detail. The light he seeks

> Revisit'st not these eyes, that roll in vain
> To find thy piercing ray, and find no dawn;
> So thick a drop serene hath quenched their orbs,
> Or dim suffusion veiled. Yet not the more
> Cease I to wander where the Muses haunt . . .
>
> (III:22–7)

The caesura, or pause, in the fourth line demonstrates and enacts the tension between the sense of loss, the eyes that 'roll in vain', and the determination, precisely *because* of this loss, to 'wander where the Muses haunt'. Loss is again invoked in the following passages, in which Milton describes the way in which he is inspired during the night, but that for him morning never comes:

> . . . not to me returns
> Day, or the sweet approach of even or morn,
> Or sight of vernal bloom, or summer's rose,
> Or flocks, or herds, or human face divine;
> But cloud instead, and ever-during dark

Surrounds me, from the cheerful ways of men
Cut off, and for the book of knowledge fair
Presented with a universal blank
Of nature's works to me expunged and razed,
And wisdom at one entrance quite shut out.
So much the rather thou celestial light
Shine inward, and the mind through all her powers
Irradiate, there plant eyes, all mist from thence
Purge and disperse, that I may see and tell
Of things invisible to mortal sight.

(III:41–55)

Once more the experience of blindness is explored, a life of 'universal blank', where light, nature, wisdom, people's cheerful ways are 'expunged and razed', 'quite shut out', as well as the urgent need, precisely because of that loss, for the 'celestial Light' to 'shine inward'. Milton is expounding perhaps the most important element in his struggle to accept his blindness. His physical sight may have gone, but in its place, his inner sight might do even more important work. The sighted see merely the surfaces of things. Milton in the 'mind's contemplation' sees 'whatever is real and permanent in them'. The phrase 'human face divine' pushes his theology close to that of the Quakers, in its suggestion that God exists within each human being.

The appeal for a light to shine inward is to enable Milton to sing *of* the world *to* the world. *Paradise Lost* does not mark a retreat into a private, internal space but an attempt to engage once more with his nation, despite his disability, despite his political defeat. This is something made explicit, or as explicit as this republican defender of regicide, this committed political servant of Cromwell, can make it, at the exact halfway point of the poem:

More safe I sing with mortal voice, unchanged
To hoarse or mute, though fallen on evil days,
On evil days though fallen, and evil tongues;
In darkness, and with dangers compassed round,

> And solitude; yet not alone, while thou
> Visit'st my slumbers nightly, or when morn
> Purples the east: still govern thou my song,
> Urania, and fit audience find, though few.[4]
>
> (VII:27–34)

When Milton writes that he sings 'unchanged', he is reminding his audience of the pamphlet writer of the 1640s, of the Cromwellian government servant of the 1650s, of the author of *The Readie & Easie Way*. When he hopes that his 'song' will find a 'fit audience', he is hoping for the poem to fulfil its political and religious aims, to reach an audience despite the 'evil tongues', the 'dangers' and his own self-proclaimed 'solitude'. Gratifyingly, his epic was published at the best moment possible for Milton to reach his imagined audience and to speak to them of religion and politics. It is no coincidence that *Paradise Lost* appeared just as Parliament reconvened in October 1667.

The nation was reeling from a succession of calamities. In a shocking blow to the national psyche, during peace negotiations the Dutch fleet launched a surprise raid on English territory on 12 June 1667. The Dutch burned the port of Sheerness to the ground, sailed up the Medway, raided Chatham dockyard and, in a final act of aggression, stole the English flagship, *The Royal Charles*. The Dutch may have withdrawn with their spoils, but the damage was done. There had been panic in London. King Charles II's leading minister Lord Clarendon remembered that Whitehall was full of 'wild despair'.[5]

In addition, the corruption and sheer immorality of Charles II's court was reaching a new height. Even those who were staunch supporters of monarchy in theory were finding it hard to stomach this monarch in practice. Now, in 1667, there was a moment of potential regime change. The naval catastrophe, coming after years of glorious victories (the occasional defeats were forgotten now), spelled doom not for the King, however, but for his minister. Someone had to be punished, and Clarendon, already a favourite subject of public anger (a gibbet was erected outside his house by rioters), was removed from power. The fall of Clarendon showed what could be done, even at the highest level.

For many, therefore, the autumn of 1667 was a moment for spiritual reflection, for the examination of conscience. Why had their nation, why had they as individuals, incurred such wrath from God? For Sir John Hobart, who had served in Cromwell's parliaments and as a supporter of any attempt to ease the position of religious dissenters, a man preoccupied with the need to 'amend our lives, and prepare ourselves for those events, which if severe, are but justly our due', *Paradise Lost* offered solace. 'Strangely' pleasing, full of 'delight', it was worth reading over and over again for its spiritual message.[6]

But the autumn of 1667 was also a moment of political opportunity, with the monarchy looking more beleaguered with every passing month, and of religious potential, when Nonconformists were optimistic that they might be able to capitalise on the national crisis. An Act of Comprehension, allowing for some new religious freedoms, was being considered. *Paradise Lost* speaks clearly on behalf of religious toleration and freedom of conscience, attacking State churches, idolatry and corruption. Even for those who could not countenance Milton's calls for religious toleration, or indeed his support for republicanism, *Paradise Lost* offered a sustained and timely critique of court culture, whether as depicted in Satan's hell or in the review of human history that closes the epic.

Milton was not alone in offering his voice to the debate about what had gone wrong in these years. The nation as a whole was trying to come to terms with the series of disasters. It had not proved sufficient to find a scapegoat for the Great Fire of London, although a mentally deficient Frenchman called Robert Hubert claimed to have started it and was duly executed. Hubert could not possibly have done so, but that was not the point. There were even dark mutterings that Charles II himself had started the fire, in order to distract attention from the scandals besetting his court. John Dryden, mouthpiece of the Establishment, responded to the plague and other disasters by emphasising the way in which these events had provided opportunities for individual heroism, and for the King to show his care for his people. Dryden's poem *Annus mirabilis: the Year of Wonders* shows that God was not punishing the nation but showing his goodness in the continued

benign rule of Charles II. Milton's student and friend, Thomas
Ellwood, had a very different perspective, spelled out (in plodding
rhyming couplets) in his poem of 1662, *Speculum Seculi or A Looking-
Glass for the Times:*

> Awhile I stood like one that's struck with thunder,
> Filled with astonishment and silent wonder.
> At length my heart, swelling with indignation
> Vented itself in such an exclamation:
> [. . .]
> Was Sodom ever guilty of a sin
> Which England is not now involved in?[7]

Both these writers, utterly divided by politics and religion, used
rhyming couplets to make their points. Not Milton. His response
to his nation's crisis was written in blank verse, unrhymed iambic
pentameter, yet another sign of his opposition to current literary
fashion. (Marvell, for one, wrote in his prefatory poem to the epic that
Paradise Lost would have allured more readers if its author had used
'tinkling Rhyme'.)[8] Milton's chosen metre is the closest to the natural
rhythms of English speech, and remains familiar now since it is the
dominant mode of Shakespeare's plays. Milton's choice suggests not
only his vision of epic as a kind of drama, not only, perhaps, a nostalgia
for the rhythms of the drama of his youth, but, most importantly, the
use of blank verse is a further indication that its author intended his
epic to do political work. Milton made this point explicitly in the note
on the 'measure' added in 1668. To use blank verse, he writes, is to
restore ancient liberty to the 'Heroic Poem from the troublesome and
modern bondage of Rhyming'. Even the choice of metre is an attempt
to free the English people from bondage. Milton's epic was designed in
both structure and content to minister to the nation in its distress.

That *Paradise Lost* has a message for the nation is indisputable. The
nature of that message is not, and it continues to be the subject of
intense debate. What is certain is that the religious and political are
inextricably linked. Tyranny, for example, is explicitly linked with

idolatry: both are established extraordinarily quickly in hell. In the closing books, good societies are those based on piety, 'freedom and peace to men', and when godly discipline collapses, disaster ensues.

> The poem leaves the reader, as it leaves Adam and Eve, with a world of choice, solitary, self-responsible, yet with Providence as their guide. The understanding of nations is much as with the understanding of individuals: free determination, subjection to correction or blessing, but within a providential frame.[9]

Above all, Milton's emphasis on private, internal transformation, the development of a 'paradise within', in itself suggests that there should be no established Church attempting to police that private belief.

This interlinking of the religious and political messages was precisely the factor that worried Milton's opponents. John Beale, a Royalist reader, was sure that Milton had not written a narrowly spiritual guide. Beale recognised that Milton was indeed singing 'unchanged', that Milton held 'to his old Principle', pointing to the Nimrod episode in Book XII as evidence of his unrepentant republicanism. (Nimrod's rule is characterised and condemned as the 'first lording of one man'.) Beale was also concerned that the blasphemies of the work, in particular the representation of Satan, would inflame readers in dangerous ways. Milton, like the Roman authors Ovid and Lucan, was 'lascivious, obscene, dissolute, or traitorous', argued Beale. For readers like him, the publication of *Paradise Lost* was a deeply unwelcome act, dangerous to the State.[10] The literary decorum evident in the poem may have kept it, at first sight, distinct from the rantings and ecstasies of groups such as the Quakers, but the content showed that John Milton was still a supporter of radical religious and political positions.

Paradise Lost explores, painfully and honestly, what went wrong from the moment that Charles I was executed. Milton shows, clinically, how systems of government descend into tyranny, how belief in God turns into idolatry, and he shows Adam's horror and his tears when he is allowed a glimpse of future humanity oppressed under a series of tyrannical rulers, worshipping false gods, forgetting to 'add love'. The poem accepts this as God's just punishment of humanity's sin. As the archangel Michael, who shows Adam this vision of the future, reminds him, 'Tyranny must be.'

In one sense, this is a darkly pessimistic acceptance of the current political and religious moment: as the Milton scholar Nicholas von Maltzahn argues, the poet's 'pessimism at the end of *Paradise Lost* about the chances of toleration shows him far less hopeful than he had been in 1659 (in his *Treatise of Civil Power*)'.[11] Yet it is a pessimism leavened with hope, since 'the ultimate aim of Michael's darkness of tone is to console Adam, to enable him to face the fallen world unflinchingly', underlining the message that 'an unflinching awareness of the difficulties to be overcome was more important than confident action without such an awareness.'[12]

As such, *Paradise Lost* offers a new conception of heroism. At first, Satan walks and talks like a hero, but the poem as a whole interrogates and satirises his form of leadership. Satanic 'perversions of the heroic' reach their height 'when Satan returns to hell intending a Roman triumph like that attending the formal coronation of Charles II – to be greeted instead with a universal hiss from his followers turned into snakes, as all of them are forced to enact a grotesque black comedy of God's devising'.[13] Milton uses these moments to 'let the reader discover how Satan has perverted the noblest qualities of literature's greatest heroes, and so realize how susceptible those models of heroism are to perversion', as indeed Charles II had perverted them in the course of his triumphal progress into London, and Cromwell had perverted them in creating a Royal court in practice, if not in name.

This moment in the poem, one of many, shows just how alert Milton wanted his readers to be, interpreting *Paradise Lost* not just through the lens of Classical and Hebrew traditions but through their own political experiences of the previous decades. Repeatedly, the poem brings the reader into the present. Belial and his sons *reign* (no past tense here) in 'courts and palaces'. The phrase 'sons of Belial' was familiar to Milton's audience as a term used, by their opponents, of

Royalists. When Satan is supported by his council of war, his hellish parliament, in his plan to corrupt new-created man, Milton angrily compares humanity's inability to live in harmony with the devils' ability to come to agreement:

> O shame to men! Devil with devil damned
> Firm concord holds, men only disagree
> Of creatures rational, though under hope
> Of heavenly grace: and God proclaiming peace,
> Yet live in hatred, enmity and strife
> Among themselves, and levy cruel wars,
> Wasting the earth, each other to destroy.
>
> (II:496–502)

Milton is attempting to rouse the political nation. As the scholar Sharon Achinstein argues, the 'final gestures in his great poem reflected not gloom at the failures of the revolution, but urgency and optimism'. This is an optimistic interpretation not only of the poem but of Milton himself: 'Milton never gave up on the people of England, and in *Paradise Lost*, the actions of a revolutionary reader become his chief concern.'[14]

The reader's involvement is critical, not just spiritually and emotionally, but politically. Milton believed that republicanism was the best mode of government for his country, but he also, by the time of writing *Paradise Lost*, knew that the English people would not, perhaps *could* not, deliver it. His élitism derived from this. The people, as a whole, were incapable of knowing what was best for the nation. Therefore, a meritocratic state run by a Council would put 'fit' leaders in place. The 'best affected', the godly few, should be running the country. The rest just dragged them down.

Yet, alongside this élitist view is a concern to *create* those leaders, to create a nation that can enjoy political and religious liberty. *Paradise Lost* seeks to create 'fit readers', not just to preach to them. The hope is that those who pick it up will, through reading it, be able, for example, to see how tyrants gain their power and, perhaps, next time, stand firm against tyranny. *Paradise Lost* therefore both demands and creates readers who will be alert to all its complexities, able to appreciate its ironies, able to share its anger and its compassion.

Paradise Lost did find a good many readers in the months and years after its publication in October 1667. The first print run of 1,300 copies sold fairly swiftly through the late autumn and winter of 1667, and was followed by three further impressions.[15] The new impressions provided an opportunity to add material. With the fourth title page, the work really started selling, with Simmons pleased to announce to his readers that, having been besieged with requests for the information, he had procured some explanatory material from his author, an 'Argument' that provided a summary of the plot and an explanation of 'that which stumbled many others, why the Poem Rhymes not'. (Simmons also made sure he recruited another book-seller, Henry Mortlack, whose shop was in Westminster Hall, thus giving a direct outlet for *Paradise Lost* at the heart of court and government.) These various steps demonstrate not only a committed publisher in Simmons but also Milton's close involvement with the publication process as he fine-tuned his verse. This kind of collaboration suggests that his emphasis on his isolation was, to some extent at least, a literary pose. In *Paradise Lost* Milton writes eloquently about the dangers facing him in the Restoration period, and, as is evident from the sufferings of Henry Vane and Thomas Ellwood, these dangers were real. Milton himself had been imprisoned, and he continued to be derided for his blindness. Yet John Milton was not quite as isolated, *could not have been* quite as isolated, as he presents himself in *Paradise Lost.* He relied on a whole network of individuals and organisations to produce his work: readers to read to him, scribes to write down his thoughts, the help of his wife, his friends, his printers, his publishers. And he relied on his daughters, who, at precisely this time, emerge from the historical shadows.

An awful lot of myths surround these daughters, very few of them verifiable, and many derived from testimonies given in a problematic legal case after Milton's death. There is an enduring impression throughout much of the literature on the subject that they, most notably his youngest daughter, Deborah, performed the roles of scribe and reader. To be able to do so, Deborah, obviously, needed to be able to read and write, and not just in English. John Aubrey reported that Deborah, whom he claimed was 'very like her father', was taught 'Latin, & to read Greek' (Aubrey then deleted the word *Hebrew*, his deletion and his syntax suggesting that she learned both to read and write Latin, only to read Greek and to do neither with Hebrew.)[16]

The facts confuse this picture slightly. Deborah was not even born at the time of her father's blindness, and, even in 1660, when Milton lost the kinds of practical support that went with his government position, and was in genuine crisis and danger, Anne, Mary and Deborah were, respectively, only fourteen, twelve and eight, with Anne disabled in some way. Moreover, the supply of male assistants did not dry up at this time, as Thomas Ellwood noted. Milton 'always kept a man to read to him which usually was the son of some gentleman of his acquaintance, whom, in kindness, he took to improve in his learning'.[17]

Milton's daughters were therefore probably not essential to his work. The fact remains that Mary and Deborah did learn to write, something that Christopher Milton's daughters, for example, did not. That the girls may have learned to read and write Latin, let alone Greek or Dutch, as some have suggested, would have made them remarkable for their time. Latin was revered for its 'masculine' qualities of order and logic over the relative chaos of English: they would have been learning, quite literally, the language of men.[18] If their father did give them this skill, in a culture that remained hostile to the education of girls and women, and saw linguistic facility as a mark of power, Milton was, on the surface at least, giving his daughters a potential weapon of liberation, acting as a man ahead of his time. It would not be until 1673 that a remarkable woman called Bathsua Makin made a compelling case for women's education. She had witnessed at first hand the achievements of women during the wars and beyond, in the absence of their menfolk, and had drawn some obvious but shocking conclusions about their abilities:

In these late times, there are several instances of women, when their
husbands were serving their king and country, defended their
houses, and did all things, as soldiers, with prudence and valour,
like men. They appeared before committees, and pleaded their own
causes with good success.[19]

Makin invited Londoners to come to a coffee shop ('every Tuesday at
Mr Mason's coffee-house in Cornhill, near the Royal Exchange') or a
pub ('Thursdays at the Bolt and Tun in Fleet Street, between the
hours of three and six in the afternoons') where they could hear her
message about the capabilities of women. Her sales pitch was cau-
tiously conservative, a wise move in a culture so hostile to women's
education. Makin, emphasising her connections with Royalty – she
had been the Royal governess – argued that education would stop
women wasting their time on frivolous things, and therefore that
women's relations would gain 'profit, and the whole nation advantage'.
She succeeded in setting up a school 'for gentlewomen at Tottenham
high cross, within four miles of London'. For just £20 a year, young
women would learn dancing, music, singing, writing and keeping
accounts for half their time. In a radical move, however, they would
spend the other half 'employed in gaining the Latin and French
tongues; and those that please may learn Greek and Hebrew, the
Italian and Spanish'. But Makin knew that there would be some who
thought that this was a step too far, and offered anxious parents the
choice: 'Those that think one language enough for a woman, may
forbear the languages, and learn only experimental philosophy, and
more or fewer of the other things aforementioned, as they incline.'[20]

Makin represented the future. When Milton's daughters were
being brought up, things were different. Education was goal-
orientated, tailored to the individual's future social role. This is
why women, generally, did not receive much of it. If its function
was to prepare a woman for her role in society, then it was clear that
women needed only the minimal instruction to prepare them for their
marital duty, household economy and the bringing up of children.
Reading was, however, seen as important, as a step to godliness. Most

educational theorists advocated that girls should learn to read English, that they 'may in their youth learn to read the Bible in their own mother tongue'. As soon as that was accomplished, the process stopped. At Banbury Grammar School, for example, girls could not stay past the age of nine, 'nor longer than they may learn to read English'. A small minority did learn to write, but again, the purpose was to make them more effective in their feminine roles. One woman described her education:

> When she did see me idly disposed, she would set me to cipher with my pen, and to cast up and prove great sums and accounts, and sometimes set me to write a supposed letter to this or that body concerning such and such things, and other times set me to read Dr Turner's *Herbal*, and in Bartholemew Vigo, and other times set me to sing psalms, and sometimes set me to do some curious work (for she was an excellent workwoman in all kinds of needle work, and most curiously she would perform it).[21]

This is very different from the education described by one diarist from the merchant class, Samuel Jeake, who (having noted that he was weaned at seven months, walked at a year and spoke at fifteen months) recorded that after his brother died when he was four he 'never went to school, but was taught by my Father'. Coming up to his fifth birthday he 'entered reading in the Bible', shortly after which he had his hair cut, one step on the road to manhood. The following year he learned to write, and by the age of seven 'could write well, several hands'.[22] By the time he was nine he was studying the Greek authors, having already tackled Latin.

If the education of girls was goal-orientated, designed to fit them for their role in society, then what were Milton's aims for his daughters? Did he share Bathsua Makin's concern that women needed to be armed with education in order to resist domestic tyranny, in order to move beyond ignorant servitude? Makin wrote, in her address to the reader that prefaced *An Essay to Revive the Ancient Education of Gentlewomen*:

Had God intended women only as a finer sort of cattle, he would not
have made them reasonable: brutes, a few degrees higher than drills
or monkeys (which the Indians use to do many offices) might have
better fitted some men's lust, pride and pleasure; especially those
that desire to keep them ignorant to be tyrannised over.[23]

There is absolutely no evidence that John Milton educated his
daughters in Latin and Greek in order to free them from ignorance,
in order to ensure that they would not be victims of tyranny, at home
or in the wider world. Any education they received was likely to have
been designed to ensure that they could fulfil their duties towards him.
Once those duties had been completed, they had no use for their Latin
or Greek. Equally, they did not need to understand the languages they
wrote or read, merely to transcribe and read them. One early
biographer claims that Deborah was forced to read to her father in
eight different languages, understanding only English.

An awareness of this context makes an assertion on the part of
Milton's most renowned twentieth-century biographer, William Parker, positively offensive. Parker argues that Anne, Mary and Deborah
were simply not very bright. He suggests that the girls were taught
languages because of Milton's commitment to a liberal education, as
espoused in *Of Education*, failing to remember that this commitment
applied only to boys. Parker sees the whole initiative resulting 'in
failure – and some would add "of course". Mary and Deborah were
never able to understand books in foreign languages'. Parker's claim is
astonishing but keeps the flame of patronising misogyny alive, his
values hurtling him back to the seventeenth century in one glib
phrase. He goes on to claim that the girls' reading would have been
painful to their father, who stopped Thomas Ellwood reading if he felt
he did not understand a passage, and happily cites Milton's reported
joke (Deborah remembered it many years later) that 'one tongue is
enough for a woman.' The picture is complete: a long-suffering John
Milton who can nevertheless laugh at his own suffering.[24]

Milton's so-called joke that one tongue was enough for a woman
instead shows him to be absolutely of his time in his attitudes towards

women, speech and education, at least when operating within his own domestic world. The tongue was seen as a pre-eminently troublesome organ by his contemporaries, 'unruly, disorderly, and likely to cause harm'. It was also seen in terms of gender. The first corrupting instrument was the tongue, Eve's tongue, woman's tongue. Add to this the fact that there was a clear link between the tongue (a 'little member') and the penis, and it is an easy step to argue that if and when a woman spoke, then she was trying to be a man. In a further leap, the tongue was also seen as a whore. These kinds of links may seem absurd now, but midwives would act upon the lore, propounded in medical books such as Jacques Guillemeau's *Child-birth, or, the happy delivery of women* (1612), that umbilical cords should be left longer in boys, because it would ensure that they had larger penises and tongues, 'whereby they may both speak the plainer and be more serviceable to Ladies'. The rule for girls – tie it short.[25]

Milton's nephew, also clear as to women's proper roles in life, gave his version of family life, and the abrupt conclusion to the daughters' 'employment' in the Milton home:

> The irksomeness of this employment could not always be concealed, but broke out more and more into expressions of uneasiness; so that at length they were all (even the eldest also) sent out to learn some curious and ingenious sorts of manufacture, that are proper for women to learn, particularly embroideries in gold or silver.[26]

Intriguingly, Betty Minshull Milton used exactly the same language when she looked back at this moment in family life, arguing that her stepdaughters were sent out to learn a method of manufacture that was 'proper for women to learn'.[27] Anne was twenty-three, Mary twenty-one, Deborah just seventeen when they left their family home to become apprentices in the lace-making industry.

This was a strange step in many ways, seeming to wipe out, in one act, the Milton family's struggle towards gentility over the previous seven decades. Diaries of the period suggest that the primary concern of most fathers was the marriage of their daughters. Even in families where there was little money, and in which there might have been anxieties about dowry payments, apprenticeships for girls were rare. Boys were far more likely to be 'placed'. It is possible that Milton wanted his daughters to be self-sufficient, to escape the limited options for most women of marriage and children, of being a governess or a midwife. Both their education and their trade would help in their escape from these roles, and their father was, perhaps, 'seeing that his daughters could be independent and cultured', refusing to force marriage upon them, as one Milton scholar has argued.[28] Then again, the step may have been Milton's way of investing in his daughters, as it were, implicitly in lieu of a dowry. In his dying words, he referred (allegedly) to what he had 'done for' his daughters, which is usually taken as a reference to their upbringing and apprenticeships. He believed he had done enough. It is just possible that the apprenticeships were a sign of the Miltons' Nonconformist zeal, one of the few things that could outweigh the social aspirations of this scrivener's son. One of Milton's supporters at Chalfont St Giles, Hester Fleetwood, came from an élite background and lived in the great house there, The Vache. Nevertheless, when she became a Quaker, it influenced the family to the extent that her son Robert would go into trade, becoming a glassmaker and -seller. Samuel Jeake, whose diary was quoted earlier, may have been highly educated in Latin and Greek by his father, but he chose to become a merchant, in sharp contrast to the professional or administrative career of his father. Jeake and Fleetwood were men, however, and there do not seem to be examples of women taking the same step. Yet in the last decades of the seventeenth century, working women were more and more visible on the streets of London, earning their own livings and often in precisely the industry into which Milton's daughters were apprenticed. Other women worked in more public spaces, selling, for example, butter, cheese, oatmeal and fruit in London's markets or, more controversially, working at the playhouses.

It would be a nice thought that John Milton wanted his daughters to join this happy throng of economically productive women, but it is unlikely. Even if he did envision them gaining economic independence, it would have been an unusual outcome. Girls were able to pursue apprenticeships, but few were able to pursue their crafts independently thereafter, firmly excluded from the most important and profitable sectors of the economy. Did Milton, or his new wife, know that female apprentices were often seriously mistreated by their master or mistress? On Christmas Eve 1680, 'a London seamstress decided to punish her thirteen-year-old apprentice for some trivial misdemeanour, and she and a male lodger tied and gagged the girl and flogged her for several hours, so brutally that she . . . died of her injuries. Neighbours observed that her cruelty had been notorious, but they had not seen fit to report her.' These cases have been described as the tip of 'an iceberg of brutality'.[29]

Whatever the reasons for the step, Anne, Mary and Deborah did move out of their father's household during 1669 or 1670. It seems that Deborah did not continue long in her apprenticeship. Her daughter recalled that her mother,

> meeting with very ill treatment from Milton's last Wife, left her Father, and went to live with a lady, whom she called lady Merian. This lady going over to Ireland, and resolving to take Milton's daughter with her, if he would give his Consent, wrote a Letter to him of her Design, and assured him, that as Chance had thrown his daughter under her care, she would treat her no otherwise than as his daughter and her own companion. She lived with that Lady, till her marriage.[30]

Again, this is a story only told many years after the events. Lady Merian has never been identified, but if this mysterious woman did take on Deborah as a lady's companion, freeing her from her lacemaker's apprenticeship, then Milton's youngest daughter ended up in a far more socially respectable role than her sisters. The move to Ireland, however, did not help to bridge the gap between father and daughter.

Christopher Milton, fighting a legal case against the daughters over his brother's will, remembered the relationship as one in which they had been 'undutiful and unkind' (meaning 'unnatural') to his brother: they were 'careless of him being blind and made nothing of deserting him'.[31] Deborah's daughter, Elizabeth, offered a rather different view when visited by Thomas Birch, who was putting together his biography of Milton, which would be published in 1753. Elizabeth recalled that her grandfather was not a 'fond father' but that it was his wife who showed the daughters actual 'ill-treatment'.[32] The dominant meaning of 'fond' in Milton's time was 'foolish and potentially idiotic', with a growing secondary meaning of 'over-affectionate'. The granddaughter's statement is not a criticism, therefore, but more a grudging acknowledgement that Milton did not spoil his daughters, practically or emotionally. In this account, he is rendered powerless against the actions of his third wife. Betty's behaviour gave John great uneasiness 'tho in his State of Health and Blindness he could not prevent it.'[33]

A servant in the Milton household, speaking in the court case, offered yet another view. According to Elizabeth Fisher, who heard it from a previous maid, when the teenage Mary Milton was informed of the marriage between her father and Betty Minshull, she replied that 'it was no news to hear of his wedding but if she could hear of his death that was something.' Worse still, the daughters had 'made away some of his books and would have sold the rest to the dunghill women'.[34]

All these differing accounts nevertheless have an explicit or implicit common theme. Milton's daughters and/or wife were out of his control, and he lived in a culture in which any wayward, disobedient or outspoken daughter or wife reflected poorly upon male authority. If his daughters were any of these things (or if his wife exploited his 'state of health and blindness' in order to impose her own rule over his daughters), it exposed a failure on his part to be suitably authoritative, a failure of his masculinity. It may have been easier to disassociate himself completely from a role in which he was so obviously failing.

On the other hand, these accounts, and indeed the circumstantial evidence of the apprenticeships, are countered by another source, far more pleasant to the ears of those who want to see 'normal' familial relationships in the Milton household. Deborah's daughter remembered that her mother was a great favourite with her father, and when 'she gave accounts of Milton's affairs . . . spoke of him with great tenderness'. Her father was 'delightful company', 'the life of the conversation' and showed 'unaffected cheerfulness and civility'.[35]

It is all intensely frustrating for the biographer. In the vast tomes of Milton's complete works, there are only the very occasional glimpses of everyday life. Apart from the record in the family Bible, there is never, ever, a mention of any of his wives, any of his daughters, not even his little son who died so young. Indeed, no letters survive between Milton and any of his family members.[36] Who or what is responsible for this, to us, strange silence? Any other figure from the seventeenth century will have letters or documents that allude to some kind of personal life. With Milton, it is absent. Was this his choice? Was the domestic, were his wives and children, 'little things' beyond his notice, to be eradicated from the documentary record? Almost everything we (think we) know about these everyday details comes from the pens of others, and these others are almost exclusively men with whom Milton worked in some way or other.

It is easier to follow his path as an author. Only a couple of years after the first publication of *Paradise Lost*, the political landscape had changed yet again. The epic had come to the press in a winter of discontent, a period characterised by ominous, apocalyptic pronounce-ments, and a sense of crisis, economic, political and military unease greater than at any time since 1659–60. The crisis had tested the relatively new monarchy to its limits, and almost to destruction. But the reactionary Parliament of 1667 had not respected the more tolerant wishes of the population at large, and soon it was business as usual once more. The crisis appeared to have been averted, and King Charles II was consolidating his power, in Church and State.

Meanwhile, the rebuilding of London in the wake of the Great Fire continued, the new City rising in stone rather than wood. John Milton's urban surroundings were being transformed, another ex-pression of the nation's new values. The old City was gone, the loss vividly evoked by John Evelyn, who described 'clambering over heaps of yet smoking rubbish, and frequently mistaking where I was' in the aftermath of the Great Fire. Presumably the sense of disorientation was even greater for a blind man. Prescriptions and regulations now abounded. The characteristic features of the old City – the jetties, bulks, projecting shopfronts and water-pipes gouting on to passers-by – disappeared almost entirely. The streets were widened, becoming thoroughfares for traffic rather than simply the way to a house. Now Ludgate Hill, leading up to St Paul's Churchyard, was more than 40 feet wide, and less steep to walk up. Markets were removed from main thoroughfares, the Fleet was dredged, and there was talk of a Thames embankment. Progress was slow, however. By the end of 1667 only 150 new premises had been built – the acceleration would come later. Over the next five years, eight thousand buildings would rise again. St Paul's itself was only patched up after the fire. It was not until 1675 that Wren's plans for the new cathedral were accepted. In 1668 the writer Samuel Rolle could still note that London looked like a 'village', 'the houses in it stand so scatteringly'.[37]

The new regime and its adherents were in the ascendant. One of its most eloquent apologists, Milton's (and Marvell's) old colleague in Cromwell's Foreign Office, John Dryden, was appointed Poet Laureate in April 1668, then Historiographer Royal a couple of years later. Even closer to Milton, the Powell family continued to thrive under monarchy, Mary Powell Milton's brother rising within the legal profession and 'reputed a rich man'. His son was following his footsteps, and so was Christopher Milton's. The Cromwellian era was beginning to look like the 'interregnum', the interruption of business as usual, the term still used by many historians.

Nevertheless, the early years of Charles II's reign were not without their problems. Charles may have been 'the best judge of manners of his time', but, as one biographer puts it, not of 'steadiness of affection' or policy. Charming, highly active, endlessly talkative, Charles hated the day-to-day business of his rule: the paperwork, the meetings, the protocol.[38]

Meanwhile, at Whitehall, his court continued to watch the City nervously. On 24 March 1668, Shrove Tuesday, there were riots when gangs of apprentices tore down the bawdy houses, or brothels, on the edge of the City 'about Moorfields'. Samuel Pepys noted that at Whitehall there was 'great talk of the tumult at the other end of town . . . And Lord, to see the apprehensions which this did give to all people at Court, that presently order was given for all the soldiers, horse and foot, to be in arms'.[39] The King and his court were right to be nervous. They did not want a close examination of their own sexual dealings, dealings vividly expressed in poems such as 'A Satire on Charles II', written by one of the King's most notorious courtiers, John Wilmot, Earl of Rochester, a few years later, but deeply characteristic of the reign.

Rochester had an extremely bad day at court in January 1674 when he, in error, gave the King a copy of a poem that viciously and hilariously satirised Charles, his government and his sexual powers – not to mention reminding the King of his declining years: the King was forty-three, the poet a mere twenty-six. 'A Satire on Charles II' (who 'love he loves, for he loves fucking much') is witty and obscene:

> His scepter and his prick are of a length;
> And she may sway the one who plays with th' other,
> And make him little wiser than his brother.
> Poor Prince! thy prick, like thy buffoons at Court,
> Will govern thee because it makes thee sport.
> 'Tis sure the sauciest prick that e'er did swive,
> The proudest, peremptoriest prick alive.
> Though safety, law, religion, life lay on 't,
> 'Twould break through all to make its way to cunt.
> Restless he rolls about from whore to whore,
> A merry monarch, scandalous and poor.
>
> (ll. 11–21)

Charles, and therefore his kingdom, are both ruled by his 'prick'. This might almost be a compliment to the merry monarch's machismo, but the poem makes absolutely clear not only that Charles is a sex addict ('Restless he rolls about from whore to whore / A merry monarch, scandalous and poor') but also that he is unable to perform. The King's current mistress, Louise de Keroualle, Duchess of Portsmouth (who had since 1671 displaced Barbara Villiers) cannot solve the problem. Even the actress Nell Gwyn's 'pains' to rouse the King's 'dull, graceless bollocks' are exposed to all: '. . . she employs hands, fingers, mouth, and thighs, / Ere she can raise the member she enjoys.' The poem ends with a straightforward attack, carrying more than a whiff of republicanism, making the libertine Rochester a strange political bedfellow to the relentlessly moral Milton: 'All monarchs I hate, and the thrones they sit on, / From the hector of France to the cully of Britain.' It was not the ideal poem to hand to one's monarch, and the result was Rochester's hasty exit from the court.

A quick stroll around the relevant room of the National Portrait Gallery in London takes the viewer into this world. The portraits are both luscious and shocking. There is Nell Gwyn, the actress and mistress to Charles II, with her nipple showing. There is Barbara Villiers, perhaps the most powerful mistress of the King, who bore him five children, portrayed, astonishingly, blasphemously, as the Virgin Mary, with one of her illegitimate children shown as Jesus.

Whitehall, where John Milton had served Cromwell and his changing governments, was of course transformed to meet the needs of this very different regime. The Duchess of Portsmouth had her lodgings torn down and rebuilt three times before they satisfied her. As Pepys put it succinctly, 'In fine, I find that there is nothing almost but bawdry at Court from top to bottom.' This did not stop him being fascinated with the sexual politics there, nor did it stop him dreaming of the gorgeous Barbara Villiers in August 1665. It was, as he put it, a comforting dream in this plague-time.[40]

As Rochester's poem makes clear, the King's sexual practices were not just a private matter. Indeed, in 1669 and 1670, the issue of his inability to produce a legitimate male heir became the subject of very public debate and provided opponents of Charles's rule with a vivid example of what was seen as his tendency towards absolutism. The King took a personal interest in the progress of a notorious divorce case between Lord and Lady Ross.[41] It is just possible that John Milton himself was consulted on the matter, for once seen as a useful ally to the crown because of his divorce pamphlets, but there is no evidence that he offered any advice in the case.[42]

It was common knowledge, however, that the King did not care about the Ross divorce case in and of itself. It only mattered as a trial run for Charles himself, who was being prompted, by some, to divorce his wife, Catherine of Braganza. The talk had been prompted by Catherine's miscarriage in 1669. Her failure to produce an heir, allied to her Catholicism, meant that many advocated the bringing in of a Protestant baby-maker. Charles's position remained unclear, but the murmurings went on. Andrew Marvell, for one, was worried, noting in a letter to his nephew that Charles had 'said in public, he knew not why a Woman might not be divorced for barrenness, as a Man for Impotency'.[43]

Marvell went on to write that he had witnessed the results of King Charles's personal involvement. In an extraordinary move the King

about ten a Clock took boat, with Lauderdale only, and two ordinary attendants, and rowed awhile as towards the Bridge, but soon turned back to the Parliament Stairs, and so went up into the House of Lords, and took his Seat. Almost all of them were amazed, but all seemed so; and the Duke of York especially was very much surprised.

As well they might be. Marvell was pretty sure that the King was there to ensure the progress of the Ross divorce. Charles himself found it all rather amusing, or so he said to justify his continued attendance in the House: '. . . the King has ever since continued his Session among them, and says it is better than going to a Play,' reported Marvell in the same letter to his nephew.

All this served to tarnish the image of the monarchy, but if his subjects had known as much about Charles's religious persuasions as they did about his sexual practices, then the situation would have been far worse. Because, in a secret treaty with the French signed on 22 May 1670, he agreed to declare his conversion to Catholicism, and to restore Catholicism to Britain.[44] Even without the knowledge of this treaty there was continued religious unrest, most notably in London. The threat to the City came not from the almost traditional rioting of apprentices on their holidays but from the coming together of those opposed to the State Church. These 'Conventicles' worried not just the government but also the City authorities:

> To say truth, they meet in numerous open Assemblies, without any dread of Government. But the Trained Bands in the City, and Soldiery in Southwark and Suburbs, harassed and abused them continually; they wounded many, and killed some Quakers, especially while they took all patiently.[45]

Such was life in the City of London in the late 1660s.

Yet, although Andrew Marvell recognised this and all the other problems in the country, he nevertheless wrote to his nephew as follows in the spring of 1670:

> It is also my Opinion that the King was never since his coming in, nay, all things considered, no King since the Conquest, so absolutely powerful at home, as he is at present. Nor any Parliament, or Places, so certainly and constantly supplied with Men of the same Temper. In such a Conjuncture, dear Will, what probability is there of my doing any Thing to the Purpose?[46]

If Marvell was struggling to find a way to do 'any Thing to the Purpose' in this climate, then how much more difficult was it for John Milton? What could he do from his modest house in Artillery Walk? It even appears that Milton sold his library off prior to moving to this house with his third wife. This seems a remarkable move for a man who loved books so intensely. Toland, one of Milton's earliest biographers, thought he took this step because the books would be no use to his heirs, and he would get a good price for them at this time. Both reasons sound (rather depressingly) plausible. That Milton had no sons, that he needed the money, does not completely explain the step, however. Is there something of a farewell to all that in the dispersal of his library, something of a blind man's acceptance of the futility of owning such a library?

Milton's only publication from these years, apart from the continued reprinting of *Paradise Lost* (two further impressions appeared in 1669) seems, at first sight, to illustrate this withdrawal from the public arena. Published in June 1669, it went under the seemingly unprepossessing title of *Accidence Commenc't Grammar Supply'd with sufficient rules, For the use of such as, Younger or Elder, are desirous, without more trouble then needs, to attain the Latin Tongue; the elder sort especially, with little teaching, and their own industry.* The work was published by Samuel Simmons, the publisher of *Paradise Lost,* and could be found by the 'elder sort' who wanted to learn Latin 'without more trouble than needs', and who had the 8d to buy it, at Simmons's shop next door to the Golden Lion in Aldersgate Street. The aim of this pocket textbook, probably put together from materials first prepared twenty years earlier, was to speed up the whole process of learning Latin: it was possible in one year, not seven. Milton was reaching out to those who had missed an education in Latin through the exigencies of life and now wanted to educate themselves. *Accidence Commenc't Grammar* is thus similar in its aims to *Paradise Lost*: it is all part of the education of a nation, allowing access to what was traditionally the sphere of the élite. All this is true, but, bluntly, this Latin primer is a somewhat bathetic contribution to the cause.

As is so often the case in Milton's life, however, there is calm before the storm. The selling of his books, the house move, the departure of his daughters: none of these events meant that he would remain silent. In 1670, he realised that for all his hopes that *Paradise Lost* would be 'exemplary to a nation' (his phrase from over twenty years earlier), that his work would justify the ways of God to man, and encourage a new commonwealth of peace and love, the grim reality was a further dangerous slide towards Royal absolutism and religious intolerance. In another characteristic step, Milton had already prepared work for this moment: three very different works in fact. One was a brief epic of four books, a sequel as it were to *Paradise Lost,* called *Paradise Regained.* The second was his *History of Britain.* The third was a drama, but unlike any drama being seen on the London stage: *Samson Agonistes. Paradise Regained*, certainly, and *Samson Agonistes*, probably, were written some years before their publication, although Milton may have been revising them right up to printing. Thomas Ellwood described how he visited Milton in Chalfont St Giles, was shown *Paradise Lost* and had the temerity to ask whether his master had considered writing a sequel:

> He asked me how I liked it, and what I thought of it, which I modestly but freely told him: and after some further Discourse about it, I pleasantly said to him, Thou has said much here of *Paradise lost*, but what hast thou to say of *Paradise found*? He made me no answer, but sat some time in a muse; then brake [broke] off that discourse, and fell upon another subject.[47]

Once the plague had abated, and Milton had returned to London, he met up with Ellwood sometime early in 1666 and showed him *Paradise Regained*. Milton, recounted Ellwood, 'in a pleasant tone said to me, *This is owing to you: for you put it into my head, by the question you put to me at Chalfont; which before I had not thought of*'. If Ellwood's story is genuine, the four books of *Paradise Regained* were completed in just a few months, and before the publication of *Paradise Lost*.[48]

With all three works completed, Milton was once again faced with the barrier of censorship. It was a matter of finding the right moment.

NINETEEN

RESURGENCE

1671

MILTON FOUND AND SEIZED his moment. These three works were prepared for the press in the autumn of 1670, having been licensed in the summer. The *History of Britain* appeared in November 1670, and *Paradise Regained* and *Samson Agonistes* came out in a joint edition in the months that followed. All three spoke powerfully to the times.

The title of *Paradise Regained* marks it out clearly as the sequel to *Paradise Lost*. Milton's new poem offered another story of temptation, of the Son of God by Satan. This time, however, Satan fails. The eloquent opening lines, with all of Milton's trademark qualities of epic invocation, authorial self-consciousness, inverted syntax and suspended clauses, culminates in the simple statement of belief that 'one man' undid the work of the Fall, that 'one man' will raise Eden again in the 'waste wilderness':

> I who erewhile the happy garden sung,
> By one man's disobedience lost, now sing
> Recovered Paradise to all mankind,
> By one man's firm obedience fully tried
> Through all temptation, and the tempter foiled
> In all his wiles, defeated and repulsed,
> And Eden raised in the waste wilderness.
>
> (I:1–7)

In *Paradise Regained*, Satan offers a series of temptations to the Son of God, who has retreated to the wilderness after his baptism by his

PARADISE REGAIN'D.

A POEM.

In IV BOOKS.

To which is added

SAMSON AGONISTES.

The Author

mary   *pills*

JOHN MILTON.

LONDON,

Printed by *J. M.* for *John Starkey* at the
Mitre in *Fleetstreet*, near *Temple-Bar.*
MDCLXXI.

cousin John. The Son will refuse all of them. The poem could be merely a succession of moments in which the Son says 'no', but, in a significant development of his biblical sources (primarily the Gospels of Matthew and Luke), Milton links Satan's temptations with the revelation of the Son's true status and destiny.

Satan certainly does not fully comprehend who he is dealing with. He only sees that the Son is 'unfriended, low of birth'. He tells his followers in hell, still ready to take his lead, that 'Who this is we must learn, for man he seems . . .' Moreover, the Son himself remains unaware of the way in which he will fulfil his redemptive purpose, how he will indeed restore Eden. Thus the poem as a whole not only celebrates 'one man's firm obedience' fully tried but shows how the trial of that obedience enables the Son to understand fully his own role in humanity's redemption.

To make the contest more real, the Son is fully human. He undergoes his temptations as a man, without any divine powers, experiencing hunger and cold, unaware at first even that the temptations are going to happen. Having endured Satan's attempts, the poem ends by saying simply, '. . . he unobserved / Home to his mother's house private returned.' Yet as he does so, this private man is being glorified by the angels in heaven as the 'Queller of Satan'. In each of his three great late works, Milton moves towards a profound simplicity of language, all the more compelling in its contrast with the often challenging complexities, of language and viewpoint, that have come before.

This is true of *Paradise Regained*, in which the quiet dignity of the Son's closing actions completes the reader's journey away from Satan's psyche. As he had done in *Paradise Lost*, Milton allows Satan a complex and compelling psychological realism, and, as in the earlier epic, he takes risks in doing so. One of the achievements of *Paradise Regained* is that the reader sees the Son of God through Satan's eyes. Satan simply does not understand, cannot begin to comprehend, what the Son is, and what he will do to redeem humankind. In Satan's view, God the Father is just another ambitious parent: '. . . what will he not do to advance his son?' Satan is equally confused and then enraged by the Son's resistance to temptations, whether of money or power, food or learning.

Milton makes sure that Satan does his very best, adding in a new, non-biblical temptation. Satan creates a glorious banquet to tempt the Son, 'A table richly spread, in regal mode'. But it is not just the food that entices, it is the company.

> And at a stately sideboard by the wine
> That fragrant smell diffused, in order stood
> Tall stripling youths rich-clad, of fairer hue
> Than Ganymede or Hylas . . .
>
> (II:350–53)

These 'stripling youths', more lovely than even the archetypal objects of desire in Classical myth, are there to tempt the Son. Milton has set it up beautifully. Earlier in Book II, Satan had been getting advice from his fellow-devils. Belial, 'the dissolutest spirit that fell', had a plan: 'Set women in his eye and in his walk.' Satan was dismissive, pointing out that just because Belial and his followers cast 'wanton eyes on the daughters of men' as they lurk 'in courts and regal chambers', it did not mean that the Son would fall to the 'assaults' of beauty. Satan suggested that the Son was interested in higher things than women, but when he actually got around to the banquet temptation, he had obviously decided that offering young boys was worth a try. Sadly for Satan, the Son remains unmoved by both the regal banquet and the decorative young men.

When the Son rejects even glory, Satan is silenced, suddenly aware of his own failings.

> So spake the Son of God; and here again
> Satan had not to answer, but stood struck
> With guilt of his own sin, for he himself
> Insatiable of glory had lost all,
> Yet of another plea bethought him soon.
>
> (III:145–9)

As Milton indicates in that final line, Satan is not silent for long. He presses on, knowing that he will fail, knowing that he will suffer from this son of Eve, but rationalising his struggle with a desperate, empty courage:

> Let that come when it comes; all hope is lost
> Of my reception into grace; what worse?
> For where no hope is left, is left no fear;
> If there be worse, the expectation more
> Of worse torments me than the feeling can.
> I would be at the worst; worst is my port,
> My harbour and my ultimate repose,
> The end I would attain, my final good.
> My error was my error, and my crime
> My crime . . .
>
> (III:204–13)

Satan cannot stop. He is compared to a swarm of flies, to waves crashing against a solid rock. He is driven on not by hope of the Son relenting but by an overwhelming desire to understand the nature of the entity he is seeking to corrupt. Even the title 'Son of God'

> bears no single sense;
> The Son of God I also am, or was,
> And if I was, I am; relation stands;
> All men are Sons of God.
>
> (IV:517–20)

So Satan's final, strange temptation is part of his attempt to get the Son to reveal his identity. He takes the Son to a high pinnacle. He expects him to fall and thus for his divine status to be revealed when angels rush to his rescue. But Milton's Son has a surprise for Satan and for the reader: 'Also it is written, / Tempt not the Lord thy God, he said and stood.' (IV: 560–61)

The simple words 'and stood' have perplexed and excited critics over the years: one has only to glance at an annotated edition of

Paradise Regained to get a flavour of the theological debates surrounding the phrase. While the Son's ability to stand firm is, in literary and spiritual terms, the culmination of his resolute defiance of everything that Satan can throw at him, the reader is left with a mystery. How and why does the Son stand? Perhaps it is not necessary for the poem to explain that he 'stood'. The reader needs only to be assured that he does.

The paradox at the heart of Christian belief runs through the poem, articulated most clearly by God himself, although with some characteristically Miltonic additions. The Son raised by 'merit' (in Milton's heterodox theology at least) will conquer Sin and Death 'by humiliation and strong sufferance': 'His weakness shall o'ercome Satanic strength.' This is something that the Son himself is still unclear about at the start of the poem, at least when he looks back at his own youth. Then he dreamt of being a great hero, rescuing Israel from its Roman oppressors, bringing down tyrannical power, 'till truth were freed, and equity restored'. Now, however, he recognises that it is more humane and more heavenly 'By winning words to conquer willing hearts / And make persuasion do the work of fear'.

The Son's thoughts about how best to restore Eden exemplify the political thinking of *Paradise Regained*. At first, the message seems uncomplicated. Unsurprisingly, given that the author is John Milton, courts and monarchies are presented as places of corruption and tyranny. The sons of Belial lurk in 'courts and regal chambers', Satan attempts his second temptation dressed as a courtier and offers the hungry Son 'a table richly spread, in regal mode'. But what should the Son, what should those who suffer the oppression of tyranny, do in response?

Milton refocuses the question. The Son does not seek an earthly sceptre. Instead he offers another model of kingship, the man who 'reigns within himself, and rules / Passions, desires, and fears'. Yet, as Satan knows full well, it has been prophesied that the Son will liberate the Jewish people, and *Paradise Regained* cannot simply dismiss earthly politics. Satan taunts the Son with this prophecy, suggesting that he is hardly going to free Judea 'by sitting still'. The Son, however, continues to refuse to engage with human military or political solutions, arguing that God will fulfil his promises in his own way and in his own time: 'All things are best fulfilled in their due time, / And time there is for all things.'

Above all, he reveals to Satan that he will deliver all humankind through his own personal suffering, through 'tribulations, injuries, insults, / Contempts, and scorns, and snares, and violence'. These are the deeds 'above heroic' with which the Son will redeem men and women. The contempt and scorn will ultimately contribute to a triumphant outcome. As the Son reminds Satan pointedly, 'my rising is your fall.'

This emphasis on the individual's responsibility to 'reign within himself' and to leave the politics, the violence and the revenge to God is utterly traditional Christian thinking, and precisely the kind of argument that Milton had eloquently overturned in order to justify the active removal of the man he saw as a corrupt tyrant, Charles I. Now, twenty years later, Milton appears to have been returning to a far more conservative view of matters. It is, however, a complicated conservatism.

Satan, demonstrating some of his old cunning, shows the Son a vision of corruption and tyranny in Rome. The Son could expel the dictator there and rule himself. Surely that would be better than letting tyranny flourish? The Son, however, has a tough-minded response. He launches a stinging attack on the Roman Empire and its people, once victorious, 'now vile and base'. They are 'deservedly made vassal', having given up their 'frugal, and mild, and temperate' lifestyles, and succumbed to the temptations of empire, governing

> ill the nations under yoke,
> Peeling their provinces, exhausted all
> By lust and rapine.
>
> (IV:135–7)

The Son makes absolutely clear that the Roman people have brought their political degradation upon themselves through their own moral degeneracy: 'Degenerate, by themselves enslaved, / Or could of inward slaves make outward free'. (IV:144–5) There is nothing for the Son to do, nothing he *should* do, until and unless the Roman people shake off their inner slavery. If applied to John Milton's England, these passages confirm the views so often expressed by him that the revolution had failed because the English people were 'inward slaves', unwilling and unable to sustain their own liberty. What is left unclear is whether it would *ever* be possible to sustain political and religious freedom. Would the English always slide back into being 'vassals', or were they capable of throwing off their slavery?

Paradise Regained's companion piece, *Samson Agonistes*, raises similar questions and offers some provocative answers. Milton retells the story of Samson and his treacherous wife, Delilah, from the Book of Judges in the Old Testament. Tricked by Delilah into revealing the source of his strength, his hair, the blind Israelite Samson eventually wreaks terrible revenge upon his Philistine oppressor. The imprisoned Samson is asked to entertain the Philistines with his great strength at a 'solemn feast', with 'sacrifices, triumph, pomp and games'. Although he refuses at first, he changes his mind, for reasons that remain deliberately obscure in *Samson Agonistes*. Once at the 'games', Samson regains his God-given strength, lost to him through the betrayal of Delilah:

> Straining all his nerves he bowed,
> As with the force of winds and waters pent,
> When mountains tremble, those two massy pillars
> With horrible convulsion to and fro
> He tugged, he shook, till down they came and drew
> The whole roof after them, with burst of thunder
> Upon the heads of all who sat beneath,
> Lords, ladies, captains, counsellors, or priests,
> Their choice nobility and flower, not only
> Of this but each Philistian city round
> Met from all parts to solemnize this feast.
> Samson with these immixed, inevitably

Pulled down the same destruction on himself;
The vulgar only scaped who stood without.

(ll. 1646–59)

It is no wonder that in recent years, *Samson Agonistes* has been described, controversially, as 'a work in praise of terrorism'.[1] The destruction of the temple is a carefully targeted terrorist atrocity in which Samson loses his own life.

Milton interestingly added the non-biblical detail that it was only the leaders of Philistine society, the 'lords, ladies, captains, counsellors' and 'priests', who were killed. The ordinary people, the 'vulgar', escape the violence, but these nuances are lost on Samson's supporters within the drama. All they feel is uncomplicated delight. 'O dearly-bought revenge, yet glorious!' they cry, insisting that Samson has 'fulfilled' his God-given 'work for which thou was foretold'. Samson's own father, who until this point has been looking for ways to free his son from imprisonment and get him home, is now equally joyous. His son is a hero.

Come, come, no time for lamentation now,
Nor much more cause, Samson hath quit himself
Like Samson, and heroicly hath finished
A life heroic, on his enemies
Fully revenged, hath left them years of mourning,
And lamentation to the sons of Caphtor
Through all Philistian bounds.

(ll. 1708–14)

Earlier, the Chorus, members of Samson's tribe, had spelled out the two options available to those who suffer from political oppression. The Chorus believed that God would enable the violent overthrow of their enemies:

O how comely it is and how reviving
To the spirits of just men long oppressed!

> When God into the hands of their deliverer
> Puts invincible might
> To quell the mighty of the earth, the oppressor.
>
> (ll. 1268–72)

But God also gives people 'patience' and may send the oppressor as a 'trial' of the people's 'fortitude'. In these cases, each individual is responsible for accepting their subjugation and maintaining their own inner freedom, 'making them each his own deliverer'.

It is this latter model that Samson struggles with in the earlier part of the drama, working painfully to achieve a patient acceptance of his bondage and humiliation. 'Eyeless in Gaza' he begins the drama in spiritual and actual darkness: 'O dark, dark, dark, amid the blaze of noon'. He is struggling psychologically: Samson can find 'ease to the body some, none to the mind / From restless thoughts'. Torments find 'secret passage' to the 'inmost mind', grief creates wounds that 'rankle, and fester, and gangrene'. As his friends tell him, 'Thou art become (O worst imprisonment!) / The dungeon of thyself.'

To dramatise Samson's struggle, both physical and mental, Milton adopts a sometimes knotty syntax, often using Latinate constructions which place the verb at the end of the phrase, packing words against each other. There is little space for lyricism. As the scholar Sharon Achinstein points out, *Samson Agonistes* imitates 'the rhythms and shapes of Hebrew poetry', resisting the neatness and conclusiveness of the fashionable heroic couplet.[2] Instead, he creates a claustrophobic and dense prosody, entirely fitting for its subject:

> Light the prime work of God to me is extinct,
> And all her various objects of delight
> Annulled, which might in part my grief have eased,
> Inferior to the vilest now become
> Of man or worm; the vilest here excel me,
> They creep, yet see, I dark in light exposed
> To daily fraud, contempt, abuse and wrong,

Within doors, or without, still as a fool,
In power of others, never in my own;
Scarce half I seem to live, dead more than half.
                              (ll. 70–79)[3]

Samson learns, slowly and unevenly, of his own culpability in his fall:
'Sole author I, sole cause'. He may have had great physical strength,
but he did not use it wisely. Over the course of the drama, he moves
beyond despair (death will be the 'welcome end' of all his pains) and
anger ('I was his nursling once' but God 'hath cast me off as never
known') to eventual action. He becomes worthy again of being God's
freedom fighter, or so Milton's drama suggests.

An important part of this process is Samson's bitter rejection of his
wife, Delilah, by whom he has been 'effeminately vanquished'. As
Samson's father, Manoa, points out, it had never been a good idea to
marry a Philistine, but Samson had been determined, believing himself
to be directed by God and having a crafty political plan besides, as
Manoa reminds him:

I cannot approve thy marriage-choices, son,
Rather approved them not; but thou didst plead
Divine impulsion prompting how thou might'st
Find some occasion to infest our foes.
                              (ll. 420–23)

Now he is imprisoned in Gaza, Delilah returns to visit her husband,
offering to intercede on his behalf with the Philistine lords, and
proposing a nice, quiet, domestic life with her away from a world
in which he needs his eyes:

At home in leisure and domestic ease,
Exempt from many a care and chance to which
Eyesight exposes daily men abroad.
                              (ll. 917–19)

To regain his masculinity, his power, Samson must reject her 'foul effeminacy', which he does, and viciously. The drama as a whole is equally harsh towards Delilah. The Chorus is particularly misogynist, extrapolating her failings to all women, just as all women in the seventeenth century were tarred with the brush of Eve. God spent too much time on the outward features of women; their 'inward gifts' were left unfinished; they lack 'judgement', are full of 'self-love', incapable of constancy – 'that either they love nothing, or not long', argues the Chorus.

Milton does something rather subtle here. Delilah proves to be quite happy with these kinds of generalisations about women. In her attempts to appease Samson, she claims that everything she did was done because she is weak, as all women are. She is simply demonstrating 'a woman's frailty'. It is, however, a pose. Once rejected, she spits out the truth. She knows she has a bad press in Judah, but

> in my country where I most desire,
> In Ecron, Gaza, Asdod, and in Gath
> I shall be named among the famousest
> Of women.
>
> (ll. 980–83)

On one level, Milton is tackling the political implications of having an idolatrous marriage partner (as Charles I had had in Henrietta Maria, and as Charles II currently had in Catherine of Braganza), and suggesting that the best thing would be to cast off this dangerous connection. To read Delilah's portrayal merely as political allegory is, however, to soften its harshness: Samson may not be Milton, but the misogyny of *Samson Agonistes* does belong to its author. There is a wider issue, however. The problem with Samson and Delilah is 'in the end their loyalties to different cultures, different nations, and religions'. Delilah should have left 'parents and country', says Samson at her marriage to him, and the drama supports that view.[4]

At first sight, therefore, *Samson Agonistes* might seem the exact opposite to *Paradise Regained,* a bloodthirsty rallying cry to the oppressed who can be inspired by Samson's example to acts of heroic, godly violence against their enemies. All this, seasoned with a dash of politically fuelled misogyny. Samson himself explicitly justifies the use of force to a Philistine visitor:

> My nation was subjected to your lords.
> It was the force of conquest; force with force
> Is well ejected when the conquered can.
>
> (ll. 1205–7)

This is resistance theory in the name of God. Samson does not fight as a private man, but as God's soldier.

> I was no private but a person raised
> With strength sufficient and command from heaven
> To free my country . . .
>
> (ll. 1211–13)

The Chorus ends *Samson Agonistes* insisting both that God has born 'witness gloriously: whence Gaza mourns' and that God's servants will learn from Samson's story, from 'this great event', and end 'calm of mind, all passion spent'.

Yet Milton asks his reader to be more wary of events within the drama than the characters are. The characters are living within the time frame of the story: Samson, for example, believes that he is part of a battle *between* gods, between the God of Israel and Dagon, the God of the Philistines. The reader, however, is asked to place Samson's moment of revenge within a much longer narrative of Israel's captivity. The reader is also asked to resist any easy conflation of John Milton and Samson, both blind, both defeated: yes, there may be parallels, but overall the drama places Samson's experiences within a larger understanding of human history.

To this end, Milton develops various elements of his Old Testament story. He makes Samson a lone, unacknowledged sufferer, unsupported by his country, which delivers him up to its enemies. The people of Judah had their opportunity, provided by Samson, but by their 'vices' they have been brought 'to servitude'; they 'love bondage more than liberty'; would rather have 'bondage with ease than strenuous liberty'. For this weakness, Israel deserves to be punished, 'whence to this day they serve'. Above all, Samson's violence does not free Israel. As Samson's father says,

> To Israel
> Honour hath left, and freedom, let but them
> Find courage to lay hold on this occasion.
>   (ll. 1714–16)

Here the parallels with the English revolution seem clearest. Necessary acts of violence may start the liberation process, but a nation needs courage to continue and perpetuate liberty. Israel, in the event, did not have that courage. Nor did the English.

This is a challenging and provocative message, and the form of *Samson Agonistes* matches its message. In an era when the theatre had exploded back into action with a multitude of sophisticated (and less sophisticated) sex comedies, performed by both men and women actors, Milton chose to write a play designed specifically to be *read* in the privacy of one's own home. The chosen form of *Paradise Regained*, a brief epic on a biblical theme written in austere blank verse, was equally out of step with contemporary poetic movements. Surrounded by the shocking literary antics of men such as the Earl of Rochester and the elegant, ambivalent rhyming verse of his old friend Andrew Marvell, John Milton's stark and passionate poetry emphasises his separation from what had become mainstream culture.

The third work to appear in 1670, the *History of Britain*, is much less well known than *Paradise Regained* and *Samson Agonistes* but was the most obvious candidate for censorship at the time, and its publication ensured that Milton remained a notorious figure. The writing of history in seventeenth-century England was never a neutral act. Not only did individuals justify their actions, however radical or conservative, with an appeal to history, but history was used to call readers to

action in the present. When Milton offered a history that he had
begun in the earliest months of the republic back in 1649, the censors
as expected decided that 'some passages' were 'too sharp against the
clergy': they interpreted Milton's critique of 'Popish Monks in Saxon
Times' as a direct criticism of Charles II's own bishops. It seems likely
that one section, a 'Digression' of 2,500 words, was cut out completely.[5]

The *History*, as much as *Paradise Lost* and the still notorious tracts
from the 1640s and 1650s, ensured that Milton remained a well-
known figure, and not just in England. Even those who did not agree
with his views had to admit that he could write well ('a very good
advocate for a very bad cause'). Old controversies kept simmering
away: a work by John Eachard went into its eighth edition in 1672,
reminding readers that Milton being 'a little tormented with an ill
chosen wife, set for the Doctrine of Divorce'.[6]

Despite or perhaps because of his difference from his literary
contemporaries, Milton was becoming something of a literary celebrity in the wake of *Paradise Lost*. John Dryden, appointed Poet
Laureate by the King in 1668, came to visit him a few years later.
Dryden was first in a long line of poets who were rather daunted by
Milton: this man, he wrote, 'cuts us all out, and the ancients too'.[7] This
did not stop Dryden continuing work on his imitation of *Paradise Lost*,
Milton's epic transformed into rhyming couplets for easier digestion
in the form of an opera. Here, for example, is Lucifer opening the
opera:

> These regions and this realm my wars have got;
> This mournful empire is the loser's lot:
> In liquid burnings or in dry to dwell,
> Is all the sad variety of hell.
>
> (I, i, 3–6)[8]

The opera, which was in fact never acted on stage (perhaps because of
the nudity of the 'human pair') but which was extremely popular in its
printed editions, was intended for the marriage festivities of King

Charles's Catholic brother, James, Duke of York in 1673.[9] One hopes that Milton savoured the irony.

Dryden's rewriting of *Paradise Lost* merely served to emphasise how far outside the literary establishment Milton stood. This may not have been a great loss for him, because the late 1660s and early 1670s were characterised by a viciousness and pettiness startling even by the usually low standards of the book world. The Earl of Rochester and Dryden engaged in a literary spat that can be tracked through plays such as *Marriage à-la-mode*, poems such as 'An Allusion to Horace', and again in the theatre, in *All for Love*. Dryden was also attacked in the play *The Rehearsal* (which appeared anonymously but was almost definitely written by George Villiers, 2nd Duke of Buckingham), while a few years later the attacks took physical form when the playwright was seriously assaulted by a group of thugs in Rose Alley, which runs behind the Lamb and Flag in Covent Garden, in revenge for *An Essay upon Satire*, in which various prominent figures (including the King, his mistresses and the Earl of Rochester) were crudely vilified. As luck would have it, the *Essay* had probably not even been written by Dryden.

Milton was separate from this court coterie, but the appearance of three works in 1670 signalled not merely that he still had a political and literary voice but that the City of London and its publishing industry were recovering from the depredations of plague and fire. London's population would double between 1650 and 1700, with a concomitant increase in readers for the books and pamphlets once again streaming from the city's printing presses.

The London publishing trade started to fight back in the last years of the 1660s. Book-sellers moved to the area north of St Paul's, between Smithfield Market and Aldersgate Street, still known as Little Britain.[10] One shop, Thomas Helder's, is advertised on the 1669 issues of the ten-book *Paradise Lost*. By 1670, the recovery in trade was complete, and 'a younger generation had begun to replace the dead and the bankrupt, and many of these returned to the traditional medieval centre of the trade, in St Paul's Churchyard.'[11]

Bookshops were designed to be pleasant places to visit in this new commercial world. Samuel Pepys, as ever, provides first-hand evidence of the pleasures of book-buying in his diary entry for 10 December 1663:

> Thence to St Paul's Churchyard to my booksellers; and having gained this day in the office, by my stationer's bill to the King, about forty shillings or three pounds, I did here sit two or three hours, calling for twenty books to lay this money out upon; and found myself at a great loss where to choose, and do see how my nature would gladly return to the laying out of money in this trade.[12]

A year later he was back at his book-sellers, again with money in his pocket. He 'spoke for several books against New Year's day', spending £7 or £8, and also found time to order some plate, spoons and forks. Another time, he headed for 'Paul's churchyard to treat with a bookbinder to come and gild the backs of all my books to make them handsome, to stand in my new presses when they come'. Pepys's progress vividly indicates the way in which book-buying was becoming another form of conspicuous consumption in a culture in which the look of the book was as important as its content.

James Allestry was Milton's printer/book-seller in 1670 (although he died only two days after the publication of the *History of Britain*), and his house expressed the wealth he had built up from the book trade. He had a 'Green Room' decorated with hangings with 'gilt scales', a 'blue Chamber', and a dining room decorated with pictures, printed hangings and gilt stars, and furnished with a Spanish table, leather carpets and eight chairs. His shop was equally well furnished, using arches to divide up the space. Allestry intended his shop as 'a meeting place for prospective authors, prestigious customers or influential members of the Royal Society (which Allestry served in an official capacity as Printer), and as a place where business deals could be negotiated'.[13]

John Milton was absolutely at the heart of this world as an author, advertised in the new catalogues offered by book-sellers to their public. In May 1671, readers were offered *Paradise Regained* and *Samson Agonistes* as well as *Tetrachordon* (one of the divorce tracts from the 1640s) and Milton's recent venture into adult education, *Accidence Commenc't Grammar.* As John Beale wrote to his friend John Evelyn on 24 December 1670, Milton was 'now abroad again, in prose and in verse, epic and dramatic'.

Around him, however, the country seemed to lurch from crisis to crisis, all sense of direction lost. Charles II sank to a new low in popularity when his treaty with France was eventually made public in December 1670. He would have been even less popular if the secret clause in which the King admitted his conversion to Catholicism had been known. For a while, the treaty seemed to offer new hope for toleration, both of Roman Catholics (perhaps unsurprising, given the King's sympathies) and of Nonconformists. Eventually, in March 1672, a Declaration of Indulgence for Catholics and Nonconformists was announced. At the same time, the country renewed its war with Holland. Again the English would be defeated in battle, and only a year after the Declaration of Indulgence, Parliament would push through a Test Act that reversed the previous small steps towards toleration, excluding all those who were not members of the Church of England from holding public office.

The King's position was beginning to look precarious. His own brother, James, Lord High Admiral, admitted that he was a Roman Catholic and thus, under the terms of the Test Act, was deemed not fit for office. Public hostility to the Anglo-French alliance, seen as a pretext for the establishment of Catholicism in England, reached a new peak. Pamphlets of the time linked France, Popery and Tyranny in a terrifying trinity.[14] Like the Earl of Clarendon before him, James, Duke of York had to be sacrificed to protect the King. He resigned from office in June and then married a Catholic princess in September 1673, in a confirmation of his people's worst fears. James was succeeded as naval commander by Prince Rupert, the old Royalist Civil War commander. Rupert was equally unsuccessful in his military efforts but blamed factions at court and the King's interference for his defeat. When even Rupert moved into opposition to the Stuart monarchy, if not monarchy itself, then things were certainly serious. (His sister Sophia, married to the Protestant Elector of Hanover, would be the mother of the future George I.) The political crisis showed no signs of abating, with stormy parliamentary sessions in the autumn and winter of 1673 and 1674 seeking to limit the power of any future Catholic monarch, and the eventual brokering of the Treaty of Westminster with the Dutch in February 1674.

John Milton's one new work from this period was the tract *Of True Religion*, published in 1673.[15] It was his last original prose work. The title page was soberly functional but also packed with eye-catching terms of which POPERY was the most boldly capitalised. *Of True Religion* states Milton's basic commitment to free speech and tolerance in religion. This short tract has been seen by critics as one of his most accomplished performances in prose, both politically canny and emotionally calm, a work seeking for consensus, demonstrating, according to the Milton scholar Martin Dzelzainis, 'a renewed and even enhanced ability to match his rhetoric to political realities'. Yet, 'to judge from the lack of response at the time . . . [it] might as well never have been published.'[16]

Why did it not have any impact? Dzelzainis offers an intriguing answer. At a time when there were some very strange alliances being formed, for example between committed Catholics such as the Earl of Castlemaine (husband to Charles II's mistress Barbara Villiers) and Nonconformists, who, Castlemaine claimed, at least looked on Catholics 'as Englishmen, and would not have us persecuted for religion', there were some figures who remained beyond the pale. John Milton was one of those figures, and Castlemaine for one showed unremitting hostility towards him. Milton's previous track record, in politics and religion, could not be forgotten. 'The somewhat depressing conclusion,' writes Dzelzainis, 'is that however much ingenuity Milton expended in contriving formulas that were acceptable to many and offensive to few, there was in truth no form of words which would allow him to break through the bonds of his own reputation.' The manner in which his name was invoked at this period suggested that he had assumed an iconic status that got in the way of anything he might still have to say.

If the image of Milton the Divorcer and Milton the Regicide cast the longest shadows in these years of restored monarchy, another image refused to fade: Milton the Sodomite. When Richard Leigh launched a sustained, detailed and vituperative attack on Andrew Marvell, focusing on Marvell's sexuality, Milton was caught in the cross-fire.[17] Leigh's *The Transproser Rehears'd* (1673) makes allegations about the homosexual activities of 'Nol's Latin Pay two clerks' – that is, Oliver Cromwell's Latin secretaries, Milton and Marvell. Marvell is a 'gelding', Milton a 'stallion', and both are 'turn'd pure Italian' (the latter shorthand for sexual perversion). The issue, of course, was not whether 'Milton sodomized Marvell in the office of the Latin secretary', in the words of the scholar Paul Hammond (who suggests this is an extremely unlikely scenario), but that in the climate of the 1670s, sexual preference could be used, explicitly, to attack both men.

Yet alongside the vilification, which in the short term may have suppressed the impact of Milton's views, there existed a kind of celebrity, which in the long term would serve to neutralise, far more effectively, his powerful political and religious vision. Famous poets such as Edmund Waller and John Dryden visited Milton; bishops visited him; it was even rumoured that the King's brother, James, Duke of York, visited him. At the same time, the Crown refused a licence for the publication of his Letters of State from the 1650s.

Milton himself to some extent fuelled this growing iconic status with a series of publications that look rather like a Complete Works, if an apparently politically neutered Complete Works. In addition to the works on language and logic, resuscitated from the 1640s, he republished his 1645 poems late in 1673 with some additions. The sonnets he had written to prominent republican figures did not, however, make it into print. Although his Letters of State could not be published, his personal correspondence could be, as well as some of his Latin poetry, with *Epistolae Familiares* (Personal Letters) and *Prolusions* appearing in 1674, the 'familiar' or personal letters advertised for sale for 1s in a catalogue of May of that year. By the end of 1674, as the catalogues informed them, readers could buy a wide range of Milton's works, from his *History* to his *Samson*, from his personal letters to his Latin primer.

This process culminated in the publication of the second edition of *Paradise Lost* in 1674. The work had been transformed in appearance from its original publication seven years earlier. First, the physical size of the book had changed from a quarto to an octavo (a far more respectable format). The ten books of the original had been changed to twelve, with the simple expedient of dividing up Book VII and Book X, the two longest books from the earlier edition. *Paradise Lost* was thus now aligned with the twelve-book Classical epics it sought to surpass. The new edition cost 3s and came complete with commendatory poems from Andrew Marvell and one 'SB', probably Samuel Barrow, the court physician. There was even a frontispiece portrait.

This run of publications masked the fact that Milton was not writing anything new. A textbook on logic that appeared in May 1672, in itself a work of little originality, had been prepared perhaps thirty years earlier. It may have been a success (it was reissued the following year), but it hardly marked a new phase in Milton's writing career. With all of his major works, and many of his minor ones, in print, he had done what he could as a writer. There was no energy to do more.

The prevalent image of Milton at this time in biographies is of a triumphantly peaceful old age, of serenity rather than exhaustion. This sanitised image of a benign elderly figure, the Grand Old Man of Letters, was initiated by the early biographers: '. . . he would be cheerful even in his gout-fits and sing,' writes one commentator, or he was 'delightful company, the life of the conversation', full of 'unaffected cheerfulness and civility'.[18] Perhaps.

The reality was that Milton spent his final year in intense and increasing pain, culminating, most probably, in death from kidney failure.[19] Contemporaries described his illness as gout: if the causes of the disease are still not understood today, it is unsurprising that seventeenth-century medical thinkers struggled to explain the condition. What was well known was its agonies. Thomas Sydenham, a sufferer, described a typical episode:

The patient goes to bed and sleeps quietly till about two in the morning, when he is awakened by a pain which usually seizes the great toe, but sometimes the heel, the calf of the leg or the ankle. The pain resembles that of a dislocated bone . . . and this is immediately succeeded by a chillness, shivering and slight fever.[20]

The pain increases with every hour, becoming 'so exquisitely painful as not to endure the weight of clothes nor the shaking of the room from a person's walking briskly therein'. Then, about twenty-four hours after the onset of the attack, there is relief, the patient 'being now in a breathing sweat he falls asleep, and upon waking finds the pain much abated, and the part affected to be then swollen'.[21]

Sydenham, a medical practitioner himself, went on to suggest that some of the more violent treatments were so dangerous that 'most of those who are supposed to perish of the gout are rather destroyed by wrong management than by the disease itself.' Some of the treatments do sound unpleasant if not horrific, based as they were on purging the body, by various means, of the bad humours thought to cause the illness. Thus copious blood-letting, forced vomiting, sweating and purging were all common, supplemented by other cures such as spirits of salts – that is, hydrochloric acid – developed by a professor at Oxford, and 'puppy boiled up with cucumber, rue and juniper' (unattributed). Most commentators emphasised the importance of diet, Sydenham advocating a barley water that he referred to as his 'diet-drink'. As with almost all illnesses, moderation in diet was seen as vital but particularly so in the case of gout, where intemperate living, overindulgence, luxury and venery were condemned. Those leading this kind of sinful life would have 'hope for no health by the use of medicines'.

Set in this context, gout was a somewhat embarrassing illness for a man of ostentatiously moderate habits such as John Milton, remembered by his granddaughter (recounting the words of her mother) as very 'temperate in his eating and drinking, but what he had he always loved to have of the best'. There were, however, some psychological compensations. Gout was at least a thoroughly masculine illness, the vast majority of sufferers being men. More importantly, there existed the view, still current in the early twentieth century, that gout occurred often in 'men of such pre-eminent intellectual ability, that it is impossible not to regard it as having a real association with such ability'.[22] It was a consolation to Thomas Sydenham for one that 'kings, princes, generals, admirals, philosophers and several other great men have thus lived and died.'[23]

Gout may have been a sign of Milton's greatness, but it was excruciatingly painful, disabling and, above all, made him even more reliant on his young wife, Betty. All this exacerbated the potential humiliations of old age, particularly for a man now aged sixty-six in a society in which the elderly were viewed as returning to childhood, even to infancy in their dotage.

John's younger brother Christopher was also growing old but was protected from many of old age's challenges by wealth, status and a sense of dynasty. He had been made a Reader at the Inner Temple (the most important legal college of its time) – a great honour and the occasion of a huge feast, the rituals accompanying the post having been triumphantly re-established with the return of monarchy after some years' interruption.[24] His duties were not onerous, and Christopher could spend most of his time in Suffolk, where, in 1671, his was named as one of the gentry families. Life had been equally kind to Milton's brother-in-law Thomas Agar. By the time of his death in November 1673, he was Deputy Clerk of the Crown Office in Chancery. Agar would be succeeded in his post by one of Christopher Milton's sons, Thomas. Agar left £200 to his Royalist 'son-in-law' (what we would call a stepson) Edward Phillips but nothing to the more anti-establishment John Phillips. The Royalists in the extended Milton family were doing well for themselves, and by each other. John Milton, in contrast, remained in his small house in the heart of the City of London, his only son long dead, his daughters gone, his library sold.

TWENTY

THE CITY

1674

I T IS, HOWEVER, entirely fitting that he spent his last months in the house in Artillery Walk. A glance at a map of Milton's London shows just how drawn he was to the small quarter of the City where he had entered the world, and where he would die. Back in 1608, he had been born in Bread Street; his school, St Paul's, was his nearest grammar school, just a few yards from his home; even when he returned from the transformational journey to Italy, he only moved to lodgings in St Bride's Churchyard, at the other end of Fleet Street, less than a mile from Bread Street. His first children, and his first pamphlets, were produced in Aldersgate Street, north of St Paul's, also the home of the Simmonses, the printing family that had been so important to his writing.

Occasionally during his working life, Milton moved out to the edges of the City. His political appointment, of course, took him to White-hall, down the river, past the fashionable and much-developed Strand. It was in Scotland Yard and nearby Petty France that his first two wives died. But his home territory was the area around St Paul's. It is probable that his secret residence after the Restoration was in the warren of streets near the cathedral.[1] And, at the last, the church he would be buried in was within a few hundred yards of so many places where he had lived and worked.

It is not difficult to understand the appeal of the area to a man like Milton. While others moved out to the fashionable modern develop-ments north of the Strand, to Covent Garden or to Drury Lane, John stayed in the dense and overcrowded streets of the City and St Paul's.

For this was the London of book lovers, the very name of St Paul's shorthand for the book trade. And although almost all the houses themselves are gone, many of the small streets keep their shape, and some of the atmosphere of the City remains.

An account survives of a visit made to Milton in 1674. He lived in a small house 'but one room on a floor; in that, up one pair of stairs, which was hung with a rusty green'. There the visitor, 'an Ancient Clergy-man in Dorsetshire, Dr Wright', found Milton 'sitting in an elbow chair, black clothes and neat enough, pale but not cadaverous, his hands and fingers gouty and with chalk stones [skin swellings on the joints]. Among other discourse he expressed himself to this purpose: that was he free from the pain this gave him, his blindness would be tolerable'.[2]

He had not long to live. In November 1674, John Milton died in this small house with its rusty green wall hangings. He was a month short of his sixty-sixth birthday. Cyriack Skinner recorded that 'he died in a fit of the gout, but with so little pain or emotion, that the time of his expiring was not perceived by those in the room.'[3] If Skinner is to be believed, it was an exemplary death, communal and calm. Ideally, 'according to Christian counsel, the deathbed would be attended by ministers and friends, neighbours and kin, who would share godly comfort and bear witness to a satisfactory passing.'[4]

Most Christians believe that death is the moment when the soul departs the body, the latter merely a vehicle or encumbrance for the former. Milton believed otherwise, on the evidence at least of *Of Christian Doctrine*, which appears to support the theory of mortalism, whereby the soul dies with the body until the final resurrection. In this belief Milton was both like and unlike his most libertine contemporary, the Earl of Rochester, who also challenged the conventional understanding of death, most provocatively in his poem 'After death nothing is, and nothing, death'. For Rochester, there was nothing to fear or to hope for from death. Humans simply became the 'lumber of the world'; '. . . devouring time swallows us whole.' The compensation for this bleak vision was the fact that threats of hellfire were meaningless, 'devised by rogues, dreaded by fools'. Hell and damnation,

continued Rochester, were merely 'Senseless stories, idle tales, /
Dreams, whimseys, and no more.'

For Milton, the writer of heaven and hell, the consolation remained
the Day of Judgement, when the Son of God would 'recover Paradise
to all mankind'.

Material, rather than theological, uncertainties surrounded Milton's death. It is unclear exactly on which day he died (most likely 9
November), although it is known that he was buried on 12 November
in the church of St Giles Cripplegate, near the altar.[5] The church still
survives, in the heart of the Barbican complex. John's nephew Edward
Phillips recorded that his uncle had a 'very decent interment according
to his quality, in the church' and was 'attended from his house to the
church by several gentlemen then in town, his principal well-wishers
and admirers'. All these details – the burial in the church (rather than
in the Nonconformist burial ground nearby), the emphasis on Milton's
social 'quality' and the 'gentlemen' who attended the funeral – place
Edward's uncle in the world in which Edward himself now operated. It
was a far cry from a Nonconformist funeral. If a Dissenter had to be
buried, the body would be placed in the graveyard, which was at least
common ground. Quakers such as Thomas Ellwood went one stage
further and had their own burying grounds, and were prosecuted for
doing so. Bunhill Fields, just by Milton's last home, was one such
place, and survives to this day.

Phillips was pleased at his uncle's 'decent interment'. Indeed,
'decent' is *the* word of these decades, signifying 'appropriateness,
fitness, seemliness, order, comeliness, good taste and the avoidance
of vulgarity or excess'.[6] As such, Phillips's use of it to describe his
uncle's funeral is yet another instance of Milton's appropriation into
mainstream, élite culture, as was his burial by the altar inside a Church
of England church.

All may not be as it seems. Milton was buried with his father, who
had died in 1647 when the ministerial leadership at St Giles Cripplegate was Independent. After a number of years when the living
remained vacant, a Presbyterian was appointed in 1658, and then, in
1662, the church moved rapidly towards conformity with the new

Church of England practices, purchasing a surplice and raising money to put rails once again around the Communion table. Despite these outward signs of conformity, on the ground the experience remained less orthodox. The minister appointed by the Crown left the parish during the Great Plague and did not return. 'It looks as if the mice played whilst the cat was away,' writes Sharon Achinstein, who notes the preaching of Dissenting ministers and the appointment of a curate with leanings towards Dissent. St Giles Cripplegate 'of Milton's day was a church in flux'.[7] Despite all these caveats, however, Milton's burial inside a Church of England church jars with so much else in his life, and remains perplexing.

Phillips's account of his uncle's funeral does not mention Milton's daughters. The deathbed was traditionally the place for dying parents to give their blessing to their children. There is no indication that this occurred in the Milton household, and events shortly after John Milton's death only served to reveal the appalling rifts between his surviving family members. Betty Minshull Milton attempted to have her husband's will probated, in which she was supported by her brother-in-law Christopher Milton. The will they presented was, however, an extremely contentious document.

Their story went as follows. In July 1674, Christopher had visited his brother in London. Betty overheard her husband reminding Christopher that he was still owed the marriage portion from his first wife, and, crucially, that he wished to change his will. John was 'ill of the gout' at the time, so with the help of Christopher, a nuncupative (orally declared) will was prepared:

Brother the portion due to me from Mr Powell my former wives father I leave to the unkind children I had by her but I have received no part of it and my will and meaning is they shall have no other benefit of my estate then the said portion and what I have beside done for them, they having been very undutiful to me. And all the residue of my estate I leave to the disposal of Elizabeth my loving wife.

Crucially for Christopher's and Betty's case, John had declared 'in a very calm manner . . . without passion, that his children had been unkind to him, but that his wife had been very kind and careful of him.'

Betty's attempt to ensure that John's daughters by Mary Powell received only the money from their mother's dowry (which everyone knew had never been paid) provides the biographer with a goldmine of family information.[8] The case was, as was normal, structured around a series of questions that each witness had to answer. Suddenly, Milton's daughters emerge from the shadows of the historical record as flesh-and-blood individuals, because it was the daughters who had the right to formulate the questions that would challenge their stepmother's case. Anne, Mary and Deborah were evidently extremely suspicious of their stepmother, and sought to expose witnesses as dependent upon her and therefore more liable to support her. Moreover, they suspected a plot between her and Christopher Milton:

> Ask Mr Christopher Milton, and each other witness, whether the deceased's will, if any such was made, was not, that the deceased's wife should have £1000 and the children of the said Christopher Milton the residue; and whether she hath not promised him that they should have it, if she prevailed in this cause? Whether the said Mr Milton hath not since the deceased's death confessed to much, or some part thereof?

Christopher Milton is seen as the figure pulling the legal strings, the one who has drawn up the will, 'hath solicited this cause, and paid fees to the Proctor about it', and it is his children who will benefit if the case succeeds.

John Milton's daughters pressed witnesses to recall the precise words used by their father, and his state of mind and health at the time, asking, 'Do you not think that the deceased, if he declared any such will, declared it in a present passion, or some angry humour against some or one of his children by his former wife?' Most important, to counter the charge of unkindness (that is, unnatural behaviour) on their part, Anne, Mary and Deborah had to prove their own reputations: 'Ask each witness whether the parties ministrant were not and are not great frequenters of the Church, and good livers, and what cause of displeasure had the deceased against them?' Finally, they raised the issue of Anne's disability, implying that she deserved to be considered in her father's estate. Witnesses were asked to confirm 'whether the said Anne Milton is not lame, and almost helpless?' These are a powerful and trenchant set of questions.

Christopher Milton, of course, had his own version of events and reiterated the reasons for the nuncupative will.[9] When pressed to admit that Anne, Mary and Deborah were good church-goers, their uncle claimed to know nothing about them because they had been 'living apart from their father four or five years late past'. Christopher presented their departure, en masse, as the daughters' intention to abandon their father (being 'careless' of his blindness), rather than what seems the more likely scenario of their being sent out from the house to start their apprenticeships.

Christopher had to acknowledge, however, that he had indeed made a deal with his sister-in-law. If she received more than £1,000, she would give any further money to Christopher's children. Although Christopher insisted that this arrangement had been discussed at an earlier time, and not on the day of the nuncupative will, it is nevertheless an important and damning admission, apparently justifying the suspicions of Anne, Mary and Deborah.

More revealing even than Christopher's assured answers are the testimonies of two servants: Elizabeth Fisher, who lived and worked in the Milton household, and her sister Mary, twenty-three years old, who happened to be in the house when the will was allegedly declared, and whose testimony in passing reveals the instability of a servant's life, with six posts in her nine years of domestic service.

Mary, visiting her sister, remembered that Betty and John had been 'at Dinner in the said kitchen' when John said, 'Make much of me as long as I live for thou knows I have given thee all when I die at thy disposal.' John was at that moment of perfect mind and memory and 'very merry'. Significantly, Mary did not know Milton's daughters at all. She 'once saw Anne Milton' but was unable to 'remember whether she was lame or helpless'.

Mary's sister, Elizabeth, elaborated further on the domestic bliss of the Milton household. She remembered her mistress cooking the perfect meal, and her master saying, 'God have mercy Betty, I see thou wilt perform according to thy promise in providing me such dishes as I think fit whilst I live, and when I die thou knowst that I have left thee all.' Elizabeth also recalled John saying several times that he had spent the best part of his estate in providing for his daughters, and they would have no more from him, a point also made by Christopher Milton, who insisted that his brother had paid quite enough money out in the 'maintenance and breeding' of his daughters, and all this without the portion he was promised from their mother. Why on earth should they receive anything at his death?

Nobody comes out of the case with much dignity. If the testimony about the daughters' treatment of their father is true, then they were actively vicious towards him rather than merely neglectful of their duty. On the other hand, Betty Minshull Milton and Christopher Milton emerge as ruthless collaborators in their attempts to cut the daughters out of their father's estate, having no compunction about defaming Anne, Mary and Deborah.

The legal outcome to the case remains unclear. It seems unlikely that the nuncupative will would have been accepted by the court, but it does appear that an out-of-court settlement was reached between the parties. Despite all the bitterness, the Powell money featured in this settlement, Milton's daughters being promised a further £200 from a deal with their maternal uncle, Richard Powell, and Christopher Milton.[10] This may have been an extremely belated acknowledgement of their entitlement to their mother's marriage portion. Betty Minshull Milton paid the daughters the money from their father's estate in February and March 1675: Anne's 'mark' is a scrawl, but Mary and Deborah both signed their names. The daughters were not forgotten by their mother's mother: Anne Powell left legacies for Mary and Deborah in her will of 24 October 1678. By then, lame Anne Milton was already dead: at some point in the intervening years she had married a master-builder, dying soon after in childbirth.

Although Milton's estate was eventually settled, the rifts evident in these legal proceedings merely pointed up the different directions in which the family members were going. Put most crudely, John Milton's daughters ended up in trade. Christopher Milton's sons, Richard Powell's sons, John Milton's nephew Edward, all ended up in the gentry. (The fragility of Christopher's status is, however, glimpsed when he was interviewed by John Aubrey. Christopher was not sure of the name of his own paternal grandfather: 'John he believes', noted Aubrey. Christopher's gentility was new-minted, a mere generation old.)[11] In Oxfordshire, the Powell family would get their estates back, although it took more than twelve years of litigation. By 1673, they had regained formal ownership of the Forest Hill property.

In contrast Mary Milton 'lived single', and Deborah was married to a weaver. Deborah's daughter, sought out by biographers because of her grandfather's celebrity, kept a chandler's shop in Cock Lane near Shoreditch Church. Meanwhile, Christopher Milton was knighted on 25 April 1686 and by May had an income of £1,000 a year. It was Christopher therefore who fulfilled the social and economic ambitions of John Milton the scrivener. But it was his eldest son John who had achieved literary immortality. The question was, who would now control John's literary legacy?

There were several key players. Thomas Ellwood was entrusted with a number of Milton's papers and would be important in the perpetuation of his reputation, but his continued commitment to his Quaker beliefs and Friends (witnessing, for example, Hester Fleetwood's will in 1714) meant that he remained an outsider. His status, as much as Milton's problematic reputation, ensured that a good edition of Milton's political letters was not published until after Ellwood's death in 1743, when the publisher received Milton's papers from Ellwood's executor. Scrappy editions of the letters had already appeared back in 1676 as *Literae Pseudo-Senatus Anglicani* (Letters of the English State; no printer identified, although the word on the ground was that it was the 'surreptitious and imperfect' work of one Moses Pitt).[12] A further edition of 1682, *Milton's Republican Letters*, was again extremely poorly produced, with inadequate translations into English.

Ellwood obviously experienced difficulties in his role as literary trustee.

Betty Minshull Milton seems to have been much more actively engaged in the dissemination and printing of her late husband's works. She passed on a copy of his *Familiar Epistles* with Milton's own corrections, and she met and talked with people interested in her husband, including John Aubrey, who found her a 'gent[le] person [of] a peaceful & agreeable humour'.[13] For Aubrey, Betty transcribed the words from the Milton family Bible: 'John Milton was born the 9th of December 1608 die veneris half an howr after 6 in the morning'.[14] In doing so, Betty was copying out, exactly, what her husband had written many years earlier, on the occasion of the birth of his first daughter, Anne.

Betty Minshull Milton also took responsibility for *Paradise Lost.* After John Milton's death, Samuel Simmons brought out one further edition of the poem, but he then assigned his rights in the epic to Brabazon Aylmer on 27 October 1680. Two months later, Simmons paid Betty Minshull Milton £8 in 'full payment' for 'all my right, title, or interest'.[15] The money was useful, but the widow Milton was not poor. She was able to loan her brother, 'a framework knitter', £300 in the same year. The following year she left London and went to live in her native Cheshire. In June 1695 she was back in London and in Mainwarings Coffee House in Fleet Street handing the copyright of her late husband's prose works (listed in full) over to Joseph Watts for a payment of 10 guineas. Milton's third wife would die in 1727, nearly fifty years after her husband, having done much both to ensure that John Milton's works would continue to reach an audience and to ensure her own financial security.

Other individuals were also important. Edward Phillips attempted to reconstitute his uncle's *History of Britain* in the early 1690s, restoring the 'Digression' and supposed cuts. Phillips was also in-volved with the publisher John Darby, who was responsible for the first complete edition of Milton's prose works. Phillips released his uncle's *Letters of State*, alongside his life, in 1694. Darby, the publisher, was a Whig, a member of the political grouping that had opposed the succession to the throne of James, Duke of York, Charles II's brother, on the grounds that he was a Catholic.[16] Charles II had died in 1685, converting to Catholicism on his death bed and leaving no legitimate heir. Even as his brother James assumed power, there were those who were looking to the Netherlands for a future leader: Charles II's niece, Mary, had married the Protestant William of Orange. These opponents of Catholic Stuart rule would embrace Milton as one of their own, yet they aspired to a far more moderate political settlement than he had done, merely seeking to curb the powers of the monarchy rather than remove it completely. Milton stayed firmly within the Whig interpretative framework for the next century and beyond. Further afield, his works continued to reach wider audiences in Europe. Many of his Latin works had, of course, already found an international readership, but now his English poems, most notably *Paradise Lost*, were being translated, a process that continued over the following centuries and that continues to this day.

And so the edifice continued to be built. Often there was little foundation. There are, for example, remarkably few reliable images of John Milton. There is the portrait when aged ten, discovered on the eve of the tercentenary of his birth. There is the so-called 'Onslow Portrait' of the twenty-one-year-old Milton, which Betty Minshull Milton owned and valued as a true image of her husband, although it was painted long before she was born. There is the engraving in the 1645 poems, which Milton himself satirised as woefully inaccurate, and the engraving by Faithorne (with no indication of his disability) in later years which prefaced Milton's works once he had gained a level of literary celebrity. There are no images of his parents, his wives, his brother or sister, or his children.

This paucity presented a problem to those who wished to create a heroic Milton. He needed to look like a poet, and a blind visionary poet at that, and thus images of sightless laureates start to appear from artist-critics such as Jonathan Richardson. As time went by, the domestic life of John Milton was incorporated into the iconic representation, most notably by William Blake, who created images of John's first wife Mary and his daughter Mary. James Barry offered a fantasy of John and Thomas Ellwood, providing a female figure in the background, sorting out his books, while Charles Lee in 1830 would paint Milton and his daughters.

At the start of the eighteenth century, Deborah Clarke, Milton's daughter, and her daughter, Elizabeth Foster (born in Ireland in 1688), began to be sought out by eager biographers searching for details of the great man's life. Barbara Lewalski is somewhat harsh about this process, suggesting that 'Milton's daughter and grand-daughter wanted to make themselves interesting to later biographers and scholars seeking personal tidbits about the great Milton.' But one can hardly blame them for supplying a few bits of domestic informa-tion to fill the void in Milton's own account of his life.[17]

Helen Darbishire, who collected together the early lives of Milton in 1932 and thought hard about the Milton industry, judged that biographers 'quarried the historical records of his time to build a formidable monument, from which in the end the living man has escaped'.[18] The escape of the 'living man' may not be entirely the biographers' fault. Despite the fact that the 'life of Milton is known to us in far more fullness of detail than that of any other major English poet before the eighteenth century', despite the clear evidence that 'Milton was intensely concerned to have his own image stand in the public eye as he himself conceived it,' there remains little of the living man.[19] Gordon Campbell, John Milton's most recent biographer, is stern in his warning against trying to find the private man: 'Serious scholars hesitate to make inferences about the private Milton who seems at times to be glimpsed through the distorting prism of an incomplete documentary record.'[20] The documentary record is indeed incomplete, and serious scholars should indeed be cautious, particu-larly in their attempts to read autobiographical significance into literary works. Yet Campbell seeks to perpetuate a division between the 'private' Milton and his 'public' self (a division that Milton himself assiduously enforced). This division is an anachronistic one to apply to the seventeenth century. In an era in which the 'private' imbues countless historical documents, from diaries and letters to newspapers and pamphlets, from legal and parliamentary proceedings to poems and plays, is it not strange that there is so little personal in Milton's own writings? The silence is telling: the distortion in the prism starts to look as interesting as the prism itself.

What remain, of course, are his writings. Far more influential to Milton's future reputation than the insights into his table habits sought by his early biographers was the way in which his poetry and prose were being presented to the public, not to mention the ways in which other authors were responding to his work. In 1688, a strikingly beautiful folio edition of his poetry would be published for Tonson, prefaced by an elegy from none other than John Dryden, with a portrait of the author, twelve engraved plates and a list of subscribers.[21] At precisely this time, Dryden's opera based on *Paradise Lost, The State of Innocence, and fall of man*, was proving to be a far greater printing phenomenon than the work it imitated. First published in 1677, it went through nine editions by 1700, easily outselling Milton's own poem.

There were other ways to bowdlerise John Milton. A 1699 version of *Paradise Lost*, designed for lady readers who could not quite manage the difficulties of blank verse, put three extracts of the poem into heroic couplets. The entire encounter between Eve and Satan in Book IX, so crucial to the poet's complex analyses of reason, free will, gender and rhetoric, is reduced to:

> At length the serpent ranges thro' the fields
> He comes. He tempts, and as he temps [sic] she yields.
> And now persuaded by a long dispute
> She boldly tasted of the forbidden fruit.[22]

Perhaps more damaging in the long run to any creative appreciation of Milton's art, religion and politics was the 1695 edition of *Paradise Lost*, complete with extensive scholarly apparatus.[23] This was the first annotated edition of an English poet and transported Milton's poetry into the protected world of Academe, where it now survives as an endangered species. Moreover, while yet further attractive editions of the poetry appeared, Milton's prose works continued to be eclipsed. *The Works of Mr John Milton* may have appeared in 1697, but there was no named place of printing or publisher, and the Latin works were excised. Milton's striking Latin prose was being lost for future generations.

Yet even as *Paradise Lost* started to be shaped into a form suitable for future undergraduates of English Literature, its author was still arousing intense political responses, both positive and hostile. When Nonconformists were experiencing severe persecution in the 1680s, they turned to Milton for solace. Elsewhere, he invoked fear, not consolation. On 21 July 1683, in Oxford, the city in which I am writing today, his books were 'publicly burnt by the hand of our Marshal in the court of our schools'. For this Oxford University book-burning, all went in their finery to the pertinent Quadrangle: '. . . scholars of all degrees and qualities in the mean time surrounding the fire, gave several hums whilst they were burning.'[24] It is not a proud moment in the University's history. There were those in Oxford, however, who could not support the book-burning and made successful efforts to hide, and therefore preserve, Milton's works.

Despite his appeal to radicals, despite the book-burnings, fifty-four years later, in 1737, a monument to John Milton was erected in Westminster Abbey. A cynic might point out that Westminster Abbey, where monarchs are crowned, the headquarters of the Church of England, was not perhaps the best place to celebrate a republican who sought the complete disestablishment of the Church. Milton himself might well have written a superb satirical sonnet on the subject.

In his lifetime, however, he never retreated into cynicism. Instead, he sustained an extraordinary creativity, allied to a powerful political and religious engagement, over many years, and in the face of the most challenging obstacles. When Betty Minshull Milton died in 1727, the dry list of her estate contained the words '2 Books of Paradise'. If her husband had only left these '2 Books of Paradise', it would have been enough. Yet *Paradise Lost* and *Paradise Regained* are only one small part of an unusually diverse and prolific series of writings. Throughout, these writings are informed by Milton's vocational commitment to writing. Despite blindness and censorship, personal losses and political defeat, he maintained and developed this commitment, invariably in the service of his country.

Milton was both a radical and a traditionalist, looking back over centuries of Classical and Judaeo-Christian thinking with his unrivalled intellectual scope, but also looking forward to many ideas that would influence both politics and literature in important ways over the coming centuries. Concerned always with the relationship between history and contemporary life, he argued again and again for the centrality of freedom of choice for the individual in religious, political and personal life. Knowing that 'tyranny must be', that we live in a world of evil, he created inspirational images of a humanity struggling heroically against oppression and moving towards lives of more liberty, more justice, more equality. No wonder he was a hero to the eighteenth and nineteenth centuries. Yet he also had a very modern awareness that in profound ways we cannot escape our selves. His emotional life, what it is possible to know of it, was marked by disappointments and bitterness, estrangements and losses. His Satan, asking 'Which way shall I fly?', echoes John's own question when he wrestled with his own unhappiness as a young man.

Satan's answer to himself is completely despairing: 'Which way I fly is hell; my self am hell.' Milton's writings and his life answer the question in other ways, never disowning or ignoring the despair, but offering also celebrations of friendship and love, of religious toleration and intellectual openness and, above all, of political 'liberty'. Although every generation will debate the terms of his arguments and their legitimacy, Milton's vision of the powerful work that can be done by the word as created by humanity remains a compelling, optimistic and necessary one:

> I imagine myself to have set out upon my travels, and that I behold from on high, tracts beyond the seas, and wide-extended regions; that I behold countenances strange and numberless, and all, in feelings of mind, my closest friends and neighbours . . . from the columns of Hercules to the farthest borders of India, that throughout this vast expanse, I am bringing back, bringing home to every nation, liberty, so long driven out, so long an exile.[25]

Notes

CPW = *Complete Prose Works of John Milton*, ed. Don M. Wolfe, 8 vols, Yale University Press, New Haven, CT, 1953–82.

Life Records = *The Life Records of John Milton*, ed. J. Milton French, 5 vols, Rutgers University Press, New Brunswick, NJ, 1949–58

Shorter Poems = John Milton, *The Complete Shorter Poems*, ed. John Carey, second edn, Longman, London 1997

Paradise Lost (Fowler) = John Milton, *Paradise Lost*, ed. Alastair Fowler, second edn, Longman, London, 1998

1 The City, 1608

N.B. John Milton's earliest poetry can be found in *Shorter Poems*.

1. See Scott Smith-Bannister, *Names and Naming Patterns in England, 1538–1700*, Clarendon Press, Oxford, 1997, p. 17. Many a John became Jack. While William Shakespeare can become Will in our world, and perhaps could in his own, it seems that John Milton never had, and never can have, that kind of familiarity applied to him.
2. Ellen (or Helen) Jeffreys was buried on 26 February 1611.
3. These early biographies are helpfully collected in a volume edited by Helen Darbishire, *The Early Lives of John Milton*, Constable, London, 1932, which includes a life written by one of Milton's nephews, Edward Phillips; another by one of his friends (Cyriack Skinner most probably, rather than John Phillips as suggested by Darbishire); and other biographical materials. None of these early biographies are completely reliable. Milton's nephew, for example, even gets the year of his uncle's birth wrong: *Early Lives*, p. 50. For the references to Sara Milton, see Edward Phillips, in *Early Lives*, p. 52; John Toland, in *Early Lives*, p. 85; John Milton, *Pro Populo Anglicano Defensio Secundo* (Second Defence), 1654, CPW IV (1) 612.
4. Richard Milton, baby John's grandfather, was a respectable churchwarden in the Church of England in 1582 but was excommunicated in the very same year. In 1600 and then again in 1601 he was fined £60 for three months of non-attendance.
5. The Brome family house, for example, just down the road at Holton, south-east of Oxford, and nearby Waterperry House were both operating as Jesuit safe houses.

6. Ralph Houlbrooke, *The English Family, 1450–1700*, Longman, London, 1984, p. 171.
7. See Gordon Campbell, *A Milton Chronology*, Macmillan, Basingstoke, 1997, for this and many other details of John Milton's life.
8. Milton, *Second Defence*, CPW IV (1) 612. As was normal, families merged in fluid ways. At the death of his wife Sara's father, and in the absence of brothers, John Milton became in effect the head of the Jeffreys family. He, for example, represented his mother-in-law in the negotiations over the marriage of her other daughter, Margaret, in 1602.
9. One early biographer records that he wrote 'an *In Nomine* of Forty Parts: for which he was rewarded with a Gold Medal and Chain by a *Polish* Prince, to whom he presented it' (Edward Phillips, in *Early Lives*, p. 51).
10. See A. L. Beier and Roger Finlay, eds, *London 1500–1700: The Making of the Metropolis*, Longman, London, 1986, p. 142 *passim*.
11. David Cressy, *Birth, Marriage & Death: Ritual, Religion, and the Life-Cycle in Tudor and Stuart England*, Oxford University Press, Oxford, 1997, p. 141. Cressy has been an indispensable source of information on family life in the period.
12. Ibid., esp. pp. 97, 106–7, 131.
13. Skinner's biography, in *Early Lives*, p. 18.
14. Aubrey's biographical notes, in *Early Lives*, p. 10.
15. Milton, *Second Defence*, CPW IV (1) 612.
16. Tradition has it that the artist was the up-and-coming twenty-five-year-old Flemish painter Cornelius Janssen. Whether he did the portrait or not, Janssen was very much a London painter, known variously as Johnson, Jensen and Janssen in this cultural melting pot of a city. He would go on to be patronised by Royalty, becoming *the* portrait painter for the country-house set until eclipsed by Van Dyck.
17. A legal document of 1626 has Anne's signature but only her mother-in-law's mark.
18. The vast majority of events in John Milton's life are under-documented, leading to heated debates among Miltonists over both major and minor issues. For a sense of the debate about Thomas Young's tutoring, for example, see Barbara K. Lewalski, *The Life of John Milton: A Critical Biography*, rev. edn, Blackwell, Oxford, 2002, p. 5. Lewalski is an excellent first stop for many, though not all, of the biographical debates. See also Gordon Campbell's revised edition of William Riley Parker's *Milton: A Biography*, Oxford University Press, Oxford, 1996, which offers superbly detailed references enabling readers to make up their minds about the biographical evidence.
19. Lina Bolzoni, *The Gallery of Memory: Literary and Iconographic Models in the Age of the Printing Press*, trans. Jeremy Pazen, University of Toronto Press, Toronto, 2001, pp. 96ff.
20. Thomas Warton, *The Life of Sir Thomas Pope*, London, 1772, pp. 73–4.
21. John Milton, *Latin Writings: A Selection*, ed. and trans. John K. Hale, Van Gorcum, Assen, 1998, p. 3. Hale's translations and notes have been essential to my understanding of Milton as Latinist.
22. See Paul Hammond, 'Classical Texts: Translations and Transformations', in *The Cambridge Companion to English Literature 1650–1740*, Cambridge University Press, Cambridge, 1998, p. 143.
23. *Pierce's supererogation, or, A new prayse of the old asse, a preparatiue to certaine larger discourses*, 1593, sig. B4v. The terms *Britain* and *England* can be confusing. The title 'Great Britain' had come into use only after 1603, when the Scottish King James VI became the English King James I, uniting under one person's rule Scotland, Wales and England. Often, Milton writes of himself as an Englishman, and addresses or speaks for 'the English people'. At times, however, he turns his attention to 'Britain' as a political and historical entity, but he did not refer to himself as British.
24. In the nineteenth century, for example, it was argued that before a truly original

Czech literature could be created, authors would have to master 'the reading and translating of excellent books'. This was not mere passive submission to cultural impulses from abroad: instead, translation of great works from other cultures was 'viewed as an active, even aggressive act, an appropriation of foreign cultural values'. See Vladimir Macura's essay in Susan Bassnett and Andre Lefevre, eds, *Translation, History, Culture*, Pinter, London, 1995, pp. 68–9.

25. *An Apology Against a Pamphlet*, 1642, CPW I 889–90.
26. Alexandra Shepard, *The Meanings of Manhood*, Oxford University Press, Oxford, 1993, p. 23.
27. Fiston, *School of Good Manners*, sig. C2v–C3r, quoted in Anna Bryson, *From Courtesy to Civility: Changing Codes of Conduct in Early Modern England*, Clarendon Press, Oxford, 1998, p. 102.
28. Quoted in Shepard, *Manhood*, p. 56.
29. *Epigram 50*, ll. 1–13, in Guy Lee, ed. and trans., *The Poems of Catullus*, Oxford University Press, Oxford, 1990, p. 49.
30. Lewalski, *Milton*, p. 9, argues that 'Diodati's precocious accomplishment probably contributed to Milton's anxieties about his tardiness in fulfilling his obvious promise', and Christopher Hill notes that the Diodati family could be seen as a symbol of international Protestantism, in *Milton and the English Revolution*, Faber, London, 1977, pp. 30–31.
31. Edward Phillips's family was from Shrewsbury, yet another example of the magnetic pull of London. In the event of her husband's death, Anne would receive as her jointure two tenements in Shrewsbury, in Milk Street and Mardall, and four others in Dog Lane, plus yet another unspecified building. The property could only be used if her husband died during her natural life.

2 Cambridge, 1625

N.B. Milton's early Latin poems can be found in *Shorter Poems*. The World's Classics edition (John Milton, *The Major Works*, ed. Stephen Orgel and Jonathan Goldberg, Oxford University Press, Oxford, 1991) has the Latin and English on facing pages. *John Milton, Latin Writings: A Selection*, ed. and trans. John K. Hale, Van Gorcum, Assen, 1998, has a new translation of *Elegy IV to Thomas Young*.

1. Quoted in *The Atlas of Historic Towns*, 3 vols, Scolar Press, London, 1975, vol. II, p. 20.
2. Alexandra Shepard, *The Meanings of Manhood*, Oxford University Press, Oxford, 1993, pp. 223–6.
3. I have drawn heavily on John K. Hale, *Milton's Cambridge Latin: Performing in the Genres 1625–1632*, Arizona Center for Medieval and Renaissance Studies, Tempe, 2005, in this chapter and elsewhere. The quotations in the following paragraphs come from pp. 1–4.
4. Some of these Latin exercises (prolusions) would be published in the last year of Milton's life. They are printed in CPW I 218–306.
5. Richard J. DuRocher, *Milton and Ovid*, Cornell University Press, Ithaca, NY, 1985, p. 43.
6. The poem, which begins '*Siccine tentasti caelo . . .*', can be found in *Shorter Poems*, p. 35.
7. See Shepard, *Manhood*, p. 120.
8. Quoted in ibid., p. 110.
9. Leo Miller argues that the *Prolusions* act as a record of John's clash with his tutor, William Chappell, and argues strongly for a date of spring 1627 for the rustication,

although it could have occurred the previous year. See 'Milton's Clash with Chappell: A Suggested Reconstruction', *Milton Quarterly* 14 (1980), pp. 77–87.

10. Skinner biography, in Helen Darbishire, ed., *The Early Lives of John Milton*, Constable, London, 1932, pp. 18–19.

11. *An Apology against a Pamphlet*, 1642, CPW I 923.

12. Aubrey's biographical notes, in Darbishire, *Early Lives*, p. 10.

13. See Barry Coward, *The Stuart Age: England 1603–1714*, third edn, Pearson, Harlow, 2003, pp. 60–61 for further details.

14. Records of St Botolph's parish, in Thomas R. Forbes, 'By What Disease or Casualty: The Changing Face of Death in London', in Charles Webster, ed., *Health, Medicine and Mortality in the Sixteenth Century*, Cambridge University Press, Cambridge, 1979, pp. 133–4.

15. These records are unreliable at times, not only because of the women's lack of medical knowledge (although it is to be doubted that many professional medical practitioners knew better) but also because they could be bribed to report incorrectly. It was in the family's interest to conceal a plague death, since the family of any victim was quarantined: no plague, no quarantine.

16. The child is not named. If it is indeed a response to a niece's death, it may be Anne Phillips, who was buried on 22 January 1628.

17. This is Carey's translation (p. 54); the phrase might be translated more precisely as 'luxuriously weeping'.

18. Hale, *Cambridge Latin*, p.11.

19. The correspondence between John and Charles can be found in CPW I 307ff. The poem, *Elegy I*, takes the form of a verse letter to Charles.

20. Anna Bryson, *From Courtesy to Civility: Changing Codes of Conduct in Early Modern England*, Clarendon Press, Oxford, 1998, pp. 114–15.

21. Circe turned men into swine, and Milton, like the Greek hero Odysseus, is protected by the herb 'moly'.

22. Shepard, *Manhood*, pp. 9, 30.

23. Bryson, *Civility*, p. 152.

24. Roger Ascham, *The Whole Works*, ed. J. A. Giles, 3 vols, J. R. Smith, London, 1864–5, vol. III, p. 106.

25. Danielle Clarke, *The Politics of Early Modern Women's Writing*, Longman, London, 2001, p. 27.

26. Shepard, *Manhood*, pp. 122ff.

3 Misrule, 1628

N.B. The early English and Latin poems can be found in *Shorter Poems. Prolusion VI* can be found in John K. Hale, *Milton's Cambridge Latin: Performing in the Genres 1625–1632*, Arizona Center for Medieval and Renaissance Studies, Tempe, AZ, 2005.

1. Matthew Wren (Master of Peterhouse) to Archbishop Laud, State Papers Domestic 1627 86.88.

2. Although the suspension officially lasted for only two lectures, it seems that Dorislaus never lectured again. See John Twigg, *The University of Cambridge and the English Revolution 1625–1688*, Boydell Press, Woodbridge, 1990, p. 13.

3. 6 September 1628, State Papers Domestic 1628 116.56.

4. A poem in Greek by Milton may allude to Gill, imagined as a philosopher condemned to death by an ignorant King. The philosopher claims that if he is killed, the King will regret the act and realise, too late, that he has deprived his 'city of a bulwark of such renown'. If it was a response to Gill's predicament, then its very opacity suggests that Milton was either unwilling or unable to express any direct opinion.

5. CPW I 314.

6. Hale, *Cambridge Latin*, p. 106.

7. Salting itself crossed the Atlantic quite early, and there were saltings recorded at Syracuse, NY, until 1919.

8. In a contemporary pornographic work, for example, a woman exclaims, speaking of language and sex, '*Salsam rem! nam salsa seminis vis*' (This is salty stuff, for the virtue of semen is salty). This reference comes from James Grantham Turner, 'Milton Among the Libertines', in Christophe Tournu and Neil Forsyth, eds, *Milton, Rights and Liberties*, Peter Lang, Bern, 2007, p. 450. I am indebted to Turner for much of the material on *sales*.

9. Turner, 'Milton Among the Libertines', p. 449. John Hale is less certain of the linguistic interconnection between *sales* and the salt of semen. In a private communication he points out that words such as 'salax' and 'salacitas' derive from the word 'salio', to leap.

10. Aubrey's notes, in *Early Lives*, p. 6. The word *fair* now, according to the *Oxford English Dictionary*, is used almost exclusively of women (epitomised in the phrase 'the fair sex'), and, although in Milton's time the term could be used to describe men and women, its primary referent was beauty in women. The secondary meaning was to describe something clean, pure and unspoiled.

11. The Onslow Portrait is named for the man who bought the picture from John's widow many years later. The original is lost, but a later copy is in the National Portrait Gallery, London. The portrait is typical of its time, the face carefully painted over a starched white collar, the head slightly misaligned with the shoulders.

12. New translation by Hale, in *Cambridge Latin*, p. 283.

13. Hale, *Cambridge Latin*, p. 273.

14. Ibid., p. ix.

15. '*Gratia sola di su gli vaglia, inanti / Che'l disio amoroso al cuor s'invecchi.*'

16. I am grateful to Dr Manuele Gragnolati of the University of Oxford for his advice concerning this translation.

17. Translation by Hale, in *Cambridge Latin*, p. 267.

18. The copy of Giovanni della Casa's *Rime e Prose* (1563) that John purchased in December 1629 survives in the New York Public Library, complete with marginal notes and text corrections in Milton's hand. These bear witness to the thoroughness of his reading, his assiduity in learning the language, and his dedication to acquiring the craft of writing poetry in it.

19. The translation can be found in CPW I 326. The original Latin is printed in *The Works of John Milton*, Columbia University Press, New York, NY, 1936, p. 24.

20. I am grateful to David Cunnington for this point, and in general for his expert help with the Latin writings.

21. The term *sodomite* was not applied exclusively to male/male sex but also to acts between men and women, and between men and animals. In Milton's time, there was little or no pressure for someone to define for himself what his sexuality was in any modern sense, since homosexuality, or sodomy, was regarded as an act, not a category of identity. Overall, it was a loose term: John Donne would make a casual conflation of all kinds of sexual indecency, talking of those who love 'whores, who boys, and who goats'. Debauchery was the key idea. See Alan Bray, *Homosexuality in Renaissance England*, rev. edn, Columbia University Press, New York, NY, 1995, p. 79 *passim*.

22. Milton scholars who do acknowledge the presence of homoerotic elements in his writing tend to view them as one of many literary voices adopted by the young poet, or as an emotional safety valve, a way of expressing and exploring feelings upon which he would never act. There are those who have denied any suggestion of homosexuality, in John or his poetry, conscious that 'sodomy' was a sin punishable by death and that Milton himself was vociferous in the defence of the chaste life. And, predictably, there are generations of critics and biographers who have refused even to address the issue. The notes, for example, to the Longman edition of the poetry resolutely avoid glossing even the least contentious references to homoerotic literature.

23. Charles had obviously apologised for the quality of his poems, making the excuse that he had been having such a good time with his friends. Critics have been dismissive of Diodati's abilities as a poet, based on a reading of his one surviving Latin verse, so it was probably for other reasons than his poetic talent that John chose to share this vision of himself with Charles. See Hale, *Cambridge Latin*, p. 152.

24. Translation from CPW I 336. The two surviving Greek letters are in the British Library, Add MS 5016. The Greek originals can be found in *Works*, vol. XII, pp. 292–4. The Columbia translation has Charles 'long for' John's 'society' and look forward to 'learned and philosophical discourse'. The great Marxist historian of the seventeenth century, Christopher Hill, has written, refreshingly directly, that Milton clearly adored Diodati more than he ever adored any human being except possibly his second wife; see *Milton and the English Revolution*, Faber, London, 1977, p. 31.

25. Both men enjoyed making teasing references to homosexual or effeminate figures, making the joke, let alone the intention, difficult to recover now. When Charles tells John to 'be joyous – though not in the fashion of Sardanapalus in Cilicia (Soli)', he seems to be warning John *against* imitating a particular seventh-century BC Assyrian King known for his effeminacy and voluptuousness. This is all very well, if a little strange, given the fact that John, unlike Charles, seems everywhere else in his writing to advocate the strictest chastity, but then Charles follows this up by suggesting that if John were with him, he 'would be happier than the King of Persia', a historical figure known for his effeminacy and good living. See the translation in CPW I 337.

26. When John writes that he rushed to find John in his rooms in London, the word he uses is *cellam*. This has traditionally been translated as 'crib', but the word can be used to mean a room in a brothel. John T. Shawcross, *John Milton: The Self and the World*, University Press of Kentucky, Lexington, KY, 1993, p. 57.

27. Ibid., p. 125.

28. CPW I 337 has 'Could I but add to these a good companion, learned and initiate, I would be happier than the King of Persia'. Bruce Boehrer, 'Animal Love in Milton: The Case of Epitaphium Damonis', *English Literary History*, 70 (2003), pp. 787–812. Boehrer adds 'cut out from the herd', p. 803.

29. The evidence suggests that illicit sexual contact with women was possible. Indeed, marriages were sometimes made, much to the horror of the King, who denounced scholars making marriage 'with women of mean estate and of no good fame'. Rather predictably, the women involved bore the blame, painted as seducers of innocent Cambridge students. See Alexandra Shepard, *The Meanings of Manhood*, Oxford University Press, Oxford, 1993, pp. 119–20.

30. John Aubrey notes, 'At Geneva he contracted a great friendship with Carolo Diodati.' He then crosses this through, and substitutes 'the learned Dr Diodati of Geneva', replacing Charles with his uncle, and missing completely the fact that Charles and John went to school together in London (Darbishire, ed., *Early Lives*, p. 2). In recent years, A. N. Wilson has acknowledged the significance of the relationship. For Wilson, Diodati was Milton's 'great love', but the emotions involved are consigned to

the 'romantic attachments of adolescence'; see *The Life of John Milton*, Oxford University Press, Oxford, 1983, pp. 15, 21.

31. John's nephew would write that his uncle's early poems 'contain a Poetical Genius scarce to be parallel'd by any *English* writer'; see Darbishire, ed., *Early Lives*, p. 54.
32. *An Apology against a Pamphlet*, CPW I 890.

4 Masque, 1634

N.B. The poems 'On The Morning of Christ's Nativity', *L'Allegro* and *Il Penseroso*, and the *Maske* at Ludlow are all in *Shorter Poems*, and appear in almost all collections of Milton's poetry. These works are available on line at http://www.dartmouth.edu/~milton, an excellent internet resource.

1. John T. Shawcross, *The Arms of the Family: The Significance of John Milton's Relatives and Associates*, University Press of Kentucky, Lexington, KY, 2004, offers a superbly detailed account of key members of John Milton's family, including his brother Christopher, his nephews John and Edward Phillips, and his brother-in-law, Thomas Agar. I do not, however, always come to similar conclusions about the evidence.
2. Shawcross, *Arms of the Family*, p. 58 *passim*.
3. It seems likely that little Anne Agar died a few years after her father's remarriage, since when Anne Milton Phillips Agar gave birth to a daughter in 1636, she was named Anne, presumably to honour her dead stepsister as much as her mother. This was a common practice at the time.
4. Horton was then in Buckinghamshire and is now in Berkshire, close to Heathrow Airport. A lovely little pamphlet entitled *Horton Parish Bucks A Short History of* [sic], published before the Second World War, describes Horton as 'a peaceful village, shadowed by large trees, and having its ancient calm apparently undisturbed by the rush of modern life, despite the fact that an omnibus route now passes through.'
5. John Milton, *Second Defence*, CPW IV (1) 613–14.
6. Edward Phillips and John Toland, in Darbishire, ed., *Early Lives*, pp. 55, 88.
7. CPW I 319–21.
8. This remarkable manuscript (the Trinity Manuscript, Trinity College, Cambridge R. 3. 4. contains handwritten copies of many of Milton's early poems, and includes his revisions. The Scolar Press have produced a facsimile (1972).
9. The key documents are detailed in Gordon Campbell, *A Milton Chronology*, Macmillan, Basingstoke, 1997.
10. See www.sph.org for the history of the church.
11. There is even a rare hint of toleration of Roman Catholicism. In 1631, John wrote an epitaph for the Marchioness of Winchester, a member of the old Catholic aristocracy.
12. *The Reason of Church-Governement Urg'd against Prelaty*, CPW I 822.
13. *The New Birth: or, A treatise of Regeneration, delivered in certaine sermons*, London, 1618, pp. 158–9.
14. Stephen Dobranski, *Milton, Authorship and the Book Trade*, Cambridge University Press, Cambridge, 1999, p. 11.
15. Travellers would set out from London near Hyde Park Corner, and then journey through Kensington, Hammersmith, Turnham Green, Brentford and Hounslow, stopping to 'bait' at Colnbrook before heading on further west, to Maidenhead, Reading and beyond.
16. As an editor of Classical Greek, Milton is superb and, astonishingly, still followed by

today's editors of Euripides. See John K. Hale, 'Milton's Euripides Marginalia', *Milton Studies* 27 (1991), pp. 23–33.

17. The music written by Henry Lawes for the entertainment, together with four additional songs, has survived in a manuscript now at the British Library, Add MS 11518. In this manuscript the date for the performance is given incorrectly as October 1634.

18. Cedric Brown, *John Milton: A Literary Life*, Macmillan, Basingstoke, 1995, pp. 45ff.

19. It is possible that John's father's connections with the London music world, and his business dealings with the Egerton family, helped to secure the commission for his son.

20. In practice the Great Hall at Whitehall became more of a Royal Presence Chamber for the formal reception of visiting dignitaries. Rubens's resplendent ceiling, painted in 1636, ensured that the room could not be used for masques because the 'ceiling richly adorned . . . might suffer by the smoke of many lights.' See Simon Thurley, *Whitehall Palace: An Architectural History of the Royal Apartments 1240–1698*, Yale University Press, New Haven, CT, 1999, pp. 82–97.

21. *Tempe Restor'd: A masque presented by the Queene, and foureteene ladies, to the Kings Majestie at Whitehall on Shrove-Tuesday 1631*, London, 1631, sig. A2.

22. John Summerson, *Inigo Jones*, second rev. edn, Paul Mellon Centre for Studies in British Art and Yale University Press, London and New Haven, CT, 2000, p. 105.

23. The fight went on. Jonson would caricature Jones in his *Tale of a Tub* (c. 1633) as an Islington cooper (barrel-maker) called In-and-in Medlay. Later, Jonson would lampoon Jones's ambitions for a peerage in a poem, 'To Inigo Marquess Would Be'.

24. For further insight into the masque form, see David Lindley, ed., *The Court Masque*, Manchester University Press, Manchester, 1984, and Stephen Orgel, *The Jonsonian Masque*, Columbia University Press, New York, NY, 1981.

25. *Mickle*, meaning 'great', was an archaic word even in Milton's time, and typical of the language of Edmund Spenser, an important influence on John's poetry through the 1620s and 1630s.

26. William Prynne, 'To the Christian Reader', in *Histrio-mastix. The Players scourge, or, actors tragaedie, divided into two parts*, London, 1633, sig. **6v, note.

27. James Sutherland, ed., *Memoirs of the Life of Colonel Hutchinson*, Oxford University Press, Oxford, 1973, p. 42.

28. There are clear verbal echoes of *Tempe Restor'd* (in which a male character speaks the following lines):

> Tis not her Rod, her Philters, nor her Herbs
> (Though strong in Magic) that can bound men's minds
> And make them prisoners, where there is no wall.
> It is consent that makes a perfect Slave. (p. 5)

29. I have drawn heavily on Annabel Patterson's thoughtful response to the *Maske*, 'Milton and Ideological Constraint', in Claude J. Summers and Ted-Larry Pebworth, eds, '*The Muses Common-weal: Poetry and Politics in the Seventeenth Century*, University of Missouri Press, Columbia, MO, 1998.

30. The very vagueness of 'haemony' leaves plenty of room for interpretations. It has been argued that the 'certain shepherd lad' who knew about haemony refers to Charles Diodati. Others, more convincingly, argue that haemony figures the word of God. Samuel Taylor Coleridge suggested the word came from *haema-oinos*, 'blood-wine', and that the herb represents the blood of Christ.

31. Catherine Belsey, *John Milton: Language, Gender, Power*, Blackwell, Oxford, 1988, p. 46.

32. From a work almost definitely read by Milton, Puteanas' *Comus, Sive Phagesiposia Cimmeria: Somnium* (or *The Cimmerian Banquet: A Dream*), 1608. See Ross Leasure, 'Milton's Queer Choice: Comus at Castlehaven', *Milton Quarterly* 36 (2002), pp. 65ff.

33. The sons of Belial demand sex with a young man sheltering in an older man's house. Instead the older man offers up his concubine, who is subjected to gang rape, and then cut up into pieces by her master. To include the boys in the threat to chastity indicates, not for the last time in his work, Milton's daring approach to sexual matters.

34. Two different manuscripts survive: the Bridgewater and the Trinity, the former shorter than the latter. The published version of 1645 has an expanded epilogue and a long speech by the Lady on 'the serious doctrine of virginity' (1. 786), together with Comus' reaction to this speech. There is some debate as to which version is closest to the actual performance at Ludlow (probably the Bridgewater Manuscript) and which version is closest to Milton's own vision of the work (probably the 1645 printed edition).

35. Only one other aristocratic entertainment by Milton survives, and it is unclear whether it was commissioned before or after the *Maske* at Ludlow. The piece was written for the Dowager Countess of Derby at her country estate, Harefield, and it was there that the victims of Mervin Touchet, Earl of Castlehaven, were cared for. The Countess was not only grandmother to the children who performed at the masque in Ludlow but also mother to the wife, and grandmother to the daughter Touchet raped. See Barbara Lewalski, *The Life of John Milton: A Critical Biography*, rev. edn, Blackwell, Oxford, 2002, p. 58; also see p. 563, n. 20 for an interpretation of the connection which emphasises the Dowager Duchess's Protestant agenda.

5 Elegy, 1637

N.B. The letters to and from Charles Diodati can be found in CPW, while the Greek originals can be found in *The Works of John Milton*, 18 vols, Columbia University Press, New York, NY, 1936, vol. XII, pp. 292–4. *Lycidas* is in *Shorter Poems*, online at http://www.dartmouth.edu/~milton and printed in most editions of Milton's poetry.

1. See Michael C. Schoenfeldt, *Bodies and Selves in Early Modern England: Physiology and Inwardness in Spenser, Shakespeare, Herbert and Milton*, Cambridge University Press, Cambridge, 1999, pp. 82–3.
2. *The Doctrine and Discipline of Divorce*, CPW II 271.
3. The Latin originals can be found in *Works*, vol. XII, pp. 18–30. I follow the translation in CPW I. The quotation here is on p. 323.
4. Letter of 1637, CPW I 326.
5. It seems absurd, as some have done, to attempt to reassure a modern readership that there was nothing improper in the relationship between the two men. Peter Levi, for example, writing of *Epitaphium Damonis* (Elegy for Damon), writes that 'a biographer is bound to note the first touch, however slight, of that conventional homoeroticism for which pastoral poetry in the period was famous. It is innocent enough, as their lives obviously were . . .'; see *Eden Renewed: The Public and Private Life of John Milton*, Macmillan, Basingstoke, 1996, p. 113. An interesting version of this attitude is the argument that the relationship cannot have been homosexual, since if it had been, Milton would have been courageous enough to act upon his feelings and announce them to the world. See William Kerrigan, *The Sacred Complex: On the Psychogenesis of Paradise Lost*, Harvard University Press, Cambridge, MA, 1983, p. 49, a fascinating and controversial book that makes provocative connections (for example, between Martin Luther's 'secret furious inviolacy' and that of Milton, p. 44) and offers a sophisticated Freudian analysis of Milton's 'feminine identification in the oedipal context', p. 49.
6. CPW I 328.

7. Shawcross is brilliant and controversial in his translation of this letter, finding puns where others fear even to look for them. 'Contention' is both 'argument' and 'sexual play'. The Latin word *partibus* refers to both the genitals and Milton's excuses. Literary correspondence (*consuetudine*) and *consuevimus* ('chat') are both also sexual intercourse. Diodati's friends are *erudituli*, 'young learned people', but also those experienced in love. See *John Milton: The Self and the World*, University Press of Kentucky, Lexington, KY, 1993, pp. 57–8.
8. My thanks to David Cunnington for this point.
9. CPW I 369.
10. Bearing in mind that John's main home was in Horton, his comment that he is looking for 'wherever there is a pleasant and shady walk; for that dwelling will be more satisfactory, both for companionship, if I wish to remain at home, and as a more suitable headquarters, if I choose to venture forth. Where I am now, as you know, I live in obscurity and cramped quarters' (CPW I 327) appears rather strange. Presumably there were shady walks aplenty in the countryside of Horton, so what was the special appeal of a place in London among lawyers? Why did John always seek the shady walks? And what kind of companionship was he seeking? Did he literally mean venturing forth – that is, going out in public – or was he talking in more metaphorical terms, about starting a career? And why were his quarters in Horton (if that was what he was referring to) 'cramped' and obscure? As is often the case, Milton's Latin phrases remain tantalisingly elusive.
11. CPW I 327 has 'So help me God, an immortality of fame'. I am grateful to David Cunnington for his advice on the translation.
12. The date of the poem is much disputed. It is linked with the strange double letter to an unknown friend, and therefore to John's early years at Horton. There is no firm evidence.
13. 'Milton's Crises', *Listener*, 19 December 1968, p. 829.
14. Indeed, there is no significant performance history for the work.
15. *Poems of Mr John Milton, Both English and Latin, Compos'd at several times*, 1645, pp. 69–70.
16. Barbara Lewalski, *The Life of John Milton: A Critical Biography*, rev. edn, Blackwell, Oxford, 2002, p. 67.
17. Theocritus, *Idylls*, trans. Anthony Verity, Oxford World's Classics, Oxford, p. vii.
18. *The Arte of English Poesie*, 1589, p. 31.
19. Lewalski, *Milton*, p. 64. Earlier biographers, such as the eminent and highly enjoyable David Masson, were happy to extrapolate from small shreds of village hearsay the vision of John Milton walking through the village with the local squire's children at his heels; see *The Life of John Milton*, 7 vols, Macmillan, London, 1881–95, vol. I, p. 556. At the time of Masson's biography, it was not known that the Miltons had previously lived in Hammersmith.
20. Marjorie Plant, *The English Book Trade: An Economic History of the Making and Sale of Books*, second edn, George Allen & Unwin, London, 1965, p. 197.
21. State Papers Domestic 1636–7 344.40.1
22. John Milton, *Second Defence*, CPW IV (1) 614.
23. Wotton to Milton, 13 April 1638, CPW I 340–43.

6 Italy, 1638

N.B. Many of the quotations in this chapter come from Milton's *Second Defence of the English People* (1654), printed in CPW and online (without annotation) at http://www.constitution.org/milton/second_defence.htm.

1. France under Louis XIII looked even more of an absolute monarchy than the regime of Charles I. Cardinal Richelieu, the King's chief minister, was viciously repressive of French Protestants, known as Huguenots. It had been Richelieu's forces which had seen off the ill-fated Duke of Buckingham's expeditions back in the 1620s.

2. Wotton to Milton, 13 April 1638, CPW I 342.

3. It has been estimated that in any given year the hospitals of Venice cared for 4,000 'perpetual poor' or nearly 3 per cent of the city's population, and the figure was similar in Florence.

4. John Milton, *Second Defence*, CPW IV (1) 615–17.

5. John A. Marino, ed., *Early Modern Italy*, Oxford University Press, Oxford, 2002, pp. 218–24. See also Barbara Lewalski, *The Life of John Milton: A Critical Biography*, rev. edn, Blackwell, Oxford, 2002, p. 91, for some helpful context.

6. Brendan Dooley, 'The Public Sphere and the Organisation of Knowledge', Marino, *Early Modern Italy*, pp. 209–28.

7. For a sceptical review of the evidence, see George F. Butler, 'Milton's Meeting with Galileo: A "Reconsideration"', *Milton Quarterly*, 39 (2005), pp. 132ff.

8. See Thomas James Dandelet, *Spanish Rome 1500–1700*, Yale University Press, New Haven, CT, and London, 2001, p. 195.

9. See Joseph Connors, 'A Copy of Borromini's S. Carlo alle Quattro Fontane in Gubbio', *Burlington Magazine*, 137 (1995), p. 588.

10. See Michael O'Connell's essay, in Mario A. Di Cesare, ed., *Milton in Italy: Contexts, Images, Contradictions*, Medieval and Renaissance Texts and Studies, Binghampton, NY, 1991, pp. 224–7.

11. CPW IV (1) 617.

12. Ibid., 618.

13. A sign of the times became apparent the following year when the most famous bandit, Giulio Pezzola, was given lodging by the Spanish ambassador when he went to Rome.

14. Anthony Low, 'Mansus: In Its Context', *Milton Studies* 19 (1984), pp. 105–26.

15. *Second Defence*, CPW IV (1) 618.

16. Ibid., 619. As the translators point out, 'Milton well knew the claims to orthodoxy asserted by the pope, and he was fully aware of the fact that he was a guest in the one city where those claims were pre-eminently accepted.' In asserting that orthodoxy lay elsewhere than Rome, Milton was being highly contentious.

17. It was probably the comic opera *Chi soffre speri*, written by Cardinal Giulio Rospigliosi, who would later become Pope Clement IX, with music by Virgilio Mazzocchi and Marco Marazzuoli, and stage design by Bernini, the most celebrated designer in Rome.

18. Milton to Lukas Holste, 1639, CPW I 334.

19. *Ad Salsillum poetam Romanum aegrotantem. Scazontes* (Scazons Addressed to Salzilli, a Roman Poet, When He Was Ill), in *Shorter Poems*, p. 262.

20. Salzilli's praise was inserted into the preface to the collection of his Latin poems published in 1645.

21. *Second Defence*, CPW IV (1) 609.

22. Ibid., 619.

23. Ibid.

24. With trade came empire, bringing its own problems. Venice struggled to maintain its stranglehold on the coastal regions of Crete, Dalmatia and the Ionian islands, while day by day, pirates harried the Venetian ships sailing through the Adriatic and beyond.

25. It was in Venice that the most notorious libertine of his generation, Ferrante Pallavicino, author of numerous novels of sex and blasphemy, plied his trade. Pallavicino would be punished for his sins but not in Venice. He was executed in Avignon in 1644.

26. The chapel on the estate is equally remarkable. The elegant eroticism of the image on the exterior speaks more of *urbanitas* and *sales* than it does of conventional piety.

27. Giovanni Diodati secretly revisited his native Italy several times and travelled to Holland and England in the Protestant cause. He had collaborated closely with the English ambassador to Venice, Sir Henry Wotton (who of course had been instrumental in helping John get to Italy in the first place) in attempts to win the Republic for the Protestant cause in 1608.

28. *Reason of Church Government*, 1641, CPW I 809–10.

29. *The Itinerary* I:392, quoted in O'Connell, in *Milton in Italy*, p. 227.

30. Shawcross speculates that the news reached Milton in a letter in Venice, at the embassy there, a place where he would be sure to receive one, 'the Embassy operating like an American Express office today'; John T. Shawcross, *The Arms of the Family: The Significance of John Milton's Relatives and Associates*, University Press of Kentucky, Lexington, KY, 2004, pp. 89–90.

7 Damon, 1640

N.B. *Epitaphium Damonis* (Elegy for Damon) is printed in *Shorter Poems* and online (with a slightly different translation) at http://www.dartmouth.edu/~milton/reading_room/damon/index.shtml. This, of all Milton's poems, deserves a new translation for contemporary readers.

1. See Matthew Curr, *The Consolation of Otherness: The Male Love Elegy in Milton, Gray and Tennyson*, McFarland & Company, Jefferson, NC, 2002, for a compelling reading within this tradition. A. N. Wilson also links Milton with Tennyson, suggesting that the friendship and intimacy Milton experienced with Diodati was 'analogous to the feeling Tennyson had for Arthur Hallam'. Wilson, quoting *In Memoriam*, suggests that after Diodati's death, Milton's life had 'some of this quality of widowhood'; see *The Life of John Milton*, Oxford University Press, Oxford, 1983, p. 93. This is a profoundly suggestive connection to make, but Wilson does not pursue the issue.

2. ll. 131–7, in Theocritus, *Idylls*, trans. Anthony Verity, Oxford World's Classics, Oxford, p. 28. Thyrsis, as has been seen, does not only appear in Virgil; he is the central character in Theocritus' *Idyll I*, where he offers a powerful lament for Daphnis.

3. James Grantham Turner, 'Milton among the Libertines' in Christophe Tournu and Neil Forsyth, eds, *Milton, Rights and Liberties*, Peter Lang, Bern, 2007, collects together the key phrases associated with Charles in Milton's writing about him, and notes the amorous connotations of *blanditiae* in *Elegy V*, l. 70 and elsewhere.

4. See, for example, Stephen Dobranski, *Milton, Authorship and the Book Trade*, Cambridge University Press, Cambridge, 1999, p. 13, for a subtle version of this argument.

5. Curr, *Consolation*, p. 32.

6. Turner, 'Milton among the Libertines', p. 452.

7. Edward Phillips, in Helen Darbishire, ed., *The Early Lives of John Milton*, Constable, London, 1932, p. 62.

8. See A. L. Beier, in A. L. Beier and Roger Finlay, eds, *London 1500–1700: The Making of the Metropolis*, Longman, London, 1986, p. 153.

9. There was no legal obligation on John Milton to take on responsibility for his nephews, at least when there were not large sums of money and land involved, and no involvement from government in the matter. In practice, however, maternal uncles often filled this role. See Ralph Houlbrooke, *The English Family, 1450–1700*, Long-

man, London, 1984, p. 219, for instances where the arrangement went horribly wrong.

10. Houlbrooke, *English Family*, pp. 51–3.
11. Many years later, Agar would leave nothing to his stepson John in his will. This probably had more to do with political differences between the two men than a personal dislike begun in childhood.
12. Houlbrooke, *English Family*, p. 45.
13. Richard Cust, *Charles I: A Political Life*, Longman, Harlow, 2005, p. 246.
14. Quoted in ibid., p. 251.
15. Ibid., pp. 263–4.
16. Barry Coward, *The Stuart Age: England 1603–1714*, third edn, Longman, Harlow, 2003, p. 193.
17. As reported in a letter from the Elector Palatine to the Queen of Bohemia. Reference from S. R. Gardiner, *History of England 1603–1642*, 10 vols, Longmans, London, 1883–4, vol. IX, pp. 366–7.
18. British Library c 57 d 48.
19. Milton, *Second Defence*, CPW IV (1) 553.

8 The Church, 1641

N.B. *Of Reformation* and *Reason of Church Government* are printed in CPW. The latter is on line at http://www.dartmouth.edu/~milton/reading_room/reason/book_1/index.shtml, and the former is at http://oll.libertyfund.org/Home3/index.php, the website of the Online Library of Liberty.

1. An invaluable account of this era is in Nigel Smith, *Literature and Revolution*, Yale University Press, New Haven, CT, and London, 1994. See also Joad Raymond, *Pamphlets and Pamphleteering in Early Modern Britain*, Cambridge University Press, Cambridge, 2003, which offers a groundbreaking analysis of the importance of pamphlet literature in the seventeenth century.
2. John Milton, *Second Defence*, CPW IV (1) 621–2.
3. *Paradise Lost*, pp. 1–3.
4. On his return from Italy, John maintained his useful connections with members of the book trade, as is evident in a 1640 invitation from the printer Thomas Cotes to provide verses for Cotes's new edition of Shakespeare's *Folio*. Cotes had moved into the printer William Jaggard's establishment at the corner of Aldersgate Street and Barbican, and was thus a close neighbour.
5. The poems that *do* get into the manuscript miscellanies are the Hobson poems from University, the elegy for the Marchioness of Winchester and one copy of 'Fly envious time . . .' See Stephen Dobranski, *Milton, Authorship and the Book Trade*, Cambridge University Press, Cambridge, 1999, pp. 78–9.
6. The excellent Hanover Historical Texts Project (http://history.hanover.edu) has the text of the Root and Branch Petition, together with numerous other historical documents. This quotation is item six in the petition.
7. It is possible that Milton had already published a ten-page, unsigned postscript to the Smectymnuan pamphlet, offering data from English history to prove the redundancy of bishops.
8. CPW I 517ff.
9. Ibid., 520.

10. Ibid., 536–7.
11. Ibid., 617.
12. *Ad Joannem Rousium Oxoniensis Academiae Bibliothecarium* (To John Rouse, Librarian of Oxford University), 23 January 1647.
13. Prynne gives his own graphic account of the proceedings in *A New Discovery of the Prelate's Tyranny,* 1641.
14. See Smith, *Literature and Revolution,* pp. 28–9.
15. Dobranski, *Milton, Authorship,* p. 9.
16. The work is *Animadversion upon the Remonstrants Defence, against Smectymnuus,* printed in July or August 1641.
17. CPW I 726.
18. See Dobranski, *Milton, Authorship,* p. 30.
19. This was the case with all the other male members of his family. See John T. Shawcross, *The Arms of the Family: The Significance of John Milton's Relatives and Associates,* University Press of Kentucky, Lexington, KY, 2004, p. 5 *passim.*
20. *Colasterion,* 1645, CPW II 724.
21. http://www.dartmouth.edu/~milton/reading_room/ddd/book_1/notes.shtml. 'Soteriologically' means 'pertaining to salvation'. This Milton website is one of the best.
22. *Second Defence,* CPW IV (1) 623.
23. Ibid., 621–2.
24. See Smith, *Literature and Revolution,* p. 66.
25. Anna Bryson, *From Courtesy to Civility: Changing Codes of Conduct in Early Modern England,* Clarendon Press, Oxford, 1998, pp. 132–3.
26. Laura Gowing, *Domestic Dangers: Women, Words and Sex in Early Modern London,* Clarendon Press, Oxford, 1996, p. 7.
27. Alan MacFarlane, *Marriage and Love in England: Modes of Reproduction, 1300–1840,* Blackwell, Oxford, 1986, p. 266.
28. The middle and upper classes usually provided hundreds, not thousands, of pounds when their daughters married. Ralph Josselin, a comfortably off minister, gave portions to his daughters of £240 and £500, with an annual income of about £100. See MacFarlane, *Marriage,* p. 266.
29. MacFarlane, *Marriage,* pp. 269–71.
30. Ibid., p. 215.
31. John Shawcross (*Arms of the Family,* p. 196) speculates that one of the reasons Milton rushed into a marriage was his knowledge that his father would be coming to live with him – perhaps marriage was another effort to please his father, or simply a wise way of getting a female household manager for a growing number of men.
32. A. N. Wilson, *John Milton,* Oxford University Press, Oxford, 1983, p. 113.
33. William Riley Parker (rev. Gordon Campbell), *Milton: A Biographical Commentary,* second edn, Oxford University Press, Oxford, 1996, p. 227.
34. The King's answer to the petition accompanying the 'Grand Remonstrance', 23 December 1641, quoted in Richard Cust, *Charles I,* Longman, Harlow, 2005, pp. 314–15.
35. Sir Edward Dering, 22 November 1641, in *A Collection of Speeches made by Sir Edward Dering Knight and Baronet, in matter of Religion,* London, 1642, p. 109.
36. Chamberlain to Dudley Carleton, quoted in Joad Raymond, *The Invention of the Newspaper: English Newsbooks 1641–1649,* Clarendon Press, Oxford, 1996, p. 8.
37. See Raymond, *The Invention of the Newspaper,* esp. the Introduction.
38. Smith, *Literature and Revolution,* p. 66.
39. See CPW I 664.

9 Divorce, 1642

N.B. *The Doctrine and Discipline of Divorce* is printed in CPW and elsewhere, including John Milton, *The Major Works*, eds Stephen Orgel and Jonathan Goldberg, Oxford University Press, 1991, and online at http://www.dartmouth.edu/~milton/reading_room/ddd/book_1/index.shtml.

1. I have found only one other work surviving from this period that uses the word *divorce* in its title, and that is a response to Milton's piece, *An Answer to a book [by J. Milton] intituled the doctrine and discipline of divorce, or, A plea for ladies and gentlewomen against divorce*, printed in 1644 in London.
2. Quoted in Bernard Capp, *When Gossips Meet: Women, Family and Neighbourhood in Early Modern England*, Oxford University Press, Oxford, 2003, p. 114.
3. CPW II 235.
4. Ibid., 244.
5. Ibid., 245–6.
6. Barbara Lewalski, *The Life of John Milton: A Critical Biography*, rev. edn, Blackwell, Oxford, 2002, pp. 168ff.
7. For a full statement of this argument, see Jason Rosenblatt, *Torah and Law in Paradise Lost*, Princeton University Press, Princeton, 1984, pp. 108–9. The second edition of *The Doctrine and Discipline of Divorce* elevates the wisdom of Moses yet higher.
8. CPW II 740.
9. See www.dartmouth.edu/~milton/reading_room/ddd/book_1/notes.shtml, and Bruce Boehrer, 'Animal Love in Milton: The Case of Epitaphium Damonis', *English Literary History* 70 (2003), p. 804.
10. This and the following quotations are all from Capp, *Gossips*, pp. 10–13, 74–5.
11. CPW II 347.
12. Ibid., 226–7.
13. Ibid., 587.
14. See ibid., 682–3.
15. Daniel Featley, *The Dippers Dippt or the Anabaptists ducked and plungd over head and eares at a Disputation in Southwark*, London, 1645, sig. B2. *Life Records* IV 356 has the same quotation in a work of Ephraim Pagitt, *Heresiography*, 1661.
16. *The Judgement of Martin Bucer concerning divorce written to Edward the sixt, in his second book of the Kingdom of Christ, and now Englisht*, 1644.
17. *Twelve Considerable Serious Questions touching Church Government*, 1644, p. 7.
18. Milton was taxed at £6 on the house, his neighbours between £3 and £8, suggesting that Mary was mistress of a substantial town house. For a sense of what she was leaving, an inventory taken on 16 June 1646 provides a fascinating glimpse of the Powell lifestyle: the trunks of linen; the piles of timber; the bedstead with green curtains and laced valences; the featherbed with a yellow 'coverlid'; the two little silver spoons and the 'one broken silver spoon'. The numerous buildings needed to sustain the estate emerge (the cellar and the cheese-press house, the boys' chamber and the wash-house), as do the livestock necessary for survival: four hogs, two ewes, one mare and foal, and one bull. See *Life Records* II 147–50. For more information on the relentless labour of domestic life at this time, see Anna Beer, *Bess: The Life of Lady Ralegh, Wife to Sir Walter*, Constable, London, 2004.
19. See Laura Gowing, *Domestic Dangers: Women, Words and Sex in Early Modern London*, Clarendon Press, Oxford, 1996, pp. 20–22.
20. See Alan MacFarlane, *Marriage and Love in England: Modes of Reproduction, 1300–1840*, Blackwell, Oxford, 1986, p. 228.

21. Capp, *Gossips*, p. 114.
22. See MacFarlane, *Marriage*, p. 228.
23. *Nineteen Propositions Made by Both Houses of Parliament to the King's Most Excellent Majestie, with his Majesties answer thereunto*, Printed by his Majesties speciall command at Cambridge: by Roger Daniel printer to the famous Universitie, 1642, p. 14.
24. The relevant quotes from the Ordinance and Proclamation are in Barry Coward and Chris Durston, *The English Revolution*, John Murray, London, 1997, pp. 9, 57.
25. Lawson Nagel, '"A Great Bouncing at Every Man's Door": The Struggle for London's Militia in 1642', in Stephen Porter, ed., *London and the Civil War*, Macmillan, Basingstoke, 1996, p. 78.
26. Anna Bryson, *From Courtesy to Civility: Changing Codes of Conduct in Early Modern England*, Clarendon Press, Oxford, 1998, p. 217.
27. Barry Coward, *The Stuart Age: England 1603–1714*, third edn, Pearson, Harlow, 2003, p. 204.
28. The traditional four London regiments had been reorganised into forty companies of eight thousand men in six regiments. The soldiers had no uniform as such but wore their normal clothing. Shopkeepers, tradesmen and merchants made up much of the soldiery: the men had to have wealth enough to pay for their own weapons.
29. Helen Darbishire, ed., *The Early Lives of Milton*, Constable, London, 1932, pp. 3–4.
30. Christopher Durston, *The Family in the English Revolution*, Blackwell, Oxford, 1989, p. 147.
31. Edward Phillips, in Darbishire, *Early Lives*, p. 65.
32. John Aubrey's notes on the marriage, made much later in the century, are interesting in this context. As he adds and deletes notes, talking to witnesses, checking his references, his scrappy, confused account accrues more and more detail. He remains uninterested in Mary in and of herself: he does not even give her name, only that she is a Powell from 'Fosthill' (i.e., Forest Hill). What does interest him is that she went to her mother at 'ye Kings quarters near Oxford' (a note he makes twice, adding the fact that Mary 'went without her husband's consent'). Fascinatingly, Aubrey returns yet again to this passage in order to prove the following tenet: 'Two opinions doe not well on the same Boulster' and then yet again, with a further comment that Mary's upbringing made it difficult for her to adapt to life in London. Aubrey also has her used to 'a great deal of company & merriment [adds dancing & c]'. Mary found it 'very solitary: no company came to her, often-times heard his Nephews cry, and beaten. This life was irksome to her; & so she went to her Parents at Fosthill.' See Darbishire, *Early Lives*, pp. 3, 14.
33. John K. Hale, 'Milton's Euripides Marginalia', *Milton Studies* 27 (1991), pp. 32–3.

10 Censorship, 1644

N.B. *Areopagitica* is printed in CPW; in John Milton, *The Major Works*, ed. Stephen Orgel and Jonathan Goldberg, Oxford University Press, Oxford, 1991; and online at http://www.dartmouth.edu/~milton/reading_room.

1. Through these difficult years, Christopher's children stayed with their mother, their grandmother and possibly other carers while their Royalist father went to the wars. When his property was confiscated, payments were then made by a Committee on Christopher's behalf to Mrs Isabel Webber, his mother-in-law, who was paid £2 14s on 1 July 1644 and then on through the following year.
2. John Milton, *Second Defence* IV (1) 621.

3. Edward Phillips, in Helen Darbishire, ed., *The Early Lives of Milton*, Constable, London, 1932, p. 64.

4. Barbara Lewalski, *The Life of John Milton: A Critical Biography*, rev. edn, Blackwell, Oxford, 2002, p. 159.

5. Milton's case for the study of agriculture is typical. Using Latin authors, and in imitation of Hercules, the boys would learn 'to improve the tillage of their country, to recover the bad soil, and to remedy the waste that is made of good'. Their book-learning would be supplemented by input from the 'helpful experiences of hunters, fowlers, fishermen, shepherds, gardeners, apothecaries; and in the other sciences, architects, engineers, mariners, anatomists, who, doubtless, would be ready, some for reward and some to favour such a hopeful seminary'.

6. CPW II 377–9.

7. The Church courts would eventually be abolished in 1646, when the land owned by the bishops and archbishops was sold off to benefit the clergy and the Commonwealth. The laws on divorce did not change.

8. For further information, see the introduction by John Morrill to John Morrill, ed., *Oliver Cromwell and the English Revolution*, Longman, London, 1990, and Peter Gaunt, *Oliver Cromwell*, Blackwell, Oxford, 1996 for a valuable overview.

9. The situation in war-torn continental Europe was hardly more stable, although at least, from the point of view of Queen Henrietta Maria, the French were in the ascendant. In September 1644, they went on the offensive against the Habsburg territories, capturing Mainz, Mannheim, Speyer, Worms and Oppenheim. They commanded the Rhine from Switzerland to Mainz.

10. State Papers Domestic 1644 503.56.10.

11. Martin Dzelzainis, in 'Milton and the Protectorate in 1658', in David Armitage, Armand Himy and Quentin Skinner, eds, *Milton and Republicanism*, Cambridge University Press, Cambridge, 1995, p. 10 *passim*, for persuasive arguments about the development of Milton's political views.

12. CPW II 479.

13. Ibid., 585.

14. The full title of *Colasterion* (1645) is as much concerned with authorship and licensing as it is with divorce: *A REPLY to a Nameless ANSWER against the Doctrine and Discipline of DIVORCE. Wherein the trivial Author of that Answer is discover'd, the Licenser conferr'd with, and the Opinion which they traduce, defended. PROV. xxvi. 5. Answer a Fool according to his Folly, lest he be wise in his own Conceit.*

15. *Tetrachordon*, CPW II 579.

16. *The Glass of God's Providence Towards his Faithful Ones*, 1644, p. 57.

17. *An Answer to a Book*, 1644, pp. 33, 16.

18. Thomas Corns, 'Ideology in the Poemata (1645)', *Milton Studies* 19 (1984), pp. 195–6.

19. See David Norbrook, 'Areopagitica, Censorship, and the Early Modern Public Sphere', in Robert Demaria Jr, *British Literature 1640–1789*, Blackwell, Oxford, 1999, p. 23.

20. CPW II 492.

21. Many fonts were 'used indiscriminately in the same work'; small printers, 'apparently men of little learning or taste', rushed into business; and overall the middle years of the seventeenth century 'found the English book industry in a broken-down condition'. See Marjorie Plant, *The English Book Trade: An Economic History of the Making and Sale of Books*, second edn, George Allen & Unwin, London, 1965, p. 33.

22. CPW II 514–15.

23. Plant, *English Book Trade*, p. 19.

24. See William Riley Parker, *Milton: A Biography*, second edn, rev. Gordon Campbell, 2 vols, Clarendon Press, Oxford, 1996, vol. I, p. 264.

25. Stephen Dobranski, *Milton, Authorship and the Book Trade*, Cambridge University Press, Cambridge, 1999, p. 31.

26. This and previous quotation, CPW II 526.

27. Written on 28 September 1654, from 'Westminster', this was John's second letter to Philaras. The first was written from 'London' in June 1652. See CPW IV (2) 869.

28. There are features of both chronic and acute glaucoma, two distinct illnesses, in Milton's account. In the former, the loss of sight is usually gradual and painless, and the nerve fibres at the sides of the eye are the first to be affected, leading to a loss of outer (peripheral) vision, which can be hard to notice. Central vision is the last to go. Acute glaucoma is more rare, and the symptoms are more painful. The eye becomes red, and the eyeball becomes hard and sore to the touch. The pupil enlarges, and becomes oval, and, as Milton notes in his own case history, vision becomes misty and haloes are often seen around sources of light. Acute glaucoma becomes more and more painful, with accompanying headaches or toothache, and sometimes nausea and vomiting. Each attack can last for a few hours, with every one causing a further loss of vision. Usually, only one eye is affected. Even now, the causes of glaucoma are not fully understood, although genetic inheritance is seen as crucial. It seems that Milton's mother had weak eyes. See Lewalski, *Milton*, p. 4, for further comment.

29. *Treatise on Painting*, quoted in Moshe Barasch, *Blindness: The History of a Mental Image in Western Thought*, Routledge, London, 2001, p. 115.

30. Michael Hunter and Annabel Gregory, eds, *An Astrological Diary of the Seventeenth Century: Samuel Jeake of Rye 1652–1699*, Clarendon Press, Oxford, 1988, pp. 120–21.

31. Ibid., pp. 124, 126.

32. Milton was 'soon dismissed', wrote Cyriack Skinner (*Early Lives*, p. 24). It is quite possible he was never there: Gordon Campbell notes that there is no record of the result of his appearance; see *A Milton Chronology*, Macmillan, Basingstoke, 1997, p. 83.

33. *Colasterion*, 1645, CPW II 727.

34. His final divorce tract, *Colasterion*, takes the name of an Athenian place of punishment, Milton punishing his enemies in print. Milton's snobbery is everywhere visible. He is savage about his opponent's lack of education and his bad spelling, and dismisses him as 'some Mechanic'.

35. Christopher Durston, *Cromwell's Major Generals: Godly Government during the English Revolution*, Manchester University Press, Manchester, 2001, p. 1.

36. It sounds unlikely, but it is just possible that John Milton was considered for military service at this time. Edward Phillips's memoir of his uncle mentions that he was considered for the post of adjutant-general in the parliamentary army, possibly by his friend Capt. Hobson. With the changes in the army, the idea, if it ever existed, was quietly dropped.

37. Thomas Edwards, *Gangraena: or A Catalogue and Discovery of many of the Errours, Heresies, Blasphemies and Pernicious Practices of the Sectaries of the time*, London, 1646, p. 62.

38. Ibid., p. 65.

39. The volume of essays *Milton and Republicanism* exposes the differences between Milton scholars. Martin Dzelzainis, for example, sees Milton's break with the Presbyterians as the first clear move towards a republican political theory. Thomas Corns, here and elsewhere, insists that Milton's republicanism, such as it was, emerged after the event. See 'Milton and the Characteristics of a Free Commonwealth', p. 25.

40. Coward, *Stuart Age*, p. 222.

41. Cromwell to a Parliamentary County Committee, 29 August 1643; see W. C. Abbott (with the assistance of Catherine D. Crane), ed., *The Writings and Speeches of Oliver Cromwell*, 4 vols, Clarendon Press, Oxford, 1988, vol. I (1599–1649), p. 256.

42. Cromwell to Colonel Robert Hammond, 25 November 1648, in Abbott, *Writings and speeches*, vol. I, p. 697.
43. See Morrill's Introduction to *Cromwell and the English Revolution*.
44. Phillips, p. 66, and Skinner, pp. 22–3, in Darbishire, *Early Lives*. The story of Dr Davis's daughter is as unsubstantiated as that of Milton being a military adviser but is taken more seriously by recent biographers, partly because it fits with their vision of him. Not only did John need a wife, but he wanted a clever one: 'This time, it seems, Milton sought a woman of wit.' See Lewalski, *Milton*, pp. 184–5.
45. It is just possible that members of John Milton's mother's family enabled the reconciliation. Hester Jeffrey, a maternal relative, married William Blackborough, a leather-seller, and John Milton often visited their house. Edward Phillips takes up the story:

> One time above the rest, he making his usual visit, the Wife was ready in another Room, and on a sudden he was surprised to see one whom he thought to have never seen more, making Submission and begging Pardon on her Knees before him: he might probably at first make some show of aversion and rejection; but partly his own generous nature, more inclinable to reconciliation than to perseverance in anger or revenge, and partly the strong intercession of friends on both sides, soon brought him to an act of oblivion and a firm league of peace for the future.' (Darbishire, *Early Lives*, pp. 66–7.)

11 Poems, 1645

N.B. The poems referred to in this chapter are all in *Shorter Poems*, and also in most collections of Milton's poetry. *The Tenure of Kings and Magistrates* can be seen online at http://www.dartmouth.edu/~milton; in John Milton, *Political Writings*, ed. Martin Dzelzainis, trans. C. Gruzelier, Cambridge Texts in the History of Political Thought, Cambridge University Press, Cambridge, 1991; and in John Milton, *The Major Works*, ed. Stephen Orgel and Jonathan Goldberg, Oxford University Press, Oxford, 1991.

1. Thomas N. Corns, 'Ideology in the *Poemata* (1645)', *Milton Studies* 19 (1984), pp. 201–2.
2. Translation in *Shorter Poems*, p. 237.
3. Ibid., p. 236.
4. Stephen Dobranski, *Milton, Authorship and the Book Trade*, Cambridge University Press, Cambridge, 1999, pp. 19–23.
5. Andrew Sharp, ed., *The English Levellers*, Cambridge University Press, Cambridge, 1998. I follow Sharp closely.
6. *Gold tried in the fire, or the burnt petitions revived*, printed in Sharp, *Levellers*, p. 80.
7. See David Scott, *Politics and War in the Three Stuart Kingdoms, 1637–1649*, Palgrave Macmillan, Basingstoke, 2004, for a clear narrative history of these complex issues, especially pp. 65–6.
8. See Sharp, *Levellers*, p. xiv. Sharp outlines (p. xiii) the key Leveller proposals: reforms in the Church-state, and a new constitution of authority to carry out those reforms, which could, and should, be instituted immediately. The Levellers insisted that the fundamental jural facts about being human justified the reforms, as well as the constitution and its institution.
9. 'Declaration of the New Model Army', June 1647, quoted in Sharp, *Levellers*, p. x.
10. See Barry Coward and Chris Durston, *The English Revolution*, John Murray, London, 1997, p. 116.

11. The members of the movement now known as the Levellers did not, therefore, refer to themselves in these terms. Nor did they use a language of democracy (although they could be described as proto-democrats). Instead, Lilburne and his fellows described themselves as 'the well-affected' or 'many thousands earnestly desiring the glory of God, the freedom of the commonwealth and the peace of all men'. See Sharp, *Levellers*, p. xxii.

12. See E. H. Evelyn White, ed., *The Journal of William Dowsing*, Pawsey & Hayes, Ipswich, 1885, p. 26.

13. The House of Commons stopped observing Christmas in 1643, and the ruling became official in January 1645, according to the Westminster Assembly's *Directory of Public Worship*. God-fearing merchants, keen to show just how little Christmas Day meant to them, stayed open for business. In response, the shops were stoned, and their owners received death threats. Elsewhere, crowds turned to violence to express their hostility to the changes.

14. One of the most entertaining accounts of travel in Italy dates from this period. John Evelyn, making the most of his escape from war-torn England, had a very different experience to that of John Milton a few years earlier. Knowing that back in England, the Christmas festival was in the process of disappearing, Evelyn made sure he attended 'the many extraordinary Ceremonies performed then in their Churches, as mid-night Masses, & Sermons; so as I did nothing all this night but go from Church to Church'. See E. S. de Beer, ed., *The Diaries of John Evelyn*, Oxford University Press, Oxford, 1959, p. 153.

15. See Mark Stoyle, *From Deliverance to Destruction: Rebellion and Civil War in an English City*, University of Exeter Press, Exeter, 1996, pp. 134–5. This is a fascinating book, packed with contemporary documents, local history at its most compelling and meaningful.

16. Robert Pye fought for Parliament and became the MP for Woodstock, a few miles north-west of Oxford.

17. State Papers Domestic 1646 23.194.

18. Powell's personal estate in corn and other household stuff amounted to £500 with timber and wood accounting for £400 more, but he owed John Milton £300 ('upon a statute') and other individuals £1,200. Moreover, he claimed to have 'lost by reason of these wars three thousand pounds'.

19. See Christopher Durston, *The Family in the English Revolution*, Blackwell, Oxford, 1999, pp. 50–52.

20. For the first eight days or so after the birth, Mary would have kept to her bed as did almost all mothers at the time. Baby Anne would have been sent away to a wet nurse during this time, since it was believed that on the second day, the baby should be put to the breast of another woman until the eighth day or so, the reasoning being that immediately after giving birth, the mother's milk was observed to be wheyish, 'Foul, Turbid and Curdy'. The rejected liquid was, of course, colostrum, and so to deny a baby this vital boost to its immune system was actually destructive.

21. Darbishire, *Early Lives*, p. 67.

22. In baby Anne's earliest months, her young mother would have had the advice and practical support of her own highly experienced mother. Later on, Mary might have consulted the huge range of advice books, often written by religious authors, telling mothers how to care for babies. There was a growing market for these publications during the seventeenth century, perhaps because an increasing number of women were becoming mothers away from their own mothers or other female relatives. See Patricia Crawford, *Blood, Bodies and Families in Early Modern England*, Longman, Edinburgh, 2004, pp. 142, 144 and 157 in particular.

23. This letter was taken to Italy by 'Bookseller James' or 'his master', possibly James Allestree, who was apprentice to George Thomason.

24. John Milton was friends with George Thomason and his wife, Katharine. Thomason's collection of pamphlets has been vital to the study of the print culture of this period. When his wife died in December 1646, John wrote a lovely sonnet in her memory (of which there are no fewer than three copies in the Trinity Manuscript, Milton's own collection of his poetry). As Milton's editor John Carey admits, '. . . very little is known of Mrs Thomason. She had nine children, and the mention of her library in her husband's will indicates scholarly leanings' (*Shorter Poems*, p. 300). Scholarly leanings or not, Milton's poem on Katharine does not provide much more detail, dealing only in brilliant but general praise. Katharine is a perfect woman, 'meekly' leaving the world, accompanied by love and faith, her two handmaids, who fly her up to heaven. There they 'speak the truth of thee', a lovely phrase, making the judgement of God into something beautiful, and allowing the judge to 'thenceforth bid thee rest / And drink thy fill of pure immortal streams'.

25. Dati to Milton, 1 November 1647, from Florence, CPW II 772–3.

26. Barbara Lewalski, *The Life of John Milton: A Critical Biography*, rev. edn, Blackwell, Oxford, 2002, p. 110.

27. The Psalms did not appear in print at their time of writing. It is possible that Milton wanted to contribute to a very current debate since the Westminster Assembly had appointed a committee to revise the Psalms, and it sat in April 1648. It is equally possible that his choice of Psalms, which focus on the need for the Church of God's guidance, expressed his private dismay at the current situation. The translations may simply have been a revelation of the academic translator in Milton. See Mary Ann Radzinowicz, *Milton's Epics and the Book of Psalms*, Princeton University Press, Princeton, NJ, 1989, esp. p. 5.

28. For one Milton scholar at least, John was still struggling to come to terms with living out the heterosexual values of his society. 'Was the anxiety potential in the married man with latent homoerotic tendencies contributory to the psychosomatic problems that seem to have advanced Milton's blindness?' asks John T. Shawcross, in *John Milton: The Self and the World*, University Press of Kentucky, Lexington, KY, 1993, p. 57.

29. See David Scott, *Politics and War in the Three Stuart Kingdoms, 1637–1649*, Palgrave Macmillan, Basingstoke, 2004 for a clear narrative history, esp. p. 188.

30. The proceedings can be seen at http://www2.wwnorton.com/college/english/nael/ 17century/topic_3/trial.htm, where all of the following quotations can be found.

31. See Sean Kelsey, 'Bradshaw, John, Lord Bradshaw (bap. 1602, d. 1659)', in *Oxford Dictionary of National Biography*, Oxford University Press, Oxford, 2004; online edn, http://www.oxforddnb.com/view/article/3201, May 2006 (accessed 21 February 2007).

32. CPW III 190.

33. Lewalski, *Milton*, p. 230.

34. Nicholas von Maltzahn, *Milton's History of Britain: Republican Historiography in the English Revolution*, Clarendon Press, Oxford, 1991, p. 36.

12 Revolution, 1649

N.B. The *History of England* (including the 'Digression'), *Eikonoklastes* (The Image Destroyer) and *A Defence of the People of England* are printed in CPW. *A Defence* can also be found in John Milton, *Political Writings*, ed. Martin Dzelzainis, Cambridge University Press, Cambridge, 1991, in a new translation by Claire Gruzelier.

1. Quoted in Martin Bennett, *The Civil Wars Experienced: Britain and Ireland, 1638–1661*, Routledge, London, 2000, p. 154.

2. Ruth Spalding, ed., *The Diary of Bulstrode Whitelocke 1605–1675*, Oxford University Press, Oxford, 1990, p. 229.

3. Matthew Henry Lee, ed., *Diaries and Letters of Philip Henry*, Kegan Paul, London, 1882, p. 12.

4. For this and the following references, see J. P. Kenyon, ed., *The Stuart Constitution, 1603–1688: Documents and Commentary*, second edn, Cambridge University Press, Cambridge, 1986, p. 306.

5. *A Single Eye All Light No Darkness*, 1650, quoted in Barry Coward and Chris Durston, *The English Revolution*, John Murray, London, 1997, pp. 136–7.

6. The Quaker leader George Fox recounts in his autobiography his meeting with some Ranters, vividly evoking the dangers of the time, as well as his own religious faith. Fox had heard of 'a people in prison at Coventry for religion', so he walked to the jail. He was happy because 'the Lord came to me, saying "My love was always to thee, and thou art in my love."' Arriving at the prison, however, 'a great power of darkness struck at me': the prisoners were Ranters. The prisoners 'began to rant, vapour, and blaspheme . . . they said that they were God . . .' Having questioned them about their biblical justification for their behaviour (from his point of view, they had none), Fox moved in for the kill: 'Then, seeing they said that they were God, I asked them if they knew whether it would rain tomorrow. They said they could not tell. I told them God could tell.' Fox, it seems, rather enjoyed this encounter. His autobiography can be found at http://www.strecorsoc.org/gfox/title.html. This episode comes in Chapter Three.

7. http://www.strecorsoc.org/gfox/title.html, Chapter Four.

8. Sig. A4r (unpaged).

9. See Andrew Sharp, ed., *The English Levellers*, Cambridge University Press, Cambridge, 1998, p. xiii. The historical conditions in which they operated meant that to hold these beliefs 'was a standing temptation to rebellion and a mutiny'. Lilburne and his allies 'exemplify the difficulties of being democratic in impossible circumstances'. The women's claims were grounded in their belief that they as much as men were created in the image of God, and had an equal interest in Christ. Therefore, crucially, women had 'a proportional share in the freedoms of this commonwealth'.

10. *To the supreme authority, the Commons of England assembled in Parliament The humble petition of divers well-affected women of the cities of London and Westminster, the borough of Southwark, hamlets, and parts adjacent. Affecters and approvers of the petition of Sept. 11. 1648*, London, 1649. Extracts are printed in Andrew Bradstock and Christopher Rowland, eds, *Radical Christian Writings: A Reader*, Blackwell, Oxford, 2002, p. 112.

11. W. C. Abbott (with the assistance of Catherine D. Crane), ed., *The Writings and Speeches of Oliver Cromwell*, 4 vols, Clarendon Press, Oxford, 1988, vol. III (The Protectorate 1653–1655), p. 438 ('His Highnesse the Lord Protector's speech to the Parliament in the Painted Chamber, on Monday, the 4th of September, 1654').

12. Ibid., vol. II, pp. 41–2.

13. In 1649 the soldiers were paid in debentures, entitling them to ex-Crown land. The regiments acted collectively to sell the land, and the cash was distributed. See Barry Coward, *The Stuart Age: England 1603–1714*, third edn, Pearson, Harlow, 2003, p. 246.

14. Guy de la Bedoyere, ed., *The Diary of John Evelyn*, Boydell Press, Woodbridge, 1995, p. 68.

15. *A Sermon Preached in Northampton*, 1607, sig. E3r–v, quoted in James Holstun, *Ehud's Dagger: Class Struggle in the English Revolution*, Verso, London, 2000, pp. 377ff.

16. Nicholas von Maltzahn, *Milton's History of Britain: Republican Historiography in the English Revolution*, Clarendon Press, Oxford, 1991, pp. 22–3, 27.

17. CPW V 441.

18. Ibid., III 192.

19. John Milton, *Second Defence*, 1654, CPW IV (1) 627–8.

20. *An Horation Ode upon Cromwell's return from Ireland*, ll. 57–64.

21. Philip A. Knachel, ed., *Eikon Basilike: The Portraiture of His Sacred Majesty in His Solitudes and Sufferings*, Cornell University Press, Ithaca, NY, 1966, pp. 137, 177.

22. CPW III 380–81.

23. Ibid., 592.

24. Ibid., 542.

25. Ibid., 601.

26. David Norbrook, *Writing the English Republic: Poetry, Rhetoric and Politics 1627–1660*, Cambridge University Press, Cambridge, 1999, p. 200.

27. In *Observations upon the article of peace*, as in *Eikonoklastes*, Milton was discreet about his own anxieties concerning the Rump's backsliding, and wrote powerfully about the dangers to be faced if the new England's enemies joined with those in Ireland or Scotland.

28. State Papers Domestic 25.63.

29. From Harold Love, 'Was Lucina Betrayed at Whitehall?', in Nicholas Fisher, ed., *That Second Bottle: Essays on John Wilmot, Earl of Rochester*, Manchester University Press, Manchester, 2000, p. 182.

30. People took their spices with them when they moved: cloves, long cinnamon, nutmegs case, long ginger, pepper case, fine mace, middle mace, all spice, marmalade, saffron, ambergris, sugar pieces, 'raisins of the sun', currants.

31. Simon Thurley, *Whitehall Palace: An Architectural History of the Royal Apartments, 1240–1698*, Yale University Press, New Haven, CT, 1999, p. 98.

32. See Joad Raymond, p. 125, and Blair Worden, p. 157, in David Armitage, Armand Himy and Quentin Skinner, eds, *Milton and Republicanism*, Cambridge University Press, Cambridge, 1995; and Nigel Smith, *Literature and Revolution in England, 1640–1660*, Yale University Press, New Haven, CT, 1994, p. 67.

33. I am indebted to www.brysons.net/miltonweb for collecting these insults.

34. John Milton, *Political Writings*, ed. Martin Dzelzainis, Cambridge University Press, Cambridge, 1991, p. 68.

35. Thomas Corns, 'Milton and the Characteristics of a Free Commonwealth', in Armitage, Himy and Skinner, *Milton and Republicanism*, p. 33.

36. See Norbrook, *Writing the English Republic*, p. 204.

37. *Life Records* III 159 has a slightly different version, noting that Brackley wrote 'the malicious rascal that wrote this book did highly deserve of the gallows' into a copy of *The Life and Reign of King Charles* (a response to *Eikon Basilike*), which he believed had been written by Milton. It was not.

38. *Life Records* III 58.

39. Ibid., III 65.

40. *Reason of Church Government*, CPW I 815.

41. *Life Records* III 42.

42. The letters can be found in CPW IV (2) 828ff.

43. For the details of property deals, legal cases and financial transactions, see Campbell, *Milton Chronology*. What follows is just one example of Milton's financial dealings. Milton bought an excise bond from one George Foxcroft. This was a useful way of

raising income in the early days of the Commonwealth. The government had raised £150,000 in excise duties through an Ordinance of Parliament in the last years of the 1640s. Some of the money was spent on government business, but it was also possible for individuals to buy into the government's excise income. So one could buy a bond, say for £400, and receive the interest on that bond at 8 per cent paid twice a year, a useful income of £16 every six months. These bonds were quite reliable sources of income, or so John must have thought when he bought his in May 1651 from a man who had bought it himself from a Maj. Alexander Elliott, who in turn had bought it from one Hugh Curtney.

44. State Papers Domestic 1651 23.110 (see pp. 595, 597).

13 Government, 1651

N.B. The poems mentioned in this chapter are printed in *Shorter Poems*, and in most collections of Milton's poetry.

1. Mylius to Milton, CPW IV (2) 837.
2. *Life Records* III 140.
3. Milton to Mylius, CPW IV (2) 835.
4. Both quoted in Ralph Houlbrooke, *English Family Life 1576–1716: An Anthology from Diaries*, Blackwell, Oxford, 1988, pp. 108, 109.
5. Quoted in Houlbrooke, *English Family*, p. 112.
6. John Toland in Helen Darbishire, ed., *The Early Lives of Milton*, Constable, London, 1932, p. 83.
7. Deborah was as radical a choice of name as, for example, Tower, the child of Levellers John and Elizabeth Lilburne (the baby had been born in the Tower of London) or indeed Prisonborn, the son of the Fifth Monarchist John Rogers, born in imprisonment in Windsor Castle.
8. British Library Add MS 32310.
9. This is, of necessity, speculation. It is equally possible that the Milton children were nursed and raised by their mother, and played with by their father, all in the family home. One father recorded just this experience in the years 1646–7. Delighted when he found that his new baby, Jane, could be nursed by his wife, a few days later he was acutely anxious when his wife thought she was going to die (she was 'weakly and faint' and suffering from toothache, while the baby had a cold). By May the baby had cut her first tooth, and, at last, in August the parents got a good night's sleep: '. . . we enjoyed our rest well in the night.' By November, celebrating her first birthday, Jane 'began to go alone', and in May 1647, when she was about eighteen months old, the father reported that 'my wife weaned her daughter Jane; she took it very contentedly; God hath given me much comfort in my wife and children, and in their quietness.' Another father recorded in detail the different dates when his young children returned home from their nurses. He took home 'my daughter Mary from nurse' when she was just two, 'she having eight teeth and having been weaned three quarters of a year before'. In contrast, Alexander, who was 'almost two year old, cannot go yet alone, but by holding he can go about the house. He hath twenty teeth, as his nurse saith'. The nurse who reported on Alexander's teeth probably cared for him in the family home. See Houlbrooke, *English Family*, pp. 110–11.
10. Guy de la Bedoyere, ed., *The Diary of John Evelyn*, Boydell Press, Woodbridge, 1995, p. 84.

11. See David Cressy, *Birth, Marriage, Death: Ritual, Religion, and the Life-cycle in Tudor and Stuart England*, Oxford University Press, Oxford, 1997, p. 383.

12. Houlbrooke, *English Family*, p. 70.

13. Ibid., pp. 70–71.

14. Darbishire, *Early Lives*, p. 71.

15. This father was mourning a ten-day-old baby. What evidence there is suggests that parents felt the death of older babies even more painfully. One father wrote that his baby died at twenty-one months, 'leaving myself and my dear wife the saddest and most disconsolate parents that ever lost so tender and sweet an infant'. He recorded that he was far more grieved than at the death of three other babies who had died shortly after birth 'who dying almost as soon as they were born, were not so endeared to us as this was'. See Patricia Crawford, *Blood, Bodies and Families in Early Modern England*, Longman, Harlow, 2004, p. 153. The familiarity of death did not diminish its impact. Sir William Brownlow recorded in his family Bible mourning texts for all his lost babies; even his last-born, George, who died at ten months in 1642, was noted: 'I was at ease, but thou O god has broken me asunder and shaken me to pieces.' Childcare practices and religious faith did not stop fathers being emotionally attached to their children and grieving intensely when they died. To make matters worse, John was Milton's only son. Historians have shown that special children, oldest sons above all, could generate a powerful commitment and equally intense grief even if they died before they had much passed infancy. See Felicity Heal and Clive Holmes, *The Gentry in England and Wales, 1500–1700*, Macmillan, Basingstoke, 1994, p. 78.

16. Quoted in Leo Miller, *John Milton and the Oldenburg Safeguard*, Loewenthal Press, New York, NY, 1985, p. 49.

17. See Ruth E. Mayers, 'Vane, Sir Henry, the Younger (1613–1662)', in *Oxford Dictionary of National Biography*, Oxford University Press, Oxford, 2004; online edn, http://www.oxforddnb.com/view/article/28086; accessed 31 January 2007.

18. Margaret Pelling, *The Common Lot: Sickness, Medical Occupations and the Urban Poor in Early Modern England: Essays*, Longman, London, 1988, p. 85.

19. This is the copy in Canterbury Cathedral Library. Noted in William Riley Parker, *Milton: A Biography*, second edn, rev. Gordon Campbell, 2 vols, Clarendon Press, Oxford, 1996, vol. II, p. 988.

20. Bernard Capp, *When Gossips Meet: Women, Family, and Neighbourhood in Early Modern England*, Oxford University Press, Oxford, 2003, p. 13.

21. The Society ceased operations in 2005. See http://ca.geocities.com/jmscan@rogers.com/History.html.

22. CPW IV (2) 859.

23. Milton to Bradshaw, 21 February 1653, CPW IV (2) 859–60.

24. Meadows in Lisbon used a mixture of bravado and common sense to save the day, and on his return his success was recognised by the Council, which voted him a ninety-nine-year lease on lands worth £100 'in consideration of the maim received . . . in execution of his duty'. In a sign of the times, the Council found it difficult to find any spare land to give him. See Timothy Venning, 'Meadows, Sir Philip (bap. 1626, d. 1718)', in *Oxford Dictionary of National Biography*, Oxford University Press, Oxford, 2004; online edn, http://www.oxforddnb.com/view/article/18479, May 2006; accessed 21 February 2007.

25. Three slightly differing eyewitness accounts are printed in Wilbur Cortez Abbott, ed., *The Writings and Speeches of Oliver Cromwell*, 4 vols, Clarendon Press, Oxford, 1939, vol. II, pp. 641–4.

26. J. P. Kenyon, ed., *The Stuart Constitution, 1603–1688: Documents and Commentary*, second edn, Cambridge University Press, Cambridge, 1986, p. 318 ('His Highnesse

the Lord Protector's speech to the Parliament in the Painted Chamber, on Tuesday, the 12th of September, 1654').

27. See Christopher Durston, *Cromwell's Major-Generals: Godly Government during the English Revolution,* Manchester University Press, Manchester, 2001, p. 2, for a superb summary.

28. Edward Hyde, Earl of Clarendon, *The History of the Rebellion and Civil Wars in England: Begun in the Year 1641,* ed. W. W. Dunn Macray, 6 vols, Oxford University Press, Oxford, 1888; 1969, vol. V (Bks XII–XIV), p. 282.

29. Barry Coward, *The Stuart Age: England 1603–1714,* third edn, Longman, Harlow, 2003, p. 261.

30. See Simon Thurley, *Whitehall Palace: An Architectural History of the Royal Apartments, 1240–1698,* Yale University Press, New Haven, CT, 1999, p. 98.

14 Defence, 1654

N.B. *The Second Defence of the English People* is printed in CPW and online (without annotation) at http://www.constitution.org/milton/second_defence.htm.

1. Milton to Philaras, 28 September 1654, CPW IV (2) 869.
2. Ibid., 870.
3. The work was *Joannis Miltoni Angli Pro Se Defensio contra Alexandrum Morum* (John Milton Englishman His Defence of Himself against Alexander More), CPW IV (2) 703. Kestar Svendsen, the editor of this work for CPW (IV (2) 687), writes that '*Pro Se Defensio* is unique among Milton's prose works because it was occasioned by the worst mistake of his public career,' his belief that Alexander More had written *Regii Sanguinis Clamor,* a belief that informs his *Second Defence.*
4. Marvell to Milton, 2 June 1654, CPW IV (2) 864.
5. Ibid.
6. Ibid.
7. Vossius to Heinsius, 21 January 1653, *Life Records* III 316.
8. Bramhall was a Royalist ex-bishop in exile. Having left the country in 1650, he administered Communion to Charles Stuart en route to a life spent moving between Royalist communities in The Hague, Antwerp, Brussels, Ghent, Utrecht, Flushing and Paris. The Royalist exiles developed their own literary and intellectual subculture. Bramhall, for example, was embroiled in a lively battle with the philosopher Thomas Hobbes, which began in Paris at the Earl of Newcastle's residence.
9. Milton to Oldenburg, 6 July 1654, CPW IV (2) 866.
10. The linguistic jokes lose what wit they have in translation. Milton puns on the Greek meaning of *morus* ('a fool') and on the Latin meaning ('a mulberry bush'): '. . . the pun on *morus* or mulberry brings on a delirium of bawdy jokes about gardening, planting, grafting, shady patches, statues of Priapus . . . In the potting shed with his landlord's maid, More shows her the *modus* of inserting the mulberry graft into the fig and many other things . . .' See James Grantham Turner, 'Milton among the Libertines', in Christophe Tournu and Neil Forsythe, eds, *Milton, Rights and Liberties,* Peter Lang, Bern, 2007, p. 452.
11. CPW IV (1) 582.
12. Ibid., 583.
13. Ibid., 638.

14. Ibid., 685.

15. The translation is from *The Works of John Milton*, 18 vols, Columbia University Press, New York, 1933, vol. VIII, pp. 13–15.

16. Scholar Joad Raymond has shown that after this date a determined newsman could get his news published, but not necessarily in newsbooks. See ' "A Mercury with a Winged Conscience": Marchamont Nedham, Monopoly and Censorship', *Media History*, 4 (1998), pp. 7–18.

17. James Holstun, *Ehud's Dagger: Class Struggle in the English Revolution*, Verso, London, 2000, p. 279.

18. Anna Trapnel, *The Cry of a Stone*, 1654, 22, 19–20, quoted in ibid., p. 285.

19. Holstun, *Ehud's Dagger*, p. 286.

20. 7 February 1654, State Papers Domestic 1653–54, 66.20.

21. Subsequently, as the Fifth Monarchist movement divided among itself, her life becomes less clear. There are glimpses of her in May 1656 in Cornwall, contemplating linking up with the Quakers, and emigrating. Trapnel was, however, still prophesying later in the decade.

22. The defeat in the Caribbean followed sharply upon a highly successful period in the Protectorate's foreign policy. By the mid-1650s, the two great powers in Europe, France and Spain, had accepted the new regime in England, and were each now seeking an alliance with Cromwell. Through 1654, he had toyed with each country, favouring overall a trading alliance with France, if only because Charles II was ensconced in Paris, and in a secret clause in a commercial treaty, the French promised to expel him. In turn, rather than declaring open war on Spain, Cromwell was plotting an attack on Spanish territories in the West Indies. The intention was to seize these regions and colonise them, boosting trade and spreading true religion. It was a good plan, and the reasons for military failure were equally good: reliance on faulty military intelligence, the deployment of pressed troops, and unexpectedly heavy surf in the Indies. But for Cromwell no explanation other than God's displeasure could be found.

23. For the instructions to the Major-Generals, see J. P. Kenyon, ed., *The Stuart Constitution, 1603–1688: Documents and Commentary*, second edn, Cambridge University Press, Cambridge, 1986, pp. 322–4.

24. See Jason Rosenblatt, *Torah and Law in Paradise Lost*, Princeton University Press, Princeton, 1994, and David S. Katz, *Philo-Semitism and the Readmission of the Jews to England*, Clarendon Press, Oxford, 1992.

25. Rumours of readmission, and Cromwell's support for the idea, encouraged the story that Cromwell intended 'to sell St Paul's' to the Jews 'for a Synagogue . . . to reward that Nation which had given the first noble example of crucifying their King'. See Ezekiel Grebner, *The Visions and Prophecies Concerning England, Scotland, And Ireland*, 1661, p. 369.

26. From the Jewish point of view, readmission to England would be another step towards the fulfilment of the prophecy in the Book of Daniel: 'And when the dispersion of the holy people shall be completed in all places, then shall all these things be completed.' The Messiah would not come and restore the Jews to Israel until they had been scattered over all the earth.

27. Mark Goldie, 'James Harrington', in E. Craig, ed., *Routledge Encyclopedia of Philosophy*, Routledge, London, 1998; retrieved 30 September 2004 from http://www.rep.routledge.com/article/S074SECT4.

28. *Mercurius Politicus*, 19 November 1657.

29. Susan Vincent, *Dressing the Elite*, Berg, Oxford, 2003, p. 21.

30. Cromwell, Speech to the Committee, 13 April 1657, in W. C. Abbott (with the assistance of Catherine D. Crane), ed., *The Writings and Speeches of Oliver Cromwell*, 4 vols, Clarendon Press, Oxford, 1988, vol. IV (The Protectorate 1655–1658), p. 473.

31. Robert Thomas Fallon, *Milton in Government*, Pennsylvania State University Press, University Park, PA, 1993, p. 139.
32. *The Works of John Milton*, Columbia University Press, New York, NY, 1933, vol. XIII, p. 159.
33. Fallon, *Milton in Government*, p. 176.
34. CPW IV (1) 676.
35. See William Riley Parker, *Milton: A Biography*, second edn, rev. Gordon Campbell, 2 vols, Clarendon Press, Oxford, 1996, vol. II, pp. 1054, 1055.
36. Katherine was the eldest of four sisters. She lived apart from her mother (who lived with another sister) and may well have supported herself in some way.
37. See Houlbrooke, *English Family Life*, p. 71.
38. Daniel Rogers, *Matrimoniall Honour: Or the Mutuall Crowne and comfort of godly, loyall, and chaste Marriage*, London, 1642, p. 45, quoted in ibid., p. 212.
39. Laura Gowing, *Common Bodies: Women, Touch and Power in Seventeenth Century England*, Yale University Press, New Haven, CT, 2003, pp. 82–3.
40. *Life Records* IV 216.
41. The account survives in the College of Arms (Painters Workbook I. B. 7, fol. 46b). 'Buck' stands for 'buckram'. The pall was to cover the coffin. Escutcheons were attached to the pall.
42. See Ralph Houlbrooke, *The English Family 1450–1700*, Longman, London, 1984, pp. 209–10, for further details about widowhood. John would not have been damaged financially in any way by his wife's death, possibly quite the opposite.
43. *Life Records* IV 217.
44. See Leo Miller, *John Milton and the Oldenburg Safeguard*, Loewenthal Press, New York, NY, 1985, for the case against Milton's governmental significance.

15 Crisis, 1659

N.B. Three of the prose works mentioned in this chapter are only available in the *Yale Complete Prose Works: Civil Power in Ecclesiastical Causes, Hirelings*, and *De Doctrina Christianae. The Readie & Easie Way* is printed in John Milton, *The Major Works*, ed. Stephen Orgel and Jonathan Goldberg, Oxford University Press, Oxford, 1991.

1. N. H. Keeble, *The Restoration: England in the 1660s*, Blackwell, Oxford, 2002, p. 6.
2. See Martin Dzelzainis, 'Protectorate', in David Armitage, Armand Himy and Quentin Skinner, eds, *Milton and Republicanism*, Cambridge University Press, Cambridge, 1995.
3. Richard Baxter, *Reliquiae Baxterianae*, ed. Matthew Sylvester, 1696, p. 100; Thomas Birch, ed., *Collection of State Papers of John Thurloe*, 7 vols, 1742, vol. VII, p. 374. Both quoted in Keeble, *Restoration*, p. 5.
4. CPW VII 241, 242.
5. Ruth E. Mayers, 'Vane, Sir Henry, the Younger (1613–1662)', in *Oxford Dictionary of National Biography*, Oxford University Press, Oxford, 2004; online at http://www.oxforddnb.com/view/article/28086; accessed 31 January 2007.
6. Keeble, *Restoration*, p. 7.
7. John Aubrey, *Brief Lives*, ed. Andrew Clark, 2 vols, Clarendon Press, Oxford, 1898, vol. I, pp. 289–91.
8. Iona Sinclair, ed., *The Pyramid and the Urn: The Life in Letters of a Restoration Squire: William Lawrence of Shurdington, 1636–1697*, Alan Sutton, Stroud, 1994, p. 6.

9. *A Letter to a Friend*, CPW VII 325.

10. Worden, in Armitage, Himy and Skinner, *Milton and Republicanism*, p. 166.

11. CPW VII 463.

12. *A Letter to a Friend*, CPW VII 324–33.

13. Robert Thomas Fallon, *Milton in Government*, Pennsylvania State University Press, University Park, PA, 1993, p. 222. The manuscript itself can be found in the Rare Book and Manuscript Library, Butler Library, Columbia University, New York, no. X823M64S62.

14. Jason Rosenblatt, *Torah and Law in Paradise Lost*, Princeton University Press, Princeton, NJ, 1994, is the best source of information on this aspect of Milton's life and work.

15. The debate continues: Oxford University Press will launch its celebration of the quartercentenary of Milton's birth with the publication of a new study of the evidence, written by Gordon Campbell, Thomas Corns, John Hale and Fiona Tweedie.

16. Aubrey, *Brief Lives*, p. 291.

17. Letter to Revd John Owen, 29 November 1659, quoted in Roger Hainsworth, *The Swordsmen in Power: War and Politics under the English Republic 1649–1660*, Sutton, Stroud, 1997, p. 259.

18. Guy de la Bedoyere, ed., *The Diary of John Evelyn*, Boydell Press, Woodbridge, 1995, p. 112.

19. Mynors Bright, ed., *The Diary of Samuel Pepys*, 3 vols, Everyman, London, 1906, vol. I, p. 30.

20. Ibid., p. 33.

21. *The Readie & Easie Way* was advertised on 8 March in *Mercurius Politicus*, edn no. 610 of this republican newsbook. This was to be the paper's final edition. The advertisement came complete with errata, indicating John's close involvement with the printing of the work, despite his blindness, and despite the pressure of time.

22. CPW VII 388.

23. Bright, *Diary of Samuel Pepys*, vol. I, p. 45.

24. John, for example, transferred an excise bond to his friend Cyriack Skinner on 5 May, only three days before the Restoration was proclaimed.

25. Sir Richard Bulstrode, *Memoirs and Reflections upon the Reign and Government of King Charles Ist and King Charles IInd*, 1721, p. 222.

26. Philip Henry, quoted in Keeble, *Restoration*, p. 48.

27. Lucy Hutchinson, *Memoirs of the Life of Colonel Hutchinson*, ed. James Sutherland, Oxford University Press, Oxford, 1973, p. 227.

28. Edward Phillips wrote that his uncle stayed in a friend's house in Bartholomew Close, West Smithfield; see Helen Darbishire, ed., *The Early Lives of Milton*, Constable, London, 1932, p. 54.

29. The book-burning process was not smooth, with different people proclaiming different things at different times. See Gordon Campbell, *A Milton Chronology*, Macmillan, Basingstoke, 1997, pp. 191ff. Parliament was probably the driving force, since Charles II was rarely vindictive, famously saying, 'I must confess I am weary of hanging except upon new offences.' In contrast, Parliament energetically 'set about the formal and public humiliation of the legislative, legal, religious and intellectual bases of the previous regimes'. See Keeble, *Restoration*, pp. 90–91.

30. Mayers, 'Vane'.

16 Defeat, 1660

1. Quoted in N. H. Keeble, *The Restoration: England in the 1660s*, Blackwell, Oxford, 2002, p. 57.
2. Ibid., p. 49.
3. For further details of L'Estrange and his methods, see ibid., p. 152.
4. Quoted in Paul Hammond, 'Dryden, John (1631–1700)', in *Oxford Dictionary of National Biography*, Oxford University Press, Oxford, 2004; online at http://www.oxforddnb.com/view/article/8108; accessed 1 February 2007.
5. *The Trial of Sir Henry Vane, knight, at the King's Bench, Westminster, June the 2nd & 6th 1662*, 1662, p. 77.
6. Gordon Campbell, *A Milton Chronology*, Macmillan, Basingstoke, 1997, pp. 199, 200.
7. Pepys did so on 1 April 1662, having earlier seen a 'pretty good play'. See John Warrington, ed., *The Diary of Samuel Pepys*, 3 vols, Everyman, London, 1906, vol. I, p. 242.
8. See Susan Vincent, *Dressing the Elite: Clothes in Early Modern England*, Berg, Oxford, 2003.
9. 23 February 1663; *Diary*, vol. I, p. 359.
10. Gordon Campbell, 'Milton, John (1608–1674)', in *Oxford Dictionary of National Biography*, Oxford University Press, Oxford, 2004; online at http://www.oxforddnb.com/view/article/18800; accessed 1 February 2007. Scholars generally agree that Milton began work on the epic at some point after 1655, although, without new evidence, there is no certainty.
11. Grub Street is now Milton Street. Nearby, Bunhill Fields was converted in 1666 from a plague pit into the burial ground for Nonconformists. It is now a peaceful spot in the centre of a resolutely commercial area of London, the resting place of men such as John Bunyan and William Blake.
12. Quoted in Ian Atherton, *News, Newspapers and Society*, ed. Joad Raymond, Frank Cass, London, 1999, p. 39.
13. Among his works are 'translations from Latin, Greek, French, Spanish, and Italian, with a suggestion that Phillips may also have known Dutch'. John T. Shawcross, *The Arms of the Family: The Significance of John Milton's Relatives and Associates*, University Press of Kentucky, Lexington, KY, 2004, p. 107, argues that Phillips's talents have been underrated.
14. 24 October 1663, in Guy de la Bedoyere, ed., *The Diary of John Evelyn*, Boydell Press, Woodbridge, 1995, p. 135.
15. Helen Darbishire, ed., *The Early Lives of Milton*, Constable, London, 1932, pp. 74, 78.
16. Felicity Heal and Clive Holmes, *The Gentry in England and Wales, 1500–1700*, Macmillan, Basingstoke, 1994, p. 90.
17. Jerrard Winstanley, *The Law of Freedom in a Platform: or, True Magistracy Restored*, London, 1652, p. 34. Winstanley actually wrote 'the first link of the chain Magistracy' [sic].
18. Ralph Houlbrooke, *The English Family 1450–1700*, Longman, London, 1984, has much material on these vexed issues; see esp. p. 21.
19. Those who found this transition difficult often had strong loyalties to their mothers: '. . . the experience of childbirth in particular held mothers and daughters together; many mothers when their own period of child-rearing was past were eager to assist at the endless lyings-in of the next generation,' according to Heal and Holmes, *Gentry*, pp. 89–90.
20. *Life Records* V 222.

21. John's niece (the daughter of his sister Anne and her second husband, Thomas Agar) did something similar when she married in 1662. When she married David Moore of Richmond, Surrey, he gave his age as thirty but was actually forty-three. Ann was twenty-six. Their first child, Thomas, born the following year and baptized on 13 October 1663 at Richmond, would go on to be a playwright of no talent whatsoever.

22. Darbishire, *Early Lives*, p. 75.

23. Barbara Lewalski, *The Life of John Milton: A Critical Biography*, rev. edn, Blackwell, Oxford, 2002, pp. 398, 411, 489.

24. The Milton scholar John Shawcross has a typically provocative view of the relationship, when he wonders 'about the sex life of an older blind man with a younger wife. Perhaps there has been a "subordination of the phallus to the tongue", but the female world in which Milton found himself, with wife, children, and servants, may have been the only answer finally to the homoerotic, to the moral strictures of carnality, to the need for companionship and avoidance of the "lonely" life'; *Self and the World*, p. 232. This 'female world' had existed for many years, certainly since the early 1650s, when John Phillips had left the household.

25. James Nayler, *The Railer Rebuked, in a reply to a paper subscribed Ellis Bradshaw, who calls it The Quaker's whitest devil unvailed*, London, 1655, p. 7, and James Nayler, *A collection of sundry books, epistles and papers written by James Nayler, some of which were never before printed. With an impartial relation of the most remarkable transactions relating to his life*, ed. George Whitehead, London, 1716, pp. 113–14.

26. See James Holstun, *Ehud's Dagger: Class Struggle in the English Revolution*, Verso, London, 2000, p. 294, from which I take the term.

27. Thomas Ellwood, *The history of the life of Thomas Ellwood. Or, an account of his birth, education, &c.*, second edn, London, 1714, pp. 191–2.

28. Keeble, *Restoration*, p. 154.

29. Ellwood, *History*, p. 156.

30. Edmund Ludlow, *A Voice from the Watch Tower Part 5: 1660–1662*, ed. A. B. Worden, Royal Historical Society, London, 1978, p. 283.

31. 15 January 1662; *Diary*, p. 126.

32. Phillips wrote that *Paradise Lost* was composed in 'a parcel of ten, twenty, or thirty verses at a time, which being written by whatever hand came next, might possibly want correction as to the orthography and pointing'. He also noted that his uncle wrote most happily during the winter months, so that 'all the years he was about this poem, he may be said to have spent but half his time therein.' See Darbishire, *Early Lives*, p. 73.

33. The correspondence can be found in CPW VIII 1–4. The comment on the Latin is from Masson, and quoted on p. 1.

34. 3 September 1666; *Diary*, p. 154.

35. Quoted in Giles Mandelbrote, 'Workplaces and Living Spaces: London Book Trade Inventories of the Late Seventeenth Century', in Robin Myers, Michael Harris and Giles Mandelbrote, eds, *The London Book Trade: Topographies of Print in the Metropolis from the Sixteenth Century*, Oak Knoll Press and the British Library, London, 2003, pp. 21–43.

36. At the same time, the contract handed over all 'benefit profit and advantage' arising from the manuscript of the poem to Simmons and gave all rights to future impressions after the third 'without let or hindrance' from the author. Peter Lindenbaum, 'The Poet in the Marketplace: Milton and Samuel Simmons', in P. G. Stanwood, ed., *Of Poetry and Politics: New Essays on Milton and his World*, Medieval and Renaissance Texts and Studies, Tempe, 1997, and Stephen Dobranski, *Milton, Authorship and the Book Trade*, Cambridge University Press, Cambridge, 1999, are both invaluable resources for an understanding of the practicalities of Milton's writing career.

37. Nicholas von Maltzahn, 'The First Reception of Paradise Lost (1667)', *Review of English Studies* 47 (1996), pp. 479–99, is authoritative on this subject; see esp. pp. 480–84.
38. See Lewalski, *Milton*, p. 454, for a summary of the issues.
39. The surviving licensed copy of Book I of *Paradise Lost* shows evidence of discretion. It omits Milton's name, while the entry of the epic into the Stationers' Register refers only to Simmons, Tomkins (the licenser) and a 'Mr Warden Royston'. Milton appears as just 'I.M.' While it is hard to believe that the censors were unaware of the work's authorship, there was no attempt to draw attention to it in word or deed.
40. Since the average rate of printing production was about one and a half to two sheets per week, and *Paradise Lost* contains forty-three sheets, the printers may well have been working on the poem for twenty-two weeks, between May and October 1667.
41. The anecdote, given by Richardson, in Darbishire, *Early Lives*, p. 295, is disputed. See Theodore H. Banks, Jr, 'Sir John Denham and Paradise Lost', *Modern Language Notes* 41 (1926), pp. 51–4. Lewalski, *Milton*, p. 456, suggests that it has 'an apocryphal ring' to it.

17 Epic, 1667

N.B. The ten-book *Paradise Lost* (1667) can be found online at http://www.uoregon.edu/~rbear/lost/lost.html and, in print, Harris Francis Fletcher, ed., *John Milton's Complete Poetical Works Reproduced in Photographic Facsimile*, 4 vols, University of Illinois Press, Urbana, IL, 1945, vol. II.

1. John Hale writes persuasively of the fusion of Milton's Greek, Latin, English and indeed Hebrew consciousnesses in *Paradise Lost*, demonstrating how Milton *thinks* in Greek or Latin 'about a Hebrew subject which he might make into an English tragedy'; see 'The Classical Literary Tradition', in Thomas N. Corns, ed., *A Companion to Milton*, Blackwell, Oxford, 2003, p. 29.
2. Line references refer to what has become the standard twelve-book version of *Paradise Lost*. When the work was first published in 1667, Milton divided his epic into ten books. See the Introduction to *Paradise Lost* (Fowler), pp. 25ff.
3. Margaret Kean, *John Milton's Paradise Lost: A Sourcebook*, Routledge, London, 2005, p.1.
4. Alistair Fowler's notes are invaluable at these moments. In this instance, he points out that Milton has made an error. Ophiuchus is not an Arctic constellation; Milton may have confused Anguitenens with Anguis, an easy error, since the Greek name for Anguis is similar. See *Paradise Lost* (Fowler), p. 146.
5. *Of Education*, CPW II 405–6.
6. See the final chapter of David Norbrook, *Writing the English Republic: Poetry, Rhetoric and Politics 1627–1660*, Cambridge University Press, Cambridge, 1999, which offers a complex but highly rewarding reading of *Paradise Lost* in its time, to which I am indebted.
7. John Leonard, 'Self-Contradicting Puns in *Paradise Lost*', in Corns, *Companion to Milton*, p. 401 *passim*.
8. *Paradise Lost* (Fowler), p. 39.
9. Christopher Ricks's study of Milton's language (in which he makes a similar argument) remains one of the best on offer: see *Milton's Grand Style*, Clarendon Press, Oxford, 1963.
10. As has been seen, Belial was one of the Old Testament devils associated with 'sodomy'. The 'sons of Belial' are not only linked with homosexuality ('worse rape') but, more importantly, with the corruption of courts and palaces.

11. See also Book VI:568–90 for some outrageously obscene punning.
12. The arguments are outlined at the start of Book X when the reader is reminded that man was 'sufficient' – strong enough – to have withstood Satan, and that humanity's failure to stand firm is therefore justly punished by God. Earlier, in Book V, the archangel Raphael instructs Adam, and the reader: 'God made thee perfect, not immutable . . .' Above all God 'requires' our 'voluntary service'.
13. The Geneva Study Bible of 1599 is less generous in its interpretation of these lines, offering the note: '. . . instead of confessing her sin, she increases it by accusing the serpent.'

18 Revelation, 1667

N.B. *Accidence Commenc't Grammar* is printed in CPW.

1. Stephen Dobranski, *Milton, Authorship and the Book Trade*, Cambridge University Press, Cambridge, 1999, p. 39.
2. Christopher Ricks, *Milton's Grand Style*, Clarendon Press, Oxford, 1963, p. 28.
3. John Hale considers this passage in his essay 'The Classical Literary Tradition', in Thomas N. Corns, ed., *A Companion to Milton*, Blackwell, Oxford, 2003, pp. 22–36.
4. This is the midpoint in both the ten-book and twelve-book versions of the poem.
5. *The Life of Edward Earl of Clarendon, Lord High Chancellor of England, and Chancellor of the University of Oxford . . . Written by himself*, 3 vols, London, 1759, vol. III, p. 799.
6. Letters from Sir John Hobart to his cousin, also John Hobart, in January 1668, quoted in Nicholas von Maltzahn, 'The First Reception of Paradise Lost (1667)', *Review of English Studies* 47 (1996), p. 490.
7. Thomas Ellwood, *The History of Thomas Ellwood, Or, an account of his birth, education, &c.*, second edn, London, 1714, p. 117.
8. In his prefatory poem to the 1674 edition of the epic, ll. 45–6.
9. See Cedric Brown, 'Great Senates and Godly Education', in David Armitage, Armand Himy and Quentin Skinner, eds, *Milton and Republicanism*, Cambridge University Press, Cambridge, 1995, pp. 58–60.
10. See David Norbrook, *Writing the English Republic: Poetry, Rhetoric and Politics 1627–1660*, Cambridge University Press, Cambridge, 1999, p. 467.
11. Von Maltzahn, 'First Reception', p. 480.
12. Norbrook, *Writing the English Republic*, p. 439.
13. Barbara Lewalski, *The Life of John Milton: A Critical Biography*, rev. edn, Blackwell, Oxford, 2002, p. 465.
14. Sharon Achinstein, *Milton and the Revolutionary Reader*, Princeton University Press, Princeton, 1994, p. 14.
15. On 26 April 1669, John received a further £5 from Samuel Simmons, and 200 copies of the work for himself, the receipt for the money signed on his behalf, possibly by Thomas Ellwood.
16. Helen Darbishire, ed., *The Early Lives of Milton*, Constable, London, 1932, pp. 2–3.
17. Ellwood, *History*, p. 88.
18. See Danielle Clarke, *The Politics of Early Modern Women's Writing*, Longman, Harlow, 2001, p. 18, for this and many more fascinating insights into women's lives at this time.

19. Bathsua Makin, *An Essay To Revive the Antient Education of Gentlewomen, in Religion, Manners, Arts & Tongues. With An Answer to the Objections against this Way of Education*, London, 1673, reprinted by the Augustan Reprint Society, no. 202, with introduction by Paula L. Barbour, University of California, Los Angeles, CA, 1980, p. 25.

20. Ibid., pp. 4, 42–3.

21. Lady Grace Mildmay, quoted in Clarke, *Early Modern Women's Writing*, p. 21.

22. Michael Hunter and Annabel Gregory, *An Astrological Diary of the Seventeenth Century: Samuel Jeake of Rye 1652–1699*, Clarendon Press, Oxford, 1988, pp. 85–7.

23. Makin, *An Essay*, p. 23.

24. There is more. If 'either Mary or Deborah Milton had evidenced the slightest aptitude for languages and the slightest desire to learn, their father would have taught them. The admirer of Queen Christina, the friend of Lady Ranelagh and Lady Margaret Ley, was no advocate of ignorance in women' (p. 586). This is a generous assessment of Milton's attitude towards learned women: the sonnet to Lady Margaret Ley, for example, is dominated by praise of her father. Margaret herself is praised only for her ability to praise him.

25. See Clarke, *Women's Writing*, p. 26.

26. Darbishire, *Early Lives*, pp. 77–8.

27. National Archive PROB 24/13.

28. John T. Shawcross, *John Milton: The Self and the World*, University Press of Kentucky, Lexington, KY, 1993, pp. 225–6.

29. Bernard Capp, *When Gossips Meet: Women, Family, and Neighbourhood in Early Modern England*, Oxford University Press, Oxford, 2003, esp. pp. 10, 143.

30. *Life Records* V 4, quoting Thomas Birch's biography of Milton from 1753. Birch had interviewed Elizabeth Foster, Deborah Milton's daughter, on 11th February 1738.

31. National Archive PROB 24/13.

32. See *Life Records* V 5. Elizabeth Foster's comment was noted by Birch but did not appear in his printed life of Milton, attached to his edition of the *Works* of 1753.

33. *Life Records* V 5, quoting the notes of Thomas Birch from an interview with Elizabeth Foster on 17 November 1750.

34. Elizabeth Fisher's deposition is the National Archive, PROB 24/13/311–313.

35. *Life Records* V 104.

36. A note about land and money might be from John, might be to Christopher: the editor of the *Life Records* warns that 'everything about this piece is highly uncertain.'

37. Quoted in John Richardson, ed., *The Annals of London*, Cassell & Co., London, 2000, p. 145.

38. J. R. Jones, *Charles II Royal Politician*, Allen & Unwin, London, 1987, p. 10; Ronald Hutton, *Charles II*, Clarendon Press, Oxford, 1989, pp. 447ff.

39. John Warrington, ed., *The Diary of Samuel Pepys*, 3 vols, Everyman, London, 1906, vol. III, p. 197.

40. Ibid., vol. III, pp. 151–2.

41. The case involved Lord and Lady Ross (or Roos), her father, an illegitimate son, violence on all sides and the couple's separation. The law as it stood could provide some sort of mechanism to resolve issues of paternity, legitimacy and separation. The problem was that now Lord Ross wanted to marry again. To do so, a special Bill needed to be passed by Parliament.

42. Cyriack Skinner mentions the case; see Darbishire, *Early Lives*, p. 33.

43. Letter to William Popple, 14 April 1670, in Andrew Marvell, *The Poems and Letters of Andrew Marvell*, 2 vols, vol. II (*Letters*), third edn, ed. H. M. Margoliouth, rev. Pierre Legouis with E. E. Duncan-Jones, Clarendon Press, Oxford, 1971, p. 317. The following quotation comes from the same letter, p. 316.

44. Charles also agreed to give the King of France, Louis XIV (also his brother-in-law), military support in Holland and Spain. Charles's conversion was undoubtedly the most contentious part of the treaty, and Louis originally offered an extra £150,000 and 6,000 troops 'for the execution of this design'. This clause was left out when the treaty was officially signed by Charles and his closest advisers on 21 December 1670.
45. Letter to William Popple, 28 November 1670, in Marvell, *Poems and Letters*, vol. II, pp. 317–18.
46. Ibid., p.315.
47. Ellwood, *History*, pp. 246–7.
48. Edward Phillips, in contrast, writes that *Paradise Regained* was written between 1667 and 1670. The stylistic and thematic concerns of *Samson Agonistes* argue for an early dating for the work, which may have been begun in the 1640s. While there is no consensus among Milton scholars, it seems plausible that Milton returned to the work in the mid-1660s. See *Shorter Poems*, pp. 349–50, and p. 417 for the debates.

19 Resurgence, 1671

N.B. *Paradise Regained* and *Samson Agonistes* are in *Shorter Poems*, and can be found in most collections of Milton's poetry. The *History of Britain* (including the 'Digression') is printed in CPW.

1. John Carey made the argument in the *Times Literary Supplement* of 6 September 2002. Although his argument was not a new one (there have always been those who have read the drama as a call to violent action), his language of terrorists and suicide bombers struck a deep chord in the run-up to the first anniversary of the 9/11 attacks.
2. 'Samson Agonistes', in *A Companion to Milton*, ed. Thomas N. Corns, Blackwell, Oxford, 2001, p. 416. Achinstein points out that Hebrew poetry was 'not based upon accentual-syllabic organisation', but 'instead vaunted parallelism, alliteration and assonance, echoing rhythms within irregular line lengths', p. 416.
3. Milton's style in *Samson* is one of the main reasons that John Carey, the editor of *The Complete Shorter Poems*, took many years to accept that the work was not written in the 1640s.
4. Cedric Brown, *John Milton: A Literary Life*, Macmillan, Basingstoke, 1995, pp. 200ff.
5. In this 'Digression', Milton took a hard look at his country on the eve of the republic, comparing the condition of the ancient British people at the time of the Roman departure with that of the English in his own day. In an extended historical parallel, he comments unfavourably on the shortcomings of State and Church in the 1640s, and concludes with his belief that only education will repair his countrymen's natural failings as citizens of a free state. This sounds very like the old republican Milton, and many of the *History*'s readers saw that his 'earlier views were still writ large'. See Nicholas von Maltzahn, *Milton's History of Britain: Republican Historiography in the English Revolution*, Clarendon Press, Oxford, 1991, pp. 1, 47, 49.
6. *The Life of the Reverend Dr John Barwick*, 1724, p. 296; John Eachard, *The Grounds & Occasions of the Contempt of the Clergy and Religion*, eighth edn, 1672, sigs A3r–v.
7. Jonathan Richardson, in Helen Darbishire, ed., *The Early Lives of Milton*, Constable, London, 1932, p. 296.
8. *The State of Innocence, and fall of man: an opera. Written in heroic verse, and dedicated to Her Royal Highness, The Duchess*, London, 1677.

9. See Vinton A. Dearing, ed., *The Works of John Dryden: Plays*, 20 vols, University of California Press, Berkeley, CA, 1994, vol. XII, p. 322, for details.

10. Along Aldersgate Street itself there were two printing presses run by widows, Ellen Cotes and Milton's publisher, Mary Simmons. In the maze of small courts and alleyways running off the street were John Wilkinson bookbinder, Robert Dakers printer, Evan Tyler printer and William Terry bookbinder.

11. Robin Myers, Michael Harris and Giles Mandelbrote, eds, *The London Book Trade: Topographies of Print in the Metropolis from the Sixteenth Century*, Oak Knoll Press and British Library, London, 2003, p. 24.

12. John Warrington, ed., *The Diary of Samuel Pepys*, 3 vols, Everyman, London, 1906, vol. I, p. 465.

13. See Myers, Harris and Mandelbrote, *The London Book Trade*, pp. 35–6.

14. *Popery and tyranny: or, The Present state of France: in relation to its government, trade, manners of the people, and nature of the countrey. As it was sent in a letter from an English gentleman abroad, to his friend in England. Wherein may be seen the tyranny the subjects of France are under, being enslaved by the two greatest enemies to reason, as well as to Christian or humane liberty, I mean popery and arbitrary power*, London, 1679.

15. It can be found in CPW VIII.

16. Martin Dzelzainis, 'Milton's *Of True Religion* and the Earl of Castlemaine', *The Seventeenth Century*, 7 (1992), pp. 53–69, esp. p. 54.

17. See Paul Hammond, 'Marvell's Sexuality', in Thomas Healy, ed., *Andrew Marvell*, Longman, London, 1998, pp. 170–204; Hammond sets these attacks in context.

18. John Aubrey, p. 5, and Jonathan Richardson, p. 229, in Darbishire, *Early Lives*.

19. The term *gout* could refer to a range of illnesses, but it seems likely that Milton did indeed suffer from what we still know as gout, an acute joint disease caused by the deposition of crystals of monosodium urate monohydrate and calcium pyrophosphate around the joints, tendons and other tissues of the body. Attacks of gout, untreated, last for days or weeks but eventually subside. Attacks are, however, recurrent, and increase in frequency until the condition is constantly present. The most common cause, in which levels of uric acid are abnormally high in the body, is that the kidneys fail to excrete uric acid quickly enough.

20. Roy Porter and G. S. Rousseau, *Gout The Patrician Malady*, Yale University Press, New Haven, CT, and London, 1998, p. 3.

21. I have drawn heavily on ibid. See esp. pp. 4, 24–7, 45–6.

22. Porter and Rousseau, *Gout*, p. 174.

23. Quoted in ibid., p. 46.

24. Unlike in earlier years, the title of Reader was no longer linked with any readings, or lectures: Readers simply paid a fine to the Temple to be relieved of their duties. By 1678 the practice had completely ended. The Inner Temple was glad of the money, and the lawyer could return to his business, or to his country estate.

20 The City, 1674

1. Helen Darbishire, ed., *The Early Lives of Milton*, Constable, London, 1932, p. 74.

2. Jonathan Richardson, in ibid., pp. 203–4.

3. Darbishire, *Early Lives*, p. 33.

4. David Cressy, *Birth, Marriage, Death: Ritual, Religion, and the Life-cycle in Tudor and Stuart England*, Oxford University Press, Oxford, 1997, p. 387.

5. Three days between death and burial was normal. Death 'was rarely sanitary, and

often left a detritus of disfigurement. Even those who died a "good death" could leave behind a cadaver defiled with sweat and vomit, urine and excrement, or pus and blood. Rigor mortis, corruption, and putrefaction would surely follow. It was therefore a matter of urgent practical necessity to prepare the dead body for burial and to transport it promptly from the deathbed to the grave' (ibid., p. 425).

6. Ralph Houlbrooke's essay, in Peter C. Jupp and Clare Gittings, eds, *Death in England: An Illustrated History,* Manchester University Press, Manchester, 1999, p. 174.

7. See Sharon Achinstein, *Literature and Dissent in Milton's England,* Cambridge University Press, Cambridge, 2003, pp. 256–7.

8. The case can be seen at the National Archive in Kew, PROB 24/13/311–313.

9. Being 'a practicer in the law and a bencher in the inner Temple but living in vacations at Ipswich', he usually visited his brother at the end of the legal term, as he did in midsummer 1674, in the forenoon because the Ipswich coach left at noon. Christopher 'found him in his chamber within his own house situate on Bunhill within the parish of St Giles Cripplegate London'. John 'being not well' and knowing he might not see Christopher for some time, declared his will. Betty Minshull Milton and the servant Elizabeth Fisher, a vital witness, were 'at the same time going up and down the room'.

10. As ever, Gordon Campbell, *A Milton Chronology,* Macmillan, Basingstoke, 1997, p. 218, lists what evidence there is. It is possible that Deborah Milton Clarke made the long journey from Ireland to London to be at the hearing, but the evidence suggests that, if she did, she had returned by March to Ireland, where she signed the documents concerning this settlement.

11. Darbishire, *Early Lives,* p. 1.

12. Letter from Daniel Skinner to Samuel Pepys, November 1676, quoted in Gordon Campbell et al., 'The Provenance of De Doctrina Christiana', *Milton Quarterly,* 31 (1997), p. 71.

13. Aubrey calls Minshull Milton's second wife; see Darbishire, *Early Lives,* p. 3.

14. Darbishire, *Early Lives,* pp. 3, 12.

15. University of Cambridge, Christ's College MS 8.

16. *Letters of State, written by Mr John Milton, to most of the sovereign princes and republicks of Europe, from 1649, till 1659,* 1694.

17. Barbara Lewalski, *The Life of John Milton: A Critical Biography,* rev. edn, Blackwell, Oxford, 2002, p. 399.

18. Darbishire, *Early Lives,* p. vii.

19. James Holly Hanford and James G. Taaffe, *A Milton Handbook,* G. Bell & Sons, London, 1929, pp. 1, 2.

20. 'Life Records', in Thomas N. Corns, ed., *A Companion to Milton,* Blackwell, Oxford, 2003, p. 483.

21. See Peter Lindenbaum, 'Dispatches from the Archives', *Milton Quarterly,* 36 (2002), pp. 46–54. Brabazon Aylmer slowly sold his rights to *Paradise Lost* to another printer, Jacob Tonson. Aylmer probably decided to offload *Paradise Lost* because he needed to raise capital for another major project, Isaac Barrow's complete theological *Works.* In hindsight this was a misjudgement. When asked many years later which poem he had made most money from, Tonson would answer simply 'Milton'.

22. John Hopkins, *Milton's Paradise Lost imitated in Rhyme,* London, 1699, p. 49.

23. *The Poetical Works of Mr John Milton. Together with explanatory notes (by P.H.) on Paradise Lost,* London, 1695.

24. 21 July 1683, Anthony a Wood, quoted in Leo Miller, 'The Burning of Milton's Books in 1660: Two Mysteries', *English Literary Renaissance,* 18 (1988), p. 432.

25. The translation is from Milton's *Second Defence,* in *The Works of John Milton,* 18 vols, Columbia University Press, New York, 1933, vol. VIII, pp. 13–15.

Select Bibliography

Primary Texts

Darbishire, Helen, ed., *The Early Lives of Milton*, Constable, London, 1932

Dzelzainis, Martin, ed., *John Milton Political Writings: Cambridge Texts in the History of Political Thought*, Cambridge University Press, Cambridge, 1991

French, J. Milton, *The Life Records of John Milton*, 5 vols, Rutgers University Press, New Brunswick, NJ, 1949–58; Gordian Press, New York, NY, 1966

Hale, John K., ed., *John Milton, Latin: Writings: A Selection*, Medieval and Renaissance Texts and Studies, Van Gorcum, Assen, 1998

Hale, John K., ed., *Milton's Cambridge Latin: Performing in the Genres 1625–1632*, Arizona Center for Medieval and Renaissance Studies, Tempe, AZ, 2005

Milton, John, *Complete Poetry and Essential Prose*, ed. William Kerrigan, John Rumrich and Stephen M. Fallon, Modern Library, New York, NY, forthcoming

Milton, John, *The Complete Shorter Poems*, ed. John Carey, second edn, Longman, London, 1997

Milton, John, *Paradise Lost*, ed. Alastair Fowler, second edn, Longman, London, 1998

The Milton Reading Room, at http://www.dartmouth.edu/~milton/reading_room/

The Oxford Dictionary of National Biography, Oxford University Press, Oxford, 2004

Wolfe, Don M., ed., *Complete Prose Works of John Milton*, 8 vols, Yale University Press, New Haven, CT, 1953–82

Oxford University Press are in the process of publishing a new *Complete Works*, of which the first volumes will appear in 2008. This exciting project will offer new 'en face' translations of the Latin works and a new two-volume biography co-authored by Gordon Campbell and Thomas Corns.

Biographical Studies

Brown, Cedric, *John Milton: A Literary Life*, Macmillan, Basingstoke, 1995

Campbell, Gordon, *A Milton Chronology*, Macmillan, Basingstoke, 1997

Dobranski, Stephen, *Milton, Authorship and the Book Trade*, Cambridge University Press, Cambridge, 1999

Fallon, Robert Thomas, *Milton in Government*, Pennsylvania State University Press, University Park, PA, 1993

Flanagan, Roy, *John Milton: A Short Introduction*, Blackwell, Oxford, 2002

Levi, Peter, *Eden Renewed: The Public and Private Life of John Milton*, Macmillan, London, 1996

Lewalski, Barbara K., *The Life of John Milton*, rev. edn, Blackwell, Oxford, 2002

The Life Records of John Milton, ed. Joseph M. French, 5 vols, Rutgers University Press, New Brunswick, NJ, 1948–58

Maltzahn, Nicholas von, *Milton's History of Britain: Republican Historiography in the English Revolution*, Clarendon Press, Oxford, 1991

Norbrook, David, *Writing the English Republic: Poetry, Rhetoric and Politics 1627–1660*, Cambridge University Press, Cambridge, 1999

Parker, William Riley, *Milton: A Biographical Commentary*, ed. Gordon Campbell, second edn, Oxford University Press, Oxford, 1996

Shawcross, John T., *The Arms of the Family: The Significance of John Milton's Relatives and Associates*, University Press of Kentucky, KY, Lexington, 2004

Shawcross, John T., *John Milton: The Self and the World*, University of Kentucky Press, Lexington, KY, 1993

Wilson, A. N., *The Life of John Milton*, Oxford University Press, Oxford, 1983; Pimlico, London, 2002

Introductions to Milton's Major Works

Corns, Thomas N., ed., *A Companion to Milton*, Blackwell, Oxford, 2003

Danielson, Dennis, ed., *The Cambridge Companion to Milton*, second edn, Cambridge University Press, Cambridge, 1999

Kean, Margaret, ed., *John Milton's Paradise Lost: A Sourcebook*, Routledge, London, 2005

See also *The Norton Anthology of English Literature* (http://www2.wwnorton.com/college/english/nael/), which offers extensive contextual materials. Lewalski's magisterial study has a lengthy bibliography, which can be further supplemented by consulting http://extra.shu.ac.uk/emls/iemls/postprint/CCM2Biblio.html, compiled by R. G. Siemens and originally published in Dennis Danielson, ed., *The Cambridge Companion to Milton*, second edn, Cambridge University Press, Cambridge, 1999

Index

N.B. Where no details are given, works are by John Milton.

Accademia degli Incogniti, 102
Accademia degli Oziosi, 98
Accidence Commence't Grammar, 363, 382, 385
Achinstein, Sharon, 347, 374, 391
Act of Comprehension, 343
Act of Uniformity, 9, 292, 297
actresses, 295, 378
Acts of Indemnity and Oblivion, 240, 280, 286
Adam and Eve, 3, 122, 147, 160, 296, 36; *see also Paradise Lost*
'After death nothing is' (Rochester), 389
Agar, Anne, *see* Milton, Anne
Agar, Anne (daughter), 54, 111, 113
Agar, Thomas, 54, 111–13, 223, 284, 287, 387
Aldermanbury, 265
Aldersgate, 112, 116, 124, 135, 151–2, 157–9, 167, 229, 245, 296, 388; and publishing industry, 124, 309, 363, 380
All for Love (Dryden), 380
Allestry, James, 381
'Allusion to Horace, An' (Rochester), 380
America, xvii, 261
Amsterdam, 138
Andrewes, Lancelot, 24–5, 30, 180–1
Annus mirabilis (Dryden), 343
Answer to a Book, An (Anon.), 167–8
Antrim, Alexander MacDonnell, 3rd Earl of, 164
Antwerp publishers, 308–9
Apocalypse, 24, 58, 205
Apology against a Pamphlet, An, 140
Appletree, Matthew, 189

Arabic, 218
Archimedes, 246
Areopagitica, xvi, 96, 165–6, 168–73, 180, 216, 256, 262, 292; publication and printing, 168, 309; reason in, 171–2; and burning of JM's books, 286; and *Paradise Lost*, 329
aristocracy, 65–6, 68; codes of love and honour, 73–4; and *Maske*, 76–7, 82
Aristotle, 13–14, 40
Army Plot, 118
Arno, River, 47, 108
Ars Amatoria (Ovid), 18
Arthur, King, 99
Artillery Walk, 300, 304, 362, 388
Arundel, Lord, 97
Assheton, Nicholas, 225
Astraea redux (Dryden), 284
Astrophil and Stella (Sidney), 238
At a Vacation Exercise, 296
Athens, 16, 157, 168–9, 219
Attaway, Mrs, 177
Aubrey, John, 155, 276, 278, 280, 296, 349, 395–6
Augustus, Emperor, 15, 32, 284
Aylesbury, 304
Aylmer, Brabazon, 396

Baillie, Robert, 177
Banbury, 155
Banbury Grammar School, 351
baptism, 3, 9–10
Baptists, 177
Barbican, 179–80, 191, 309, 390
Barbon, Praise-God, 241

Barebones Parliament, 241–2, 259
Baroni, Leonora, 101
Barrow, Samuel, 385
Barry, James, 397
Bastwick, John, 128–9
Beale, John, 345, 382
Bemerton, 62
ben Israel, Menasseh, 261
Berkshire, 88
Bernini, Gian Lorenzo, 97
Bible, 48, 64, 73, 127, 169, 296, 351;
    Hebrew, 12, 195; Italian, 19; and sexual
    anxiety, 78; and fundamentalism, 144;
    Milton family Bible, 190, 193, 226–7,
    357, 396; and republicanism, 201;
    Polyglot, 231; Dutch, 237; *see also* Book
    of Deuteronomy; Book of Genesis; Book
    of Isaiah; Book of Judges; Book of
    Proverbs; Book of Revelation; Gospel of
    John; Gospel of Luke; Gospel of
    Matthew; New Testament; Old
    Testament; Psalms; Scriptures
Billing, Edward, 302
Birch, Thomas, 356
Bishops' Wars, 102, 116–17, 155
Blackfriars Playhouse, 7
Blake, William, 316, 397
blindness, 236–8, 244–5, 251–4; JM's, 231,
    236–8, 242, 244–5, 248, 251–4, 256,
    270, 283–4, 286, 294, 299, 311, 340–1,
    348–9, 356, 377
Bodleian Library, 63, 129, 194–5, 286
Bohemia, 12, 91
Bologna, 102
Bolt and Tun coffee house, 350
Book of Common Prayer, 9
Book of Deuteronomy, 141–2
Book of Genesis, 122, 142, 312, 321
Book of Isaiah, 315
Book of Judges, 75, 227, 372
Book of Proverbs, 301
Book of Revelation, 57–8, 78, 109, 258
Borgia, Cardinal, 93
Bradshaw, John, 199, 211, 238–9, 245, 265;
    loss of influence, 231, 241, 255, 257;
    death, 283; leaves JM money, 285;
    retribution at Restoration, 287, 291
Bramhall, John, 247, 284
Bread Street, xvi, 3–5, 7, 28, 55, 111, 388
Breda, 24–5
Bremen, 222
Brentford, 63

Bridewell, 259, 301
Brief Notes Upon a Late Sermon, 283
Bristol, 178, 301
Britain (the name), 16
British Library, 118, 190
Brutus, 16
Bucer, Martin, 150, 165
Buckingham, George Villiers, 1st Duke of,
    38–40
Buckingham, George Villiers, 2nd Duke of,
    380
Buckinghamshire, 138, 304
Bunhill Fields, 304, 308, 390
Buonmatthei, Benedetto, 95
Burton, Henry, 128–9
Byrd, William, 8

Cade, Jack, 153
Calabria, 92
Calvin, John, 12
Calvinism, 38, 103
Cambridge, 21–2, 30–2, 90
Cambridge University, 95, 264; JM's
    education, 21–7, 33–4, 40–1, 52, 74, 131,
    133; town and gown conflicts, 22; and
    JM's poetry, 24–6, 30, 40, 128; bullying,
    26–7; JM's rustication, 27, 247; religious
    divisions, 38–9; JM performs at salting,
    41–4, 95, 99; exclusion of women, 51–2;
    JM leaves, 55, 62; and *Lycidas*, 83–6, 106
Campbell, Gordon, 57, 398
Capp, Bernard, 147
Cardogni family, 104
Carew, Thomas, 74, 184
Caribbean, 260
Cartwright, William, 184
Castlemaine, Earl of, 383
Catherine of Braganza, Queen, 361, 376
Catholic Church, 6, 9, 24–6, 97, 257
Catholicism, 6, 10, 39, 62; JM and, 98–100,
    104; and civil war, 163, 178; and
    censorship, 171; and attacks on
    Commonwealth, 211; and Piedmont,
    257–8; under restored monarchy, 297,
    361, 382–3, 397
Catullus, 18, 30–1
censorship, 96, 121, 167–72, 216; under
    restored monarchy, 292–3, 364, 378–9;
    and *Paradise Lost*, 310–11
Chalfont St Giles, 304, 354, 364
Chamberlain, John, 138
chapels of ease, 57

Chapman, Livewell, 282

Chappell, William, 27, 31

Charing Cross, 202–3

Charles I, King, 20, 38–40, 217, 271, 371, 376; and court masques, 65–6; and Caroline literary culture, 73; Personal Rule, 88, 115; and approach to civil war, 113–18, 125, 136–9, 153; and civil war, 149, 154–6, 159, 163–4, 178–9, 186, 189–91, 197; 'secret cabinet', 178; held in captivity, 186, 213; trial and execution, 198–9, 202–3, 206, 210–12, 216, 234, 345; and *Eikon Basilike*, 212–13, 215

Charles II, King, 220, 233, 257; as Prince of Wales, 178, 204; crowned in Scotland, 205; Dryden and, 284, 293, 343–4; Restoration, 280–7, 292, 303; assassination urged, 293; attends sermon against JM, 294; mistresses, 295–6, 360, 380; and religious tolerance, 297–8, 382; and Great Fire, 308, 343; and *Paradise Lost*, 310, 346; immorality at court, 342, 359–60; coronation, 346; reign of, 357–61, 363, 382; Catholicism, 361, 382, 397; and *Samson Agonistes*, 376; and *History of Britain*, 379; vilified in *Essay upon Satire*, 380; death, 397

chastity: JM's commitment to, 17–18, 27, 32–4, 78–9, 110, 133, 145; in *Maske*, 74–8, 83

Chatham, 342

Chaucer, Geoffrey, 75

Cheshire, 300, 396

Child-birth (Guillemeau), 353

Christ's College, Cambridge, 21, 39, 42

Christianity, 221; and homosexuality, 51, 110; and paganism, 58–9, 61, 110; assurance of salvation, 85; consolation, 86; manly, 132; spread of, 170; JM's heterodoxy, 280, 370, 389; and *Paradise Lost*, 323, 338; and *Paradise Regained*, 370–1; and death, 389–90

Church of England, 6, 9–10, 12, 55, 57, 400; and ritual, 21, 38–9, 87, 136; and university education, 41; JM considers priesthood, 61–3; licensing of ministers, 62; and sexual anxiety, 78, 80; opposition to, 113, 115–16, 150, 234, 362; corruption in, 125, 128, 181, 204, 233; increasing orthodoxy, 125, 175–6; reform and abolition of episcopacy,

126–8, 130–2, 136, 139–40, 161, 164, 273, 275; radical reform and iconoclasm, 137, 188; and divorce, 141; Presbyterian establishment, 175–6, 185; link with State, 179, 187, 232–3, 235, 265, 275, 345; under Commonwealth, 206, 228; re-establishment, 292, 297; and providential signs, 311; and Test Act, 382; and JM's burial, 390–1

Cicero, 13–14, 233

City of London, 55, 57, 63, 112, 179, 194; and JM's early life, 3, 6–9, 27–8; and opposition to King, 37, 114, 116–18, 136–8, 154; urban life, 151–2; and civil war, 175; radicals increase influence, 199; at Restoration, 297; impact of fire, 307–8, 380; Shrove Tuesday riots, 358–9, 362; revival of publishing industry, 380–1; and JM's later life, 387–9; *see also* London

city of London's resolution, The (Anon.), 139

Clarendon, Edward Hyde, Lord, 241, 342, 382

Clarke, Deborah, *see* Milton, Deborah

Claxton, Laurence, 205

Cobham Heath, 208

Coelum Britannicum (Carew), 66, 74

coffee houses, 276–7, 280, 293, 295, 298, 350

Colasterion, 145, 150, 172, 174

Colchester, siege of, 197

Colnbrook, 63

Colne, River, 88, 109

Committee for the Propagation of the Gospel, 232, 234

commonplace books, 13–14, 64, 80, 187, 280

Commonwealth of Oceana, The (Harrington), 261

Company of Merchant Taylors, 4

Company of Scriveners, 6, 57

Company of Stationers, 129; and licensing of print, 167, 172, 292

Comus, see *Maske Presented at Ludlow Castle, A*

Considerations Touching the Likeliest Means to Remove Hirelings, 274–5

Conventicle Act, 297

Coppe, Abiezer, 205

Coptic, 218

corantos, 138

Cornwall, 164

Correggio, Antonio Allegri da, 98

Coryate, Thomas, 94

Council of State, 208, 234, 245, 259–60, 262, 265; establishment of, 203; JM's appointment, 210–12, 215, 217–18, 221, 231, 238, 262

Counter-Reformation, 97, 101

Court of Chancery, 242

Court of Star Chamber, 121, 129

Covenanters, 113–14, 163–5

Cromwell, Elizabeth, 261

Cromwell, Mary, 262

Cromwell, Oliver, 73, 163–4, 186, 189, 197, 211, 384; rise to power, 175, 177–9, 231–3, 240–2; military abilities, 178, 205, 233, 248, 264–5, 303; opposition to radicals, 187, 206, 208, 259; and execution of King, 199; campaign in Ireland, 205; Marvell and, 212, 265; JM's attitude to, 231–3, 255, 264–5; dissolves Rump Parliament, 240–2; millenarian beliefs, 241; installed as Protector, 242, 257, 259–61, 268; and Piedmont, 257–8; assumes absolute power, 261–2, 268; refuses kingship, 262, 268; vision of Protestant unity, 263–4; political pragmatism, 264; death and funeral, 271–2, 280; Dryden and, 272, 293; retribution at Restoration, 287, 291; *Paradise Lost* and, 316, 341, 346

Cromwell, Richard, 272–3, 277–8

Cropredy Bridge, Battle of, 163

Cry of the Royal Blood to Heaven, The (Anon.), 248

Cust, Richard, 114

Custom House, 308

dance, 66, 68, 70

Dante, 16, 75

Darby, John, 396

Darwen, River, 232–3

Dati, Carlo, 95, 193–4

Davenant, William, 231

Davis, Mr, 179

Days of Public Humiliation, 190

De Fide Concubinarum (Anon.), 42

death, 29–30, 52, 389–90; in childbirth, 225–6; decline of rituals, 228; of children, 230

Declaration of Indulgence, 298, 382

Defence of Himself (Defensio Pro Se), 250

Defence of the English People, The (Pro Populo Anglicano Defensio), 218–21, 231; editions and translations, 220; revised edition, 272; denounced, 286

Defence of the Reign of Charles I (Defensio Regio Pro Carolo I) (Salmasius), 218, 298

Denham, Sir John, 311

Deptford, 228

Diggers, 208–9

Diodati, Charles, 169; friendship with JM, xv, 19, 34–6, 45–52, 79–81, 85, 133; family, 19; and JM's poetry, 30–1, 34–5, 45–9; letter-writing, 49–50; leaves to study in Geneva, 54; death and *Elegy for Damon*, 105–11, 118

Diodati, Giovanni, 19, 103, 105

Diodati, Theodore, 19

Dippers Dipt (Featley), 184

Dissenters, 297–8, 390–1

divorce, 152–3; JM and, 141–2, 144–53, 159–62, 165, 167–8, 172, 174, 176–7, 181, 187, 194, 262, 274, 294, 304, 379; and remarriage, 161–2, 187–8; Charles II and, 360–1

Dobranski, Stephen, 130

Doctrine and Discipline of Divorce, xvii, 140–51, 177; opposition to, 149–51; proliferation of editions, 150, 172, 174; printing and publication, 172, 309

Don Quixote (John Phillips translation), 298

Donne, John, 27–8, 62, 86, 89, 121

Dorislaus, Isaac, 39

Dowsing, William, 188

Dryden, John, 265, 295–6, 384; and Cromwell, 272, 293; and Charles II, 284, 293, 343–4; appointed Poet Laureate and Historiographer Royal, 358, 379; imitation of *Paradise Lost*, 379–80, 399; spat with Rochester, 380; elegy for JM, 399

Dunbar, Battle of, 233

Dunkirk, 271

Dury, John, 231

Dutch, 241; wars, 234–5, 281, 311, 382–3; Jewish community, 260; and Vaudois community, 263; loss of New Amsterdam, 303; attack England, 342

Dutch (language), 112, 220, 231, 349

Dzelzainis, Martin, 383

Eastern Association, 163
Eclogues (Virgil), 83–4, 87, 107
Edgehill, Battle of, 154–5
education, 159–61, 352, 363; women's, 11–12, 34, 160, 349–52
Edward VI, King, 150
Edwards, Thomas, 176–7
Egerton, Alice, 66, 72
Egerton, John, 66, 72
Egerton, Thomas (Lord President), 64–5, 69, 71–2, 74–6
Egerton, Thomas (son), 66, 72
Egypt, ancient, 237
Eikon Basilike, 212–13, 215
Eikonoklastes, 213–16, 231, 236, 284, 304, 309, 311; denounced at Restoration, 286, 294
Electra (Euripides), 157
Elegy I (Elegia Prima), 30–1, 34–6
Elegy III (Elegia Tertia), 24–5, 30
Elegy IV (Elegia Quarta), 24–5, 45
Elegy V (Elegia Quinta), 44–5
Elegy VI (Elegia Sexta), 48–9, 108
Elegy VII (Elegia Septima), 44, 182
Elegy for Damon (Epitaphium Damonis), 106–11, 118, 180
Elements of Architecture (Wotton), 89
Elizabeth, Princess, 19, 91
Elizabeth I, Queen, 6, 9, 64, 76; education, 14–15
Ellwood, Thomas, 300–5, 344, 348–9, 352, 364, 390; and JM's literary legacy, 395–6; image of, 398
England: and Classical culture, 16; use of Latin in, 22; growing political and religious crisis, 87–8; descent into civil war, 101–2, 111, 113–18, 153; and JM's political vision, 127, 171–2, 255–6, 344, 347, 372; and civil war, 149, 154–60, 162–4, 172, 174–5, 177–9, 185, 197; Commonwealth established, 203–11; pre-Conquest, 221; Protectorate established, 242, 248, 257, 262, 271–2; Jews and anti-Semitism, 260–1; political pragmatism, 264
England's New Chains Discovered (Lilburne), 206
English, 99, 118, 122, 218, 349, 351–2
English Channel, 25, 271
English literature, 13, 399–400; influences on JM, 29, 60; sexualisation of, 80

episcopacy, 12, 126–8, 130–2, 136, 139–40, 144, 161, 273, 275
Erasmus, 150
Essay to Revive the Ancient Education of Gentlewomen, An (Makin), 351–2
Essay upon Satire, An (Dryden), 380
Essex, Robert Devereux, 3rd Earl of, 155, 164
Eton College, 90
Euclid, 246
Euripides, 13, 63–4, 157, 168, 170, 252, 269
Evans, Margery, 75
Eve, *see* Adam and Eve
Evelyn, John, 97–8, 209, 228, 282, 298, 382; on plague and Great Fire, 303–4, 308, 357
Excise Bank collapse, 298
Exeter, Bishop of, 149
Exeter, 158, 188–9, 191
'Expostulation with Inigo Jones, An' (Jonson), 68

Faerie Queene, The (Spenser), 29
'Fair Oriana in the Morn' (John Milton senior), 7
Fairfax, Thomas, Third Lord, 163, 189, 196–7, 239, 255
Faithful Statement against the False Accusations of John Milton (More), 250
Faithorne, William, 397
Fallon, Stephen, 263
Familiar Epistles, 396
fathers, 297, 299, 353
Fawkes, Guy, 25
Featley, Daniel, 184
Felton, John, 39–40
Ferrara, 102
Ficino, Marsilio, 95
Fifth Monarchists, 205, 234–5, 258, 276, 297
Finsbury Fields, 154
First Protectorate Parliament, 257
Fisher, Elizabeth, 356, 393–4
Fisher, Mary, 393–4
Fiston, William, 17
Five-Mile Act, 297
Fleet, River, 358
Fleet Street, 273, 350, 388, 396
Fleetwood, Anne, 304
Fleetwood, George, 304
Fleetwood, Hester, 354, 395

Fleetwood, Robert, 354
Florence, 47, 94–6, 100, 102, 194, 204
Florio, John, 59
Forest Hill, 116, 134, 163, 189, 192, 222, 395
Foster, Elizabeth (JM's granddaughter), 355–6, 386, 395, 398
Fowler, Alistair, 321
Fox, George, 205–6
Foxe, John, 14
France, 39, 114, 164, 250; papermaking in, 88; JM visits, 91–3; and Italy, 96–7; Prince of Wales flees to, 178, 205; JM's books burned in, 220, 248, 250; war with England, 222; Marvell visits, 239; English Resident appointed, 262; alliance with England, 271; influence on English fashion, 295; treaty with, 382
French, 15, 112, 168, 231, 350
Fulham, 57

Gaddi, Jacopo, 95
Gag for Long Haired Rattleheads, A (Anon.), 154
Galilei, Vincenzo, 96
Galileo Galilei, 96
Gangraena (Edwards), 176–7
Garden of Eden, 3, 122, 296; restored in Paradise Regained, 365, 367, 370; see also Paradise Lost
Geneva, 12, 54, 103–5, 251
Genoa, 92, 94
George I, King, 383
German, 224
Germany, 12, 93, 222, 231, 245
Gesualdo, Carlo, 102
Gill, Alexander, 19, 39–41, 62
glaucoma, 173
godly man's choice, The (Grantham), 139
Gold tried in the fire (Walwyn), 185
Gospel of John, 4
Gospel of Luke, 367
Gospel of Matthew, 141, 283–4, 367
gout, 385–7, 389, 391
Grand Remonstrance, 137
Grantham, Caleb, 139
Greece, 101, 105; ancient, 16, 237, 255
Greek, 12–13, 15, 20, 55, 63, 122; and same-sex love, 48–51, 81, 106; translations of, 95, 112; and women's education, 168, 349–52; verses added to Poems, 184; Marvell and, 239; JM plans

dictionary, 264; Samuel Jeake and, 351, 354
Grotius, Hugo, 91–2
Grub Street, 298
Guerret, Elizabeth, 250
Guillemeau, Jacques, 353
Gunpowder Plot, 25–6, 40
Gunther, Count Anthon, of Oldenburg, 221–2
Gwyn, Nell, 360

Habsburgs, 12, 91, 96
'Hail native language . . .', 99
Hale, John, 15, 22, 30, 45, 157
Halifax, 229
Hall, Joseph, 126, 130–1, 139
Hamburg, 12, 24
Hamilton, James Hamilton, 1st Duke of, 233
Hammersmith, 55–7, 62
Hammond, Paul, 384
Hampden, John, 81
Hampton Court Palace, 138, 261–2
Hanover, Ernst August, Elector of, 383
Harrington, James, 261, 276
Harrison, Colonel Thomas, 241
Hartlib, Samuel, 160
Harvey, Gabriel, 16
Hearth Tax, 309
Hebrew, 12–13, 15, 19, 218, 242, 280, 346; women and, 168, 349–50; poetry, 374
Heimbach, Peter, 305, 307
Heinsius, Nicholas, 220, 247
Helder, Thomas, 380
Henley, 175
Henrietta Maria, Queen, 65, 118, 138, 164, 188, 376
Henrietta, Princess, 189
Henry VIII, King, 6, 9
Herbert, George, 62, 125
Herculaneum, 99
Heroic Stanzas (Dryden), 272, 293
Heywood, Oliver, 228–9, 266
High Holborn, 194, 197
Hippely, Sir John, 216
History of Britain, 210, 212, 363, 365, 378–9, 381, 385, 396; 'Digression', 210, 379, 396
history of the Inquisition, The (Servita), 93
Histrio-mastix (Prynne), 73
Hobart, Sir John, 343
Hobson, Captain John, 159

Hodgkin, Roger, 297
Holborn, 287, 291
'Hold your hands, honest Men' (Anon.), 146
Holdenby House, 186
Holland, 218, 234, 239, 382; see also Dutch
Holmby, 213
Holstein, Lucas, 98, 102
Holy Communion, 9
Homer, 13, 237
homosexuality, 35, 51, 80, 83, 110; and vilification of JM, 247, 251, 384; and *Paradise Lost*, 326; see also male friendship and love; sodomy
Horace, 15–16, 104, 222, 246
'Horatian Ode upon Cromwell's Return from Ireland, An' (Marvell), 212
Horton, 55, 63, 88–90, 109, 111, 116
Hounslow, 155
House of Commons, 186, 213, 311
House of Lords, 178; bishops in, 132, 137–8; and licensing of print, 172, 174; abolished, 203
Howard, Thomas, Earl of Berkshire, 38
Hubert, Robert, 343
Huguenots, 298
Hull, 154, 265
Humanist traditions, 13, 42, 63
Humble Petitions, 185, 276–7
Huntingdonshire, 178
Hutchinson, Lucy, 73, 285

iconoclasm, 137, 188
Idylls (Theocritus), 60, 84, 107
Il Penseroso, 59–61, 74, 84
Ile de Ré, 39
Inferno (Dante), 75
Inner Temple, 54, 63, 81, 287, 293, 387
Inquisition, 93, 96
Instrument of Government, 257, 268
Ireland, 64, 114, 117, 284; Irish Rebellion, 136–7, 190; and civil war, 163–4, 178; under Commonwealth, 205, 211, 216, 241
Ireton, Henry, 205, 291
Irish Rebellion, The (Temple), 136
Islington Fields, 295
Italian, 15, 19, 45–8, 112, 350
Italy, 16, 118, 171, 194–5, 312; JM's visit, 89–105, 108, 111–12; literary reputation, 92–3, 101, 104; hospitals, 94; intellectual life, 94–5, 103, 133, 197;

English in, 100, 104; JM returns from, 101–2, 105, 111–14; Marvell visits, 239

James I, King, 6, 9–10, 37–8, 40, 136; statue of, 112
James II, King (Duke of York), 204, 271, 303, 361; marriage, 380; Catholicism, 382, 397; reputed visit to JM, 384
Jeake, Samuel, 173–4, 351, 354
Jeffreys, Ellen, 4
Jeffreys, Paul, 4
Jesuits, 6, 98, 100
Jesus Christ, 3, 126, 206, 301, 360; Second Coming, 21, 241, 260, 276; birth of, 58–9, 61; and divorce, 141–2, 144; and Simeon, 307
Jewin Street, 296–7, 303
Jewish thought, 280
Jews, readmission of, 260–1
John Milton Englishman Second Defence of the English People, see *Second Defence of the English People*
Jones, Inigo, 37, 65, 68, 216
Jones, Richard, 245
Jonson, Ben, 28, 68, 74
Josselin, Ralph, 225
Judgement of Martin Bucer, The, 174

Kean, Margaret, 314
'Keep a Good Tongue in your Head' (Anon.), 146
Keller, Helen, 237
Kelso, 114
Kent, 173
Kermode, Frank, 82
Kineton, 155
King, Edward, 83–5, 87
King's Musick, 65
kingship, see monarchy
Knox, John, 12
Koran, 171

La Rochelle, 39
La Tina (Malatesti), 95, 101
L'Allegro, 59–61, 74, 84
Lambe, Dr John, 38
Lambert, John, 233, 276, 278–80
Lambeth Palace, 116
Langport, Battle of, 178
Latin, xv–xvi, 12, 15–16, 18, 56, 122, 224, 303, 307; performance in, 22–3, 26, 33–4, 41–4; use by European Protestants,

23; JM's poetry in, 24–6, 30, 41–4, 106–11, 181–2, 195, 246, 250, 384; and same-sex love, 47–50, 52, 79, 106–7, 109; JM's self-descriptions in, 80, 101, 104; translations of, 95, 112; and women 's education, 168, 349–52; and JM's work for Commonwealth, 211, 216, 220, 231, 263; Marvell and, 239; JM's dictionary and primer, 264, 363, 385; and *Paradise Lost*, 315, 323; Samuel Jeake and, 351, 354; and *Samson Agonistes*, 374; JM's works in, 397, 400

Laud, William, 38–9, 57, 87, 115–16, 121, 126, 128; execution, 175–6, 181

Lawes, Henry, 65, 82, 90–1, 124

Lawrence, Edward, 245–6

Lawrence, William, 277

Lee, Charles, 398

Leghorn, 94

Leigh, Richard, 384

Leonard, John, 319

Leonardo da Vinci, 38, 97, 173

leprosy, 57

Leslie, Alexander, 114

L'Estrange, Roger, 240, 280, 283, 292, 298

Letter to a Friend, 279, 282

Letters of the English State (Literae Pseudo-Senatus Anglicani), 384, 395–6

Levellers, 185–7, 206–9, 259, 281

Lewalski, Barbara, 88, 144, 194, 201, 300, 398

Ley, James, 159

Ley, Lady Margaret, 159

Licensing Act, 292

Life and Death of Sir Henry Vane (Sikes), 294

Life Records of Sir John Milton, The, 192

Lilburne, John, 185, 206

Limerick, siege of, 205

Lincoln, 223

Lincoln's Inn Fields, 194

Lisbon, 240

Lisle, Sir George, 197

Little Britain, 309, 380

Little Swaffham, 188

Livy, 204

Lockyer, Robert, 206–7

London: immigration and population growth, 6, 28, 152, 297, 380; theatres, 7, 31, 295–6; brothels, 8; expansion, 8–9; and ancient Rome, 16; as Troynovant, 16, 32; civic life, 27–8; book trade, 28,

124; in JM's poetry, 30–2, 42; increasing volatility, 37–8; hospitals, 57; literary and musical network, 65; politics and approach to civil war, 116–18, 121, 126, 135–8, 151–2, 154; urban life, 151–2; and civil war, 154–9, 162, 175, 185, 193; Humble Petition, 276; Charles II enters, 285; Restoration lifestyle, 295; Great Plague and Fire, 303–4, 307–8, 343, 357–8, 380; working women in, 354–5; under restored monarchy, 358–9, 362; *see also* City of London; Westminster

London Bridge, 297

Long Parliament, 282

Lords Lieutenants and Deputies, 137, 153

Lostwithiel, Battle of, 164

Louis XIII, King, 96–7, 114

Louis XIV, King, 96, 220, 263

Love's Triumph through Callipolis (Jonson), 68

Lucan, 345

Lucas, Sir Charles, 197

Lucca, 94, 102–3, 105, 108

Ludgate Hill, 358

Ludlow, 64–5, 69, 71–2, 74–6, 90, 124, 171, 220

Luther, Martin, 94

Lycidas, 83–8, 106, 180–1, 233; religious and political concerns, 87–8; publication and authorship, 90, 124; in Trinity Manuscript, 124

Machiavelli, Niccolò, 101, 204

'Mackerels rejoice . . .', 250

Madrid, 240

Maimonides, 280

Mainwarings Coffee House, 396

Major-Generals, 260, 265, 268

Makin, Bathsua, 349–51

Malatesti (Italian poet), 95, 101

Maldon, grain riots, 38

male friendship and love, 35–6, 47–52, 106–9, 145, 326

Maltzahn, Nicholas von, 346

Manchester, Edward Montagu, 2nd Earl of, 163–4, 175, 179

Manchester, 154

Manso, Giovanni Batista, Marquis of, 98–9, 101

Mansus, 99

Maratti, Carlo, 98

Marenzio, Luca, 102

marriage, 133–5, 274; without sex, 78; companionate, 145–6; and Protestantism, 146, 148–9; remarriage, 161–2, 187–8, 266–7; and sex, 266–7; polygamy, 280; and JM's daughters, 299–300, 353–4; *see also* divorce

Marriage à-la-mode (Dryden), 380

Marseilles, 92

Marshall, William, 184

Marston Moor, Battle of, 163, 178

Marten, Henry, 285

Marvell, Andrew, 78, 245–6, 358, 361–2, 378; and Cromwell, 212, 265; JM recommends, 239; helps JM, 287, 298; commendatory verses to *Paradise Lost*, 344, 385; vilified by Leigh, 384

Mary II, Queen, 397

Maske Presented at Ludlow Castle, A, 64–77, 104, 171, 220; sheet music, 67; and chastity, 74–8, 83; and criticism of aristocracy, 76–7; publication and authorship, 82–3, 90, 124; in Trinity Manuscript, 124; and *Paradise Lost*, 314, 318, 329

masques, 65–6, 68, 73–4; anti-masques, 77; publication of, 82

Massachusetts, 234

Massacre at Blackfriars, 40

mathematics, 56

Mazarin, Cardinal, 100–1, 220, 263

Meadows, Philip, 239–40

Mede, Joseph, 21, 39

Medici, Cosimo de', 95

Medway, River, 342

memory, 14, 305

Merchant of Venice, The (Shakespeare), 36

Mercurius Aulicus (newspaper), 218

Mercurius Politicus (newspaper), 217–18, 257, 259, 261, 273–4

Mercurius Pragmaticus (newspaper), 217

Merian, Lady, 355

Mermaid tavern, 28

Metamorphoses (Ovid), 32

Michelangelo, 97

Middlesex, 88

Midrash, 280

Milan, 94, 103

militias, 137–8, 153–5, 179, 199, 297, 362

millenarianism, 241, 258, 260, 276

Milton, Anne (daughter), 194, 224, 226–7, 264, 268; birth, 190, 193; disability, 192, 227, 231, 296, 349, 393; and

Restoration, 285; and JM, 298–300, 348–57; apprenticeship, 353–6; and contested will, 391–5; death, 394

Milton, Anne (sister), 4, 11–12; marriage and children, 20, 28–9; widowhood and remarriage, 54, 63, 111; death, 111–12

Milton, Christopher (brother), 10–11, 27, 31; studies law, 54, 63, 81, 121; marriage, 111; attacked in London, 116; and civil war, 158, 188–9, 191; and Restoration, 287, 293; his daughters, 349; contests JM's will, 355–6, 391–5; old age and social status, 387, 395

Milton, Christopher (nephew), 293, 358

Milton, Deborah (daughter), 264, 268; birth, 226–8; and Restoration, 285; and JM, 298–300, 348–57; apprenticeship, 353–6; travels to Ireland, 355; her daughter, 355–6, 386, 395, 398; and contested will, 391–5; marriage, 395

Milton, Elizabeth (née Minshull), 387, 397; marriage, 300, 356; and JM's daughters, 353, 355–6; contests JM's will, 391–5; and JM's literary legacy, 396; death, 396, 400

Milton, John (father), 4, 28, 253; family and religious background, 6, 10, 62; business dealings, 6–8, 10, 34, 55, 116; social status, 7, 11, 20, 111, 395; musicianship, 7–8, 65, 82; and son's education, 10–11, 15, 20, 34; gradual retirement, 55–7; and son's career, 62–3; life as widower, 116; returns to London, 158; death and burial, 191, 390

Milton, John (nephew), 158

Milton, John (son), 223–4, 227–8, 387; death, 230–1, 234

Milton, John: birth and baptism, 3–4, 7, 9; social status, 7, 11, 15, 19, 31, 121, 181, 219, 269, 354; childhood and adolescence, 8, 10–20; school education, 11–20; appetite for literature, 16–17; and chastity and sexual restraint, 17–18, 27, 32–4, 78–9, 110, 133, 145; friendship with Diodati, 19, 34–6, 45–52, 79–81, 85, 133; earliest English poems, 19–20; university education, 21–7, 33–4, 40–1, 52, 74, 131, 133, 160; mastery of Latin, 22–4, 30, 52, 211; early religious zeal, 24–6; rustication and return to London, 27–36; money-lending business, 34, 89, 116, 131, 134, 266; performs at

Cambridge salting, 41–4, 95, 99; appearance, 43, 251; approaches twenty-third birthday, 52–3; graduation and return home, 55–6, 62–3; psychological crisis, 56; Protestantism, 57–8, 73, 100–1, 104; considers priesthood, 61–3; reading, 63–4, 81, 131–2; handwriting, 63; quest for patronage, 65, 77; sexual anxiety, 78–81, 110; poetic ambitions, 80–2, 101, 111, 121–2, 312; and *Maske* publication, 82–3; and mother's death, 89; visits Italy, 89–105, 108, 111–12; attitude to Catholics, 98–100, 104; sense of Englishness, 101; return from Italy, 101–2, 105, 111–14; and death of Diodati, 105–11; and sister's children, 112–13, 159, 298; turns to prose, 118; financial resources, 121, 131, 133, 162–3, 188, 192, 222–3, 264, 266, 284–5, 298–9, 362; engagement with print culture, 121–2, 124–5, 128–31, 139–40, 170, 172; literary plans, 122–4, 221; book collection, 124; opposition to episcopacy, 126–8, 130–2, 144, 156, 177, 180; political vision for England, 127, 171–2, 255–6, 344, 347, 372; finds public voice, 132–3; marriage to Mary Powell and separation, 133–5, 151, 155–6, 161–2, 172, 192; and divorce, 141–2, 144–51, 159–62, 165, 167–8, 172, 174, 176–7, 181, 187, 194, 262, 274, 294, 304, 379; political radicalisation, 148–9, 156; and civil war, 156–9, 194–5, 197–8; and Margaret Ley, 159; and education, 159–61; professional tutoring, 159, 162, 245; and Powell family property, 162–3, 188, 191–2, 222–3, 264; attitude to Parliament, 164–5, 167–8; attacks censorship, 167–72; deteriorating eyesight, 173–4, 197, 216, 224, 244; attitude to authorship, 174, 180–1, 194–5, 310, 338–9; break with Presbyterianism, 177, 185; republicanism, 177, 197, 201, 210, 215, 219–20, 227, 234–5, 265, 278–9, 282–3, 293–4, 343, 347; first marriage and children, 179, 182, 189–90, 192–4, 223; publishes Complete Works, 180–5, 384–5; complains of loneliness, 193–4; and execution of monarch, 198–9, 201–2, 210, 213–16, 227; disappointment with Commonwealth, 209–10; role in Commonwealth government, 210–13, 215–22, 231, 238–40, 248, 252, 257–8, 262–4, 278–9; family life under Commonwealth, 216–17; becomes *cause célèbre* in Europe, 220–1, 231, 379; books burned, 220, 248, 250, 286, 400; and death of first wife, 227–32; blindness, 231, 236–8, 242, 244–5, 248, 251–4, 256, 270, 283–4, 286, 294, 299, 311, 340–1, 348–9, 356, 377; attitude to Cromwell, 231–3, 255, 264–5; friendships of middle age, 245–7, 252; vilified, 247–8, 250–5, 384; marriage to Katherine Woodcock, 265–70; advocacy of religious liberty, 273–6; fears for future, 278–9; copies government papers, 279–80; heterodox beliefs, 280, 370, 389; responses to Restoration, 282–5; goes into hiding, 285–6; and his daughters, 285, 296–300, 348–57, 387, 391–5; escapes death sentence, 286–7; arrested and imprisoned, 287, 291, 348; life under restored monarchy, 291–8; marriage to Elizabeth Minshull, 300, 356; friendship with Ellwood, 300–5; and underground print network, 302–3; leave London, 304; return to poetry and publication of *Paradise Lost*, 305, 307–11; self-representation in *Paradise Lost*, 338–41, 348; sells library, 362–3, 387; and revival of publishing industry, 381–2; bound by his reputation, 383–4, 395; failing health, 385–7; death, 389–90; burial, 390–1; disputed will, 391–5; literary legacy, 395–7; images of, 397–8; early biographies, 398–9

Milton, Katherine (née Woodcock), 265–8; death and funeral, 268–71, 296

Milton, Katherine (daughter), 267–8

Milton, Mary (née Powell), 296, 392, 397; marriage and separation, 133–4, 151, 155, 155–6, 161–2; age, 134–5, 151–2; appearance, 135; politics, 156; marriage and children, 179, 182, 189–90, 192–4, 223–4; family life, 216–17; death and burial, 227–32, 269

Milton, Mary (daughter), 194, 224, 226–7, 264, 268, 397; birth, 193; and Restoration, 285; and household duties, 296–7; and JM, 298–300, 348–57; apprenticeship, 353–6; and contested will, 391–5

Milton, Sara (née Jeffreys), 4, 6, 10–11, 20, 28, 89, 111
Milton, Sara (sister), 4
Milton, Tabitha (sister), 4
Milton, Thomas (nephew), 189, 387
Milton, Thomasina (née Webber), 111, 116, 158, 189
Milton's Republican Letters, 395
Minshull, Elizabeth, *see* Milton, Elizabeth
misogyny, 146–7, 230, 352; and *Paradise Lost*, 333–5; and *Samson Agonistes*, 376
monarchy (kingship): divine right, 68; and State Church, 136; analogy with marriage, 148–9; and civil war, 164; and trial of Charles I, 198–9; abolished, 203–4, 206; and *Defence of the English People*, 219–20; restoration of, 280–7
Monck, General George, 281, 283
money-lending, 34, 55, 89, 116, 131, 134, 266
Monteverdi, Claudio, 102
Montrose, James Graham, 1st Marquess of, 164
More, Alexander, 250
Morland, Sir Samuel, 258
Morley, Thomas, 8
Morrill, John, 179
Mortlack, Henry, 348
Moryson, Fynes, 104
Moseley, Humphrey, 93, 180, 184–5
Mucklestone, Rowland, 146
music, 7–8, 56, 60–1, 65; Italian, 102; JM's ability, 135; and education, 160
Mylius, Herman, 221–2, 224, 232

Nantwich, Battle of, 163
Naples, 92–3, 98–9, 101–2, 105
Naseby, Battle of, 178
National Portrait Gallery, 360
natural phenomena, 311
Navigation Act, 234
Nayler, James, 301
Nedham, Marchamont, 217–18, 259, 261
neighbourliness, decline of, 126
Netherlands, 24, 64, 91, 222, 281
New Birth, The (Whately), 62
New Law of Righteousness, The (Winstanley), 208
New Model Army, 178–9, 186–7, 189, 197–8, 202; under Commonwealth, 206–8, 241; and Protectorate politics,

273, 276–8; Humble Petition, 277; and Restoration, 281; disbanded, 292
New Palace Yard, 199, 276
New Testament, 4, 13, 258
New World, 294
New York, 303
Newcastle, 116–17, 164
Newgate Prison, 301
newsbooks and newspapers, 124, 138–9, 176, 216–17
Nice, 93
No Blinde Guides (L'Estrange), 283–4
Norbrook, David, 220
Norman Conquest, 221
Northamptonshire, 186
Norwich, 236
Nottingham, 154
Nottinghamshire, 189
nurses, 192, 225, 227–8, 230

Oath of Covenant, 189, 191
Observations, 216
Of Christian Doctrine (De Doctrina Christiana), 280, 389
Of Civil Power in Ecclesiastical Causes, 273–4, 286, 346
Of Education, 160–1, 187, 211, 352
Of Reformation Touching Church Discipline in England, 126–7, 129–31, 136, 139, 180
Of True Religion, 383
Old Bailey, 286
Old Testament, 75, 150–1, 312, 372, 377
Oldenburg, Henry, 245, 247–8
Oldenburg Case, 221–2
'On the Death of a fair Infant dying of a Cough', 29–30, 86
On the Fifth of November (In Quintum Novembris), 25
On the Law of War and Peace (Grotius), 91
'On the Morning of Christ's Nativity', 48, 57–9, 61, 110
'On the New Forcers of Conscience', 177
On the Platonic Idea (De Idea Platonica), 40–1
'Onslow portrait' (of JM), 43, 397
Ottoman Empire, 171
Outcry of London Prentices, The (Anon.), 281
Overton, Richard, 206
Overton, Robert, 265
Ovid, 13, 18, 24, 30–2, 37, 48, 110, 315, 330, 345

Owen, John, 205
Oxford, 6, 40, 116, 151, 286; and civil war, 154–5, 158–9, 164, 175, 189–91, 218; JM's books burned, 400
Oxford University, 22, 154, 245, 264, 386, 400
Oxfordshire, 90, 284; and Milton family, 6, 62; and Powell family, 34, 116, 135, 139, 151, 153, 161, 395; JM's properties in, 188, 191–2, 222–3, 264

Paget, Nathan, 300
Palladio, Andrea, 102
Palmer, Herbert, 150, 167
pamphlets: and mid-century print culture, 122, 125, 128–31, 138–40, 159, 170, 221; print runs, 129; prices, 168; Royalist, 217–18; comparison with Putney Debates, 186; and Restoration radicalism, 298, 382; and revival of publishing industry, 380
Pandectae Locorum Communium (Foxe), 14
paper and papermaking, 88–9, 129
Paradise Lost, xvi–xvii, 305–48, 357, 364, 379–80, 396, 400; plans for, 122, 296; composition, 305; publication, 305, 309–11, 342, 348; publishing contract, 309–10; reception by readers, 311, 345, 348; character of Satan, 314–21, 323–4, 326, 345, 367, 400; 'grand style', 315; uses of Latin, 315, 323; politics, 317, 343–7; character of God, 321–2; and free will, 322, 327, 399; women and gender in, 324–6, 333–5, 399; sex in, 325–6, 328–9; title page, 328, 348; and JM as author, 338–41, 348; choice of blank verse, 344; reprintings, 363; Dryden's imitation, 379–80, 399; second edition, 385; translations, 397; later editions, 399–400
Paradise Regained, 363–4, 365–72, 376, 382, 400; simplicity of language, 367; character of Satan, 367–8; politics, 370–1
parenting, 193, 227–7
Paris, 91–2, 100, 220, 248
Parker, William Riley, 135, 352
Parliament, 39, 189–90; abolishes Star Chamber, 121, 129; and Church reform, 126, 130–1, 161, 164; and approach to civil war, 115, 117–18, 137–8, 153–4; and licensing of print, 140, 168–9, 216,

257, 275; and divorce pamphlets, 140, 148, 150, 165; and civil war, 156, 158, 163–5, 175, 178–9, 193, 223; JM's attitude to, 164–5, 167–8; and radical sects, 185; and second civil war, 197; and trial and execution of Charles I, 189–9, 201–3; establishes Commonwealth, 203–4, 206–8, 218; Cromwell dissolves, 240–1; under Protectorate, 257, 265; under Second Protectorate, 273, 276–82; and Restoration, 284, 287; under restored monarchy, 297–8, 303, 342, 357, 362
Pattison, Mark, 250
Paul III, Pope, 93
Paul's Cross, 27
Pennington family, 302
Pepys, Samuel, xv, 238, 276, 282, 284, 295–6, 359–60, 381
Personal Letters (Epistolae Familiares), 384–5
Petition of Right, 39
Petrarch, 16, 45, 194
Petty France, 224, 229, 238, 256, 264, 266, 388
Philaras, Leonard, 244, 252
Phillips, Anne, *see* Milton, Anne
Phillips, Anne (daughter), 28
Phillips, Edward (father), 20, 28, 54
Phillips, Edward (son), 29, 54, 111–12, 298; memoirs of JM, 179, 192, 230, 296, 300, 305, 353; receives legacy, 387; and JM's burial, 390; social status, 395; and JM's literary legacy, 396
Phillips, Elizabeth, 28
Phillips, John, 28–9, 54, 111–12, 262, 298, 387
Piedmont, 257
Pindar, 63
Pisa, 94
Pitt, Moses, 395
plague, 22, 28–9, 88–9, 105; in Italy, 96, 102; Great Plague, 303–4, 307, 343, 364, 391
Plato, 40–1, 95, 145, 182
Pleasure Reconcil'd to Virtue (Jonson), 74
Plutarch, 157
Poems of Mr John Milton, 180–5, 201; engraving, 184; printing, 184–5; deposited in Bodleian Library, 194–5
poetry: meters, 26, 30, 49, 56, 195, 344, 374, 378, 399; pastoral, 50, 60, 84–7,

106, 109–10; coteries and authorship, 82, 90; detachment in, 84; in Italy, 95–6, 101; nationalist, 99; manuscript miscellanies, 124–5; and education, 160

Pompeii, 99

Poor Robin (almanac), 294

Popish Plot, 118

Portsmouth, Louise de Keroualle, Duchess of, 360

Portugal, 222, 239–40

Powell, Anne, 189–92, 222–3, 225, 264, 285, 394

Powell, Mary, *see* Milton, Mary

Powell, Richard (father), 34, 134, 189–92, 284, 287, 358, 394

Powell, Richard (son), 158, 293, 358, 395

Powell family, 116, 134, 154, 179; politics, 156, 158, 162, 358; property, 162–3, 188–92, 222, 395

power of love: a sermon, The (Anon.), 139

Prerogative Courts, 203

Presbyterianism, 12, 164, 175–7, 185, 189, 234, 390–1; *see also* Covenanters

Preston, Battle of, 197, 233

Pride, Colonel Thomas, 198, 240

prisons, 301–2

Privy Council, 203

'Prolusion I', 41

'Prolusion II', 41

'Prolusion VI', 47

'Prolusion VII', 41

Prolusions, 384

propaganda, 178, 248, 275

prostitutes, 149

Protestantism, 6, 9–10, 24–5, 62, 125, 204; and Scripture, 12, 144; international, 12, 19, 64, 103; nationalist, 20, 26; and Milton family, 57; and poetry, 58; emphasis on Bible study, 63–4; and hostility to theatre, 73; in continental Europe, 91–2, 96, 146; and marriage, 146, 148–9; and civil war, 163; and freedom of speech, 171; and Nonconformity, 297–8

Prynne, William, 73, 128–9, 150

Psalms, 19–20, 176, 181, 195–6, 242–3, 280

puns, 80

Putney Debates, 186

Puttenham, George, 87

Pye, Robert, 189

Pym, John, 117–18, 137–8, 178

Quakers, 205, 281, 300–4, 341, 345, 354, 362, 390, 395

Rainsborough, Colonel Thomas, 186

Ralegh, Sir Walter, 16

Ranters, 205, 235

rape, 75, 163, 197

Raphael, 97

Raworth, Ruth, 180

Readie & Easie Way to Establish a Free Commonwealth, The, 282–3, 342

Reading, 116, 155, 175, 188

Reason of Church-government Urg'd against Prelaty, The, 132–3

recusants, 6, 62

Reformation, 9, 127, 168; Scottish, 113; radical, 137; godly, 185, 228, 260

Rehearsal, The (Buckingham), 380

religious sects, 150, 176, 184, 205–9, 234

Rembrandt van Rijn, 237

Remonstrance (Hall), 130–1

Renaissance, 45, 94, 204

republicanism, 186, 261, 280; JM's commitment to, 177, 197, 201, 210, 215, 219–20, 227, 234–5, 265, 278–9, 282–3, 293–4, 343, 347; in Italy, 204; army and, 273, 276–8; and Restoration, 284, 293–4; and *Paradise Lost*, 310, 343, 347; Rochester and, 360

Restoration (the word), 295

Restoration Comedy, 295

Richardson, Jonathan, 397

Richelieu, Cardinal, 39

Robinson, John, 192

Rochester, John Wilmot, Earl of, 359–60, 378, 380, 389–90

Rogers, Daniel, 141

Rolle, Samuel, 358

Rome, 93, 96–102, 104

Rome, ancient, 15, 32, 37, 219, 255; represented in *Paradise Regained*, 371–2

Root and Branch Petition and Bill, 126, 130

Rose Alley, 380

Rospigliosi, Cardinal, 101

Ross, Lord and Lady, 360–1

Rous, John, 194–5

Royal Charles, The (flagship), 342

Royal Exchange, 308–9, 350

Royal Society, 381

Rubens, Peter Paul, 38, 216

Rump Parliament, 198, 203–4, 206, 208,

210, 216–17; dissolved, 240–2, 279–80; restored, 278, 281–2
Rupert, Prince, 163, 382

Sabbath observation, 206
St Bartholomew Close, 286
St Bride's Churchyard, 111, 388
St George's Hill, 208
St Giles Cripplegate, 191, 300, 390–1
St Giles-in-the-Fields, 287
St James's Park, 224
St Martin-in-the-Fields, 34, 89
St Paul, 144, 146
St Paul's Cathedral, xvi, 8, 20, 40, 55, 63, 112, 286, 380; churchyard, 27–8, 93, 124, 273, 308–9, 358, 380–1, 388–9; John Donne and, 27–8, 62; alterations to cathedral, 37; converted to barracks, 185; and Great Fire, 308–9
St Paul's School, 13, 19, 21, 29, 39, 63, 106, 388
sales, 42–4, 95, 110
Salmasius (Claude de Saumaise), 218–19, 247–8, 250–1, 275, 287, 294, 298
Salzilli (Italian poet), 101
Samson Agonistes, 364–5, 372–8, 382, 385; politics, 373, 376–8; misogyny in, 376
Sandys, George, 93
'Satire on Charles II, A' (Rochester), 359–60
Savoy, Duke of, 257–8, 263
Schoole of Good Manners, The (Fiston), 17
Scotland, 12, 113, 163, 205, 241, 265, 281
Scotland Yard, 216–17, 229, 388
Scots, 113–14, 116–18, 136, 163–4, 186, 197, 233
Scripture, 12, 14, 110, 127–8, 144, 274
Scudamore, Viscount, 100
Second Defence of the English People (Pro Populo Anglicano Defensio Secunda), 100, 248–51, 254–7, 264
Selden, John, 81
Self-Denying Ordinance, 175, 178
Seneca, 210
Servita, Paul, 93
Seventh Eclogue (Virgil), 60
sexual anxiety, 78–81
Shakespeare, William, xv, xvii, 23, 28, 60, 73, 344; Venus and Adonis, 29, 35; The Merchant of Venice, 36; 'Th'expence of Spirit', 78–9; Twelfth Night, 81; The Comedy of Errors, 81

Sheerness, 342
Sheldonian Theatre, 22
Shepherd's Calendar, The (Spenser), 58
Shirley, James, 184
Short Parliament, 115
Shotover Woods, 116
Shurdington, 277
Sicily, 101, 105, 109
Sidney, Henry, 64
Sidney, Sir Philip, 29, 58, 64, 238
Sikes, George, 294
Simmons, Mary, 309, 388
Simmons, Matthew, 172, 309, 388
Simmons, Samuel, 309–11, 348, 363, 388, 396
Skinner, Cyriack, 159, 246–7, 252, 254, 276, 389
Skippon, Philip, 138, 154–5
Skipwith, Henry, 76
Socrates, 35, 145
sodomy, 50–1, 75–6
Solemn League and Covenant, 163, 185
Somerset, 156
Somerset House, 272
Sonnet II ('Donna leggiadra, il cui bel nome onora'), 45
Sonnet IV ('Diodati, e te 'l dirò con maraviglia'), 45
Sonnet VII ('How soon hath time'), 53, 56
Sonnet VIII ('Captain or colonel, or knight in arms'), 156–7
Sonnet XII ('I did but prompt the age to quit their clogs'), 181
Sonnet XV ('Fairfax, whose name in arms through Europe rings'), 196–7
Sonnet XVI ('Cromwell, our chief of men'), 232–5
Sonnet XVII ('Vane, young in years'), 235, 294
Sonnet XVIII ('On the late Massacre in Piedmont'), 257, 264–5
Sonnet XIX ('When I consider how my light is spent'), 253–4
Sonnet XX ('Lawrence of virtuous father'), 246
Sonnet XXII ('Cyriack, this three years' day these eyes'), 254
Sonnet XXIII ('Methought I saw my late espoused saint'), 269–70
Sophia, Electress of Hanover, 383
Spain, 20, 37, 261; and Italy, 91–4, 96–8; Charles I seeks support of, 114,

118; Marvell visits, 239; loses Dunkirk, 271

Spanish, 112, 350

Speculum Seculi (Ellwood), 344

speech, freedom of, 121, 165, 167–72, 275–6, 320

Spenser, Edmund, 29, 58, 60

State of Innocence, The (Dryden), 379–80, 399

Strand, 8, 388

Strange and horrible news (Anon.), 139

Strange Wonder or a Wonder in a Woman, A (Anon.), 147

Suckling, John, 73–4, 184, 197

Suffolk, 387

Surrey, 208–9

Svogliati Academy, 95, 102

Swan Alley, 297

Switzerland, 263

Sydenham, Thomas, 385–7

Symposium (Plato), 145

Tacitus, 39

Talmud, 280

Tarabotti, Arcangela, 102

Tasso, 98

taxation, 37, 125, 260

Tears or Lamentations of a Sorrowful Soul, The (music anthology), 7

Tempe Restor'd (Townshend), 66, 68, 74

Temple, Sir John, 136

Temple, The (Herbert) 125

Tenure of Kings and Magistrates, The, 199–202, 210–11, 213, 216, 293, 309

Test Act, 382

Tetrachordon, 148–50, 161, 167, 172, 174, 382

Thames, River, 8, 16, 31, 47, 57, 109, 138, 175, 186, 358

theatre, 7, 31, 60, 66, 73; under restored monarchy, 295–6, 378; *see also* masques

Theocritus, 60, 84–5, 107

'Th'expence of Spirit' (Shakespeare), 78–9

Thirty Years War, 12, 91, 114, 125, 222

Thurloe, John, 239, 257, 272, 284

Tibbermore, Battle of, 164

Tintoretto, 38

tithes, 125, 176, 242

Titian, 38

To His Sacred Majesty (Dryden), 293

'To John Rous', 195

To My Father (Ad Patrem), 82, 85

Toland, John, 310, 362

Tonson, Jacob, 399

Totnes, 16

Tottenham, 350

Touchet, Mervin, 2nd Earl of Castlehaven, 75–6

Toulouse, 220, 250

Tower of London, 118, 207, 307

Townshend, Aurelian, 66, 74

Trained Bands, *see* militias

translations, 16, 112; *see also* Psalms

Transproser Rehears'd, The (Leigh), 384

Transylvania, 263

Trapnel, Anna, 258–9

travel books, 89, 93, 98

Treatise of the Execution of Justice (Anon.), 292–3

Treaty of Newport, 197

Treaty of Westminster, 383

Trinity College, Cambridge, 26; Trinity Manuscript, 122–4, 232, 238, 296

Trinity College, Oxford, 39

Troy, 16

Tudors, 117

Turk's Head coffee house, 276

Turner, James Grantham, 42, 108, 110

Turnham Green, 155

Tuscany, 92, 94, 108

Tweed, River, 281

Twyn, John, 292

Tyburn, 291

Tyler, Wat, 153

Underhill, Thomas, 129

United Provinces, 281

Upon Appleton House (Marvell), 239

Urban VIII, Pope (Cardinal Barberini), 93, 96–8, 100

Van Dyck, Sir Anthony, 262

Vane, Sir Henry, 234–5, 240, 242, 261, 276–7; arrested and executed, 287, 294, 348

Vaudois community, 257, 263

Venice, 89, 94, 102–3, 105, 204

Venner, Thomas, 297

Venus and Adonis (Shakespeare), 29, 35

Verona, 103

Veronese, Paolo, 102–3

Vico, Marquis of, 92

Vigo, Bartholomew, 351

Villa Barbaro, 102–3

Villiers, Barbara, Countess of Castlemaine, 296, 360, 383
Virgil, 60, 83–4, 87, 107, 315
Vossius, Isaac, 221

Wales, Prince of, *see* Charles II, King
Wales, 64, 69, 74, 175
Waller, Edmund, 184, 197, 384
Wallington, Nehemiah, 225
Walwyn, William, 185
Warwick Castle, 155
Warwickshire, 138
Watch-word to the City of London and the Armie, A (Winstanley), 209
Watts, Joseph, 396
Webber, Thomasina, *see* Milton, Thomasina
Wells, 158
Wentworth, Thomas, 114, 117–18
Westminster, 8, 65, 115, 117, 138, 210, 276; Gunpowder Plot, 25; and plague, 28; pillory at, 40; and Charles I's execution, 202–3; and Lockyer funeral, 207; JM and, 221, 224, 247, 262–3, 273; Monck arrives, 281; regicides' heads displayed, 291; effect of plague, 304
Westminster Abbey, 199, 400
Westminster Assembly of Divines, 140, 161
Westminster Hall, 348
Whately, William, 62
Wheatley, 188, 192, 222–3
Whigs, 396
Whitehall, 199, 201, 241–2, 262; Banqueting Hall, 38, 65, 216; JM and, 216–17, 221, 238, 273, 388; Anna Trapnel prophesies at, 258–9; General Monck enters, 281; under restored monarchy, 295–6, 342, 358–60
Whitelocke, Bulstrode, 202
Wild Gallant, The (Dryden), 295–6

Wilkinson, Robert, 209
William III, King (William of Orange), 397
Wilson, A. N., 135
Wiltshire, 257
Winchester, Bishop of, *see* Andrewes, Lancelot
Windsor, 88
Winstanley, Gerard, 208–9, 299
Woman's Doctor, The (advice book), 266–7
women: education, 11–12, 34, 160, 349–52; physiology, 33, 193; and male friendship, 35, 51–2; social status, 54, 133–4; professional performers, 101, 295, 378; and marriage, 133–4, 141, 146, 149, 152–3; and misogyny, 146–7, 230, 376; and war, 156, 187–8; JM's attitude attacked, 168; printers, 180, 309; present petition to Parliament, 207; and childbirth, 225–6; advice to widows, 266–7; dress, 295; domestic sphere of influence, 297; obedience, 299; representation in *Paradise Lost*, 324–6, 333–5; and speech, 352–3; and apprenticeships, 354–5; working, 354–5
Wood, Anthony, 288
Woodcock, Elizabeth, 266
Woodcock, Katherine, *see* Milton, Katherine
Worcester, Battle of, 205, 233, 240
Works of Mr John Milton, The, 399–400
Wotton, Sir Henry, 89–92
Wren, Sir Christopher, 358
writing, 11–12, 192, 349

Yates, Jane, 112
York, Duke of, *see* James II, King
York, 116, 164
York House, 38
Yorkshire, 163, 229, 301
Young, Thomas, 12, 19, 24–5, 35, 126